Teacher's Resource Guide for

BRITISH AND WESTERN LITERATURE

A Thematic Approach

G. Robert Carlsen · Miriam Gilbert

Contributor

Lee Davis

WEBSTER DIVISION, McGRAW-HILL BOOK COMPANY
New York, St. Louis, Atlanta, Dallas, San Francisco

Editorial Direction: John A. Rothermich
Editor: Martha Alderson
Editing and Styling: Marnie Hauff
Design: Virginia Copeland
Production: Tom Goodwin

SERIES EDITORS

General Editor

G. Robert Carlsen

Editors

- Focus • Insights • American Literature: A Thematic Approach • American Literature: A Chronological Approach

  Anthony Tovatt
  Patricia Tovatt

- Perception • Encounters • British and Western Literature • English Literature: A Chronological Approach

  G. Robert Carlsen
  Ruth Christoffer Carlsen

- American Literature: A Thematic Approach • American Literature: A Chronological Approach

  Edgar H. Schuster

- British and Western Literature

  Miriam Gilbert

Contributing Editors

- Encounters • English Literature: A Chronological Approach

  Carroll Moulton

- American Literature: A Chronological Approach • English Literature: A Chronological Approach

  Ken Pitchford

- English Literature: A Chronological Approach

  John A. Rothermich

2 3 4 5 6 7 8 9 10 EB EB 93 92 91 90 89 88 87 86 85 84

ISBN 0-07-009822-0

G. Robert Carlsen, former Professor of English and Professor of Education at the University of Iowa, has taught English in the public schools of Minneapolis and at the Universities of Minnesota, Colorado, Texas, Hawaii, and Iowa. He has served as a consultant in curriculum revision to a number of school systems in Texas, Iowa, Colorado, California, Oklahoma, and Virginia. For many years he was the book review editor of young people's books for the *English Journal* and was a coauthor of an edition of *Books for You.* Dr. Carlsen is a past president of the National Council of Teachers of English. He has written some seventy articles for professional journals and is coauthor of *The Brown-Carlsen Test of Listening Comprehension* and of the National Council of Social Studies' publication entitled *Social Understanding Through Literature.* He is also the author of *Books and the Teen-Age Reader.*

Ruth Christoffer Carlsen is a coauthor with Dr. Carlsen of several anthologies for young readers. She has also written successful juvenile books. Her research was of particular value in the development of the anthology series. As a coauthor with her husband she works on the development of anthology materials, in particular, for the texts *Perception* and *Encounters.*

Anthony Tovatt, former Professor of English in Burris Laboratory School, Ball State University, has been the director of an extended research study on the teaching of composition under the Program for English of the United States Office of Education. For eighteen years he edited the column "This World of English," which appeared regularly in *The English Journal.* Active over the years in the National Council of Teachers of English, he has made many contributions to materials that the NCTE has published and made available to classroom teachers. His articles have appeared in professional journals and his poetry has appeared in magazines and newspapers. Dr Tovatt's colorful career began in a rural, one-room high school near a western Indian reservation where teachers before him had been intimidated by the students and beaten off before the school year ended. His stories of four happy years there read like some of Jesse Stuart's accounts of his early teaching experience.

Patricia O. Tovatt has taught English at both high school and junior high school levels in Colorado and Indiana. She works as a coauthor with her husband on the development of anthology materials, in particular for the texts *Focus* and *Insights.*

Edgar H. Schuster, Language Arts Coordinator for the Allentown (Pa.) School District, has taught English in urban and suburban high schools in the Philadelphia area. He has also taught at the college level. He has written articles for many professional journals, including the *Clearing House,* the *English Journal,* and *Educational Leadership.* Dr. Schuster has been a Master Teacher at Harvard University and is a recipient of a Lindback Foundation Award for Distinguished Teaching. He is a coauthor of McGraw-Hill's *American English Today.*

Miriam Gilbert, Professor of English at the University of Iowa, has taught English and American Literature at Iowa since 1969. Her primary work, both as a teacher and a director, has been with Shakespeare's plays. She has presented papers and led discussions on the teaching of Shakespeare, including two workshops at the Institute of Renaissance Studies in Ashland, Oregon. Under the sponsorship of the National Endowment for the Humanities, she has offered two seminars for college teachers on Shakespeare and has just given one of the first NEH summer seminars for high school teachers. At Iowa she has been a frequent teacher in the Literature Semester.

Kenneth Pitchford has published five books of poems: *The Blizzard Ape* (Scribners), *A Suite of Angels* (Chapel Hill), *Color Photos of the Atrocities* (Atlantic-Little, Brown), *The Contraband Poems* (Templar), and his version of Rilke's *Sonnets to Orpheus* (Purchase Press). He has written a short novel, *The Brothers* (Lippincott), and a play, *The Wheel of the Murder,* which was produced by Joseph Papp at The New York Public Theater. His work has been anthologized in *A Controversy of Poets, The New Yorker Book of Poems, A Geography of Poets, New York: Poems,* and *The Poetry Anthology.* He was featured in the movie *Not a Love Story,* produced by the Canadian Film Board. His work has appeared in *Poetry* (Chicago), *The New Yorker, The New England Review, Ms., Saturday Review, American Poetry Review, The New York Times Book Review, The Village Voice, The Nation, The New Republic.* He has given readings at Harvard, Yale, Oxford, Cambridge, the Universities of California (Berkeley), Kentucky, Massachusetts, Minnesota, Washington, the YW/YMHA Poetry Center in New York, The Poetry Center in San Francisco, and Shakespeare & Co. (Vienna). His poetry has been set to music by Ned Rorem, Robert Phillips, and Lockrem Johnson. He has taught poetry workshops at the New School, New York University, and St. Clement's Poetry Festival.

Carroll Moulton has taught classical and English literature at Yale, Princeton, and Duke Universities and has been a visiting fellow of Christ Church, Oxford. In addition to books on Homer, Menander, and Aristophanes, his writings include two textbooks: *Teaching English Literature* (a survey for teachers) and *Speaking for Yourself: The Student Workbook for Speech and Communication.* From 1972 to 1977 Dr. Moulton was editor of the journal, *Classical World.* He helped to establish the New Jersey Scholars' Program for high school students of that state, and has taught English at Stoughton High School, Stoughton, Massachusetts. He has served as general editor of a number of sound filmstrip series for high school students on English, Spanish, and Greek and Roman literture, and is the author of numerous reviews and articles in scholarly journals.

John A. Rothermich has taught English and Latin at St. Louis University, Webster College, and the city and suburban high schools in St. Louis. He has served as a curriculum consultant to a number of school systems and has given workshops and in-service training for elementary and secondary teachers throughout the United States. For the past twenty years he has held various editorial positions in the Webster Division of the McGraw-Hill Book Company.

Contents

Introduction

Conflict of Wills

Medieval British Poetry: Understanding Poetry

Renaissance British Poetry: The Elizabethan Age

Choice and Consequence

Seventeenth- and Eighteenth-Century British Poetry: An Age of Contradictions

Foibles

Nineteenth-Century British Poetry: Revolution and Imagination

Critics of Society

Twentieth-Century British Poetry: The Present and the Past

Know Thyself

Introduction

The subject matter of literature is life itself. The writer's task is to preserve our tragedies and triumphs, our fears and foibles, our insights and insufficiencies. The writer seeks to discover and portray the essence of human existence.

Good writers have the gift of exceptional insight. They are able to see more clearly than most people. They have been given the power to make enduring statements about the human condition. Whether they put their statements into the form of a novel, an essay, a short story, or a poem is secondary to the significance of the statement itself.

THEMES

One who becomes familiar with Western literature discovers that there are certain statements about the human condition that are continually repeated. The discovery that certain themes appear again and again is one of the great joys of reading. The editors of this anthology have arranged the selections to foster the discovery of the universal themes that have engrossed Western civilization and motivated its literature.

This book contains five vital themes: CONFLICT OF WILLS, CHOICE AND CONSEQUENCE, FOIBLES, CRITICS OF SOCIETY, and KNOW THYSELF. Each theme begins with one of the five major works contained in this book: *Antigone, Macbeth, The Miser, An Enemy of the People,* and *The Metamorphosis*. These are arranged chronologically beginning with a fifth-century B.C. play by the great Greek dramatist Sophocles and ending with a twentieth-century short novel by the modern Czech author Frank Kafka. The major work in each unit frames the basic question that will be the concern of all of the selections within the unit. Each of these works crystallizes a major human dilemma that has been the focus for many of history's most influential writers. Each is long enough and rich enough to permit the reader to discover and assess the dominant concern of each unit.

The editors have carefully structured each theme to promote the progressive understanding of its meaning. After encountering the theme in the major work, the reader then traces the theme through the shorter selections that make up the remainder of each unit. Shorter prose selections—biographies, essays, and short stories—contribute to the impact of the theme and enable the reader to trace the theme through the works of different writers of varying historical periods.

CHRONOLOGY

Four interludes of poetry are interspersed among the five thematic units. Each is chronologically and thematically related to the major selection immediately following it. The early period of English poetry leads into *Macbeth*. The poetry of the seventeenth and eighteenth centuries expresses the spirit of that time, which is echoed in *The Miser*. The concerns of the poetry of the nineteenth century are the concerns of *An Enemy of the People*. And the poetry of the twentieth century prepares for the changes of style and content of *The Metamorphosis*. Each poetry interlude begins with a short introduction that presents the major poets of the period, discusses poetic development and briefly relates the poetry to the history and thought of the period. There is also a short biographical introduction to each poet. The teacher wishing to present a brief survey of British poetry may present all four interludes sequentially.

GALLERIES

Each major theme is further illuminated by representations of paintings and sculptures that complement the thematic concerns of the literature. The galleries of fine art that accompany all the themes represent the unique contributions of art historians and teachers of literature. The interaction of the graphic and the literary arts extends the teaching of literature into the teaching of the humanities. The exploration of each theme is heightened by the vision of major artists and sculptors of the Western world.

STUDY NOTES

The study material in this text is divided into four and sometimes five major sections. Each is designed to produce a greater understanding of the reading selections and the themes that they illustrate.

The first section comments upon the selection, guiding the student in understanding its content and in relating the selection to the general theme of the unit.

The second section probes the implications of each selection through a series of thought-provoking questions and propositions. The reader is encouraged to think deeply about the ideas expressed by the selection and to relate these ideas to personal experience.

The third section provides a framework for developing competence in understanding literary techniques. Two or three elements of literary style selected for special study in each unit are traced through all the selections within each theme. The student is led in a step-by-step manner to an understanding of the essential components of the writer's art.

The fourth section contains an orderly sequence for vocabulary growth. The areas chosen for exploration and practice include context clues, connotation, imaginative language, and semantic change.

Occasionally, a composition section is included in the study notes. These sections provide stimulating suggestions for larger reading-related writing assignments.

The organization of the selections into thematic units helps broaden the student's understanding of literature. Focusing attention upon the thematic concerns of memorable writers gives students a method of literary analysis to use in reading beyond this text. A deeper understanding of literature is one of the results that can derive from careful thematic structuring.

The vitality of literature arises from the stories that it tells, the emotions that it arouses, and the visions of human striving that it presents. A relationship exists among literary works that extends beyond chronology and form. This book is designed to enable readers to study the most important themes of Western literature and to probe the mystery of their enduring appeal.

UNIT TEACHING

Each unit begins with a major work that embodies the central human concern of the unit. This work should intrigue students and provoke them to think about questions involving this aspect of life. Then each work throughout the unit offers in turn one facet of the unit theme. Each provides a new dimension of the idea, a dimension not treated in earlier selections.

After reading the introduction to the theme and discussing with students the basic idea of the unit, it is usually good to crystallize four or five major questions for which they should seek answers. These questions may be placed on the chalkboard or on the bulletin board so that they are constantly in front of students as they work on the unit. They should also be used at the conclusion of the unit, when the class can offer their answers.

It is important in unit teaching that the whole unit be treated almost as if it were a single work in itself. After introducing the unit, many teachers find it desirable to have the class skim through the materials to gain a bird's-eye view of the kinds of things that they will be reading. After the discussion of each selection, the teacher needs to keep asking these questions: What does this selection show that we have not seen before? What new ideas come to mind? What new kinds of possibilities in human relationships are apparent? Rather than assuming that each selection is an entity in itself, the teacher should keep reminding the class of the theme and get students to recognize similarities and differences between the new selection and the ones that they have read earlier in the unit.

Ordinarily, a selection will be assigned as homework for the next day's lesson. The next class period can be used for discussing the selection. However, many variations are possible.

1. It is often profitable to allow students a day in class to read the selection itself.

2. Reading a selection aloud is a very simple, old-fashioned technique that almost always has excellent results. The teacher should prepare for this oral reading in advance so that he or she is familiar with the selection. Sometimes an able student may be asked to prepare a selection for oral reading. However, under no circumstances should the teacher go around the class asking individual students to read small sections. This destroys the flow of the selections and hinders rather than increases understanding.

3. The buzz session is an interesting variation to use occasionally. The class is divided equally into groups consisting of about five students. Grouping may be random or it may be by ability levels within the class. The task for the group may be one of several kinds.

a. Each group may be assigned a separate selection. They may read it and then work out the study notes through discussion.

b. All groups may work with the same selection, but each group should be given a different study question to work on.

c. All groups may work on the same study notes. Through groupings, differences in points of view often emerge. Groups may meet for a part of the period. Then a recorder in each should be responsible for reporting the conclusions reached.

4. Writing is another approach to a selection. Frequently, it is good to state a proposition (one of the implications in the study notes) and have everyone write about it for 10 to 15 minutes. Then have several students read what they have written. This provides practice in composition directed toward a goal and also serves to provoke thinking on the part of everyone in the class. The material produced can also serve as a springboard for many interesting discussions.

For most of the units, one or two outside composition assignments should be made. Topics may be selected from the study notes. In addition, a number of composition activities related to the unit are given in this resource guide at the end of each unit.

Often in unit teaching each student is asked to choose a book to read in conjunction with the selections that she or he is reading in common with the rest of the class. If so, the list of titles should be presented early in the unit. Try to have as many of the books as possible available in the classroom. Sometime before the end of the unit a discussion can be conducted in which you ask students to share ideas about the unit theme that they have discovered in their independent reading. This kind of discussion can be systematically planned around the following general questions:

1. What situations related to the theme of the unit?
2. What reactions did the characters show to the situations presented?
3. What new ideas about this theme did you gain that were not presented in the short selections that you read?
4. In what ways were the ideas in your book similar to those presented in the shorter selections?

There is a cliché associated with the construction of a good speech: Tell them what you are going to say; tell them what you are saying; tell them what you have said. Unit teaching—in fact, all good teaching—makes use of these principles. Be sure that the students know what they are about to study. As they study, keep underlining what they are learning; at the end, help them realize what they have studied.

The organization of material into units is basic to good teaching. Psychologists sometimes refer to the mind as a computer that can be programmed to handle various kinds of information. The human mind operates by organizing stimuli from the external world into conceptual frameworks. It must see similarities among variant things and classify them under larger groupings. For this reason, reading literature in a piecemeal fashion usually results in utter confusion for students. Only a small handful of the selections that they are required to read makes an impression. The rest they quickly forget. The unit attempts to put materials together so that several major concepts will emerge that will genuinely affect students and make the reading of literature a really meaningful experience for them.

READING LITERATURE

This reading program focuses on reading to learn and to appreciate rather than on mastering the mechanics of reading. In this anthology, reading is a handmaiden to the literature program rather than the literature serving as a handmaiden to the reading program. The thematic structure of *British and Western Literature: A Thematic Approach* literally forces the student to encounter literature in terms of its central purpose—to record and communicate the intellectual and emotional life of human beings.

Central Meaning The thematic organization of the book helps students to encounter the whole problem of finding the central meaning, or theme, of literature. Because of the way that reading is taught in our schools and because of the way that it is used in many academic subjects, students are inclined to be far more competent in reading for detail than for central meaning. Transferred to the literature class, this means that most frequently students have been drilled on the details of a story: What happened to whom and under what circumstances? The organization of this anthology, in concentrating on the larger threads—the themes—that bind human experience together, forces students to consider the central meaning of each work and to examine how it is similar to or different from the meaning of other works in the same unit. Thus students using this anthology are encouraged to consider the whole of a work and to ferret out its underlying human content.

Documentation of Interpretation One of the major problems in reading literature is that different untrained readers may give a single work widely varying interpretations. Sometimes teachers have responded, "Well, if that's what it means to you, all right." In contemporary criticism this attitude has been seriously questioned. The critic insists that a work of literature is a unified whole. That interpretation is best that takes into account the greatest number of elements in the work. An interpretation that cannot explain a relatively prominent detail of the work is almost necessarily an incorrect interpretation. The study notes in this text continually ask students to document their opinions and interpretations from the details of the work itself.

Awareness of Literary Techniques Moreover, by examining only two or three literary techniques in each unit, students are given systematic practice in observing how master writers successfully clarify and intensify their messages. Thus students are able to acquire the tools necessary for more readily discovering the central meaning of a work and for deepening their appreciation and enjoyment of literature.

A reference list of appropriate literary terms under the heading *Handbook* precedes the teaching notes for each selection. The terms are defined in the Handbook of Literary Terms in the students' book. After you have called students' attention to the terms for a selection, you might remind them that they can refer to the back of their texts for definitions of the terms.

Vocabulary Program The vocabulary program complements the study of literary techniques and provides students with systematic approaches to vocabulary and its significance. It takes students considerably beyond the mere "word attack" skill taught earlier and stimulates an interest and a curiosity about words.

Words that could cause students difficulty and words that might be used for special study are included in the Glossary in the students' book. For each selection those words that might require special attention are listed in your resource guide under the heading *Glossary* along with the location of the words and a brief definition of the words as used in the context of the selection. You will probably want to list and discuss these words before assigning the selection.

The Application of Reading Finally, an act of reading is not really complete until one has judged the relevance of what one has read to personal situations. Too much of our instruction in reading stops short of this point. The study notes, particularly the implications presented for discussion and for composition topics, provide the bridge between the literary work and the students' own concerns. They ask them to look at the selection and what it says and then to look at their own lives to see what it means to them.

The reading emphasis in *British and Western Literature: A Thematic Approach* does not deal with phonic analysis or with speed reading. Instead it is concerned with those skills essential to the understanding and enjoyment of reading literature.

At the beginning of the notes for each of the five major themes is a Scope and Sequence Chart. This chart lists the reading skills that are most involved in the understanding of the selections in the following sections of the text. Although it would be impossible to define absolutely all of the reading skills for any selection, the essential ones are listed under the headings Language/Vocabulary, Comprehension, and Critical/Literary Skills. There is also a heading for Composition.

EVALUATION AND TESTING

A good test begins with a clear definition of the objectives of teaching a particular unit. The next step is to determine what kinds of student behavior indicate that each objective has been achieved. Test items are then constructed to determine whether students exhibit such behavior patterns. Each unit has four major objectives:

Understanding the Factual Content This objective is fundamental to everything else, but it is only the beginning point. The teacher may well construct test items designed to elicit recall of the content of various selections contained in the unit. There is no reason to include questions on every selection. Such items may be multiple-choice, true-false, or short-answer items.

Understanding the Central Theme of the Unit In CONFLICT OF WILLS, for example, students should understand what is meant by a clash of strongwilled persons. It is probable that an essay question will best test their understanding of this problem. It may well be that students' ability to recall and explain the conflict of wills in three or four works will be highly indicative of their understanding of the theme.

Understanding the Literary Techniques Emphasized in the Theme Questions that ask for specific definitions and illustrations of setting, characterization, conflict, climax, and so on will show whether students have grasped the literary concepts.

Vocabulary Concepts A half dozen or so words that have been emphasized in the vocabulary lessons may be tested through the construction of multiple-choice items, by having students write definitions, or by having them use the words in a composition.

Check Tests There is a Check Test for each selection or in the case of short selections or poems, a Check Test covering several short selections or poems. The Check Tests are on blackline masters available in a separate test booklet, ISBN 0-07-009823-9.

Unit Tests There are several options for testing your students' grasp of the unit. You may use the Summing Up section in the anthology—either whole or in part—as the unit test. For a second approach, you may select questions at random from the study notes at the end of each selection as a basis for constructing a final examination covering the complete unit. For a third option you may choose to use the comprehensive unit test already prepared on blackline masters available in a separate test booklet, ISBN 0-07-09823-9.

THE RESOURCE GUIDE

This resource guide follows the general plan and the headings of the anthology. It provides suggestions for introducing each theme and major writer and for approaching each literary work or group of poems. It also provides many suggestions for handling the Commentary, Implications, and Techniques sections that follow each selection. It supplies sample answers for these sections and for the Words and Composition sections. It includes suggestions for using the galleries of fine art, suggestions for relating the humanities (i.e., music and films) to the literature, and a bibliography of additional literary works.

This resource guide is not intended as a prescription for the course. The approaches, discussions, and answers that it supplies are merely suggestions that may in some cases help supplement the teacher's own valuable and proved techniques.

Conflict of Wills: Scope and Sequence

Selection	Language/Vocabulary	Comprehension	Critical/Literary	Composition
ANTIGONE	context, usage, abstract/ concrete words	details, point of view	tragedy, conflict, identification, diction	exposition*
"The Little World of Don Camillo"	usage	details, inferences, point of view	conflict, comedy, identification, diction	exposition*
"The Jar"	context, synonyms, simile	details, inferences	conflict, identification, diction	exposition*
"The Lumber Room"	context, descriptive words, synonyms	details, logical argument	conflict, identification, diction	exposition, description, the paragraph
"The Way Up to Heaven"	context, noun and verb forms	details, sequence, inferences, drawing conclusions	conflict, identification, diction, irony	exposition, justifying conclusions
"Shooting an Elephant"	slang	details, inferences, point of view	essay, conflict, diction, identification	exposition*
"The Prisoners"	synonyms (rephrasing)	details, point of view, inferences	conflict, identification, diction, irony	exposition*
"On Guard"		details, sequence, inferences	conflict, identification, diction, satire	exposition*
"Life Sentence"		details, sequence, inferences	conflict, identification, diction	exposition*
Summing Up	usage, descriptive words	details, inferences, supporting conclusions	conflict, identification, diction	dialogue, exposition
Relating Composition, the Gallery, and Humanities			identification, conflict, diction, point of view	exposition, dialogue

Medieval and Renaissance British Poetry

Selection	Language/Vocabulary	Comprehension	Critical/Literary	Composition
Medieval Lyrics	imagery, homophones, alliteration, assonance, onomatopoeia	details, inferences, contrast, conclusions	ballad	exposition*
Chaucer's Poetry	imagery, description, context	details, inferences, conclusions	characterization, satire, irony, metaphor, simile	exposition*
Renaissance Poetry	imagery	details, inferences	tone, alliteration, personification	
Spenser's Poetry	imagery, description	details, inferences, supporting conclusions	narrative poetry, allegory	
Shakespeare's Sonnets	imagery	details, inferences, theme	sonnet, satire	sonnet

*Teachers can use the Implications in the study notes as writing assignments.

Conflict of Wills

In virtually all of the selections in this unit the reader will meet strong-willed persons in conflict with other strong-willed persons. Such conflicts provide a great deal of tension as the reader comes to realize that something or someone will have to give. Not all of the conflicts, however, are of equal seriousness: "The Little World of Don Camillo," "The Jar," and "On Guard" are relatively light pieces, although they nonetheless reveal important truths about human nature.

Most classes will benefit by following the order of the stories given in the anthology. In some classes, however, it may be better to open the unit with a shorter, lighter piece than *Antigone.* "The Jar" may be a good substitute. It is easy to read and almost certain to entertain; it is also a first-rate piece of writing. If you open with *Antigone,* for your own information you may wish to read the comments under Techniques on page 37 of the student text.

OBJECTIVES

1. To identify conflicts in literature between two strong-willed people.
2. To experience how a conflict between people affects the lives of those involved.
3. To learn that in a conflict right is seldom on one side alone.
4. To pinpoint the center of the reader's identification in a literary work.
5. To perceive how varied diction produces different effects.
6. To practice verbalizing one's reaction to literature in discussion and in composition.
7. To develop vocabulary.

MOTIVATING THE UNIT

If you are teaching more than one class, you may want to try more than one of the approaches listed below. Of course, how well an approach works will depend as much upon the class that you are teaching as upon the approach itself.

Pattern I Ask students to think of a real-life clash between two strong-willed persons. Ask them to discuss the reasons for the conflict and to explain why the individuals took the positions that they did. Ask them how the conflict was resolved and what could be learned from it—either by the participants themselves or by an observer of the conflict. Finally, let students discuss the dramatic possibilities of such conflicts—why such conflicts may make particularly good materials for writers. Make your first reading assignment, and suggest that students can expect to find the same kinds of conflicts in their reading that they have discussed.

Pattern II If students are unwilling or unable to discuss conflicts of wills on a personal level, you may wish to deal with the matter on a community level or even on an international level. Community or national conflicts of wills occur at any given time. Ask students how such conflicts are resolved. Do battles or riots often bring permanent solutions? If not, what are some potential solutions? To what extent can conflicts on a community, national, or international level be applied to clashes between individuals? It is interesting to note that the conflict in *Antigone* is partly rooted in a conflict that extends beyond the individual level, for Polyneices is denied a religious burial because he has led an allied force against Thebes.

Pattern III Tell students that you are going to write a phrase on the board and that they should write everything that comes to their minds when they see the phrase. Write the words "Conflict of Wills" on the board, and let the class write for five or ten minutes. Then ask some students to read their papers aloud, or collect the papers and select some at random to read to the class.

A good classroom discussion can stem from this technique of free association. The discussion should lead naturally into the reading of the introduction to the unit and the assignment of the first selection.

Pattern IV Propose yourself or ask a student to propose a situation in which two strong-willed persons clash. Then ask each member of the class to write a resolution to the conflict. Discuss which resolutions are most realistic, most dramatic, and most satisfying morally. Try to get students to see how such conflicts and their resolutions are especially interesting to both writers and readers.

Pattern V Read aloud to the class the introduction that starts on page 1 in the student text, pausing after each paragraph to be sure that students understand the points being made. You may, for instance, ask them for examples from their reading or from real life of the types of conflict mentioned in the second paragraph. Also, try to provoke some discussion of the two questions posed just after the middle of the introduction. Make certain that students understand that conflicts between strong-willed persons do not necessarily have to end seriously or tragically. Point out that regardless of how they end, such conflicts can teach us a good deal about life and human nature.

Antigone

PAGE 9

Sophocles

Glossary Words

prerogative (page 10, col. 1) A right or privilege that nobody else has; special right or privilege such as may derive from an official position, office, etc.

panoply (page 11, col. 1) A complete suit of armor; complete equipment or covering; any splendid array

edict (page 12, col. 2) A decree or law proclaimed by a king or other ruler on his or her sole authority

requite (page 13, col. 1) Pay back; reward; repay

belie (page 16, col. 2) Show to be false; prove to be mistaken; give a wrong idea or impression of

imprecations (page 17, col. 2) Curses; a calling down of evil, etc., upon someone or something

fell (page 21, col. 2) Fierce; savage; ruthless; deadly; destructive

censure (page 22, col. 2) Express disapproval of; find fault with; criticize

augury (page 28, col. 2) Art or practice of foretelling events by interpreting such signs and omens as the flight of birds, thunder and lightning, etc.

calamitous (page 32, col. 2) Dreadful; ruinous

Handbook

conflict, diction, identification, metaphor, point of view, simile

Check Test 1

Check Tests for each selection—in the form of blackline masters—are available in a separate test booklet, ISBN 0-07-009823-9. Each test is titled and numbered for easy filing after use.

Give the Check Test after students have read the selection(s) and before you begin the discussion of the work(s).

Antigone tells the story of the clash between two strong-willed and strong-principled individuals—Antigone, daughter of Oedipus and sister of Eteocles and Polyneices; and her uncle Creon, king of Thebes. Antigone feels bound, as Polyneices's sister, to seek a proper burial for him. Creon as leader of Thebes, feels compelled to order that Polyneices shall lie unburied and unmourned. Death is the penalty for disobedience. The essence of the conflict is set forth in the first scene of the drama as Antigone tries to persuade her sister Ismene to join her in giving proper burial to their brother.

In the First Ode, the Chorus sings of the victory of Thebes over Argos and of the fight between Eteocles and Polyneices in which both were killed.

Creon enters and enunciates his philosophy of the supremacy of the state. He is obviously a person of principle. He then repeats his edict regarding Polyneices, whom he regards as a traitor to the state. A guard then arrives and reveals that someone has "buried" Polyneices by throwing dust over the body. Creon becomes enraged and threatens all the guards with death unless they can discover the culprit.

The Chorus then sings the Second Ode, hailing human beings as the most wonderful of wonders; at the same time, it warns that people can turn their cunning in evil directions and that when they do they are dishonored.

The drama moves swiftly ahead, as Antigone is brought in by a guard. She was captured as she tried to rebury the body after the guards had swept aside the dust that she had originally scattered over it. Under questioning by Creon, Antigone asserts that she disobeyed his edict in order to obey a higher law—the law of Heaven. This particularly antagonizes Creon, who believes that she is trying to glorify her crime as virtue. It is also clear that Creon especially resents the fact that a woman is defying him.

Creon then orders Ismene brought forth, assuming that she must have been an accomplice. The latter offers to share Antigone's fate, but Antigone will not permit it. In the course of this dialogue we learn that Antigone is betrothed to Creon's son Haemon, but this fact does not alter the king's resolve to execute her.

In the Third Ode, the Chorus bewails the curse that the gods put on the house of Oedipus. They point out that humans are powerless to avert the will of Zeus.

Haemon enters and with the phrase "good government" sets his father off on a long speech. Creon therein reveals his belief that the ship of state will founder unless there is total obedience to lawful authority—even when the authority is wrong or unjust. He also reveals again—especially at the end of his speech—his fear of being defeated by a woman. His son then tells him that public opinion is on Antigone's side; Creon sees his son's pleading as another threat to his power: "What? men of our age go to school again/And take a lesson from a very boy?" He grows increasingly angry and finally causes Haemon to lose control; the latter rushes out determined to share Antigone's fate. Creon resolves to put Antigone in a cave with very little food and thus to let her die by starving.

The Chorus sings of the power of love, and when Antigone returns under guard, they commiserate with her over her fate. She sees that fate to be intertwined with the past tragedies of her family, but she remains adamant in defending her act as just, claiming that she has kept a law that is holy.

The Chorus laments others who have suffered imprisonment as Antigone is taken away under guard.

Teiresias, the blind soothsayer, enters and tries to tell Creon that the gods are angered and the city is polluted because of his refusal to allow Polyneices to be buried. Creon angrily accuses the soothsayer of having been bribed to say such things. Teiresias in turn is angered and is moved to reveal his "dark secret"—that Creon will atone for what he has done by the death of his son Haemon. After hearing this, Creon turns to the Chorus leader for advice and accepts his suggestion that he (Creon) should release Antigone from her prison. As he goes to do so, Creon reasons that it is best to observe established laws.

In the Sixth Ode, the Chorus sings a hymn to Dionysus, protector of Thebes.

A messenger arrives and, lamenting human fortune, tells the Chorus of Haemon's suicide. At this point Creon's wife Eurydice enters and asks that the messenger tell the whole story. The latter relates how after Creon had buried Polyneices, he proceeded toward Antigone's tomb only to find that she had already hanged herself. Haemon was in the cave lamenting her death. When he saw his father, he tried to kill him, then suddenly turned and killed himself. Eurydice leaves without a word.

Creon enters with Haemon's body; he knows that he has done wrong, and he is full of remorse. But his troubles are not at an end; soon a messenger comes from the palace to announce that the queen has committed suicide. Creon prays for death for himself and laments that his grief is more than he can bear. The Chorus ends the play by urging wisdom and reverence for the gods. They attribute Creon's downfall to his pride.

Antigone is generally acknowledged to be among the greatest tragedies ever written. Its comparative simplicity and brevity make it an ideal introduction to classical Greek tragedy. Although the importance attached to proper burial may be a somewhat foreign idea to students, other elements of the play are properly described as timeless. The clash between allegiance to the law of a country and allegiance to the laws of God or of one's own conscience, for instance, may be seen in many contemporary manifestations.

It is hardly necessary to point out that the play provides an excellent example of our theme. The conflict of wills is not confined to the Creon-Antigone clash but may also be seen in the clashes between Creon and Haemon, Creon and Teiresias, and Antigone and Ismene.

INTRODUCING THE SELECTION

You will probably want your students to read all of the introductory material in the text on pages 3–8. The remarks under the heading "The Greek Theater" include some very useful commentary on the Greek Chorus, a dramatic element with which most students will be unfamiliar. It is especially important to have students read the discussion on "The Background of *Antigone*." The remark that *Antigone* is "part of a series of three plays" is not meant to imply that it is part of a trilogy like Aeschylus' *Oresteia.* The so-called Theban Trilogy—*Oedipus the King, Oedipus at Colonus,* and *Antigone*–is a trilogy only in the sense that all three plays are related to the Oedipus legend. *Antigone,* the last play relating to the legend, was actually written first. It was produced in 442 or 441 B.C. *Oedipus the King* was written next; it was produced some time between 430 and 411 B.C. *Oedipus at Colonus* may have been the last play that Sophocles wrote; in any case it was first produced after his death in 406 B.C.

Care should be taken in trying to fit *Antigone* into the framework of Aristotle's notions on tragedy. The very question of who is the tragic hero is difficult to answer. Thus the title and perhaps the sympathies of many readers would tend to mark Antigone as the hero. But—as H.D.F. Kitto notes—Creon is the agent, and his character, faults, and merits are those "which are immediately relevant to the play." Creon is also the focal character with respect to the conflict of wills, for his will clashes with the strong will of several characters. Furthermore, the question of precisely what Aristotle meant by such terms as "hamartia"—usually translated as "tragic flaw"—is still being debated by scholars. In any case, with high school students it is probably better to discuss Sophocles' play rather than Aristotle's theory.

USING THE STUDY NOTES PAGE 36

I. HOW INSECURE IS HUMAN FORTUNE

This phrase—spoken by a messenger—could well stand as the epilogue to nearly all of classical Greek tragedy. It is important to see, however, that in Sophocles' work the insecurity is not caused primarily by chance. At the end of *Antigone,* the Chorus speaks of the need for wisdom and reverence. The clear implication is that Creon could have averted his downfall if he had possessed these qualities in greater measure.

Reverence in this play refers specifically to a respect for unwritten divine laws and perhaps, as well, for unwritten human laws—to what a sister owes her brother. Wisdom, in Sophocles' philosophy—Professor Kitto tells us—implies "knowing what you are, knowing your place in the world, being able to take the wide view, with a due sense of proportion."

That Creon did not have the security that comes from self-knowledge and knowing his place may be discerned throughout the play. We can see it, for instance, in his somewhat strained and public philosophizing over the role of the king; it is as if he were testing himself in a strange role. We can also see insecurity in his strong fear of being overruled by a woman and by a youth. His inability to take the wide view may be inferred from the fact that the citizens of Thebes—public opinion, we would call it today—are opposed to his actions; yet he does not see this.

In the conflict of wills there is a kind of irresistible force (Antigone) set against an immovable object (Creon), and the former is stopped. But, as in most conflicts between strong-willed antagonists, tragedy could have been avoided if one of the participants had adopted "the wide view, with a due sense of proportion."

II. IMPLICATIONS

To the questions asked in the Implications sections of the text, there are no clear-cut right or wrong answers. The comments that we make in this guide are therefore merely suggestive; frequently they are not the answers students will give. Students will answer in terms of their own experience, not in terms of your experience or of ours.

1. Students are asked to consider the statements below and to judge whether they are antiquated or still relevant today.

a. But why attempt a hopeless task at all? (Ismene)

This question should have a familiar ring to students; they may find a different wording still more familiar: "Why fight city hall?" or "You can't fight city hall." And of course the same spirit pervades this question: "What can a single individual do?"—with the emphasis on *single* and usually delivered in either a whining or a hopeless tone. Students should realize that if some "single individuals" do not act, they will be forced to accept the decisions that other "single individuals" make for them.

b. ...love of gain
Has often lured a man to his destruction. (Creon)

Obviously, the statement applies today, but less obvious may be the variety of ways that love of gain may lead to destruction. Ask students to give examples. And point out that the word *destruction* need not be taken literally. Thus, for instance, dehumanization of the personality is a kind of destruction, too, and some forms of "love of gain" may lead to this deterioration.

c. **Nor could I think that a decree of yours—**
A man—could override the laws of Heaven
Unwritten and unchanging.
(Antigone)

In this country there are legislative bodies to make laws, but one could argue legitimately that some of the laws attempt to override the unchanging laws of Heaven. We presume that there is a law of Heaven that decrees that an individual's skin color should in no way affect the rights that the person is entitled to enjoy; yet decrees made by mortals have challenged this unwritten and unchanging law of Heaven. Other examples may be offered by students, all proving that the statement of Antigone is still relevant.

d. **No man can rule a city uprightly**
Who is not just in ruling his own household.
(Creon)

If one accepts the notion that a person is all of a piece, one could say that this statement is still relevant today. Students, however, are likely to be familiar with contradictions between public and private personalities—as well as split personalities. They will probably believe that there is nothing at all unusual about an individual who governs a city very democratically and yet is a tyrant at home, or vice versa.

e. **There's no disgrace, even if one is wise,**
In learning more, and knowing when to
yield. (Haemon)

The statement is obviously still relevant, but the discussion may center on the word *disgrace.* Why is it difficult for authority figures to admit to changing their minds; for instance, the parents who object to their son or daughter marrying a person of a different religion, or the manufacturer who resists environmentalists' demands to stop polluting the air. Do the so-called "wise" people fear that they will be disgraced if they change their opinions, or is something else involved as well?

f. **. . . how insecure**
Is human fortune! Chance will overthrow
The great, and raise the lowly . . .
(Messenger)

It is still true that chance can cause chaos even in the lives of the great because our control over nature —especially human nature—is still imperfect. Try to have students contribute their own examples. Some may cite the assassinations of the Kennedy brothers, Martin Luther King, Jr., or Malcolm X. Others may draw on more recent reports in the news about a prominent local person, a respected politician, or a government worker who has been found stealing, bribing, or cheating. Are they brought down merely by chance or by their own human flaws?

2. Students are asked to determine which of the following motives or qualities could belong to Antigone and which to Creon:

courage	**patriotism**
duty	**power**
pride	**selfishness**
logic	**stubbornness**
loyalty to family	**revenge**
religious belief	**anger**

In addition, they are asked the following questions, based on their distribution of the foregoing motives or qualities.

a. Does your examination of Creon's and Antigone's motives indicate that one is all right or all wrong? Is there some right on each side?

b. Which motives do you consider the better ones?

One ought not to be categorical in attributing the motives or qualities. Both characters, for instance, are courageous, proud, and angry. We could say that Antigone shows a sense of duty and loyalty to family and to religious beliefs, whereas Creon displays patriotism, power, and stubbornness. These motives or qualities, however, are not attributed to either character exclusively.

There is certainly some right on each side, but Antigone comes off the better of the two because of the relatively high value that we place on her qualities. Furthermore, Creon possesses negative qualities such as selfishness, stubbornness, revenge, and anger to a greater extent than does Antigone.

3. Students are asked to consider the following statements and to tell whether they agree or disagree with them.

a. The playwright shows Creon as a typical villain and gives him no "saving virtues." This is obviously false. Creon's greatest "saving virtue" is that he is able to recognize that he has been wrong.

b. Sophocles presents Antigone as both unfeeling and aggressive. Support your opinion with lines from the play. We would agree that Antigone is presented as an aggressive, self-assertive person. Numerous examples of aggressive behavior can be cited. At the beginning of the play, Antigone asserts, "No one shall say *I* failed him" (line 45). Later, in discussion with Creon after her capture, we see her strong will and confidence in lines such as:

> And if you think it folly, then perhaps
> I am accused of folly by the fool.

Also, she intimates that it may be the gods and not she who may have erred (lines 894-900).

Although at times Antigone seems to behave in an unfeeling way—for example, treating Ismene harshly —we do not agree that she is an unfeeling person. She is motivated by a sense of duty and by loyalty, not by cruelty.

c. The Chorus, representing the opinion of the townspeople, sides sometimes with Creon and sometimes with Antigone. The Chorus leader speaks for the Chorus, and for this question we speak of them as a single entity. The Chorus does side sometimes with Creon and sometimes with Antigone, although its position is rather more consistent than this statement may suggest. The Chorus is *for* Antigone when it sees her as obeying unwritten laws, but it is *against* her for boldly defying the authority of the king. As for Creon, the Chorus is quite reluctant to go against his will, and—unlike Antigone—it never openly defies him. It respects him as the king. On the other hand, the Chorus recognizes that he may be acting against his own and the state's best interests, and it attempts on several occasions to suggest this to him.

It is difficult to agree that the Chorus represents the townspeople. The Chorus is rather like a conservative group of diplomats, whose main concern is the welfare of the state and the defense of the values of what we today may call "the establishment." Characters such as the Guard and the Messenger are more representative of townspeople. Contrast their concerns and their tone with the concerns and the tone of the Chorus.

d. The conflict of wills in this play results from the conflicting motives of the characters. Use one of these pairs to demonstrate your opinion.
Antigone and Ismene
Creon and Haemon
Creon and Teiresias

Students should see that motives in fictional lives are likely to be as numerous and as complex as motives in real lives often are. The more important the character, the more numerous and complex the individual's motives are likely to be. Antigone and Ismene may be used to illustrate the point. Ismene's motive for not wanting to help her sister is that she is too weak to act against the will of the city, and she states this directly (lines 79 to 80). Antigone's motives, on the other hand, include her sense of duty, her love of her brother, her religious beliefs, her desire to perform a "glorious deed," and her hostility toward Creon and perhaps toward authority in general. These motives are not only multiple, they are also not always fully spelled out. In any case, the reader is left to infer which of them are comparatively powerful and which weak.

Much the same may be said of Creon in his struggles against the comparatively one-dimensional characters of Haemon and Teiresias. On the other hand, we should stress the word *comparatively.* In great literature, even the less-than-major characters may be rather complexly motivated. Thus, we know from his later actions that Haemon's chief motive in arguing with his father must be his love of Antigone; yet knowing his father as he does, Haemon does not appeal to him on this basis but acts rather as if he had Creon's well-being in mind.

III. TECHNIQUES

Identification

Students are asked to discuss the following:

1. As you read the play did you identify with Antigone? With Creon? With both? There may be considerable individual variation, but it seems clear that Sophocles expected his audience to identify with—or sympathize with, at any rate—Antigone, especially from the middle of the play onward. The author also seems to have intended us to sympathize with Creon near the end of the play. This is not to say that readers will inevitably feel sympathetic toward these two characters at the appropriate times. But if they do not, they are probably not going to get the effects that Sophocles intended.

2. Is there any shift in your sympathy as the play progresses? Again, there will be individual differences. Some students, for instance, may be immediately sympathetic with Antigone and may retain that sympathy until the end. Others may take an initial attitude similar to Ismene's. In the latter case there would be a shift; in the former there would not.

3. Try to imagine what the play would have been like if Sophocles had chosen either Haemon or Ismene as his major character. There are many possibilities here. With Ismene as the focal character, for instance, Sophocles might have portrayed Antigone as a less sympathetic character, perhaps by showing her as selfish. The effect of this would be to transfer sympathy to Ismene. The main purpose of this question, of course, is to help students to see the importance of identification. If they do see that, it matters very little what particular imagining they volunteer.

Diction

Students are asked to label the quotations below by choosing from each pair of the following adjectives:

plain—flowery
conversational—oratorical
abstract—concrete

a. Know *what?* Why do you preach at me like this?

Adjectives: *plain, conversational, concrete.*

b. For, as ivy grows on a tree,
Strangling it, so she slowly turned to
Stone on a Phrygian mountain-top.

Adjectives: *flowery, oratorical, concrete. Flowery* has connotations that do not apply here, but we do not want to classify the quotation as *plain. Oratorical,* too, may not be the best word to characterize the lines, but the "as...so..." structure is certainly not *conversational.*

c. **...Lawful authority**
Must be obeyed in all things, great or small,
Just and unjust alike.

Adjectives: *plain, oratorical, abstract.* The neat parallelisms with which the statement ends make it *oratorical,* as opposed to *conversational.*

d. **Thou spirit whose names are many,**
Dionysus,
Born to Zeus the loud-thunderer,
Joy of thy Theban mother-nymph,
Lover of famous Italy:
King art thou in the crowded shrine
Where Demeter has her abode...

Adjectives: *flowery, oratorical, concrete.*

e. **Then think: once more you tread the razor's edge.**

Adjectives: *plain, conversational, abstract.*

IV. WORDS

A. Students are to use context clues to determine the meaning of the following words by checking their answers in a dictionary.

prerogative—a special right, power, or privilege
pretext—an appearance assumed in order to conceal the real intention or situation
sated—satisfied by having indulged to the full
edict—official proclamation having the force of law
requite—repay; avenge
connive—conspire
belie—to present a contrasting appearance to
imprecations—curses

B. The first usage of *ordained* (line 20) obviously suggests that Creon's order is arbitrary and cruel. The second usage (line 363) is appropriate, and the conventional meaning is intended. A comparison of the two meanings suggests that Creon has usurped the power of the gods.

1. **Brave** (line 8) is used facetiously. Antigone means that he is anything but brave.
2. **Pure** in "this *pure* crime" (line 72) means "lawful."
3. **Double doom** (line 169) refers to the fact that both brothers have died at each other's hands.
4. **Graced with every rite** (line 195) means accorded every honor given to those who die in battle.

C. For maximum effectiveness, this assignment ought to be made before the play is read. The scope of the exercise can be narrowed to the odes spaced throughout the play. Here is a partial list of similes and metaphors.

similes: lines 113, 115, 139, 809, 891, 917, 949, and 995
metaphors: lines 130 and 949

D. An examination of the odes will provide many examples of concrete language.

E. It is worth noting that not all the meanings of *orb* are considered archaic.

The answers to this exercise vary. It may be a good idea to discuss why some words become archaic.

The Little World of Don Camillo: Rivalry

PAGE 46

Giovanni Guareschi

Glossary Words

sacristy (page 47, col. 1) Place where the sacred vessels, robes, etc., of a church are kept; vestry

domicile (page 47, col. 2) A dwelling place; a house; one's home

dissension (page 48, col. 1) Disagreement in opinion that produces strife; discord

infernal (page 48, col. 2) Of or having to do with hell; hellish; fiendish; outrageous

carillon (page 48, col. 2) A melody played on a set of bells arranged for such playing

audible (page 50, col. 1) Loud enough to be heard

skeptical (page 51, col. 1) Inclined to doubt; not believing easily

Handbook

comedy, conflict, diction, identification

Check Test 2

INTRODUCTION

The Little World of Don Camillo is a collection of short stories, nearly all of which focus upon two strong-willed characters: Don Camillo, parish priest of a village in the valley of the Po River in Northern Italy, and Peppone, the Communist mayor of the village. "Rivalry" is the seventh episode in the book.

The conflict begins when Peppone aims a loudspeaker at the walls of Don Camillo's church so that he will hear the speech of the Communist big shot who has come to the village. Don Camillo retaliates by ringing the church bells so loudly that he drowns out all objectionable parts of the speech. Peppone then arranges to have an amusement park set up right next to the church square.

Don Camillo complains to Christ—with whom he confers in most crises—but the latter tells him that it is "democracy," provided that the mayor remains within the law. The conflict intensifies when Peppone scores very high on a game that measures the strength of one's blows. He boasts of this so loudly that Don Camillo hears him. When this happens a third time, Don Camillo rushes into the amusement area, strikes the pad on the machine, and scores higher than Peppone. The latter takes still another turn and he ties the priest's score. When Don Camillo talks with Christ afterward, we learn that Don Camillo had hoped that the mayor would tie his score and that it was Christ who had arranged it that way. We learn, too, that Peppone himself had hoped that Don Camillo would at least equal Peppone's own high score.

This selection—along with the next—will provide some comic relief for students. In this selection the readers discover at the end that the joke has been on them in the sense that it only *seems* that the two men want to prevail over one another. In short, although we would *expect* that a Communist mayor and a Catholic priest would be unable to get along, the fact is that they do; and the conflict of wills between them is all in the spirit of fun.

You will want to be sure that students know in advance that Peppone is a Communist mayor and that Don Camillo is a Catholic priest in the same village. If your students are unfamiliar with the Don Camillo stories, you may want to engage them in a discussion about the kind of conflict that they might expect between two such characters. Do not, however, point out in advance that the conflict is all in fun; students will enjoy the story more and perhaps gain more from it if they themselves discover its ultimate point.

USING THE STUDY NOTES PAGE 51

I. CONFLICT AND COMEDY

A comedy must, of course, have a happy ending; but this fact should not be taken to mean that comedies have no serious messages. Try to encourage students to talk about the meaning of this story. Ask them to compare their expectations with what actually occurred. The fact that the chief characters bear the labels of Communist and Catholic does not necessarily mean that they must seek to hurt or destroy one another, as the reader tends naturally to assume.

II. IMPLICATIONS

Students are asked to explain why they agree or disagree with the following statements:

1. Peppone and Don Camillo are basically alike in temperament and character. In many ways they are, and that is one of the sources of the humor—they are so alike, and yet they are so opposed in position and politics. Their alikeness is pointed up at the end of the story when it is revealed that both wished for the same thing.

2. The story shows that it is possible to fight in public an individual that you respect in private. The story clearly does show this. It may be that one of the chief reasons why the two fight in public is that the public expects them to. At any rate, we know that the public is easily led and misled by labels such as Communist and Catholic. Frequently, one sees individuals who claim to dislike a particular group getting along very well with an individual member of that group.

3. Conflict is intensified when people try to prove themselves right. Yes. Peppone could have let the conflict drop after the speech was drowned by the bells; instead, he intensified it by bringing in the amusement park in an effort to prove himself right and to gain the upper hand.

4. It is not easy to see that an opponent's point of view has any validity. Clearly, this is true; indeed, it often seems as if we do not make even the slightest effort to try to see the points of view of our opponents. Students could profit from a discussion of why this is true. Some causes that they may discover are (a) the tendency to think in terms of black and white, or right and wrong, and (b) the fact that our ideas are frequently bound up with our emotions.

III. TECHNIQUES

Identification

Students are asked the following questions:

1. What characteristics of Don Camillo tend to make the reader identify with him? Don Camillo is a very human character. Like most of us, he gets angry rather easily, he finds it hard to control his emotions, he speaks or acts first and thinks afterward, he enjoys baiting his antagonists, and so on. He is also generally good-humored, clever, and strong—all qualities that we admire and presumably find easy to identify with.

2. Are there points in the story in which you identify with Peppone? If students know only this story in *The Little World of Don Camillo,* they may not be able to identify with him very readily. If they know other stories in the series, they are likely to identify with Peppone when he is "down," just as much as they identify with Don Camillo. Students may also identify with Peppone when they learn that he "nearly died for fear" that Don Camillo would not reach nine hundred fifty-two.

3. How do the dialogues with Christ make you more or less sympathetic with Don Camillo? Answers may vary on this question. In general, we would say that they make us sympathize with Camillo. Christ tends to take a superhuman point of view of things and tends to require the same of the priest. The reader may feel sympathetic toward Don Camillo because more is being asked of him than is being asked of Peppone. This is especially true when Christ insists that the priest remain within the law and when Christ calls the amusements and the din "simply democracy."

Diction

Students are asked to select from a list the words that best describe the language that Guareschi uses. They are also asked to find examples in the story to support their choices. The list is as follows:

1. **Slangy**
2. **Visually precise**
3. **Exaggerated**
4. **Colloquial**
5. **Archaic**
6. **Delicate**
7. **Simple, straightforward**

Answers may vary somewhat, but examples of all but five and six are available. *Big Shot* in the first sentence is slangy. *Mushroom* is an example of visual precision. The speech of the Communist Big Shot could be considered exaggerated, as could the phrase *violation of domicile.* Colloquial language is seen in phrases like *got down to business* and *stop talking nonsense.* Much of the language in the story could properly be classified as *simple, straightforward.* There are, of course, many examples other than those given here.

The Jar

PAGE 52

Luigi Pirandello

Glossary Words

vented (page 54, col. 1) Let out; expressed freely

stipulated (page 55, col. 1) Demanded as a condition of agreement; arranged for as a condition of agreement.

indignation (page 55, col. 1) Anger at something unworthy, unjust, unfair, or mean; resentment

contrivance (page 56, col. 1) Thing invented; a device

carousal (page 58, col. 2) A noisy revel or drinking party

Handbook

absurd, conflict, diction, identification, simile

Check Test 3

INTRODUCTION

A bumper crop of olives causes Don Lollo to order a new, very large earthenware jar to hold the oil of the harvest. Some time after the costly jar arrives, his workers discover that it is broken. Don Lollo flies into a rage, but when his anger is spent, the workers persuade him that the jar can be repaired and that

Zi' Dima with his marvelous cement is the person to do it. Don Lollo, however, insists that Zi' Dima use rivets as well as cement. After Zi' Dima has fixed the rivets from inside the jar he finds that he cannot get out.

This time the jar will have to be broken for good, but before releasing Zi' Dima, Don Lollo runs off to his lawyer to discover what recompense he can legally demand. The lawyer declares that Zi' Dima should pay the price that he himself decides the jar to be worth at the present time. Zi' Dima, however, declares that he would sooner stay in the jar until he rots. That evening he uses the wages that Don Lollo has paid him to have a party with the latter's farmhands. The noise of the party awakens Don Lollo, who discovers his roaring drunk workers dancing around the jar while Zi' Dima remains inside, singing at the top of his voice. Don Lollo attacks the jar and sets it rolling down a hill. The jar breaks against an olive tree, leaving Zi' Dima the winner in the dispute.

Like the previous selection, this is a comic variation on the theme CONFLICT OF WILLS. The chief source of amusement lies in the fact that it is largely Don Lollo himself who is responsible for bringing mischief on his own head. The reader sympathizes with the underdog, Zi' Dima, and enjoys watching Don Lollo suffer.

There are two points that you may want to make before assigning this story. First, be sure that students understand that the jar in the story is made of clay. If they do not read carefully, they will miss this point, think that the jar is glass, and wonder how rivets can be put into it. Second, students should pay close attention to the early descriptions of Don Lollo and his character because so much of the humor depends upon knowing the kind of person that he is.

USING THE STUDY NOTES — PAGE 59

I. GRAND EMOTIONS FROM TINY CAUSES

Ask students to discuss the tiny causes that led to the grand emotions in the story, in particular the causes that led to Zi' Dima's imprisonment in the jar. Careful rereading will show that he was trapped because he was preoccupied by his grievance against Don Lollo. Had Don Lollo not insisted upon the rivets or had Zi' Dima agreed goodnaturedly to put them in, the whole problem could have been averted.

Ask students to think of examples from contemporary life or from their own experiences that demonstrate this point; for instance, a fan's anger at a player who misses the shot that would have won the basketball game.

II. IMPLICATIONS

Students are asked whether they would agree or disagree with the following statements:

1. Pirandello illustrates this point: sometimes the "letter of the law" applied rigidly becomes ridiculous. This seems to be a point illustrated in the story. It is ridiculous for Don Lollo to ask Zi' Dima what he thinks the jar is worth and to expect him to pay that amount. Clearly, the jar is worth nothing with Zi' Dima in it, and the only way to get him out is to break it—in which case the jar would also be worthless. Don Lollo's paying Zi' Dima is another instance, one that is neatly turned against him at the end of the story; indeed, this rigid application of the letter of the law is indirectly responsible for Don Lollo's losing the conflict of wills.

2. "Life is a very sad piece of buffoonery." This quotation from Pirandello, mentioned in the headnote on page 52, is a reflection of the writer's philosophy. Students are asked to decide if "The Jar" expresses these sentiments. Perhaps students will need to check the precise meaning of buffoonery. They will probably agree that the story does have posturing, farcical pranks, and coarse jokes. But is it "very sad"? This will be a matter of opinion. Some may agree that it is sad indeed when a person makes the protection of material possessions the dominant concern in life.

3. The conflict in "The Jar" is triggered because Don Lollo and Zi' Dima have similar personalities. For the most part, this statement is accurate. Both characters want things done *their* way, and both are easily upset when their way does not prevail. There could not have been any conflict unless the two characters had shared these traits.

4. While this story is amusing, it contains no "truth" of general human significance. This story is like a cartoon that makes significant comments but in an amusing way. Students may be misled by the grotesque actions of the characters into presuming that the section is a piece of fluff. Hence it is important to pin down what Pirandello is saying about anger, about the need to be right, about worship of the law, and about blowing up trifles into causes.

III. TECHNIQUES

Identification

If they take the word *identification* literally, students will probably not identify with either main character. The age, appearance, and personality of each person would make such identification difficult. Students should, however, *sympathize* more with Zi' Dima than with Don Lollo, for the latter has some decidedly unpleasant characteristics, notably his tendency to tyrannize his inferiors. Zi' Dima, in contrast, enjoys the company of the farmhands, and he is in many ways the underdog in the conflict.

Diction

Students are asked the following questions:

1. Compare the kind of language used by the author himself with that used by his characters. What distinctions do you find? First, there is the difference normally found between written language and spoken language (or the representation of spoken language)—that is, the language of the author is more formal. The author uses longer sentences, more periodic sentences, more "grammatical" sentences, and so on. Second, because it is the language of a good short-story writer, it is often vivid or colorful; it is also marked by freshness and the (relative) abundance of imagery. The language of the characters also contains many more questions and exclamations than that of the author.

2. Find examples of the way in which Pirandello chooses words to bring action and vivid pictures into his prose. For example: "His eyes glared about him wolfishly. . ." Examples are abundant: (a) "His fury made his eyes more piercing and bloodshot and his face became green with bile," (b) "His wild gesticulations made those who saw him galloping past think that he might well be hastening to shut himself up in a lunatic asylum," (c) ". . . he could see in the moonlight what looked like a gang of devils on his threshing floor," and (d) ". . . looking for all the world as if someone had caught hold of the bulging front and cut it off with a sharp sweep of the knife." Students should be able to find many more instances.

3. What is the earliest point in the story at which the choice of language suggests that "The Jar" will probably be a comic tale? We find it at the end of the first paragraph with the reference to the "breast-high and pot-bellied" new jar that would be "the mother superior to the little community of five other jars."

IV. WORDS

A. Answers vary slightly. Strong context clues are not always present.

1. **dissension**—disagreement of opinion
2. **skeptical**—doubting
3. **stipulated**—specified
4. **indignation**—anger at something believed unjust
5. **carousal**—drunken revel
6. **intoxicated**—drunk; exhilarated

B. The effect of the various synonyms could profitably be discussed in class.

1. **infernal**—hellish
2. **satellites**—followers; adherents; partisans; disciples
3. **bellowed**—shouted; bawled
4. **dispute**—argument; debate; controversy
5. **squeaking**—creaking; squealing
6. **console**—comfort

C. Students are given an example of a simile from *The Little World of Don Camillo* by Guareschi and one from "The Jar" by Pirandello.

What other similes do Guareschi and Pirandello use?

Guareschi uses "a voice like the wrath of God," "fists like sacks of potatoes," and "Don Camillo went to his peephole in the window as though he were on his way to the scaffold."

Similes in the Pirandello story include "cursing like a trooper," "it rang like a bell," "old man with swollen crooked joints, like the stem of an ancient Saracen olive tree," "Zi Dima . . . was struggling like a wild animal in a trap," and "Don Lollo . . . rushed down like a mad bull."

The Lumber Room

PAGE 60

Saki

Glossary Words

alleged (page 60, col. 2) Declared as a fact, often with the suggestion that the person's truthfulness is in question

tactician (page 61, col. 1) A person skilled in planning, especially of military operations

asperity (page 61, col. 1) Harshness or sharpness of temper, especially as shown in tone or manner

germinated (page 61, col. 2) Grown or developed

illumination (page 62, col. 1) A lighting up; light

consign (page 62, col. 1) Hand over; put for safekeeping

transfixed (page 62, col. 1) Pierced through

vociferation (page 62, col. 2) Loud, noisy cries or shouts

sauntered (page 63, col. 1) Strolled; walked slowly

punitive (page 63, col. 2) Inflicting punishment

Handbook

conflict, diction, identification

Check Test 4

INTRODUCTION

"The Lumber Room" details incidents in an ongoing conflict between a bright, imaginative child and his "self-styled," prosaic aunt. Nicholas has slipped a frog into his breakfast cereal thus proving the adults wrong who tell him he is just imagining a frog in his cereal. As punishment, he is kept at home while his cousins go off to the beach. The aunt then announces that Nicholas is not to go into the gooseberry garden. To make sure he does not disobey her, she engages in trivial garden chores in order to keep an eye on the doors into the garden. Nicholas makes several aborted attempts just to make sure the woman will remain on guard. Then he hastens to get the key to the lumber room (storage room) and in a moment is in that forbidden place. He finds all sorts of fascinating discards on which his imagination can work. Hearing the aunt calling him, he returns outside to find that she has slipped into a dry rainwater tank in the gooseberry garden where she had been hunting for him. Now she wants him to bring a ladder so that she can climb out. He responds that he is forbidden to enter the garden. She argues with him. He then pretends that he thinks the voice he hears is the devil trying to tempt him and simply wanders away. The aunt is rescued by a kitchen maid. The other youngsters return from the beach where things have gone badly. Nicholas is the undeniable victor in the conflict having had a splendid time at home.

USING THE STUDY NOTES PAGE 63

I. LOGICAL ILLOGICALNESS

The conflict of wills continues because each of the arguments has traces of illogicalness built into it. What are they? Nicholas' argument is illogical in that he has no reason to assume that this one time the aunt's voice would be the devil. He has apparently never made that assumption before. The aunt's argument is illogical in that her kind of punishment is not effective with Nicholas since no form of punishment seems to get through to him, not even the fearsome silence at the dinner table. Nicholas has his own inner resources to keep him occupied.

II. IMPLICATIONS

Students are asked to discuss the following statements using the details in the story or experiences in their own lives.

1. The story could have been called "The Gooseberry Garden" instead of "The Lumber Room." This statement is intended to get the students to examine the role of the lumber room in the story. Though the aunt thinks that the gooseberry garden is the spot where he wishes to play, it is really the storage room that he has been preparing to visit for some days and it is this room that provides the stimuli to Nicholas' imagination. Notice that at the end, he is not upset by the silent treatment he is getting, because he is off in his mind trying to solve the mystery of what was happening in the screen he had seen.

2. **The fact that things work out in unexpected ways for the aunt is her own fault.** The details of the story seem to support the statement. If the aunt had checked the cereal bowl immediately, she would have known there was a frog there. If she had not acted in anger, she might have realized that the tide would be in at the beach. If she had listened to the little boy complaining of his boots, she would have realized that he'd get blisters if he walked on the beach. If she had not ordered Nicholas to stay out of the gooseberry garden, the rest would not have followed. She seems to be beset with the need to carry punishment to its furthest extreme.

3. **Nicholas is the kind of child whom it is fun to read about, but who would be difficult to handle in real life.** The conflict here is set in motion by the implacable rigidness of the aunt who has a set picture in her mind of how a child must behave. Nicholas is a bright, imaginative youngster with an amazing ability to detect an adult's illogicalness. A different kind of adult might have a thoroughly enjoyable time with Nicholas instead of the running battle that is pictured here.

III. TECHNIQUES

Identification

If you think of the story as a play, who is on stage the most? Nicholas. And in the theater this usually indicates the character with whom the audience will identify. **How do the descriptions of Nicholas and the aunt make the one more appealing than the other?** She is depicted as a woman of few ideas and immense powers of concentration, a self-styled aunt who looks for a few tears from Nicholas when the others leave for the beach, who ends in the water tank because she is so determined to keep Nicholas from having a little fun in the garden, who promises him strawberry jam if he will bring the ladder but has no intention of keeping the promise, etc. Nicholas is described as a skilled tactician, who chuckles in a cheerfully grim way, imagines treasures, enjoys golden minutes, and feels perfectly capable of being in disgrace and in a gooseberry garden at the same moment.

Diction

Examine the opening paragraph. Look at the following phrases in their context and then try to express what the choice of words does to the style: wholesome bread and milk, seemingly frivolous ground, older and wiser and better people, veriest nonsense, the alleged frog, profoundly in error, utmost assurance. The adjectives and adverbs give a heroic, grandiose, stately, important quality to the incident which in view of the action makes the piece humorous.

IV. WORDS

A. Use context clues here and in the story to determine the meaning of each word.

1. **alleged**—claimed (without proof); supposed
2. **tactician**—an expert in battle tactics or maneuvering
3. **debarred**—shut out; prevented from entering
4. **asperity**—harshness
5. **obstinacy**—stubbornness
6. **germinated**—grown; developed
7. **consign**—assigned; committed
8. **vociferation**—noisy clamoring
9. **punitive**—inflicting punishment

B. Students are to use substitutes for these words and then decide why the author chose the words he did.

1. **scrambling**—climbing, stepping. *Scrambling* suggests a child's haste and clumsiness.
2. **reposed**—lay; rested. *Repose* suggests a quietness and contains the irony of excitement at rest.
3. **illumination**—light. The meaning of *illumination* suggests the divulging of mystery. Also this longer word in comparison to *light* has softer sounds that help to build some suspense.
4. **transfixed**—fastened; pierced and held. *Transfixed* explains the scene fully with one word.
5. **springing**—jumping; leaping. *Springing* gives a better idea of the sudden forward movement.
6. **leapt**—come; jumped. *Leapt* indicates an extreme action and calls to mind that she should have heeded the adage to "look before you leap."
7. **sauntered**—walked slowly. *Sauntered* suggests an attitude of coolness and unconcern, an attitude Nicholas certainly exhibits.
8. **partaken**—taken; drunk. *Partaken* is a more stilted word and suggests the formality of the event. The word contributes to a humorous effect.

V. COMPOSITION

Students are asked to write a descriptive paragraph about Nicholas' personality. Most of the descriptions will probably be favorable to Nicholas. Remind students that a paragraph should stick with one basic idea.

The Way Up to Heaven

PAGE 65

Roald Dahl

Glossary Words

foible (page 66, col. 1) A weak point; weakness; a little fault or failing
disconsolate (page 68, col. 2) Without hope; forlorn; unhappy
oppressive (page 72, col. 1) Close; sultry. Also, hard to bear; burdensome

Handbook

conflict, diction, identification, irony

Check Test 5

INTRODUCTION

Mrs. Foster has a phobia: the fear of missing a train, a plane, or even the opening moments at the theater. The fear is manifested by a twitching muscle in the corner of her eye. As the story opens, the Fosters' sixth-floor apartment is being closed up because Mrs. Foster is flying to Paris to visit her daughter's family and to see her three grandchildren for the very first time. The servants are being sent on vacation and Mr. Foster is moving to his club while his wife is gone. The rented limosine is waiting to take Mrs. Foster to the airport, and she is nervously pacing up and down, afraid to call out to her husband and urge him to hurry. He arrives in the hall and then goes back to wash his hands. As she waits nervously in the car, he ambles down the front stairs. A dense fog sets in and she is frantic with worry about missing the plane. At the airport, she finds the flight is delayed, but she elects to stay and wait and her husband goes on home. After six, the flight is postponed and reluctantly Mrs. Foster returns to her house. Her husband orders a car again for the next morning, but dumbfounds her by announcing that she can drop him at the club on the way to the airport. She protests that it's in the opposite direction, but gives in. The next morning the same scene is played out with his usual delaying tactics. After getting into the car, he races back inside for a package he claims to have forgotten. She finds it tucked down behind his seat as if deliberately shoved there. Much distressed for now she feels he did it on purpose, Mrs. Foster leaps from the car, runs up to the door, inserts her key, and then stands there listening. Then without entering she runs back down and orders the driver to take her to the airport saying her husband can get a cab. Six weeks later, at the arranged time on the arranged date, she returns. There is a strange odor in the front hall. She goes to the elevator, finds it isn't working and goes to the telephone and calls the repair man. The implication is that she has murdered her husband by leaving him in the nonfunctioning elevator for six weeks.

You could introduce this story by asking the class to write down on a piece of paper the kinds of things people do which annoy them. Give three or four minutes for jotting down some ideas. Let a half dozen or more students read their lists. Then discuss whether these are big, dramatic actions or simply little tics that seem to cause annoyance. If the annoyance continues, does this build pressure, perhaps setting up a psychological tug of war? Ask the class to open their books and read the story ''The Way Up to Heaven'' to see what happens to two people when an annoying habit goes on and on and on.

USING THE STUDY NOTES

PAGE 72

I. THE BREAKING POINT

This discussion should reveal how readers pick up clues to what is going to happen. Different people will have different moments at which they realize what is happening. The hints are rather subtle so there may even be a few who aren't sure at the end what has happened.

II. IMPLICATIONS

Students are asked to discuss the following statements:

1. The conflict that is operating between husband and wife is shown only by the muscle twitching in Mrs. Foster's eye. This is not an accurate statement. Mrs. Foster's nervous rushing about, her questions to the butler about whether there's still time to make the plane, her urging her husband to please let her go by herself, her frantic questions about whether she'll make the plane and his comments to her, the way she clasps her hands tightly together under the lap robe, and her determination to stay right at the airport until the flight takes off are all visible signs of her reaction to the conflict.

2. A repeated annoyance usually brings one to a point of eruption either with words or actions. The story supports this statement. Ask if students can remember an annoyance of some kind that finally made them either speak up or strike out. There will probably have been some childhood events when they broke under teasing and attacked the teaser or at least tried to do so.

3. The title is ironic. What do students think the title means? Was Mrs. Foster helping her husband get to heaven? Could she possibly believe that she had guaranteed herself a place in heaven? Or is being able to live near her daughter and grandchildren enough of heaven for her? The title is, of course, ironic. In some cases it may be necessary to discuss irony before opening the discussion.

III. TECHNIQUES

Identification

It is suggested that Mrs. Foster's anxiety about being on time could have been used in a comedy and the reader's sympathies might then have been with the husband. Students are asked how the author makes us side with the wife?

The obsession is made to seem very small. Mrs. Foster has served her husband well, and he has disciplined her not to question his actions. It is also suggested that Mr. Foster has rages. Notice that she had to have permission to go to Paris. Surely she could be indulged this one time without his making her life miserable up till the last moment. Mr. Foster is portrayed as a cat playing with a mouse. Our sympathies naturally are with the mouse.

Diction

Read the phrases that follow and then reread the first four paragraphs to see the phrases in context. Discuss the effect that Dahl's choice of words has on you as a reader. What quality does it give to the telling?

It was nothing much—....
It is really extraordinary....
Mr. Foster may possibly have had a right....
Mind you, it is by no means certain....
He had disciplined her....
Assuming (though one cannot be sure)....
....there had been times recently....

The tone of these comments suggests that the narrator is trying very hard to be fair. They also convey the idea that Mr. Foster is a bit of a tyrant and uncaring. As a counter to these statements of impartiality, Dahl in the fourth paragraph says that Mrs. Foster has been a good and loving wife, served her husband loyally and well, is a very modest woman, but that even she, after thirty years of refusing to admit the possibility, is coming to believe that her husband is deliberately tormenting her. Still the other comments predominate making the author seem very fair.

IV. WORDS

A. Use context clues here and in the story to define each word.

1. **pathological**—unhealthy; sick; caused by disease
2. **apprehension**—fear of danger
3. **foible**—weakness
4. **disconsolate**—unhappy; forlorn
5. **oppressive**—heavy; burdensome

B. Students are asked to supply noun or verb forms for words that were used in the selection.

Noun	**Verb**
obsession	**obsess**
discipline	discipline
distribution	distribute
supervision	supervise
operation	**operate**
resemblance	**resemble**
suspicion	**suspect**

V. COMPOSITION

Students are to write three paragraphs which will end with their conclusion about which main character is more at fault in this conflict. Remind students to support this conclusion in their third paragraph.

Shooting an Elephant

PAGE 74

George Orwell

Glossary Words

imperialism (page 75, col. 1) Policy of extending rule of one country over other countries

labyrinth (page 75, col. 1) Many winding passages through which it is hard to find one's way; maze

garish (page 76, col. 2) Glaringly bright

Handbook

essay, conflict, diction, identification

Check Test 6

INTRODUCTION

This essay reads like a story because it has a beginning conflict, a rising action, a climax, and a denouement. The author is serving in Burma as a British police officer during the days of strong British imperialism. Unfortunately, he dislikes his job because he is disgusted with the superior airs of his countrymen and with imperialism, and he is sensitive to the hatred of the Burmese. An event happens that crystalizes his thinking about imperialism.

He gets word that an elephant in its period of "must" has become temporarily wild. He sets out to find the elephant, confident that by now it has passed through its violent state. Confronted by the elephant, which has just killed a native, he feels tremendous pressure from the crowd to shoot the animal. But the author is aware that the elephant is harmless and merely grazing. Suddenly, in this situation, he realizes that the essence of imperialism is a loss of freedom for those who rule, since they must constantly impress those who are ruled. Freedom of choice vanishes. Actions must be prescribed by "the ruled." Against all his moral convictions, Orwell shoots the elephant and then suffers as it takes a long half-hour to die.

In this essay, the conflict of wills is between that of the narrator and the collective will of the crowd. The crowd's pressure wins out for the act of killing the elephant. Through this experience the narrator comes to know a truth that he might not have recognized otherwise.

A world map indicating the location of Burma is a good way to begin this selection. Ask the students what they know about the British rule in Asia. What characterized the British attitudes toward the people of the "ruled" lands? You might tell them that Britain gradually took over Burma, taking different sections at different times from 1826 until 1885, when they occupied the last pieces. From 1919 until 1937, Burma was governed as a province of India, a situation not too palatable for the Burmese.

Captured by the Japanese in 1942 and ruled by them until 1945, the Burmese refused at the time of their liberation to return to British rule. In 1948, they refused to join the British commonwealth, an indication perhaps of their deep-lying bitterness and animosity toward the British. Yet, strangely enough, most British living in Burma were so isolated and insulated against the Burmese feelings that they lived in ignorant bliss.

Ask the class about the kinds of conflicts that arise from there being a "ruling" group and a "ruled" group. Then assign the essay.

USING THE STUDY NOTES

PAGE 78

I. THE PUBLIC AND THE PRIVATE LIFE

What are the conflicts Orwell faces in this essay? Orwell is from a Western culture and the townspeople are of an Eastern culture. Orwell is a member of a ruling group and the townspeople are the ruled. But Orwell is of the minority group while the townspeople are the majority. Orwell's conflicts include dealing with these great differences between him and the Burmese townspeople. He is one man living several lives, and his public life is suddenly in conflict with his private life.

II. IMPLICATIONS

How do the following quotations show the conflicts of wills in the situation?

1. **"...I was stuck between my hatred of the empire I served and my rage against the evil-spirited little beasts who tried to make my job impossible."** This individual who hates his employer and eagerly wants to help those oppressed by the employer feels terrible pressures when those he wants to help hate him as well.
2. **"...I could feel their two thousand wills pressing me forward irresistibly."** Here is an external pressure. He feels their eyes upon him demanding that he kill the elephant. Yet in his mind he feels it is murder.
3. **"And my whole life, every white man's in the East, was one long struggle not to be laughed at."** In a strange culture, it is hard to appear at ease. And laughter is one of the most effective and terrible weapons that an oppressed people can use.
4. **"But I did not want to shoot the elephant."** This terrible inner conviction that it is wrong to shoot the elephant is opposed by the external pressure of the Burmese. Try to get the students to express in their own words the conflict of the situation and why it puts stress on Orwell.

III. TECHNIQUES

Identification

Students are to list briefly those qualities in the author's personality that they find admirable and then those that they find offensive or unsympathetic. Then they are to sum up their opinion of him. This should provoke an interesting discussion. Of course, the answers will be varied, for different students will find different qualities admirable or offensive. Many will admire Orwell's concern for the Burmese, his forward-looking ideas about empire, his integrity, his eagerness to do the right and sensible thing. Students will probably dislike his giving in to the pressure and shooting the elephant, feeling it shows a lack of conviction and courage. Perhaps they may be helped to see that most people faced by massive opinion cannot find the nerve to stand against it. In other words, Orwell is very human. Perhaps the fact that he writes about this incident indicates how deeply troubled he is by it.

Diction

George Orwell's diction can be characterized as fresh, direct, clear, and simple. It should be noted that his use of slang contributes to the effect of directness and simplicity. After studying the style of this essay, the students should realize that Orwell avoids triteness, euphemism, and superficial language. In short, he is sensitive to language and is well aware of its power when properly handled.

The Prisoners

PAGE 79

Guy de Maupassant

Glossary Words

obstinately (page 80, col. 1) Stubbornly

admonition (page 81, col. 1) Earnest advice; a warning

voraciously (page 81, col. 2) Greedily; gluttonously

ecstatically (page 82, col. 2) With overwhelming joy or delight; joyously

catapult (page 88, col. 2) An ancient weapon for shooting stones, arrows, etc.

Handbook

conflict, diction, identification, irony

Check Test 7

INTRODUCTION

"The Prisoners" takes place during the Franco-Prussian War (1870-1871), one of the series of bitter wars between France and Germany. German troops pushed into France and surrounded Paris. Rather than attack the city directly, they decided to starve the inhabitants into submission. Meantime, the peasantry of France rose to the defense of the city with a kind of guerrilla warfare. "The Prisoners" is a dramatic account of a rural French citizen's success in outwitting six German soldiers.

Obviously, war is a prime example of a conflict of wills on the national level that becomes an individual conflict for each citizen. In the story, Berthine, the daughter of a ranger, is alone with her mother in the forest cottage where the family lives. Six Prussian soldiers arrive—lost, tired, hungry—and demand food and shelter. Berthine feeds them; they behave like well-mannered guests. After the men have fallen asleep in front of the fire, and the girl and her mother have retired upstairs, there is the sudden sound of shots being fired. Berthine appears, tells the soldiers that there are at least two hundred French outside, and urges them to hide in the cellar. After securing the heavy trap door, which is the only exit from the cellar, Berthine laughs to herself, for it is she who had fired the shots. When her father returns late that night, she tells him of her exploit and urges him to get help from Major Lavigne and his troops in order to take the Prussians prisoner. When the prisoners refuse to surrender, the major orders water pumped into the cellar, and they are thereby forced out.

In introducing the story it may be well to discuss the historical background of conflict between France and Germany. Be certain to point out to the students that war spawns thousands upon thousands of conflicts of will, for the will of the nation becomes the will of each individual citizen, and that will is the will to win.

USING THE STUDY NOTES PAGE 85

I. CONFLICT OF WILLS IN WAR

The student is asked to explain why the reader wants Berthine to succeed in capturing the Prussians.

The Prussians are invaders, and Berthine is on her own territory. We generally believe that protecting one's own property is more worthy than trying to wrest something away from others. The author has also told the story from Berthine's point of view, which tends to direct sympathy toward her. In addition, we tend to be on the side of the underdog—and Berthine is one person against six.

II. IMPLICATIONS

Students are asked to give opinions about the following statements and to use the story to support their opinions whenever possible.

1. It is hard to conceive of Berthine and her mother being so very different. The mother is timorous, retiring, and a worrier. Berthine is just the opposite. Notice that she is barearmed and chopping wood outdoors even though it is winter. When her mother worries about their being all alone in the cottage, Berthine says that she could kill either a wolf or a Prussian. The daughter shares this spirit of independence with her father—called "High Horse" because he had refused to leave his home for the greater security of the city.

2. The Prussians do not realize the kind of person that Berthine is. Yes, this is probably true until the incident of the wolves. The soldiers are incredulous (and somewhat appalled) that there should be wolves outside the door, but Berthine is calm and unperturbed. Her attitude should have warned them that she was spirited and competent, but perhaps their exhaustion and hunger dulled their intuitions.

3. The story is a good illustration of Hemingway's definition of courage: "grace under pressure." The answer turns on the definition of "grace." Have students look it up. There are many meanings given for the word. One is, "skill in avoiding the inept or clumsy course—a sense of fitness or propriety." Berthine's capture of the Prussians seems to fit Hemingway's definition.

4. It is surprising that Berthine is not decorated for her part in the capture of the Prussians. Opinions may differ on this. Some may think that the French have always made much of their unusual women: Joan of Arc; George Sand, the writer; Madame Curie, the discoverer of radium, to name a few. Others may think that few governments would recognize a peasant woman's part in a war action that occurred more than a century ago. The question of recognition leads into the next implication.

5. The last paragraph of the story is intentionally ironic. No one can actually say that this paragraph is intentionally ironic, but because de Maupassant is noted for his irony, it would be safe to surmise that such was his intent. After all, it was through Berthine's clever ruse that the soldiers were imprisoned in the first place. There is obvious irony in the fact that Major Lavigne was decorated, the fat baker was awarded the military medal, and Berthine received no recognition of any kind.

III. TECHNIQUES

Identification

The readers' center of interest in the story is Berthine. Do you identify with her, or do you find her

to be an interesting stranger? One can find a character interesting and admirable without feeling any personal identification. Most students will probably be on Berthine's side, and some will actually identify with her. But many students will probably feel that Berthine, who lived in circumstances far different from their own, is not a character with whom they can easily identify.

Diction

Just as individual writers have characteristic ways of writing, so certain word choices or expressions seem characteristic of the period in which they were written. Since this is a nineteenth-century story, it contains phrases, such as those following, that would be expressed differently by a modern author. Try to rephrase them in modern diction. Here are some suggested answers, but obviously, other answers could be equally correct.

1. A daughter of the woods: She grew up in the forest.

2. A wrinkled old woman whom age had made timorous: a frightened old lady

3. An admonition to barricade themselves in the house: a warning to lock all the doors

4. ...they were waiting, well-behaved, like children on school benches: like patients in a doctor's crowded office

5. It would have resisted blows from a catapult: It would have resisted the blows of a wrecking ball.

6. The way coachmen do to keep warm: the way football fans do to keep warm

On Guard

PAGE 86

Evelyn Waugh

Glossary Words

astute (page 86, col. 1) Shrewd, especially with regard to one's own interest; wise

longevity (page 88, col. 2) Long life

phlegmatic (page 89, col. 2) Not easily aroused to feeling or action; indifferent

transfigured (page 89, col. 2) Made more beautiful or glorious; changed in form or appearance

capricious (page 90, col. 1) Likely to change suddenly without reason; changeable; fickle

oblivion (page 90, col. 1) Condition of being entirely forgotten

obtruded (page 90, col. 2) Thrust forward; stuck out

chagrin (page 91, col. 2) A feeling of disappointment, failure, or humiliation; annoyance

artifice (page 92, col. 2) A clever device or trick

irreparable (page 92, col. 1) That cannot be repaired, put right, or made good

Handbook

absurd, conflict, diction, identification, satire

Check Test 8

INTRODUCTION

A young man named Hector takes a fancy to the nose of a Miss Millicent Blade. Hector can find no employment in England and is forced to leave his intended to seek his fortune in Africa. Suspecting that it will require from three to eighty-one years to succeed, Hector buys a dog named Hector to stand guard over Millicent until he can send for her.

As soon as the first Hector is gone, Millicent's nose attracts other young men—largely because it reminds them of noses they had known in their school days. Hector develops a large repertoire of tricks by which he successfully defeats all competitors for his mistress's attention until finally he encounters a really formidable antagonist in the person of Sir Alexander Dreadnought, Bart., M.P. Sir Alexander has been mistreated for decades, and he accepts Hector's worse behavior as naturally due to him.

Hector realizes that the game is up, unless he takes extreme measures. He bites off his mistress's nose. A plastic surgeon is able to patch her up flawlessly, but the new nose is not the old nose. Men no longer seek her out. Thus Hector's mission is accomplished. He ages along with Millicent as she settles into her single life.

With this selection we return to a lighter treatment of our theme. Unlike the earlier comic selections, however, "On Guard" is zany and is a rather sophisticated piece of work. It is also biting social satire, criticizing British manhood, womanhood, courtship, love, and marriage.

The headnote in the text on page 86 is a good introduction to Evelyn Waugh and his special kind of humor. The wildness in his writing can be appreciated by examples such as the speech in which Hector tells Millicent how terrible Africa is going to be—"blinding sun, lions, mosquitoes, hostile natives, work from dawn until sunset single-handed against the forces of nature, fever, cholera"—and concludes, "...but soon I shall be able to send for you to join me." Or consider the sales clerk's remark that tortoises are "very safe in traffic."

USING THE STUDY NOTES PAGE 93

I. WOMAN'S BEST FRIEND?

The idea of a dog "on guard" and doing all the things that Hector does certainly is bizarre, but students should not conclude from this that the story is pointless or entertaining only. The fact is that the behavior of the human characters in the story is occasionally all too close to reality.

II. IMPLICATIONS

Students are asked to give their reactions to the following statements:

1. **The conflict of wills reaches the heights of ridiculousness in this story because one of the antagonists is a dog.** Most students will probably agree with this statement. It should be pointed out, however, that the human characters also behave ridiculously.

2. **A conflict of wills must result in violence.** No. A conflict can end in a nonviolent draw, as it does in the Don Camillo story. Some students may consider the end of "On Guard" nonviolent. (Ask them how they would characterize it if *their* noses had been involved.)

3. Students are asked to discuss which of the following Waugh is attacking.
   a. **British womanhood**
   b. **The courting habits of the British**
   c. **The position of a dog in a society household**
   d. **The ineffectiveness of the British male**

   All are targets. Ask students to cite evidence from the story.

III. TECHNIQUES

Identification

Students are to discuss the following questions:

1. **By making the reader identify with a dog, how does Waugh bring out the absurdity of the situation?** The implication would seem to be that dogs are superior to people, for the dog succeeds, whereas the people fail. Identification with the dog is therefore preferable.

2. **Where does your sympathy shift from Hector to Millicant?** In the very last part of the story, some students may shift their sympathies because of Hector's physical attack on Millicent. The sympathy of some students, however, may remain with Hector.

Diction

Students are asked to read the names of the characters out loud and to discuss how well the names fit the characters. "Hector," of course, was the defender of Troy. "Dreadnought" is a perfect name for Sir Alexander because he is so formidable. "Millicent Blade" seems quite comic and ironically fitting since she is anything but sharp.

IV. WORDS

Students are asked to describe the language of the characters and its effectiveness.

Waugh chooses a level of language that is appropriate to the characters that he is depicting. Both Millicent and Hector use a type of speech that one can readily identify with the upper class. In addition, Millicent's speech has a "lightness" about it that would suggest that she is not a deeply serious person.

Life Sentence

PAGE 94

Martin Andersen Nexø

Glossary Words

galling (page 95, col. 1) Bitter and hateful; irritating

filial (page 96, col. 1) Due from a son or daughter toward a father or mother

pedagogue (page 97, col. 2) Teacher of children; a schoolmaster

incessantly (page 98, col. 1) Continually or repeatedly without interruption; unceasingly

indictment (page 98, col. 1) A formal written accusation of a crime; an accusation of wrongdoing

irately (page 98, col. 1) Angrily; furiously

retribution (page 98, col. 1) A deserved punishment; return for evil done; a reckoning

opaline (page 98, col. 2) Having a play of colors such as those in a rainbow

inveigle (page 98, col. 2) Entice; wheedle

rumination (page 99, col. 1) Meditation; reflection; deep thought

Handbook

balanced sentence, conflict, diction, identification

Check Test 9

INTRODUCTION

"Life Sentence" is a story based on the conflict between a son and his parents, a conflict that springs from the wide difference in their ages and from opposing views of what the son should do with his life. Mattis Lau is a high-spirited child born late in life to a worn-out, rather dull couple. He spends a childhood of deprivation and misery, dreaming of that day when he is old enough to go to sea. A bachelor uncle, regarded as the head of the family because he is the only property owner, offers to bequeath his farm to Mattis on the condition that Mattis marry the old man's faithful housekeeper, Bodil. Although Mattis struggles to resist the pressures, so accustomed is he to doing his duty that he marries Bodil and has a son named Hans. Because of his resentment of what life has done to him, Mattis treats his son in the same cruel fashion that his parents had treated him. However, unlike his parents, Mattis finally realizes what he is doing to his son; it takes time, but he and the boy become good companions. Now he is determined that the boy will get away to the sea even though he himself will feel an awful loss. The boy goes to sea but returns to live with his father. The uncle has at last died, and Mattis's old parents and Bodil move to the farm. But Mattis and Hans continue to live in a shack near the sea while Hans completes a carpenter's apprenticeship. Dreading the boy's departure but determined not to do to his son what his parents had done to him, Mattis finds Hans a job as a ship's carpenter. Although the boy invites Mattis to accompany him to sea, Mattis realizes that he will be a drag on the young man. The story ends with Mattis sitting alone in the shack.

In introducing the selection, you may want to use the title as your springboard. Ask the class what images come to mind when they hear the words "life sentence"? Are there life sentences other than the ones handed down in a criminal court? Try to get the class to expand the idea. A physical handicap could be a life sentence; one's size, coloring, and physical features could be a life sentence. And what about race, sex, nationality? Students may suggest many varied things that can be viewed as life sentences. Then turn to the story and ask them to see how the phrase is used in this selection.

USING THE STUDY NOTES PAGE 101

I. THE POINT OF NO RETURN

At the end of the story, Mattis is described as going back into his prison. At what point did Mattis receive his life sentence? At birth? At the moment he accepted his uncle's offer? Or at some point in between? Some may argue that the die was cast the moment Mattis was born to such an old, defeated couple. Others may think that he could have gone to sea and sent money to his parents, that his inability to leave was the cause of his entrapment. (A point worthy of discussion is *why* he was unable to leave.) Still others may insist that Mattis was free to go until he accepted his uncle's offer.

Did he actually assist in his own imprisonment by his lack of will? Mattis's strong sense of duty and responsibility would not let him leave. But was he so locked into his pattern of self-sacrifice that he could not see alternatives?

II. IMPLICATIONS

Students are asked to give their reactions to the following statements:

1. This story is a classic picture of the conflict between parents and child. If the statement means that the conflict is "classic" because of the differences in ages, goals, and desires that always exist between generations, most students would probably agree. But in today's society there are few parents who actually expect their children to stay home and take care of them; in that sense, the picture is not classic.

2. People tend to do to others exactly what they hated having done to them at an earlier time. The class might consider the hazing of a new member of a gang, a club, or even a class. What breeds this need to continue unpleasant experiences? Do students think that they will treat their own children as they have been treated? Most will probably believe that they will behave in a very different fashion. You could mention that children who have been victims of child abuse usually mature into adults who abuse their own children. What does this fact say about Mattis's behavior toward Hans?

3. Hans is really not as eager to go to sea as his father seems to believe. There is a certain ambiguity here. Hans returns home after his first trip to sea, explaining that the sloop had sprung a leak and was to be laid up. But Mattis knows that the boy could have looked for another seagoing job. Then after the winter has passed, Hans decides to learn carpentry and stay with Mattis during his apprenticeship. Still, Hans does not go out and look aggressively for a job. And yet, when his father has him hired as a ship's carpenter, "a sudden joy" lights the young man's face. Perhaps Hans was also obligated to stay with Mattis, but with a difference—he stayed because of loving concern and Mattis had stayed for duty.

4. There is a profound difference between the quality of Mattis's sacrifice in letting Hans go and his sacrifices for his parents and wife. Yes, Mattis's sacrifice for his son is done out of love and the wish not to stand in Han's way. But what he did for the others was only based on a sense of duty, and he begrudged every sacrifice. The first is an ennobling act, but the second tends to degrade and destroy the doer. Some students may, of course, differ with this interpretation.

III. TECHNIQUES

Identification

The reader's sympathies are definitely with Mattis and against his parents. What has Andersen Nexø done to make the reader feel this way? Have students point out some of the descriptions of the parents: "two people already in fear of age," "the wails of his mother and his father's bleary eyes"; "He was allowed to do neither this nor that"; "they rated dead things above the living child"; "The stick hung over his childhood like a constant threat." Obviously, all the comments about the parents are negative.

What might he have done if he had wanted readers to identify with the parents? The author could have used less caustic, downgrading descriptions. Perhaps the parents were right to urge Mattis to accept the farm. If they had been presented in a more favorable light, their viewpoint about the farm could have been interpreted by readers as having some merit. After all, readers often have sympathy for and identify with people who are even less appealing than the Laus.

Diction

Point out the balanced elements in the sentences that follow.

1. God's gift	young, hot-blooded couple
tardy hand-out	two people already in fear of age
2. He had to do his share of work	which did not bother him at all
3. He	was afraid of no boy in the fishing village
the parents	whimpered when they heard of his recklessness and foolhardy pranks

4. The ones who had something in them	went to sea
the others	took jobs in the capitol or on the far side of the island

This kind of sentence gives a certain quality to the writing. What is that quality? This kind of sentence gives writing rhythmic flow, almost like the surge and the ebb of waves on a beach. It would be good practice for students to write similar kinds of sentences to see what happens to the quality of their writing.

SUMMING UP: CONFLICT AND THE STORY

Students are given pairs of characters from each selection and then are asked to answer a series of six questions, all of which deal with the conflict between the characters. The following are suggestions for variations on this assignment.

Ask students to answer the questions but to do so in the form of an essay on "The Importance of Conflict" (or let them choose a title of their own).

Instead of assigning students one pair of characters, let them choose two pairs and compare and contrast the two. This approach may be particularly interesting if one of the selections is humorous and the other serious. Although you may wish to assign essays, it is not necessary to do so. You could ask students simply to list answers, not necessarily in sentence form, to the questions. When they have completed their answers, they could reread their opinions and then write a paragraph or two on how the conflict of wills affected the characters.

IMPLICATIONS

Students are asked to discuss the following statements by citing examples from the selections in the unit.

1. While a conflict of wills may be settled, the individuals involved never really change their opinions about what they believe. Although the majority of the selections seem to support this point of view, there is a notable exception in the case of Creon. Based on the selections, then, one's conclusion could be that although it is extremely difficult for people to change their minds about the rightness of what they believe, it can happen.

The reluctance to change our opinions may stem from a fear of changing our identities, especially because many of us feel insecure about our conceptions of self.

2. The most devastating kinds of conflict spring from emotions rather than from reason. Perhaps the best approach to this statement would be to ask students to identify the source of conflict in each of the selections. Is it emotion, reason, or a bit of both?

Reason	**Emotion**
Antigone	*Antigone*
"The Prisoners"	"The Little World of Don Camillo"
"On Guard"	"The Jar"
"Life Sentence"	"Life Sentence"
"The Lumber Room"	"The Way Up to Heaven"
	"The Lumber Room"
	"Shooting an Elephant"

With this list before them, students may conclude that emotion plays a part in creating most conflicts. Although emotions do not always create devastating results, when devastating results occurred in this group of readings, the conflict sprang from emotional sources.

3. Conflict is the means by which we test our own values. Conflict is *a* means by which we may test our values. Antigone's values, for instance, were tested in her conflict with Creon, as were Mattis's in his conflict with his parents. But we do not normally seek out a conflict for the purpose of testing values. (Once the conflict has begun, however, it may help those involved to sharpen and define their beliefs.) We may discover a great deal, too, about our own values by observing a conflict, for we often sympathize with the individual whose principles we admire.

4. A conflict of wills may be humorous to the observer, but it is never so to the people involved. "The Little World of Don Camillo," "The Jar," and "The Lumber Room" suggest that there may be moments in which a conflict may seem humorous to at least one of the participants. It is usually a moment when one person feels that he or she has the upper hand or when the opponent is acting like a fool. A conflict also may be seen as humorous after it is over. Don Camillo's concluding remark, for instance, indicates that he is capable of looking upon the preceding incidents good-humoredly. In general, however, the struggle tends to appear far more humorous to the observer than to the participants—which is another way of saying that we have to stand outside ourselves in order to appreciate how funny we are at times.

TECHNIQUES

Identification

The students are to discuss the following questions:

1. For each selection, describe the person or persons with whom you most closely identified. You may want to ask students to read some of the descriptions aloud. This will give them a chance to discuss the *whys* of identification, especially as they discover that two students may identify with the same character for different reasons. You may also want to ask students if they notice any patterns of identification on the part of the class. How do they account for these patterns?

2. Take *one* of the selections. Discuss the approach or approaches by which the writer involves your sympathies with the leading character. Is it by

a. selection of incident?
b. reactions of others toward him or her?
c. description?
d. direct comments about him or her?

NOTE: *Direct comments* refers to direct comments by the author, and *description* refers to word portraits of the character by the author.

Try to arrange it so that at least several students select *Antigone.* They will observe that the last two methods are not used in drama. You may want to point out that the first two methods are often called "dramatic" methods of character development. It is true that in modern dramas methods *c* and *d* are used in the printed play; but, of course, they are not used on the stage.

Diction

Students are asked to describe the dialogue, the vividness of the descriptive passages, and the total effect of a particular selection. To ensure that all selections will be discussed, assign specific ones to students.

WRITING FROM READING

1. This activity is intended to reinforce the unit's theme by asking students to write a dialogue of their own imagining. Students should get their audience to identify with one of the two characters in conflict. Diction and length of sentence will be important in creating the tone of the piece. You might assign a few students to read their dialogues aloud to see if the class identifies with the correct person.

2. This assignment is designed to help students see how important word choice is in creating a reaction in the reader.

3. Students are to write a paragraph using specific sensory words to create a word picture presenting a mood.

Suggestions are made as to the kinds of scenes or interior sets they may choose to describe. Diction plays an important part here. But the last part of the assignment, the introduction of two people performing one swift action, may enhance or destroy the mood. It should be interesting to the class to see what different choices are made and their effect on the piece of writing.

UNIT TEST

There are several options for testing your students' grasp of the unit. You may use the Summing Up section in the pupil's anthology—either whole or in part—as the unit test. For a second approach, you may select questions at random from the Study Notes at the end of each selection as a basis for constructing a final examination covering the complete unit. For a third option, you may choose to use the comprehensive unit test prepared on blackline masters available in a separate booklet, ISBN 0-07-09823-9.

RELATING COMPOSITION TO THE UNIT

SUGGESTED ACTIVITIES

1. Describe an incident from your own life which illustrates the theme CONFLICT OF WILLS.

2. Imagine that you are one of the following characters:

Antigone in *Antigone*
Don Lollo in "The Jar"
Nicholas in "The Lumber Room"
Mattis in "Life Sentence"

Explain whether or not you would have acted differently from the original character in the story. If you would have behaved in a different manner, explain how that behavior would have affected the conflict of wills and how it would have changed the final outcome of the story.

USING THE GALLERIES

The Galleries in each unit are more than collections of fine art. The grouping forms an intrinsic part of the structure of the unit. Each work of art has been deliberately selected not only to serve as a dramatic visualization of the unit theme but also to depict scenes, situations, or persons that students will recognize or find personally stimulating. The works of art are tools that teachers can use—practically, validly, and creatively—to define, present, and personalize the thematic content of this anthology.

Consequently, the old "aesthetics" approach to art that demanded an extensive knowledge of painting, sculpture, and art history on the part of the teacher (and an inordinate amount of patience on the part of the student) has been deliberately avoided. Instead, the galleries are designed as an extension of the structure of the unit. They add extra dimensions to the printed words. The captions and the editorial commentary in the galleries provide all that the teacher needs to know to use and discuss the gallery effectively.

It is recommended that you do not treat the works of art as representations of a distinct and separate art form. Instead, use them as artistic *expressions* that are as valid as writing, music, or any of the other creative arts.

There are, of course, many ways of using these galleries. Your own ingenuity, creativity, and purposes will dictate your approach. However, the following are some suggestions that you may want to consider.

1. Introduce the unit by surveying the works in the gallery.

2. Sum up the unit by relating the works of literature to the works of art.

3. Reinforce the unit themes revealed in the literature through references to the works of art in the galleries.

4. Change the pace by spending class and assignment time on parts of the galleries.

ACTIVITIES

To expedite your planning and to help you to make the galleries part of your teaching strategy, activities have been provided to accompany the galleries.

Some of the activities can be divided into two parts. First, there is an informational or expositional part that is comprised of the first few sentences of the activity. This section can be used if you are merely *discussing* the galleries. The second part contains specific directions for assignments that treat the works of art as expressions of the unit theme. These assignments will permit students to enter into real artistic "experiences" that will encourage them to become involved with the concepts of the theme. Use this part of the activity to gain extensive, creative involvement.

RELATING THE GALLERY TO THE UNIT

PAGE 39

The gallery for this unit emphasizes the art and architecture of the Golden Age of Greece. It is an unusual gallery for the *McGraw-Hill Literature Series* because in all other units the gallery is closely related to the theme of the unit.

1. Rather than merely reflecting the unit theme, this gallery will introduce the concept of human beings as intelligent, reasoning, creative creatures who define themselves through contention, which in turn results in form and meaning. The Golden Age of Greece was certainly an age of conflict between old and new values. The certainties associated with the ancient gods were being challenged by the uncertainties introduced by philosophers. The basic message of Sophocles' *Oedipus Rex* is that humans cannot defy the gods and their prophecies without fatal results. Still, human beings try, and despite some tragic consequences, they do gain a measure of knowledge concerning the form of existence. Form was important to Greek thinkers and creators, but this order was expressed in human terms, as the strict structure of the tragic theater of Greece attests. Within that theater, tragic heros struggled, questioning their own motives, rewards, and tragic ends. It was thus a period in which human beings searched for answers in specific ways. The similarity of the Greek period to our own should remove some of the distance that students may initially feel from the remnants of buildings and statuary that Stephen Sondheim, in *Follies,* describes as "... that lovely debris."

As a general introduction, survey the various ruins, and speculate on the record that our own civilization would leave behind, if future historians were to sift through its ruins. What parallel might there be for the Parthenon? The Acropolis? The Temple at Delphi? Hercules? Pericles? Socrates? The paintings on vases? Is our civilization one in which artists and philosophers can flourish? Why, or why not? As a follow-up activity, direct students to create, through collected artifacts, an exhibition of some of the debris that could be left as a clue to the values that we hold.

2. The role of art in Greek society should be examined through the gallery. Art in Greece gave a form to existence and thus was a comfort to both the artist and to those who exprienced that art. The notion that form in art gives order to the chaos of existence is one argument for the existence of art. This notion should be discussed. Ask students the following questions: Can you think of art that has no form? Would formlessness be satisfying to you? Is it important to you that a story ends satisfactorily? That a piece of music ends without merely drifting off? Could you live a day without structure? Does agreement on the need for form give you a clue about the importance of art for human well-being and comfort?

As a follow-up exercise, pick a general topic such as friendship, defeat, fulfillment, and so on, and instruct students to express this topic in artistic forms. Students should use whatever artistic expressions they wish—songs, poems, stories, paintings, drawings, collages. Note that in translating this general topic into artistic terms, each student will be imposing a form on a formless topic.

3. If you can find the time, you might collect illustrations from newspapers and magazines of conflicts between strong people or groups. Students might assist by seeing what they can find in their reading materials at home. After viewing the collection, discuss what the illustrations say about conflict...how are they the same or different from those reported in the drama and stories?

RELATING THE HUMANITIES TO THE UNITS: THE EXPANDED EXPERIENCE

The Expanded Experience is a humanities approach to the unit topic that is designed to increase the dimension of your teaching and of the students' learning experience. As realists in our shrinking but complex world realize, compartmentalization is an untruth. Experience occurs simultaneously and in groupings of impulses. If American students of the past have been more naive than their European counterparts have been about the entire spectrum of artistic expression and experience, that naïvete can perhaps be attributed to the insistence of the educational community upon specialization through subject matter disciplines.

Perhaps some valid lessons can be learned from the educational experience of the old one-room schoolhouses in which education was based on the spectrum of experience that existed in the world beyond the classroom. Consequently, various abstractions, facts, and concepts were taught and retained because they were, of necessity, presented in a realistic context of interrelationships. The Expanded Experience is really a one-room-schoolhouse approach to each unit theme.

The various disciplines involved in the activities in this section are listed in abbreviated form—see the key below. In addition, the skills involved in each activity are also listed because skills taught in context have generally proved to be skills retained.

SYMBOLS

Disciplines		**Skills**	
M	music	PS	public speaking
A	art	Rd	reading
E	English	Log	logic
SS	social studies	Org	organization
TA	theatre arts	LS	library skills
F	film	Wr	writing skills

The activities have been constructed like building blocks. Each is presented in its ideal or most complete form. Modifications are endlessly possible, depending upon individual needs and/or wishes.

The following are ways to approach and use these activities:

First, you may select one of the activities or you may ask the class to choose one of the activities.

Second, you may use the activities as class exercises or as outside research projects.

Third, you may use the activities as *group* or *individual* projects. If groups are designated, no more than three students should be assigned to any one activity. If the activity is designated as an individual project, only a part of the activity should be assigned.

Fourth, you may use all or part of the activity. Each activity is designed to be used in segments to fit the needs of the class. A comparatively creative class that enjoys working on projects will profit from using the activities intact. Other groups of students will do better using only segments of each activity. For these students eliminate the inappropriate sections, working from the end of the activity back to the beginning. The activities are structured to permit this kind of adaptation without a loss of impact.

Personalization, skill development, and creative expression are the goals of the activities. They are designed to appeal to and to be handled by a variety of students who possess different aptitudes and interests. Some of the projects are designed for students who have verbal skills; some for less verbal students; some for students with artistic skills; some for those with no artistic skills whatsoever. Each activity should provide students with unique, personal opportunities for extending their skills while at the same time developing their comprehension of the unit theme by *doing,* rather than by merely reading.

THE EXPANDED EXPERIENCE: RELATING THE HUMANITIES TO THE UNIT

1. Disciplines: E, SS, TA. Skills: Rd, PS, Org.

Read Ken Kesey's novel *One Flew Over the Cuckoo's Nest.* Using Kesey's story as a model, fashion your own parable—through dance, mime, or improvisation—about a conflict between an individual and the representatives of arbitrary authority. Kesey meant his book to be a symbolic comment on contemporary society, and your parable should be one, too. After the performance, discuss the point of view presented and accept arguments from the rest of the class.

2. Disciplines: TA, E, SS, F. Skills: Rd, PS.

Read selections from Dostoevsky's *The Brothers Karamazov,* or view the film version of the novel. Consider the major conflicts in the work to be those between the values represented by each brother and the father. Translate these values and the story into contemporary terms, and in a series of improvised scenes, present situations that parallel those of the novel or the film. After the performance, ask for reactions from the class. Consider: With whom did class members most easily identify? Did the conflicts portrayed parallel conflicts of values that students have personally had?

3. Disciplines: M, E, F. Skills: Rd, Org.

Ask students to look back at one of the short stories in the unit. Suggest that they try to visualize the story as a movie. If this story were a film, what kind of background music would be used? Students will probably conclude that more than one type of music would be necessary: perhaps lighthearted, melodic music at the beginning and dramatic, exciting music at the climax. (Students should select music appropriate to the excerpts.) What does the addition of music do to the action in the written word?

4. Disciplines: M, E, SS. Skills: PS, LS.

Invite students to bring in records containing lyrics that deal with a conflict of wills. Country music and ballads should prove excellent sources. After a song is played, allow students to lead a discussion of what the lyrics say about conflict. Does the music intensify the comment? Is there a similar conflict in any of the stories? How are the two presentations different or the same?

5. Disciplines: E, SS. Skills: PS, Rd, Wr.

Some of the ideas of Socrates (as recorded by Plato in his *Dialogues*) should be explored in connection with the gallery. The contentions explicit in these dialogues in which Socrates almost always demolished his critics should be explained to the students. Explore some of the ideas by reading aloud the confrontations between Socrates and his students, and ask your students to react to these ideas. On which side do they find themselves? Would they be able to defend themselves against the reasoning, probing mind of Socrates? Have they ever thought of these ideas before? The role of philosophy in civilizing human beings should then be examined: Humans are thinking creatures, but how often do they exercise this capability—as Socrates and his students were willing to do? As a follow-up assignment, students could write and perform a modern meeting in academe between Socrates and his students, speculating abrasively on problems that are vital to your students today.

RELATING ADDITIONAL READING TO THE UNIT

SUGGESTED BOOKS

Barrett, William. *Lilies of the Field*
Brontë, Emily. *Wuthering Heights*
Dürrenmatt, Friedrich. *The Physicists*
Forester, C. S. *The African Queen*
Golding, William. *Lord of the Flies*
James, Henry. *The Turn of the Screw*
Hemingway, Ernest. *The Old Man and the Sea*
Ibsen, Henrik Johan. *Hedda Gabler*
Kesey, Ken. *One Flew Over the Cuckoo's Nest*
Knowles, John. *A Separate Peace*
Lawrence, D. H. *Sons and Lovers*
London, Jack. *Sea Wolf*
du Maurier, Daphne. *Rebecca*
Melville, Herman. *Moby Dick*
Nordhoff, Charles; Hall, James. *Mutiny on the Bounty*
Park, Charles. *True Grit*
Schaefer, Jack. *Shane*
Shakespeare, William. *The Taming of the Shrew*
Swarthout, Glendon. *God Bless the Beasts and Children*
Wharton, Edith. *Ethan Frome*
Williams, Tennessee. *Cat on a Hot Tin Roof*
Wouk, Herman. *The Caine Mutiny*

MEDIEVAL BRITISH POETRY: Understanding Poetry

Check Test 10

In this first of the poetry units that chronologically present British poetry, students are introduced to poetry from the medieval period. They are also introduced to the subject of poetry and the ways in which we talk about poetry. Material concerning language, imagery, meter, and sound effects is gathered in units that are narratively connected but may also be read separately or referred to throughout the course. This preliminary material emphasizes the interconnection of form and feeling. We are suggesting that *what* a poet says is really inseparable from *how* the poet says it. Students need to learn how to deal with both the emotion and the expression of that emotion in poetry.

The first unit is therefore designed to be taught sequentially. We think that you will find it easiest to work through each section and the poems included within it, perhaps bringing in some examples of your own choosing.

The first section, Approaching a Poem, addresses the questions "What is poetry?" and "How do we read it?" Here the short medieval lyric "Western Wind" appears as an example of an intensely emotional poem that seems extremely direct and simple but that becomes more meaningful when one understands *how* it works.

The next three sections, The Language of Poetry, Imagery in Poetry, and Meter in Poetry deal with these formal aspects as the primary components of poetry. The next section, Understanding "Western Wind," returns to that poem, analyzing it in light of the preceding discussion. This analysis may also help students to see how formal terms can be used to arrive at the emotional dimension of a poem.

The next section, Medieval Lyrics, includes "Now Go'th Sun Under Wood," "I Sing of a Maiden," and "Corpus Christi Carol." These lyrics provide excellent material for students to try to analyze on their own.

Another discursive section, Narrative and Drama in Poetry, is followed by three poems that can be discussed in relation to all of the preceding sections: "The Wanderer," "Sir Patrick Spens," and "Edward." The unit concludes with a brief discussion of sound effects.

The major writer Geoffrey Chaucer is represented by excerpts from *The Canterbury Tales* which follow this unit on medieval poetry and maintain the chronological survey.

The following annotated bibliography lists useful sources for the study of British poetry. It includes general books on British history, on British literary history, and on reading and teaching poetry. It also includes sources for each of the chronological periods covered in the text.

SUGGESTIONS FOR FURTHER READING

General Sources: Encyclopedias

Collier's Encyclopedia.
Encyclopedia Americana.

Both contain good essays on the political and literary history of England. *Encyclopedia Americana* divides English literature into periods and furnishes a short bibliography after the essay on each period.

Political and Social Background

The Pelican History of England. Individual titles are: A. R. Meyers, *England in the Late Middle Ages;* S. T. Bindoff, *Tudor England;* Maurice Ashley, *England in the Seventeenth Century;* J. H. Plumb, *England in the Eighteenth Century;* David Thomson, *England in the Nineteenth Century.*

Literary Background

Baugh, A. C. (ed.) *A Literary History of England.* NewYork: Appleton-Century-Crofts, 1948.

Hopkins, Kenneth. *English Poetry: A Short History.* Philadelphia: J. B. Lippincott, 1962.

Norton Anthology of English Literature: useful period introductions and comments on individual authors.

Oxford Anthology of English Literature: useful period introductions and comments on individual authors.

Oxford History of English Literature: a multivolume set, with individual volumes by H. S. Bennett *(Chaucer and the Fifteenth Century),* C. S. Lewis *(English Literature in the Sixteenth Century),* Douglas Bush

(English Literature in the Earlier Seventeenth Century, 1600-1660), James Sutherland *(English Literature of the Late Seventeenth Century),* Bonamy Dobree *(English Literature in the Early Eighteenth Century),* W. L. Renwick *(English Literature, 1789-1815),* Ian Jack *(English Literature, 1815-1832),* and J. I. M. Stewart *(Eight Modern Writers).*

On Reading and Teaching Poetry

Brooks, Cleanth and Robert Penn Warren. *Understanding Poetry.* New York: Holt, Rinehart and Winston, 1961. A classic textbook with long and helpful explanations of imagery, meter, and theme, and explications of many poems.

Koch, Kenneth. *Rose, Where Did You Get That Red?: Teaching Great Poetry to Children.* New York: Random House, 1974. Although Koch worked with elementary school children, his methods can be adapted for any age group.

______. *Wishes, Lies, and Dreams: Teaching Children to Write Poetry.* New York: Random House, 1970. Frequently, we recommend using poetry writing as a way to get students closer to the poem; Koch's examples will suggest many teaching ideas to you.

Nims, John Frederick. *Western Wind: An Introduction to Poetry.* New York: Random House, 1983. A recent classic, combining explanation of poetic terms with marvelous illustrations, poems, and thoughtful explications and questions.

Scholes, Robert. *Elements of Poetry.* New York: Oxford University Press, 1969. Short, precise, imaginative.

Medieval British Poetry

David, Alfred. *The Strumpet Muse: Art and Morals in Chaucer's Poetry.* Bloomington: Indiana University Press, 1976. A comprehensive book on Chaucer's poetry. The chapter on the *Prologue* is fine. The same author has an article in *College English,* 27, (1965), 39-44 on "Criticism and the Old Man in Chaucer's *Pardoner's Tale.*"

Davies, R. T. (ed.). *Medieval English Lyrics.* Evanston: Northwestern University Press, 1964. An anthology, with a good historical and generic introduction, many poems, and helpful footnotes.

Donaldson, E. T. *Chaucer's Poetry.* New York: Ronald, 1958. An edition containing many of the tales with slightly normalized spelling. The notes in the back amount to short, critical essays.

Hoffman, Richard L. and Maxwell S. Luria. (eds.). *Middle English Lyrics.* New York: Norton, 1975. An anthology, with a fine introduction and many poems and critical essays.

Shoeck, Richard and Jerome Taylor (eds.). *Chaucer Criticism. The Canterbury Tales.* Notre Dame: Notre Dame Press, 1960.

Wagenknecht, Edward (ed.). *Chaucer: Modern Essays in Criticism.* New York: Oxford University Press, 1959.

Renaissance British Poetry

Booth, Stephen. *An Essay on Shakespeare's Sonnets.* New Haven: Yale University Press, 1961. A superb book on the sonnets, showing in detail how they work, metaphorically, grammatically, technically. The book not only analyzes many sonnets but teaches the reader how to read them carefully.

Shakespeare, William. *The Sonnets.* Signet edition, (1964), William Burto, (ed.), with an introduction by W. H. Auden. Good footnotes.

Smith, Hallett. *Elizabethan Poetry: A Study in Convention, Meaning, and Expression.* Cambridge: Harvard University Press, 1964.

Spenser, Edmund. *The Faerie Queene, Books I and II.* Robert Kellogg and Oliver Steele (eds.). New York: Odyssey, 1965. A fine modern edition (from which our selection has been taken). The explanatory notes, both in the introduction and in the text, are quite helpful.

Seventeenth- and Eighteenth-Century British Poetry

Fish, Stanley E. *Surprised by Sin: The Reader in Paradise Lost.* Berkeley: University of California Press, 1971. Like Booth's book on the sonnets, Fish's reading is both an explanation and a model for how to read Milton.

Keast, William R. (ed.). *Seventeenth-Century English Poetry: Modern Essays in Criticism.* New York: Oxford University Press, 1962. Good essays on Donne, Jonson, Marvell, and others.

Paradise Lost appears in two modern editions, one edited by Merritt Y. Hughes (Odyssey Press), with a long, historical introduction on Milton's thought, and one edited by Scott Elledge (Norton), with a number of critical essays at the end of the edition. Both have helpful footnotes.

White, Helen C., Ruth C. Wallerstein, and Ricardo Quintana (eds.). *Seventeenth-Century Verse and Prose* (2 vols.). New York: Macmillan, 1952. Extremely good period introductions.

Nineteenth-Century British Poetry

The closer we get to our own century, the more accessible the poems become. Therefore we mention only a few titles that may be of interest.

Bate, Walter Jackson. *John Keats.* New York: Oxford University Press, 1963. A superb biography and critical work combined. The chapter on the writing of the great odes is helpful in showing how the odes fit into Keats's life and how he developed the particular form that he used for them.

English Romantic Poets: Modern Essays in Criticism. New

York: Oxford University Press, 1960. This anthology of essays, compiled by M. H. Abrams is especially fine. There are essays on each of the major figures: Blake, Wordsworth, Coleridge, Byron, Shelley, and Keats plus several introductory essays on romanticism in general. Abrams's own essay, "The Correspondent Breeze: A Romantic Metaphor," is most helpful.

Langbaum, Robert. *The Poetry of Experience: The Dramatic Monologue in Modern Literary Tradition.* New York: Norton, 1963. The book focuses on Browning but also develops the fascinating idea of the tension between sympathy and moral judgment that is produced by a work such as "My Last Duchess."

Twentieth-Century British Poetry

Brooks, Cleanth. *Modern Poetry and the Tradition.* Chapel Hill: University of North Carolina Press, 1939. Essays on the relationship between modern poetry and earlier works, with special emphasis on Auden, Eliot, and Yeats.

Hollander, John (ed.). *Modern Poetry: Essays in Criticism.* New York: Oxford University Press, 1968. Essays on all the major poets, both English and American.

Unterecker, John. *A Reader's Guide to William Butler Yeats.* New York: Farrar, Straus, Giroux, 1959.

Williamson, George. *A Reader's Guide to T. S. Eliot.* New York: Farrar, Straus, Giroux, 1957.

Medieval Lyrics

PAGE 107

Handbook

couplet, metaphor, refrain, stanza

Check Test 11

INTRODUCTION

The three medieval lyrics (pages 107-109) work on at least two levels at once. Each is centered in the real world, a world where one may see a sunset or feel dew falling or even, in the Middle Ages, behold a wounded knight. And yet each of these lyrics implies a religious experience as well. They are therefore good poems to start with; the religious implication is reasonably clear in each case, and yet each poem does not reduce to a symbolic reading. Moreover, the poems offer an introduction to the use of simple, repeated phrases and the ways in which this kind of language can be poetic. Students will also note the dependence on understatement that marks each of these poems, as it did "Western Wind." Perhaps an exercise in which students are asked to convey a feeling through a metaphor or through a description will give them a sense of how difficult it is to achieve the emotion—and how successful these poems are in doing precisely that. Finally, we should note that each poem preserves a kind of mystery about itself. We cannot be absolutely sure of the poet's meaning, perhaps because the poet is not trying to present a moral lesson but is working instead toward projecting the emotional quality of the experience. Consequently, students will have to exercise a certain amount of tact—these poems cannot be *totally* explicated—and that is something worth learning very early in the study of poetry.

USING THE STUDY NOTES

PAGE 108

NOW GO'TH SUN UNDER WOOD

1. Some editions give this poem the title "Sunset on Calvary." Why doesn't the speaker just refer to that moment? What details in the poem create that reference? Much of the poem's force comes from the fact that the Crucifixion is *not* referred to. In the first line, the speaker seems to be describing a sunset with the sun (sonne) going under or into the woods. The introduction of an emotional reaction by the speaker in the second line, "Me reweth," and the fact that the woman addressed is named Mary makes us rethink the first line. We begin to wonder *why* the speaker pities Mary. We are aware of some contrast between the darkening of the day and the fairness of Mary's face. The repetition in the third line of the sunset metaphor sets up the fourth line in which the pun on *sun* and *son* finally becomes clear. The speaker's compassion is for Mary's son suffering on the cross and also for Mary witnessing that suffering. By holding off the sun/son pun until the last line, the poet makes us sense that something pitiful is happening, but that something is not fully experienced until the end of the poem.

2. This poem is made up of two couplets that are similar, but not exactly the same. What is the emotional force of the repeated words? What is the emotional force of the different words? The repetition, especially of "Me reweth," which is the only explicit feeling in the poem, stresses the speaker's compassion. The repetition in lines 1 and 3 is carefully set up to emphasize the difference between *wood,* which could be a natural object (the sun seems to set behind or go into a wood, for example) and *tree,* which is a single, isolated part of that wood. Both *wood* and *tree* are words that together remind us of Christ's cross. By introducing them singly, the speaker preserves both their actual identity as natural objects and their symbolic force. Similarly, the repetition of *sonne* is designed to make us hear that word in one context—that of the *sun.* We later realize that it is a sound pun for quite another word, *son.* The fact that *sun* and *son* should sound the same stresses their symbolic relationship; the sun lights the natural world, as Christ brings light to the spiritual world.

I SING OF A MAIDEN

1. What are the details in the poem which imply that the maiden is really the Virgin Mary? Why is that revelation kept for the last line? The pun on *makeless* is our first indication: The maiden is without a mate and also without equal. The biblical flavor of line 3, "King of alle kinges" lets us know that she is probably the Virgin. The poet plays with the paradox suggested in the first stanza and then spelled out in the last stanza, "Mother and maiden." By delaying the revelation, he makes us supply it for ourselves in order to understand the rest of the poem. The middle stanzas create our emotional reaction to the special event. The last stanza ("Well may such a lady/ Godes mother be") tells us what we have already sensed and so provides a conclusion.

2. The second, third, and fourth stanzas are very much alike, with only a slight variation in the metaphor. What is the emotional effect of those three stanzas? Students may have a number of different reactions to these stanzas. Some may find them hypnotic in a gentle way. The repetition of "He came also stille" tends to lull the reader into a sense of the quiet intimacy of Christ's conception. Other students may find that the repetition of "dew in Aprille" emphasizes spring as the season of rebirth and dew as an emblem of grace; this phrase therefore stresses the spiritual aspect of the scene. Still other students may be struck by the natural quality implied in each of the three metaphors—grass, flower, spray—and by the progression from the earth and grass, to a single flower, to a spray (a group of flowers). There is also something mysterious about these three stanzas—the event described seems to be the same because it is introduced with the same ritual phrase, "He came also stille." But it is not quite the same; perhaps the poet is telling us that all metaphors are, in some way, appropriate but all are inadequate to describe this moment.

THE CORPUS CHRISTI CAROL

1. The poem begins with a refrain that we are intended to hear after each of the stanzas. What effect does the refrain create? The first line creates the sense of a lullaby, a kind of soft and crooning tune that is sung repeatedly. The second line reminds us of the loss of the "make" (mate) that cannot be forgotten. The effect of the refrain is thus both accepting and mournful at the same time.

2. What is the actual situation implied in the poem? What details might suggest a religious significance in that situation? On the surface, there is a maiden mourning by the side of a wounded knight. However, there are many symbolic details in the poem—the title and the last line, the association of the colors (purple, gold, red) with priestly vestments, and the continual bleeding of the wounds. All of these details imply that the knight is Christ and that the communion service, in which Christ dies again, is being celebrated.

3. What is the emotional force of the following: "an orchard brown," "purple and pall," "gold so red"? We note a progression from the contradictory "brown" of the orchard (which gives us a feeling of a dead place) to the funeral associations of "purple" (which are also contradicted by the royal associations of purple) to the final contradiction of "gold so red." That last phrase suggests both the triumph of the royal gold and the defeat of the bleeding knight. As with so many other features of this poem, students may develop different interpretations of those phrases.

4. One might describe this poem in cinematic terms: The camera (speaker's voice) moves closer and closer to the scene, focusing first on the setting, then on the characters, and finally on the stone and its inscription. What is the effect of this progression? The technique of narrowing is a sophisticated form of the understatement that we have seen in the previous poems. It is also a way of controlling our understanding and our response. We are asked, first, to note the outside signs (the orchard, the hall, the bed), then, to see the knight and the maiden weeping for him, and, finally, to understand that he is Christ. The poet does not want only an emotional response, although the refrain reminds us of mourning. Rather he wants us to discover the meaning of Christ's sacrifice as we discover what the poem is actually describing.

The Wanderer
Sir Patrick Spens
Edward

PAGE 111

***Glossary Words** (for "The Wanderer")*

wretchedness (page 111) Condition of being very unfortunate, unhappy, miserable

winsomeness (page 112) Quality of being charming, attractive, and pleasing

redress (page 113) A setting right; relief; a remedy

Handbook

ballad, conflict, imagery, narrator, stanza

***Check Test 12** (for "The Wanderer," "Sir Patrick Spens," "Edward")*

INTRODUCTION

"The Wanderer," "Sir Patrick Spens," and "Edward" are grouped together because they followed naturally after the discussion of narrative and drama in poetry. They are all early poems. "The Wanderer" dates from the tenth century, and the two ballads were written somewhere between 1200 and 1700. "Sir Patrick Spens" may even be an eighteenth-century poem written in the style of the medieval ballads. The important point, however, is that all three of these poems present immediately evocative characters, or stories, or both.

"The Wanderer" is frequently called an *elegaic* poem because it mourns the death of a way of life—the cheerful, secure circle around a feudal lord. The Wanderer of the poem's title begins as a wretched man, "weary of exile," remembering what has happened to him. In spite of his statement that "the mark of a man/Is keeping his counsel and locking his lips," (lines 12–13) he feels impelled to speak. It is as if his sorrow bursts out of its "grave," "deep in the breast" (line 17), or breaks from the chains (line 19) that have restrained his speech. Even in dreams, his memories of happier days turn into elusive visions, almost like nightmares. From personal sorrow he passes to a more generalized sorrow; it is not only *his* world that is transitory, but the joys of all the world. Perhaps, although this is not explicit, the realization that "All the foundation of earth shall fail," (line 102) is what gives him the impetus to look toward God. God is here described as a "Fortress"—a strong, secure building in contrast to the storm-battered ramparts and the failing foundation of earth.

Certainly the poem is firmly rooted in the Old English version of security, but this notion is not really so different from ours today. We place a value on the family, whereas the Old English warrior placed value in the *comitatus* (the warrior band or family assembled around a lord who gave treasure to his followers and protected them). Those who have read *Beowulf* will find this idea familiar. Students might be encouraged to make a list of the things that they associate with security and love and then ask to compare their lists with the Wanderer's.

"Sir Patrick Spens" and "Edward" are more familiar to both teachers and students than is "The Wanderer." The dramatic qualities in these poems are obvious, and the ways in which the poets work by excluding certain details and including others are useful approaches on which to focus. One may want to compare the ballads, asking what would be lost if "Sir Patrick Spens" were constructed entirely in dialogue or if "Edward" had narrative passages. This kind of experimentation is usually interesting for students: it encourages them to practice manipulating form and thus to discover why a poem is put together as it is.

USING THE STUDY NOTES

PAGE 117

THE WANDERER

1. What are the positive images that the Wanderer remembers? What kind of life does he value? In concrete terms, he remembers his "dear lord" (line 21), later specified as a "gold-lord" (that is, a giver of treasure) and a comforter (line 25). He values treasure not only for itself but because it is associated with a way of life that included feasting and companionship (lines 31–32). The emphasis on companionship becomes stronger in lines 35–47. Here the dreams of vowing loyalty to his liege lord are contrasted with the bitter reality of cold, wet loneliness. Also, he dreams here of his kinfolk, only to have their shapes "melt into air." In addition to the values of friendship and security *implied* in the above images, he *explicitly states* some of his other values: silent stoicism (lines 12–17); loyalty (line 37); moderation, patience, and humility (lines 59–63); acceptance of fate (lines 64–65); and, finally, faith in God (line 102).

2. What are the natural images in lines 1–51 that suggest the Wanderer's state of mind? There is a chain of images of cold, wet loneliness expressed in the following phrases: "wintry seas" (line 4); "icy wave" (line 5); "dark earth" (line 21); "a heart that is frozen" (line 29); "gray stretches of tossing sea" (line 40); "sea-birds bathing" (line 41); "While hailstorms darken, and driving snow" (line 42); and "tossing sea" (line 51). The images emphasize the Wanderer's sorrow and despair.

3. What advice does the Wanderer offer for coping with life's sorrows? There are a number of possible solutions. At first he seems to recommend quiet suffering, noncomplaining. Travel, the ceaseless exile that he seems unable to leave ("And grimly he spurs his weary soul / Once more to the toil of the tossing sea."), may be another antidote. The description of the wise man (beginning on line 59) offers yet another solution—finding the moderate way to live. And from that moderation will come acceptance by seeing that the entire world is composed of transitory buildings, people, and pleasures.

4. Lines 78–100 are built on a familiar medieval motif referred to as *ubi sunt?* ("where are they now"?). Why do you think this melancholy listing comes near the end of the poem? One can argue that the poem moves from the particular to the general, from the loss experienced by one man to the loss that we all must feel. Therefore the *ubi sunt?* passage would naturally come when the speaker sees the universality of his sorrow. Or one could say that, psychologically, the speaker begins by considering his own loneliness in a world where nothing seems to last. He sinks into a deeper despair when he begins to believe that the whole world is like that. One can also find a different psychological movement, a movement away from a sense that only he is afflicted and toward a realization that everything is fleeting. And from that realization comes a degree of comfort for him. The concrete details of the passage—the "bright ale cup," the "byrny-clad warrior" and that curiously decorated wall—help to make it emotionally powerful. The evocation of the past is made quite specific and is stated in terms that could apply to all men not just to the Wanderer; the reader can thus feel the beauty and the warmth of that vanished civilization. In this sense the passage balances lines 20–51 in which the Wanderer remembers his particular loss. The poem returns to a cataloging of loss so that we, as readers, can share the Wanderer's feelings.

5. Consider the following statements from the poem. Do you agree or disagree with them? Why?

a. **I have learned truly the mark of a man**
Is keeping his counsel and locking his lips,
Let him think what he will!

b. **No man may know wisdom till many a winter**
Has been his portion.

c. **Wretchedness fills the realm of earth,**
And Fate's decrees transform the world.

These statements are likely to be challenged by students, who may thus reveal many of their own values. In response to the first quotation, students may argue that it is psychologically harmful to keep things "bottled up" inside. Discussion could focus on whether there are situations in which not speaking is the best thing to do. The second quotation will probably be especially provoking to high school students. How can one say that you have to be older in order to develop wisdom? Here the discussion could look at the extent to which the statement may be true—what kinds of things do we learn from experiences that usually come later in life (a job, marriage, birth of a child, death, and so on). The third quotation is extremely pessimistic and yet not entirely beyond our understanding, especially in a world faced with the threat of thermonuclear weapons. You may want to use this question to provoke students to think about the problem of fate. To what extent are we controlled by some outside force and to what extent do we control our own lives?

SIR PATRICK SPENS

1. How does the picture of the king, told in the first two lines, show his attitude toward the job he is assigning? It may be assumed by most students that the king is careless in the job that he is assigning because he is sitting and drinking at the time; however, the next two lines indicate that he will not accept an ordinary sailor for the job. Recall, too, that the sailor is to take many Scotch nobles with him. Perhaps the king is more worried than careless, and the drinking may signal his concern.

What is the significance of the fact that the king does not seem to know the best sailor in his kingdom? That the king does not know the best sailor in his kingdom may indicate that his life has been spent exclusively with lords and rulers. He may have little time for common men or sailors—even for a "guid sailor."

Who suggests the name of Sir Patrick to the king? Why is it significant that he "sat at the king's right knee"? An elderly knight suggests Sir Patrick. The fact that the knight is at the king's right side may indicate that he is a favorite; the fact that he is sitting at the king's knee could indicate that the king has no peers (that is, everyone sits below him) or that the knight is not a peer of the king.

2. The fourth stanza has a vivid contrast between the first two lines and the last two. How has Sir Patrick's attitude changed in the last two lines? Sir Patrick's attitude changes from one of disbelief to one of deep sadness, as signaled by the shift from laughter to tears.

3. Is Sir Patrick really asking a question in the fifth stanza or is he simply raging against an unjust fate? He is most probably doing the latter, but it would be difficult to establish the point with certainty. It is possible that Sir Patrick has enemies at court and that the elderly knight is one of them.

4. Why doesn't the narrator describe the storm? How do the images in the eighth stanza convey the scene and the emotional effect of the drowning? This is an instance in which understatement is more powerful then mere statement. The poet does not create a chaotic scene in which the ship sinks and the lords try frantically to save themselves. In the absence of such description, we are struck by the inevitability of the tragedy. Because we are not told about the storm, it is almost as though there is no chance to stop it. We are told that the nobles were "richt laith" to get their shoes wet; the understatement is so extreme here that it forces us to imagine the opposite, namely, that they are going to their deaths with horror and fear. The picture of the hats floating on the waves reminds us necessarily of the bodies sunk below. We do not need a graphic picture—the single detail is gruesome because it is so underplayed.

5. Where do the narrator's sympathies lie? Clearly, they lie with the "guid," loyal, and courageous sailor. Students may also feel that there is sympathy for the dead nobles or at least for their ladies, but the concrete details in lines 29-32, 34, 38, and 44 make this seem improbable.

6. Is the basic conflict between the king and Sir Patrick or between Sir Patrick and the elder knight? Is it between a simple man of action and a group of politicians or between duty and common sense? Or is it between each of these pairs? On the personal level, the basic conflict is between the king and Sir Patrick. The elder knight simply offers Sir Patrick's name, and there seems to be no evidence in this version of the poem to indicate any guile on his part. Each conflict may be seen in the poem, but the conflict between the simple man of action and a group of politicians is the most significant.

7. Ballads often represent the voice of the common people protesting against the social order in which they live. If you look at this ballad from this point of view, what is it saying? It is saying that a person should be judged by deeds, not by rank, and that a relatively common person may be a king of a sort. To put this point dramatically, ask students to compare line 6 with line 44. Moreover, the poem suggests that a common person may be much better than a king—physically, morally, and spiritually—and that the social order should be based on a person's worth rather than hereditary position.

EDWARD

1. Dialogue makes up the whole poem. Who are the two speakers? Edward and his mother are the two speakers.

2. What is Edward's rank in society? What lines in the song supply this information? The sword, hawk, and steed suggest that Edward was a knight. The towers and hall (line 33) were probably inherited from his father, who was presumably a member of the nobility.

3. Is the mother really seeking information? Or does she know the answer all along? She knows that he has killed his father. However, she is seeking information about what he is going to do. A particular concern is what he is going to leave to her.

4. Why does Edward try to avoid telling the truth to his mother? The chief reason is that he does not want to admit it to himself; line 24 indicates that it is very painful for him to do so.

5. The poem represents an intense moment of conflict between mother and son, but not the whole story that led up to this moment. Can you reconstruct the essential story from hints given in the poem? What kind of woman is the mother? What do you suppose were her motives? Edward's mother advised him to kill his father, perhaps suggesting to him that he would then gain the father's estate. She presumably did not love her husband and wanted him out of the way. She must also have thought that she would be in a better position with her son in control of the estate. Or, possibly, she foresaw how the murder would affect him and hoped that she would gain control herself.

Geoffrey Chaucer

The Canterbury Tales: Prologue

PAGE 123

Glossary Words

engendering (page 123, col. 1) Bringing into existence; producing
solicitous (page 126, col. 1) Showing care or concern; anxious; concerned
prelate (page 127, col. 1) Clergyman of high rank
palfrey (page 127, col. 1) A gentle riding horse, especially one used by ladies
verity (page 127, col. 1) Truth; a true statement or fact
accrue (page 127, col. 2) Increase gradually, like the interest on money
secular (page 128, col. 2) Not religious or sacred; worldly
felicity (page 129, col. 2) Great happiness; bliss
abstrusest (page 134, col. 2) Most hard to understand; most difficult
prevarication (page 137, col. 2) Turning aside from the truth; a falsehood; a lie

Handbook

characterization, irony, satire

Check Test 13

INTRODUCTION

The "Prologue" to *The Canterbury Tales* is a literary masterpiece that has withstood all shifts of taste, all tests of time. It remains a portrait gallery virtually unparalleled in the history of literature; it offers the reader a catalog of virtues and vices and of human types that describes not only Chaucer's own time but also our time.

Students should read the introduction in the text—with the possible exception of the material presented in the section Chaucer's Language—before beginning the selection. The account of Chaucer's life will show him to be the kind of person most Americans admire—well-rounded. The material on page 122 will provide useful background for the reading of the "Prologue."

The ability of the students that you are teaching, as well as your own background, will probably determine how much time you will spend on Chaucer's language, but we would like to make two observations. First, consider deferring extensive discussion of Chaucer's language until your students have read at least some of the "Prologue." Indeed, we believe that students should read the entire selection before much is said about Chaucer's language, for it is what Chaucer says rather than how he says it that will be the primary interest of most high school readers. Second, it is true that nearly all students will be interested in hearing Chaucer's own English. Therefore, do get a reading of some selections of the "Prologue" if at all possible or read the selection given on page 121 if you are able.

How you break the reading up will depend upon the ability of the classes that you are teaching, but even the best classes should not be given the whole "Prologue" in a single assignment. They will be *able* to read it all, of course, but they will hardly be likely to appreciate it. Point out to students that the selection is not a story. For slower readers the first assignment may be page 123 only or, at most, this page and the first two portraits. As students get used to the language and the rhythm, you will probably be able to increase the length of assignments, but overly long assignments will almost certainly lead to blurring of the individual portraits.

USING THE STUDY NOTES PAGE 139

I. PORTRAITS IN A FRAME

First, it would be advisable for students to make a list of Chaucer's characters. The list should include a summary of what each character does, if that is not obvious from the individual's name. Students should then be able to discuss such questions as the following:

1. Which of the professions named are still important in our own society? Here the students must be careful about the terms that Chaucer uses. Thus, his Plowman is equivalent to our farmer and his Franklin could be considered the equivalent of our real estate tycoon, or some such term.

2. Which professions do not exist at all in contemporary American society? Students may also wish to speculate on *why.* They should be able to discern that the breakdown of the class system has, by and large, eliminated the need for such persons as reeves and manciples, and they should perceive that increasing secularization (and other causes as well) has eliminated the need for Pardoners.

3. Which professions exist but are much less prominent than they were in Chaucer's time? In this case, it should be clear that modern technology has lessened the role of tradespeople and that increasing secularization has decreased the prominence of prioresses, monks, and friars.

4. What professions are important in contemporary society and are not listed by Chaucer? Here again, the emphasis should be on the *why.* Thus in asking why salespersons are relatively important in our society and were much less important in Chaucer's, we can learn a good deal about both societies. Of course, it should not be assumed that Chaucer set out to list every profession of his time. Certainly, there were teachers in Chaucer's society. Still, his failure to include a teacher among his pilgrims may indicate that teaching was a profession practiced by far fewer individuals than it is in our society, in which education is compulsory.

II. IMPLICATIONS

Students are asked to discuss the following statements and to cite evidence from their reading of the "Prologue."

1. Chaucer the poet does not admire the Monk as completely as does Chaucer the pilgrim.

It is easy to see that Chaucer the pilgrim does admire the Monk a good deal. He calls him "a prelate fit for exhibition"; he agrees with his modern views; he calls him "one of the finest sort." To document the assertion that Chaucer the poet admires the Monk less, students will have to do a little reading between the lines. They may note for one thing that the Monk is physically unprepossessing. Gluttony is also implied in his preference for whole fat swans, not to mention all the food imagery used in the description: "plucked hen," "fish," and "oyster." (And note his *greased* face.)

Another contrast between Chaucer the poet and Chaucer the pilgrim is in the attitudes displayed toward the Monk's failure to obey his vows. The poet indicates his disapproval of this disobedience by inserting such details as the fact that the Monk's bridle has bells, that he has "many a *dainty*" horse in his stable, that—in general—"he spared for no expense" in pursuing sport. In short, the reader learns that the Monk not only disobeys his vows but does so in a flagrant manner.

The argument about leaving the world on a shelf—with which Chaucer the pilgrim agrees—lacks force, for that was precisely what Benedictine monks were supposed to do. Chaucer the poet would have observed that if the Monk did not want to leave the world on a shelf, he should not have entered a monastery in the first place.

2. From his portraits of the religious figures on the pilgrimage, we can be sure that Chaucer admired the Church of his day wholeheartedly.

In discussing this statement, students should be careful to distinguish between the Church and the people of prominence in the Church. Chaucer disapproves, and harshly at times, of most of the church-people on the pilgrimage. He gently chides the prioress, whose vanity is only partly submerged in her role as a nun. He blasts the Monk, who swaggeringly dismissed all the rules of monastic life, and also the Friar, who lives contrary to the purpose and spirit of the Franciscan order. He bitterly satirizes the Summoner and the Pardoner, both hideous frauds. He disapproves of these church figures principally because they fail to live up to the ideals of the Church. Thus the Church, or at least some of its institutions and ideals, is the norm against which these people are measured and found wanting.

Help students to realize, for example, that the Monk flaunts almost every rule of monastic life. Have them note that the rules themselves are not criticized. On the contrary, the Monk "damns" himself by totally rejecting the labor with soil and with book that characterizes the work of a monk and the life of poverty, chastity, and obedience that did so much to civilize a barbarous world, preserve the Greco-Roman heritage, and foster economic, political, social, intellectual, and spiritual growth. Likewise, Chaucer does not criticize the ideals that the Friar should have aspired to uphold. The Friar is despicable because he deviates from those worthy norms set by St. Francis. The norms are not in error; the Friar is.

By implication, Chaucer compares the "worthy" clerics to the Parson, whose Christlike charity and humility constitute a positive statement of the religious ideals that Chaucer himself seems to espouse. The Parson is a church official whom Chaucer does seem to admire wholeheartedly. Chaucer criticizes the others to varying degrees. Insofar as these people are the Church, Chaucer dislikes the Church of his time. But he obviously does admire the ideals embodied in the Parson and implied in the norms against which the deviations of the other religious leaders are satirized. In this sense Chaucer does admire the Church and its principles.

3. One of the most famous poems of the twentieth century, T. S. Eliot's *The Waste Land,* opens also with a passage about April and spring:

> April is the cruellest month, breeding
> Lilacs out of the dead land, mixing
> Memory and desire, stirring
> Dull roots with spring rain.

Contrast this with the opening of the "Prologue." What are the implications of each as to the attitudes of the twentieth century and the attitudes of the fourteenth century toward nature, spring, and love?

In Chaucer's poem there is obvious delight with spring and with nature. It is the season of physical rebirth, and it prompts the pilgrims to seek spiritual rebirth. In Eliot's version of the modern world there is a loss of faith and spiritual values. People prefer the "death" of winter to the "life" of spring. There is a fear of the kind of change that spring brings, of "mixing/Memory and desire." Of course, Eliot's is *a* view of the twentieth century, just as Chaucer's is *a* view of the fourteenth century.

III. TECHNIQUES

Characterization and Contrast

Students are given a list of attributes that Chaucer used in making his character sketches. Then they are asked to compare one pair of characters from a group of six pairs. To the extent that it is possible, students should have a choice, but you will probably want to discuss all six pairs (and perhaps some others of your own choosing). Try therefore to get at least one volunteer for each of the pairs. Also, do not overlook the possibility of small group assignments. Each group could be assigned two pairs, and the judgments of one group could be compared with those of another about the same pair of characters.

Students are also asked to tell which pilgrims are presented without satire or irony. The only ones are the Parson and the Plowman.

The Pardoner's Tale

PAGE 141

Geoffrey Chaucer

Glossary Words

pallor (page 142, col. 2) Lack of color from fear, illness, death, etc.; paleness

prating (page 143, col. 1) Empty or foolish talk

parley (page 143, col. 2) A conference or informal talk

miscreants (page 144, col. 1) Base or wicked persons; villains; rascals

perdition (page 144, col. 1) Damnation; loss of one's soul and the joys of heaven

apothecary (page 144, col. 1) Druggist; pharmacist

Handbook

dialogue, irony, mood, short story

Check Test 14

INTRODUCTION

Three rioters are drinking in a tavern and hear a funeral procession going by. Upon learning that the deceased is a friend of theirs, they decide that they will catch and kill Death. Early in their mission they meet an old man—he is really Death—who tells them that they will find Death at a nearby oak.

Rushing to the tree, they find gold. After some consultation among themselves, they resolve to send one person to town for provisions while the others watch over the gold until nightfall. The two who remain behind then agree to stage a wrestling match with the third when he returns; during the match they will stab him to death. Meanwhile, the third man has been hatching his own plot. He buys some poison in town and puts it in two of the three wine bottles that he has purchased. When he returns, he is killed in the wrestling match, and the other two are killed by the poisoned wine. Death has had his day.

This selection, though in verse, is a good example of the early "short story." Of special note is Chaucer's heavy reliance on dialogue to establish character and the tight structure and the economy of the tale.

Point out that the story is arranged in stanzas. (This is not immediately obvious.) Also remind students that when a new stanza begins, quotation marks are repeated at the beginning, even though the speaker does not change. Students can see that the speaker has not changed by noting the absence of quotation marks at the end of the preceding stanza. Good instances of this may be pointed out in lines 67–68 and again in lines 81–82. The old man is the only speaker in this portion of the poem.

This tale is relatively short and simple. Ask students to read it in a single session.

USING THE STUDY NOTES

PAGE 144

I. A SHORT STORY IN VERSE

Evidences of Chaucer's restraint are found throughout the tale. Most conspicuous, of course, is the ending, where—the point having been made—he closes quickly, without fully rendering the fight scene or the poison drinking. Another good instance is the opening. Note how the initial remarks of the Pardoner give only the barest minimum of detail: the time, the place, the "actors," and the funeral hand-bell for atmosphere. Then he plunges at once into dialogue. For a third instance, note how quickly the rioters make and seal the plan to kill Death (lines 34–45).

II. IMPLICATIONS

Students are asked to defend or refute the following propositions:

1. The portrait of the Pardoner in the "Prologue" doesn't suit a person who could tell such a sensitive tale as this. Students should first ask themselves in what sense the tale is sensitive. Second, they would do well to reread the sketch of the Pardoner (pp. 141–142); they should observe (lines 705 ff.) that he has become a storyteller of some competence because his livelihood depends on it.

2. The details given about the old man in the story clearly indicate that he is Death. The details may not "clearly" indicate to all students that the old man is Death, but the indication is certainly there. Notice the greeting that he uses (line 56); notice that when the proudest rioter asks him, "Isn't it time to die?" he looks the rioter straight in the eye; notice that the old man shows only his face and that he cannot himself die; notice that he walks alone; notice the veiled threat in line 90. And even these imitations do not complete the catalog.

III. TECHNIQUES

The Short Story, Dialogue, Details

Students are asked to respond to the following statements:

1. The characters in this story have ironic speeches. Cite several instances where they are saying far more than they think they are. The following are some instances: "Isn't it time to die?" (line 60); "And you're his spy, by God!" (line 98); "Who would have thought / This morning was to be our lucky day?" (lines 125–126); "For later on there'll be the corpse to bury" (line 229). The students may find other instances as well.

2. Explain how the simple, natural dialogue increases the terror of the supernatural forces that are effortlessly achieving their end. The terror arises from the reader's perception of the *contrast* between the human people and the supernatural forces that are working against them. The reader continuously sees beyond the present moment, sees more than the participants perceive in their natural actions and motives. Incidentally, the terror would increase still more if the reader were to identify with the rioters.

3. How can Chaucer's power to give meaning to details be seen in the first rioter's excuse to the apothecary when asking for poison? The rioter says that he has rats and a polecat to kill, and these animals aptly describe his friends. The "vermin that destroy a man by night" are at that very moment planning just that—just as he, another rat, is planning to do the same to them.

IV. WORDS

A. Students are to determine the meanings of these words from context clues. Answers will vary slightly.

1. **engendering** (p. 127, l. 4)—begetting; procreating
2. **engages** (p. 127, l. 11)—involves
3. **hostelry** (p. 127, l. 23)—inn; hotel

4. **baldric** (p. 129, l. 120)—a shoulder cord or band
5. **solicitous** (p. 130, l. 147)—eager
6. **verity** (p. 131, l. 231)—truth
7. **accrue** (p. 131, l. 253)—accumulate
8. **secular** (p. 132, l. 303)—worldly or temporal

B. Students are to use their dictionaries to determine the meanings of the words as used in the selection.

liquor—a bath
strands—shores or beaches
chivalry—knightly skill
gentle-knight—a proper knight
cadet—a younger member of a family
embroidered—ornamented
saucy—bold; impudent
proper—excellent
counterfeit—pretend; assume

C. Even a cursory search will reveal many similes. The Yeoman's head was "like a nut"; the Monk's greyhounds were "as swift as birds"; the Friar's neck was "whiter than a lily-flower"; the Franklin's beard was "white as a daisy-petal"; the Wife of Bath's hat was "as broad as is a buckler or a shield." The work is also full of metaphors as well as many more similies.

UNIT TEST

You may select questions at random from the Study Notes at the end of each selection as a basis for constructing a final examination covering the unit Medieval British Poetry. You may also choose to use the comprehensive unit test prepared on blackline masters available in a separate test booklet, ISBN 0-07-009823-9.

RENAISSANCE BRITISH POETRY: The Elizabethan Age

INTRODUCTION

The Renaissance lyrics in this section are by Wyatt, Surrey, Marlowe, Raleigh, Sidney, and Shakespeare. For each poet one poem is included, with the exception of Shakespeare, for whom five sonnets are included. Spenser is represented by an excerpt from *The Faerie Queene,* specifically, the fight between the Red Cross and the monster Error.

There are a number of ways in which you can work with these poems. If you have a class that is particularly interested in matters of form, you can certainly use these poems as examples of experimentation with language, with metaphor, and with complicated stanza forms. You may want to have students try to write sonnets. This may be a difficult exercise for them, but it is one worth trying. Another suggestion is to introduce your class to Renaissance music or Renaissance painting—art that will demonstrate the period's emphasis on forms that are both repetitious and varied.

Because a central subject of Renaissance lyrics is love, you may want to pull these poems together by focusing on the questions of love and of how people in love express themselves. Ask students to talk about what a love poem should be. (They may wish to bring to class examples of modern love poems that they find appealing.) After reading some of the poems, students could compose personal statements about love or even some love poems of their own. (Certainly there are other summing up techniques, but this subject, of primary interest to the poets, should interest students also.)

You may want to use the following implications in discussing the poems in the unit.

1. Love makes me unhappy and frustrated.
2. Love comforts me when I am unhappy.
3. Love leads inevitably to deceit and rejection.
4. The only thing a rejected lover can do is complain.
5. Love enables me to see reality.
6. Love makes me a better person.

NOTE: For some suggested reference sources, see the bibliography in the introduction to the first poetry unit, pages 34–36 in this Teacher's Guide.

Blame Not My Lute

PAGE 147

Sir Thomas Wyatt

Glossary Words

wit (page 147) Intelligence, good sense, etc.

perforce (page 147) By necessity; necessarily

Handbook

imagery, point of view, realism, tone

Check Test 15 *(for "Blame Not My Lute," "The Soote Season," "The Passionate Shepherd to His Love," "The Nymph's Reply to the Shepherd," "Sonnet 31")*

INTRODUCTION

Other Elizabethan poets seem somewhat colorless in comparison to Wyatt, whose personality and feelings are strongly expressed in his poetry. "Blame Not My Lute" presents Wyatt, the rejected lover, being wittily cynical as he taunts the woman who has left him. He has sung uncomplimentary songs about her, and in his poem he addresses her and her complaints. Yet he remains cool, even when she breaks his lute strings. He knows that she cannot stop him for long—he has more strings and more songs to sing.

This poem provides a good example of tone in poetry. The speaker begins with a reasonably cool attitude, but he becomes increasingly more upset. A good method for finding the tonal shifts is to read the poem aloud, perhaps, first, in a calm manner, and, then, with more strong emotion. Should students find the speaker of "Blame Not My Lute" too self-satisfied, you may wish to ask them to compose a stanza of the woman's rejoinder.

USING THE STUDY NOTES

PAGE 150

BLAME NOT MY LUTE

1. What is the implied dramatic situation in this poem? What is the speaker's relationship to the listener? What actions are implied in the poem or between the lines? The speaker is probably a member of the court, skilled at playing the lute and composing songs. He is replying to a woman who once loved him (or so he thought) and who is now cool toward him. To pay her back for her change of heart, he has made up songs about her and has sung them publicly. She understandably complains, and he argues that his lute is not responsible, nor, by extension, is he. Rather, it is her own behavior that is the cause of her embarrassment. Between the second and third stanzas, she seems to reach out and break the strings in an attempt to stop him from playing. Between stanzas five and six, he seems to restring the lute. At the end of the poem it is clear that he plans to exit strumming.

2. What changes of tone do you hear in the poem? How are they signaled? The poet starts out in a reasonably controlled mood. We can ascertain this from his description of the woman's behavior: It is called a "change" (line 6); her behavior is described as gently deceitful ("use to feign" line 13), and he intends to keep on singing (lines 4, 11). But when she breaks the lute strings, he becomes angrier. Expressions such as "wrongfully" (line 17), "rightful spite" (line 20), "falsed faith" (line 23), "fault so great" (line 24), and finally "evil" (line 31) suggest that he is losing control and accusing her of greater and greater wrongdoing. In the last stanza, he regains his calm and becomes somewhat flippant. He can even afford to call his poem "foolish," for he knows that she is embarrassed by it.

3. What is the effect of the repeated short line "Blame not my lute" in terms of the poet's argument? In terms of his emotional state? This conversational line starts off the poem in a casual way. Considered purely as an argument, the statement "Blame not my lute" has two major implications. First, it points to the speaker himself, for he is clearly the player of the lute and therefore the composer of the offending songs ("to give such tunes as pleaseth me"). But it points also to the real cause of the songs, the woman and her behavior. Line 29 makes this second point clear, "Blame but thyself." The repetition of the phrase "blame not my lute" becomes a way of reminding her who is really to blame. It is a short line that follows six longer lines; it thus tends to come as a kind of surprise, perhaps expressing the speaker's anger (a kind of "so there" tone) or his quiet but pointed insult to the woman. The repetition may suggest either that he is totally in control or that he needs to regain control by repeating the line.

4. With whom in the poem do you sympathize? Why? Readers are intended to sympathize with the witty speaker, who can continue singing a poem to a woman who is getting so angry that she breaks the lute strings. Some may find him too smug and therefore, in reaction, start to sympathize with the woman.

The Soote Season

PAGE 148

Henry Howard, Earl of Surrey

The Passionate Shepherd to His Love

Christopher Marlowe

The Nymph's Reply to the Shepherd

Sir Walter Raleigh

Glossary Word

madrigals (page 149) Songs, especially love songs

Handbook

imagery, tone

Check Test 15 *(for "Blame Not My Lute," "The Soote Season," "The Passionate Shepherd to his Love," "The Nymph's Reply to the Shepherd," "Sonnet 31")*

INTRODUCTION

These three poets have been grouped together because they offer a view of the minor, but interesting, poems of the period. These poems include an almost rigidly structured sonnet by Surrey and poems by Marlowe and Raleigh that wittily state and rebut the traditional appeal of the pastoral wooer. The Surrey poem poses some problem in language because he has chosen a number of words that are closer to Middle English than to modern English. The Marlowe and Raleigh poems suggest themselves as a teaching unit, perhaps to be read aloud to stimulate a discussion of tone.

The trick with all of these poems is to get students to recognize convention and yet to hear the personal voice speaking within the conventional phrases and structures. You could ask them to think of situations in which they, too, turn to conventions, to particular ways of speaking and acting. They are likely to mention occasions such as marriage, death, applying for a job, and so on. If they can think of the conventions that we use today, they are less likely to find the idea of convention so formal and rigid. Instead, they will be able to see that we turn, almost instinctively, to particular formulations as ways of dealing with complicated emotional situations.

USING THE STUDY QUESTIONS

PAGE 150

THE SOOTE SEASON

Students are asked how they would demonstrate the inadequacy of the following statements about "The Soote Season."

1. The sonnet merely lists details about spring in a random order. At first, one could agree with this statement, but a closer look reveals that there is some patterning. The poet begins by describing a green and flowering landscape, and then he starts to bring that landscape alive. He moves from birds (the nightingale, the turtledove) to deer in the forest to fish and snakes and then, in a circular motion, back to flying objects (the swallow and the bee). The first two lines could be seen as an introduction, coloring the picture. Line 5 could be viewed as a transition through repetition and line 12 as a summary, standing in a parallel relationship to line 5 ("Summer is come" juxtaposed with "Winter is worn").

2. The sonnet is limited because there are only two rhyming sounds. The English sonnet normally offers the poet seven rhyming sounds, but Surrey has chosen to use only two rhymes. One of the ways in which he breaks away from possible monotony is to emphasize adjectives and nouns with alliteration, thus returning to the older tradition of alliterative half lines. In fact, the first line could almost be from "The Wanderer" ("The soote season, that bud and bloom forth brings"), and we find alliteration in every other line as well. The repetition of the rhymes, like the circular movement suggested in the pattern of detail, is related to the cycle of the year. Every year we see these kinds of activities, just as every year spring returns to the earth after winter. Thus, the repetition of rhyme enhances rather than detracts from the poem's success.

3. **The sonnet is an impersonal description and tells us nothing about the poet's feelings.** Once again, we find a technique familiar to us from the medieval lyrics, that of keeping the personal note subdued but important because it has to be so firmly hidden. In this case, Surrey manages to express his personal feelings eloquently with one magnificent pun in the last line. After thirteen lines describing the beauty of returning spring, he compares his own lot—"and yet my sorrow springs." We feel the uncoiling of emotion in that last word. If *spring* is the word that we are thinking of throughout the poem (as well as hearing, echoed in the repetitious rhyme scheme—possibly another reason that Surrey chooses not to vary the rhymes), then we are both surprised and moved when he reveals that there is another meaning to spring, a meaning that stands in opposition to the cheerful burgeoning of life that he has been depicting.

THE PASSIONATE SHEPHERD TO HIS LOVE
THE NYMPH'S REPLY TO THE SHEPHERD

Students are asked if the following statements seem true or false or neither.

1. **One of the poems expresses the point of view of a dreamer; the other, that of a realist.** If all students think that this is true, you may enjoy playing devil's advocate by saying that you are glad they all agree that Marlowe is the realist and Raleigh the dreamer; for Marlowe's shepherd will surely get a nymph, whereas Raleigh's will just as surely be left with dreams. This should provoke some interesting discussion that should lead to the discussion of the other questions.

2. **Most men in love are impractical like the shepherd; most women remain practical like the nymph.** Experience suggests that neither sex in itself is more practical than the other. Actually, a more interesting question to explore is the value that students give to practicality in love. If they seem to be arguing for practicality, you could intrude into the discussion the question of why they value practicality so highly. Maybe a person in love ought to be impractical; maybe love fares better if both parties are impractical.

3. **True love fares better if both parties retain a mixture of romance and realism.** Students will probably find little to debate about on this issue—unless you provoke them by asking what *percentages* of each quality they would recommend. This may lead to quite an interesting discussion.

4. **Marlowe leaves himself open to Raleigh's reply. He deserves the implied criticism.** Students will probably agree that Marlowe's portrait is overidealized and that he does deserve the criticism that Raleigh gives him. But Marlowe's poem is, after all, fundamentally based on emotions that live in all of us, and Raleigh himself acknowledges these emotions at the end of his reply. Furthermore, you may wish to ask whether anyone can say for sure that a given person will not find a love forever young, with dateless joys. And perhaps the selves that we know when we are in love are more truly our "real" selves than those that we know in our everyday, humdrum existence.

Sonnet 31

PAGE 151

Sir Philip Sidney

Glossary Word

languished (page 151) Being weakened or weary; dropped

Handbook

imagery, personification, sonnet

Check Test 15 *(for "Blame Not My Lute," "The Soote Season," "The Passionate Shepherd to His Love," "The Nymph's Reply to the Shepherd," "Sonnet 31")*

INTRODUCTION

What makes Sidney particularly interesting is the combination of highly crafted art and intensely personal feelings that we find in his poetry. The famous "Sonnet 31" is a good example of this expression. Sidney starts in a fairly detached tone. He addresses the moon but implies his own feelings by attributing them to the moon. Then, in the last six lines, he turns to questions that suggest his own great unhappiness.

USING THE STUDY NOTES PAGE 151

SONNET 31

1. The section on Imagery (page 105) mentions the first two lines of this sonnet as an example of personification. What other details in the poem help to personify the Moon? We need to remember that all the human attributes that Sidney gives to the Moon are really being transferred to it from the persona of the dejected lover. Thus, the Moon has been wounded by Cupid's arrows; the Moon sympathizes with the lover (line 6); the Moon's "looks," its "languished grace," make clear its emotional state—which is really the speaker's, "to me that feel the like." The mention of "fellowship" (line 9) suggests that the speaker and the Moon are somehow friends, as if they are both courtiers seeking love.

2. "Sonnet 31" demonstrates Sidney's version of the sonnet form. What is the formal structure he chooses? How is this particular structure related to his argument? This question requires that students review the various rhyme schemes for sonnets (see page 147 of the pupil text). Sidney writes a version of the Italian sonnet; he begins with the Italian octave, *abbaabba,* then shifts into a sestet *cdcdee.* Yet this sestet is, in effect, the English form of a quatrain and a couplet. The eight/six division works in this sonnet because Sidney can form a companionship with the Moon in the first eight lines and then, once that is established, turn to the problem by asking questions in the last six lines. He sets up an interesting tension in the last six lines because although they divide into a quatrain and a couplet, Sidney does not let the syntax stop with the rhymes. That is, the questions in lines 10 and 11 cease at the end of the line, but the question in line 12 runs on into the next line, thus overrunning the normal separation between quatrain and couplet. This overrunning has the effect of separating the last line from the preceding one. Usually, in a couplet, the two lines flow together, but here the last line stands on its own and so has a somewhat stronger, perhaps harsher effect.

3. How would you describe the tone of the last six lines? Is that tone different from the tone of the opening lines? In what ways? The first eight lines are descriptive, gently inquisitive, and sympathetically friendly; the last six change noticeably. It is as if the real questions pour out in these later lines, after the sense of kinship with the moon has been created. And we can hear hurt verging on bitterness in the questions. The speaker feels that he is constantly in love, but he fears that the woman may find such constancy merely foolish "want of wit." He accuses her of pride and of selfishness (wanting to be loved and yet rejecting the one who loves her). The last line can be paraphrased in several ways; it may mean, "is my virtue (my truth) considered unpleasing in heaven?" or, more bitterly, "is her rejection (ungratefulness) considered a virtue above?" The first reading works more easily with the syntax of the line and suggests self-deprecation. The second reading seems closer to the poet's bitter feelings in the last lines but demands that we add some words to the last line: "Do they call virtue there [what we call] ungratefulness?"

from The Faerie Queene PAGE 152

Edmund Spenser

Glossary Words

beguile (page 154) While away (time) pleasantly

revoke (page 154) Take away; withdraw

disdain (page 155) A feeling of scorn; contempt

aghast (page 155) Struck with horror; dumbfounded; horrified

perplexity (page 156) Puzzlement; bewilderment; great confusion

Handbook

allegory, allusion, irony, stanza, symbol

Check Test 16

INTRODUCTION

Like Milton, who is represented in a later poetry section, Spenser is a great though rarely read poet. Teachers and students have somehow acquired the mistaken notion that a great deal of background about complicated subjects such as allegory is necessary before one can enjoy Spenser. But Spenser is a delightful poet to read because he is so full of vivid description, so sensitive to human psychology, and so skilled at constructing a narrative that is interesting to read and to think about. The excerpt from Book I of *The Faerie Queene* shows Spenser's ability to get a good fight going, while simultaneously showing us that the fight is representative of a spiritual struggle. He cunningly leads the reader into the Wandering Wood, just as he leads Red Cross and Una. He skillfully characterizes the young knight with his eager desire for battle; the sensible Una whose advice, of course, the knight rejects; and, in a line and a half, the "fearful dwarf." Error is the first of the monsters Red Cross meets. She seems both fierce and cowardly; she conquers and yet is finally devoured by her own ugly children; she is both a real dragon and an emblem of human pride, greed, and ignorance. Reading Spenser, who presents significant and characterizing details so clearly, may help your students read Chaucer's Prologue more carefully—or vice versa. The only major problem may be the language, because Spenser deliberately chose archaic words to give his narrative the old-fashioned quality associated with the mythical and romantic tales of earlier times.

The excerpt is particularly interesting as an example of narrative which works both as action and as symbol. Spenser chose a dragon/woman to represent Error. You might ask students what monsters would be constructed today to personify Error—or other human failings.

USING THE STUDY NOTES PAGE 158

from THE FAERIE QUEENE (Book 1, Canto I)

1. Spenser is famous for his descriptive passages, yet one might argue that the catalogue of trees (stanzas 8–9) is not really useful for the narrative. Can you justify the inclusion of these two stanzas? Just as the shady grove "seems" to promise "fair harbor" to Red Cross and Una (7:9), so the catalogue of trees lures the reader away from the darker implications of stanza 7. After all, a "shady grove" whose trees hide "heaven's light" and which is full of "paths and alleys wide" (cf. Matthew, 7:13, "for wide is the gate, and broad is the way, that leadeth to destruction, and many there be which go in thereat") might well be an evil place. But when we read about all the various trees (and one might imagine that Red Cross and Una are admiring them too), most of them with uses of particular value to human beings (shipbuilding, house construction, making of bows), we forget the "shady grove" as well as the tempest. We are "led with delight" (stanza 10) and are lost, as are Red Cross and Una.

2. Sometimes Spenser lets a character announce the allegorical level very plainly as when Una says, "This is the Wandering Wood." But by the time she says where they are, the reader has already been warned that the characters are lost. What words and phrases in stanzas 7–12 suggest this symbolic world? The darker implications of stanza 7 are discussed above. One might note the repetition of the verb "seem" in stanza 8. ("Seeming" is always a hint from Spenser that things aren't what they should be.) Stanza 10 makes the confusion evident: "They cannot find that path which first was shown." They "wander to and fro." The paths seem to multiply so that they question their own sanity and their own feelings. Stanza 11 increases the problem; they aren't merely lost but are in a "labyrinth" (the maze from which no one could escape). Once more they take a path "that beaten seemed most bare" and, as in stanza 7, a well-worn path should be a sign of danger. By this time, the action of Red Cross giving the dwarf his spear seems foolish—and "champion" may seem an ironic word. Una's warning, stanza 12, makes the danger more evident, since she suspects "the danger hid, the place unknown and wild." But perhaps her proverbial way of stating the problem, "Oft fire is without smoke" may still be a device to hide the reality from us.

3. What qualities of Red Cross make him vulnerable to Error? And what does he need to help him escape from her clutches? Red Cross is "full of fire and greedy hardiment" (stanza 14); his eagerness to fight gets him in trouble, as does his youth. He doesn't listen to Una's advice or to that of the dwarf (although perhaps we too discount his "fear"); thus he rushes in and is caught in "Error's endless train" (stanza 18). Hitting the monster doesn't help at first, but only enrages her so that she traps him. To escape, he must follow Una's advice as he did not do at first. When she counsels him, "Add faith unto your force," she is speaking spiritually; the human being trapped by Error must believe that one can escape. His attack on Error's throat causes the monster to vomit out her poison—and it is significant that this second attack again weakens the knight, "well-nigh choked with the deadly stink" (stanza 22). But once again he gathers courage, "Resolved in mind all suddenly to win" (stanza 24), and thus manages to kill her.

4. The description of Error and her progeny is full of vivid details. Which of these imply a symbolic value as well? Error lives in a "darksome hole," and her ugly brood cannot stand the "uncouth light"; her hatred of light ("the deadly bale") represents the association of error and ignorance. The many children suggest that Error is found in a thousand small ways, "each one / Of sundry shapes." Thus there are many kinds of error. Her retreat from Red Cross implies cowardice. The constant reference to the tail, the knots, the coiling, remind us of a snake and of the first great error in the world, the Fall. Internally Error is full of poison, and the references to books and papers suggest that one way in which error is constantly spread is through false, even heretical writing. The image of the Nile overflowing Egypt reminds us of the constant spreading of evil through error. Most striking of all is the way in which the little errors, sucking up the mother's blood, kill themselves. Ultimately, Error is self-destructive.

Sonnets 18, 29, 65, 116, 130

PAGE 159

William Shakespeare

Glossary Words

impregnable (page 160) Able to resist attack

impediments (page 160) Hindrances; obstructions

Handbook

couplet, imagery, metaphor, sonnet

Check Test 17

INTRODUCTION

What we present here is, of course, only a small sampling of Shakespeare's sonnets, but you will find a variety of emotional attitudes and sonnet structures to work with. Sonnets 18 and 65 both express the poet's confidence in his ability to preserve beauty against the ravages of time. (Sonnet 18 gives more emphasis to beauty through a comparison with the fading of summer, whereas Sonnet 65 stresses the destructive nature of time.) Sonnet 29 presents a small drama in which the speaker moves from despair to happiness; that movement is made possible by thoughts of the beloved. Sonnet 116 is one of the most famous of Shakespeare's poems. It is also one of his most subtle. It seems to be a poem that asserts the value of constancy in love, and yet there are so many negative statements in the poem that we begin to question the poet's faith in the value that he so desperately seeks. Negative statements are also the key devices in Sonnet 130, but they are used for a marvelously humorous turnabout: The poet seems to be dispraising his beloved but shows us at the end that his love is more "real" because he does not use fancy (and therefore false) poetic descriptions.

These selections offer a chance to focus on the construction of the sonnet. There is a variety of structures within the characteristic pattern (three quatrains and a couplet) of the English sonnet. Sonnets 18 and 29 show how the Italian pattern of eight lines and six lines is superimposed on the English pattern, for in these sonnets the change of idea or of mood begins at line 9. Sonnets 65 and 130 essentially place the twelve lines of the three quatrains against the couplet; the last two lines offer the resolution (in Sonnet 65) or a surprise ending (in Sonnet 130). Sonnet 116 is, not surprisingly, more difficult to analyze structurally, for its form fits with its emotional complexity. But we can see that Sonnet 116 divides into three quatrains, each organized around a central idea. The problem is that the middle quatrain is the only one that contains positive statements, whereas the first and third quatrains define love by what it is not rather than what it is. The final couplet throws the preceding twelve lines into question: "If this be error."

You will certainly want to start any discussion of the sonnets with some reading aloud. It takes only a short time to read a sonnet and yet students may find it difficult to convey the thought and, at the same time, give needed emphasis to the rhyme scheme and organization. You could try having the poem read aloud at the beginning of the discussion and then again at the end.

This section is also the ideal place to get students to write sonnets. It is, admittedly, a difficult form, but the English sonnet, with its seven rhymes, offers more possibilities than the Italian one—and trying to write a sonnet gets one to appreciate the complexity of matching thought and rhyme scheme. One problem that you may encounter is that students are not always sensitive to the sound of iambic pentameter and so write lines that are too long or unrhythmical. Reading aloud is the best way to counter this problem.

USING THE STUDY NOTES PAGES 159, 161

SONNET 18

Students are to consider the following statements:

1. The poet knows that nature's beauty passes. Students may want to alter this proposition in some ways. The first line of the poem tells that the comparison is going to be between "thee" and summer, not between "thee" and nature's beauty in an absolute sense. Then, students may prefer the verb *changes* to *passes.* The words and phrases dealing with nature's beauty are *shake,* the short *lease* of summer, *dimmed, declines,* and *changing course.*

2. The poet's real need is to preserve his own feelings about the woman, not her beauty. This raises the question of how one is to define *real* need. Some students may note that all of us desire immortality, Shakespeare included, and that this must have been one impulse behind the writing of the poem (even though he may have been only dimly aware of it —or not consciously aware of it at all.) There is no way to defeat such an argument because it cannot be proved false. On the other hand, this does not guarantee that the argument is true.

Perhaps it is best to look closely at the poem itself. We do not find any serious attempt there to describe physical beauty specifically. Thus one could argue that the preservation of beauty alone was not the primary intention. However, we would still be reluctant to say that preservation of the poet's feelings was the primary intention because the idea of preserving beauty or emotion eternally was something of a convention at the time. We suggest that the primary intention of the poet was simply the *expression* of his emotions rather than their preservation. Support is given to this notion by the fact that the best evidence indicates that Shakespeare never authorized the 1609 publication of the sonnets nor any other publication. If he had really wanted to immortalize his own feelings, he would presumably have seen to it that the sonnets were published.

3. The fact that you are reading this poem more than 350 years after it was written indicates that Shakespeare succeeded in his purpose. As we have said, his true purpose was probably not to preserve beauty or his feelings eternally; yet this is certainly what he has done. As long as humans breathe or eyes see, this sonnet will live. Of course, however, it lives largely because it is great art rather than because it preserves the loveliness of a particular person.

SONNET 29

1. Do you think the details of unhappiness in the first eight lines are causes of the poet's sorrow or results of it? Both possibilities are present in the sonnet. The opening line suggests a generalized misery, "in disgrace with Fortune and men's eyes," without making clear if the speaker is responsible for it. And the mention of "outcast state" and "fate" implies that he is somehow the victim of other people and of destiny in general. But the second quatrain brings in the speaker's own problems: He is envious and discontented, wishing himself like other people. At least he is aware of his own problem—"with what I most enjoy contented least"—but he does not seem to acknowledge the possibility that he does not *have* to feel as he does.

2. The poet needs to convince us that his mood has changed in the last six lines. How does he do this through language, imagery, and sentence structure? There are words in the last six lines that remind us of the despair of the octave: "despising," "sullen." But basically the language changes so that we get "sweet love," "such wealth," "my state" (instead of "my outcast state"). There is the image of the lark, seen at "break of day" (the metaphor of sunrise and thus a new beginning), ascending to the sky—and the lark is not merely a bird flying but a singer of "hymns," sacred songs, at "heaven's gate." The implication of salvation need not be taken on the Christian plane, but we sense that something special, something holy, is happening. The lines have been almost relentlessly end-stopped through line 9.

Line 10, although it ends with a comma, really cannot be stopped because the thought continues (the verb does not come until line 12). And line 11 forces the reader to carry on to the middle of line 12, thus giving the feeling of swift movement, as in flight. That rhythmical ascent in the middle of these six lines is balanced by the couplet which returns to the dominant end-stopped pattern of the whole poem. However, the couplet is not a return to despair but suggests a cheerful acceptance of "my state," found both in the diction and in the couplet's resolution.

SONNET 65

1. What things does Shakespeare mention in the poem which we think of as permanent? Shakespeare mentions brass, stone, earth, sea, rocks, and the gates of steel.

2. What are the contrasting things he mentions which are usually thought of as fragile or fleeting? Beauty, a flower, and love are the major contrasting things; the first and the third are what the poem is about.

3. Do you agree that both sets of objects—those that seem fragile and those that seem permanent—are ultimately destroyed? Ultimately? Who can tell what "ultimately" will be destroyed? It is a good bet, though, that beauty—as represented, for instance, by Shakespeare's sonnets—and love will be around as long as human beings will be.

4. Do you agree or disagree that the "miracle" the poet seeks has come to pass? That is, that his love ("Time's best jewel") still shines brightly more than 300 years later? Not all students will agree, perhaps, that his love shines brightly, but no one can question the fact that the love has endured. Our own view is that Shakespeare's love shines more brightly today than even he would have guessed.

SONNET 116

1. What metaphors does Shakespeare use to express love's permanence? He calls it "an ever-fixed mark," like a star. He says that it cannot be cut down (killed) by Time's "bending sickle." In the first quatrain he says that true love does not alter when it finds cause for alteration or when the other has ceased to love.

2. In lines 1–4, the poet says that love will not change if it is really true love. In lines 5–8, he indicates that it is a permanent guide. In lines 9–12, he says that time cannot shift love. What one element is common to all three groups? What value is the poet seeking from love? If students say that love is the common element, point out to them that this is the subject of the poem. What the question asks for is the predicate, as it were—the theme or thesis. Students should be able to see that the "common element" is the idea of permanence. It is permanence in a world of change that the poet is seeking in love.

3. Do you have any doubts about the poet's confidence in love's constancy? Does he? The pervasive negative statements in the poem are curious; the poet seems to be much more articulate about what love is *not* than about what love *is*. "Alteration" and removal, although set up as charges that constant love does not produce, still remind us that love is, in fact, subject to possible alteration and removal. Similarly, Time as a death figure (with a sickle) is present in the poem, as is "the edge of doom." These images of destruction give the poet's assertions a somewhat fragile quality. So does the envelope structure of the poem, in which the one quatrain of positive statements is surrounded by two quatrains of negative statements. All these factors may make us question the poet's confidence. His couplet may (but not necessarily) suggest his own questions: If he is wrong, then he has written to no effect, and no man has ever loved. For the poet to be willing to disavow all of his own work may be taken as proof of his confidence in his search for value; it may also be taken as a desperate cry.

SONNET 130

1. This poem might be considered a parody of poems which praise (or overpraise) the loved one's beauty. What are the words and phrases that specifically suggest this humorous/satiric tone? The whole idea of negating a beloved is funny, and the details here are carefully chosen. Expressions such as "wires," "reeks," "dun," and "trends on the ground" are chosen for their shock value; "reeks" gets special emphasis because it is also a rhyme word.

2. What feeling is built up by the poet's series of negatives? Honesty, conviction, and forthrightness.

3. How does this feeling help the effect of the final couplet? It places the beloved beyond the necessity of empty rhetoric; the speaker accepts her as she is.

UNIT TEST

You may select questions at random from the Study Notes at the end of each selection as a basis for constructing a final examination covering the unit Renaissance British Poetry. You may also choose to use the comprehensive unit test prepared on blackline masters available in a separate test booklet, ISBN 0-07-009823-9.

Choice and Consequence: Scope and Sequence

Selection	Language/Vocabulary	Comprehension	Critical/Literary	Composition
MACBETH	context, semantic change, definition, simile and metaphor, pronunciation	details, inferences, contrast, supporting conclusions, sequence	drama, tragedy, imagery (simile and metaphor), soliloquy, characterization	exposition*
"Witness to the Truth: Socrates"		details, inferences, supporting conclusions	characterization, imagery (metaphor), biography	exposition*, summaries
"The Death of Socrates"	context, connotation, denotation	details, inferences, conclusions	characterization	exposition*
"The Hint of an Explanation"	metaphor	details, inferences, conclusions, cause and effect	characterization, imagery, style (story within a story)	exposition*
"The Stamp Collection"	abstract and concrete words	details, inferences, conclusions, cause and effect	characterization, imagery, irony	exposition*
"The Little Bouilloux Girl"	definitions; semantic change	details, inferences, sequence, cause and effect	characterization, imagery, irony	exposition*
"To Please His Wife"	descriptive words	details, inferences, summary, cause and effect	characterization, imagery, contrast	exposition*
"The Duchess and the Jeweller"	descriptive words, metaphor	details, inferences, generalizations, cause and effect	characterization, imagery, style (stream of consciousness)	exposition*
"The Guest"	sensory words	details, inferences, cause and effect	characterization, imagery	exposition*
"How Much Land Does a Man Need?"	definition, metaphor	details, inferences, cause and effect, conclusions	characterization, imagery	exposition*
Summing Up	descriptive words	details, inferences, cause and effect	theme, characterization, imagery	essay
Relating Composition, the Gallery, and Humanities		cause and effect, conclusions, generalizations	characterization, drama, journal	journal, selection of passages, drama, log

Seventeenth- and Eighteenth-Century British Poetry

Selection	Language/Vocabulary	Comprehension	Critical/Literary	Composition
Donne, Jonson, Herbert, and Herrick Poems		details, inferences, conclusions, order of parts, comparing and contrasting	metaphor, pun, sonnet, personification, shaped poetry, author's purpose	epigrams
Lovelace, Marvell, Milton Poems	definition	details, inferences, logic, contrast	verse patterns, hyperbole, purpose, epic, sonnet, metaphor, mood	exposition, couplets
Dryden, Pope, Gray Poems		details, inferences, comparison	satire, tone, metaphor, alliteration, assonance, couplets, irony	

*Teachers can use the Implications in the study notes as writing assignments.

Choice and Consequence

Although all the selections in this unit focus upon choices that lead to important consequences, there is great variation within the theme. In some cases, for instance, the consequences of the choices are known beforehand, whereas in others they are not known at all. Graham Greene's young hero, for example, could not have realized that his decision to swallow the wafer would ultimately lead to his becoming a priest; Socrates, on the other hand, knew precisely the consequences of his choice. Another variation concerns the role of chance or fate. It plays a very large role in the Hardy story but a comparatively small role in the tale by Tolstoy. Motive is still another variable. Macbeth, Hardy's Joanna, and Woolf's Oliver Bacon are motivated by ambition, spite, and the need for status, but characters in some other selections are prompted by commendable motives.

Whatever the variables, the important thing for students to see is that the consequences of our choices are shaped by, and, in turn, shape our personalities. Choices cannot be made in a vacuum; choices invariably have consequences. As adults we know that our choices have made us what we are. This unit should serve to help students to realize that the choices that they make will affect what sorts of persons they will become.

OBJECTIVES

1. To help students to see that the choices one makes are determined by character and that they, in turn, also mold one's character.
2. To stimulate students to a greater awareness of the role of fate or chance in human affairs.
3. To study relationships between motivation and choice.
4. To illustrate how moments of decision bring forth the strengths and weaknesses in one's character.
5. To show the reasons why writers are especially attracted to the theme of choice and consequence.
6. To develop sensitivity toward techniques of character development and the use of imagery in writing.
7. To develop vocabulary.

MOTIVATING THE UNIT

Pattern I Tell students that you are going to write a phrase on the board and that they should write down on a sheet of paper everything that comes to their minds when they see the phrase. Write the words "Choice and Consequence" on the board, and let the class write for five or ten minutes. Ask some students to read their papers aloud or collect the papers and select some at random to read to the class.

This technique can lead to the raising of questions related to the objectives just stated. Do not try to answer the questions yourself, but tell students that the selections that they will read in this unit will suggest some possible answers.

Pattern II Ask students to discuss—orally or in writing—important choices that they had to make and the consequences of their decisions. Let them discuss matters such as the following: things that happened that they could not foresee; how the consequences changed them; the role that fate or chance played; their motives in making the choices that they did; and anything else that they consider relevant.

You can add interest by asking students how they would go about building stories around the choices and their consequences, giving extra credit to those who actually write stories. Point out that the selections in the unit are built around the issue of choice and consequence, and discuss why this theme is particularly attractive to writers.

Pattern III List a number of pairs of alternative choices on the board, and have students speculate on how the choice of one or the other alternative could lead to radically different consequences. The following are some suggested choices: (1) take a job or go to college; (2) marry in late teens or in middle twenties; (3) take a job that one would not like but that offers money and prestige or take a job that one would like but that pays much less and offers less prestige; (4) tell a lie to escape punishment for a wrong that one has done or tell the truth and take the punishment; (5) tell a friend an unpleasant truth about yourself and risk destroying the friendship or keep the truth to yourself. Be sure to discuss how even apparently simple solutions to problems have consequences of one sort or another, and be sure that students do not overlook internal consequences. Point out that in the first selection, the internal consequences are as important as the external consequences.

Macbeth

PAGE 167

William Shakespeare

The major choice in this drama is made by the end of the first act; thus the play may be thought of primarily as a dramatization of the consequences of an evil act. The consequences themselves lead to the need to make further choices that would not have been required if the initial choice had been different. Moreover, it is the internal consequences that Shakespeare probes and illustrates most brilliantly; the best reading of the play will focus upon these consequences, both in the character of Macbeth and Lady Macbeth.

Even if students' previous experience with Shakespearean drama is slight, it is probably unwise to begin by extensive lecturing on Shakespeare's life and work or on the Elizabethan theater. The notes in the text are probably a sufficient introduction for most classes. In a thematic approach to literature, the work itself should occupy the center of attention.

Shakespeare's plays were meant to be seen, not read, and it is obvious that the more your class can dramatize the play, the better. Let students take roles, if they are at all capable of reading the dialogue. (In some cases it may be advisable to give students at least a night to study their parts.) Still better, let them act out parts. Perhaps some students would be willing to make simple costumes for some of the actors. The witch scenes, in particular, can be dramatized effectively, and they do not require much in the way of props or costumes.

Notice that the greatest amount of study notes follows the play. It is probably not a good idea to pause long between acts. Indeed, you may not wish to pause at all if you think that your class has a clear notion of the play's meaning. You can always discuss the questions later. On the other hand, the students' answers to these questions will give you a good idea of the extent to which they are appreciating the drama. Try not to spend too much time on discussion between the acts, for students ought to have a sense of continuity. One aid to understanding is to point out before the reading begins which characters are major and which are minor.

ACT I

PAGE 168

Glossary Words

brandished (page 169) Being waved or shaken threateningly

smack (page 169) Have a taste, trace, or touch (of something)

deign (page 170) Condescend to give; lower oneself

corporal (page 172) Being or having a body

interim (page 174) The time between

harbinger (page 175) One that goes ahead to announce another's coming

surcease (page 179) An end

plague (page 179) Vex; annoy; bother

Handbook

metaphor, personification, semantics, simile

Check Test 18 (for Act I)

Check Tests for each selection—in the form of blackline masters—are available in a separate test booklet, ISBN 0-07-009823-9. Each test is titled and numbered for easy filing after use.

Give the Check Test after students have read the selection(s) and before you begin the discussion of the work(s).

USING THE STUDY NOTES

ACT I PAGE 182
TEMPTATION IN A PROPHECY

1. What are we told about Macbeth's life and character up to the time the play begins? What opinion do others have of him? Before Macbeth appears, we learn that he is a brave and formidable soldier, that he is a cousin of the king, and that he is a captain in the Scottish army. He is very much admired by his fellow soldiers and by the king, who refers to him with such adjectives as *valiant, worthy,* and *noble.*

2. Look carefully at the witches' original prophecy to Macbeth and Banquo. Do the witches indicate that they have any power to turn their predictions into reality? At the time that they utter the predictions, they do not indicate that they have power to turn them into reality; Macbeth is responsible for turning the prophecies into reality.

a. If you were in Macbeth's and Banquo's positions, what meaning would you draw from the witches' prophecies? Students would probably draw from them the same meaning as Macbeth and Banquo do. There may be some question about the meaning of *hereafter* in the third prophecy to Macbeth, however, and the first two prophecies to Banquo are somewhat paradoxical.

b. What is the difference in Macbeth's and Banquo's reactions to the witches? Macbeth is less concerned than Banquo with the question of whether the witches are real and whether they are speaking the truth; he is more concerned with drawing them out and having them explain themselves. His reaction to their prophecies is a mixture of shock and fear (page 171, line 51). It is as if he had already thought about the points that they bring up.

3. How does Shakespeare contrast Macbeth's character with that of Lady Macbeth in Scenes 5 and 7? The contrast is forcefully revealed in the soliloquies on pages 177 and 179. Lady Macbeth thinks in imperatives; Macbeth, in conditionals. He is all for thinking things over; she is all for immediate action.

What arguments does Lady Macbeth use to force Macbeth to a decision? Lady Macbeth argues that her plan cannot fail and details how they can escape detection by pinning the crime on Duncan's guards and by making their own "griefs and clamor roar." She forces him to a decision by implying that he would be cowardly not to do the deed.

4. What choices does Macbeth make during this act? He first chooses not to kill the king (page 180, lines 31–35); then he shifts and resolves to do it (page 181, lines 79–80).

5. How is the Macbeth we see at the end of this act different from the Macbeth we saw and heard about at the outset of the play? The early Macbeth was good, loyal, and a person of action; the later Macbeth is evil, disloyal to his king, and fearful of acting in his new cause. The shift is brought about by the witches' prophecies, which provoke his ambition, and even more so by Lady Macbeth.

WORDS

A. Students are to use context clues to infer the meanings of these words.

1. **furbished**—polished
2. **vantage**—benefit; gain
3. **battlements**—parapets with open spaces that surmount walls; used for defense

B. Students are to find the meanings of these words as used by Shakespeare.

Scene 2:
broil—a quarrel
quarrel—to find fault
slave—an unimaginative, dull person
survey—to appraise
memorize—to bring to memory once again
dismal—unlucky
lavish—abundant; defiant
composition—an armistice
present—imminent

Scene 3:
poster—a traveler
fantastical—imaginary
post—a report
earnest—a token as a pledge
addition—new (rank)
line—assist
soliciting—counseling

C. Students are asked to explain selected lines from the first act.

1. The valor of Macbeth and Banquo is likened to the power of a cannon loaded with double the normal charge of powder.

2. Ross explains that the Norwegian banners, being numerous, dominate the sky. He likens them to fans that, at first, fan Duncan's troops cold, inspiring in them a dislike for battle.

3. The witch explains that she will so enkindle Macbeth's ambition that sleep will never close his eyes.

D. Many contemporary dictionaries do not attach the labels *archaic* or *obsolete* to these words.

E. Students are to try to read lines from *Macbeth* using Shakespearean pronunciation.

ACT II

PAGE 183

Glossary Words

cleave (page 183) Hold fast; cling

palpable (page 184) Readily seen or heard and recognized; obvious; actual; real

knell (page 184) A warning sign of death, failure, etc.

surfeited (page 185) Having eaten or drunk to excess; gluttonous

appalls (page 186) Fills with consternation and horror; terrifies

minions (page 191) Darlings; favorites

invested (page 192) Installed in office with a ceremony

Handbook

scene, stage action

Check Test 19 (for Act II)

USING THE STUDY NOTES

ACT II

PAGE 192

A KING IS KILLED

1. If you were staging a production of *Macbeth,* would you have the dagger that Macbeth sees in Scene 1 visible to the audience? A generation raised on television programs that leave very little to the imagination would presumably prefer a visible dagger. However, it is important to point out that both Macbeth and Banquo saw the witches, and yet here Macbeth alone sees the dagger, as later on in the play he will be the only one to see Banquo's ghost. The question then really pivots on whether the dagger is intended to be real or to represent the workings of Macbeth's conscience. If it represents the workings of his conscience, then it is probably better not to have the dagger actually appear.

2. How does Macbeth's conscience react before and during the murder? And Lady Macbeth's conscience? After the murder how does each of them react? The reaction of Macbeth's conscience before the murder is best revealed in his soliloquy on page 184; the dagger is put in the air by his conscience, of course. His reaction during the murder is detailed in the second scene of his dialogue with Lady Macbeth; it was his conscience that presumably cried, "Sleep no more? / Macbeth does murder sleep." His conscience also kept him from pronouncing "Amen." Lady Macbeth's conscience seems much less troublesome; still, we may observe that she does not murder Duncan herself. What keeps her from the deed is the thought that the King resembles her father. This may be a bit of conscience-inspired rationalization. After the murder Macbeth is very much troubled: He sees things, and he cannot get his mind off the deed. Lady Macbeth, in contrast, is untroubled: "A little water clears us of this deed." (Of course, we know how heavily charged with irony this remark is.)

3. Why does Lady Macbeth faint? Her faint can be interpreted in three ways. It may be feigned, in which case it was done in order to keep suspicion from her and her husband. Also, she perhaps made a slip in saying, "What, in our house?" She seems conscious of this possibility because she is silent in the interval between making her remark and her faint. The faint breaks off the scene. Does she realize that Macbeth is overdoing his grief and so chooses this means of silencing him? On the other hand, her faint could have been caused by the first stirrings of conscience. She may have been overcome by Macbeth's description of the scene.

It is also possible to view Lady Macbeth's faint partly as a natural manifestation of her frail constitution. Although she managed to summon great energy in order to goad her husband into murder, the ordeal must have affected her physically. Although most directors have preferred to portray Lady Macbeth as strong, she is probably more dramatically pictured as being somewhat physically weak. There is every reason to believe that the contrast between a massive but fainthearted Macbeth and a frail but determined Lady Macbeth would appeal to Shakespeare and his audience.

4. What evidence is there that Banquo, Macduff, and others do not trust Macbeth? Macduff directly asks Macbeth why he killed the guards; Banquo speaks of "treasonous malice." It is fairly clear that the guards would not have murdered the king on their own initiative, that they would have been acting on orders, for pay. In killing them, Macbeth has removed all possibility of getting to the bottom of things. Malcolm and Donalbain are suspicious of the whole gathering, including Macbeth.

5. Why do Duncan's sons flee rather than remain to inherit the crown? They suspect that whoever killed their father did so in order to gain the crown himself; it follows logically that they will be the killer's next target. Better to be alive and just a noble than dead but a King.

ACT III — PAGE 193

Glossary Words

scepter (page 194) The rod or staff carried by a ruler as a symbol of royal power or authority

incensed (page 195) Made very angry; filled with rage

assailable (page 197) Capable of being attacked and overcome

jocund (page 197) Cheerful; merry; gay

nonpareil (page 200) Person or thing having no equal

infirmity (page 201) Sickness; illness

thralls (page 205) Persons in bondage

malevolence (page 205) The wish that evil will happen to others; ill will; spite

rue (page 205) Be sorry for; regret

Handbook

metaphor, semantics, simile, soliloquy

Check Test 20 (for Act III)

USING THE STUDY NOTES

ACT III — PAGE 206

MOUNTING CONSEQUENCES

1. What is the difference between Macbeth's behavior in the murder of Duncan and his behavior in the murder of Banquo? What changes in the character of Macbeth does this show? Macbeth behaves in a much colder, much more calculating manner than he did in killing Duncan; he is much less concerned about the morality of his act. He is changing to an evil character; he is losing all moral scruples and is becoming dehumanized.

2. What signs are there that Macbeth's conscience is troubling him? The clearest sign is his seeing the ghost of Banquo, but several other signs are mentioned in his conversations with Lady Macbeth, notably at the end of Scene 2. He is troubled by terrible dreams; he eats his meals in fear; he is not comfortable in the company of others.

3. How has the relationship of Macbeth and Lady Macbeth changed? She is no longer the aggressive one; ideed we find her markedly subdued in this act. He is the leader, the hatcher of plans.

4. What unforeseen consequences have followed the choices Macbeth has made? He did not foresee the consequences that would affect him personally—the "murder" of sleep, the "scorpions" in the mind, the hallucinations, the dehumanizing. He did not foresee the need to keep spies in the households of all his friends and the paranoia that this implies. He did not foresee that Fleance would escape the murderers, that Duncan's sons would voluntarily exile themselves, or that Macduff would go to England to raise an army against him. Neither did Macbeth foresee at the time of the murder of Duncan that he would have to murder Banquo.

5. What signs are there that Macbeth's character and personality are beginning to crumble? The hallucinations constitute the primary sign; note especially what he says in Scene 4, lines 110–115; in the same scene, note the reference to "strange things . . . in head," line 139. His determination to consult with the witches may be taken as another sign of his crumbling, suggesting that he feels he can no longer depend upon his own wit.

WORDS

A. Students are to find the meanings of these words from context clues.

1. **surfeited** (p. 185, ll. 5–6)—satiated
2. **multitudinous** (p. 186, ll. 61–62)—innumerable
3. **suborned** (p. 192, ll. 23 and 25)—bribed
4. **benison** (p. 192, l. 40)—blessing
5. **scepter** (p. 194, ll. 60–61)—a staff signifying the sovereignty of a king
6. **jocund** (p. 197, l. 40)—merry; happy
7. **nonpareil** (p. 200, l. 19)—having no equal

B. Students are to give the meanings of these words as used in Shakespeare's day.
franchised (p. 183, l. 28)—stainless
sensible (p. 184, l.36)—tangible
charge (p. 185, l. 6)—responsibility
unruly (p. 188, l. 43)—stormy
combustion (p. 188, l. 46)—tumult

C. Students are to explain the following similes and metaphors:

1. (p. 186, l. 36) Sleep is compared to a knitting needle. Sleep banishes care in the same way as a needle restores the raveled sleeve of a garment.

2. The metaphor is explained in side note 32, page 189.

3. (p. 191, l. 130) Just as daggers are potentially dangerous weapons, so also are the smiles of the men who surround us here, explains suspecting Donalbain. The smiles are but external appearances.

4. (p. 197, l. 13) Macbeth explains that he has managed to injure only temporarily those who threaten his throne.

5. (p. 198, l. 47) Macbeth likens the effect that the longed-for approach of night will have upon the day to that of a scarf wrapped about the eyes.

6. (p. 184, l. 50) Macbeth explains that wicked dreams disturb his sleep in the same way that one might disturb a shielding curtain.

7. The figure is explained in side note 28, page 189.

D. Lady Macbeth merely suggests that a little water will sove the problem of Macbeth's guilt.

E. The change in meaning is an example of broadening (extension).

F. The pronunciations are similar to those of *fad, mad, hat,* and *rat.*

ACT IV PAGE 207

Glossary Words

commend (page 208) Speak well of; praise
potent (page 209) Having great power; powerful; strong
pernicious (page 210) Fatal; deadly
diminutive (page 211) Very small; tiny; minute
laudable (page 213) Worthy of praise
sundry (page 215) Different; various; several
avaricious (page 215) Greatly desiring money or property; greedy for wealth
interdiction (page 216) Formal order forbidding something
abjure (page 217) Deny or give up

Handbook

characterization

Check Test 21 (for Act IV)

USING THE STUDY NOTES

ACT IV PAGE 220

MURDER COMPOUNDED

1. What are the three new prophecies the witches make to Macbeth? In essence, the prophecies are that he should look out for Macduff, that "none of woman born" shall harm him, and that he shall not be defeated until Birnam wood shall move to Dunsinane hill.

What questions do they refuse to answer? Questions addressed to the apparitions are not answered. There is also no direct answer to Macbeth's question of whether Banquo's children shall ever rule, but when Macbeth interprets the apparitions of the kings to mean that Banquo's progeny shall someday rule, the First Witch tells him that it is as he has guessed.

What is the meaning of the three apparitions Macbeth sees in the witches' cave? The Armed Head is the head of Macduff, who will invade Scotland and defeat Macbeth. The Bloody Child would probably be Macduff at birth—he was "untimely ripped" from his mother's womb. The Child Crowned would presumably be Malcolm, who is young and who becomes the next king.

2. Explain these lines:

"From this moment
The very firstlings of my heart shall be
The firstlings of my hand."

Macbeth is saying that the first things that he feels or thinks he shall immediately carry into action; he'll do things as soon as they occur to him, without thinking them over.

3. How does the murder of Macduff's family differ from the murder of Duncan? From the murder of Banquo? The chief differences between the murder of Macduff's family and the earlier murders is that the former is a wanton act and one that will not advance Macbeth's cause in any way. Also, it is carried out almost instantly and by "professional" killers.

4. What has happened to the Kingdom of Scotland since Macbeth took the crown? The general disorder is well summed up by Macduff in Scene 3, lines 4–8, and by Ross in the same scene, lines 164–173.

5. In this act, is Macbeth acting with greater decision than in Act I? Is he more or less in control of himself and of events? Macbeth is acting with greater "decision"—and with a great deal less deliberation. He is much less in control of himself and events than he was formerly, as shown by the senseless murder of Lady Macduff and her son. The general disorder just referred to is another sign that events are out of his control.

ACT V — PAGE 221

Glossary Words

perturbation (page 221) A thing, act, or event that causes disturbance or agitation; condition of being greatly disturbed; great distress; worry; anxiety

pristine (page 225) Original; pure

Handbook

characterization, imagery, metaphor, semantics, simile, tragedy

Check Test 22 (for Act V)

USING THE STUDY NOTES

ACT V — PAGE 232

THE PROPHECY FULFILLED

1. What are the memories that Lady Macbeth cannot rid herself of? She cannot rid herself of the memories of the murders; she refers to those of Duncan, Lady Macduff, and Banquo. The blood on her hands and the knocking at the gate are specific details of the first murder that she cannot get out of her mind.

2. Trace Macbeth's changes of mood throughout this act. How does Macbeth react to Lady Macbeth's death? Macbeth's changes of mood are very swift. As Scene 3 begins he seems to be in a mood of arrogant self-confidence, but in lines 11–19 his quick-tempered anger shows him to be a good deal less confident. Then in the middle of line 19 his mood shifts again—to one of sickness at heart. His courage flashes forth momentarily in lines 32–33; then in his next brief speech (ll. 34–37) his mood shifts in virtually every sentence, terminating in an expression of concern for his wife. This concern is also seen in his next speech (ll. 39–45), but his tone in addressing the doctor is not gentle, and when the doctor replies to him, Macbeth flies into a rage: "Throw physic to the dogs, I'll none of it!" He displays bitterness in the remainder of his speech to the doctor.

As the fifth scene opens, Macbeth is arrogant, boastful, courageous; but the cry of the women causes another shift in his mood, making him rather meditative, and he expresses sadness at the change that has come over his personality since he became king. When he hears of the death of the queen, it touches him for a moment, but he quickly shifts into his speech on the futility of life: "Tomorrow, and tomorrow. . . ." After this speech his anger flares again as he speaks with the messenger. At the close of the scene, his mood shifts from anger to fierceness to weariness to fierceness again.

In his fight with young Siward, Macbeth shows both courage and boastfulness. Finally, in his encounter with Macduff he first expresses a kind of sympathy for him—he really does not want to kill him since he has already done him so much harm. Then for a brief moment he seems fearful, but his fear quickly yields to his courageous will to fight on in spite of what he knows fate has in store for him.

What does this suggest about the changed relationship between them? What does it show about Macbeth's own character at this point? Macbeth's reaction to Lady Macbeth's death may seem stoical—even cold—to many readers. The problem, of course, is that he is so beset by his own problems—both inner and outer—that he has neither the time nor the inclination to think much of her. He has become dehumanized, but not wholly so: He can still wish that there had been time to speak with her before her death.

3. How is each of the witches' prophecies fulfilled? Macbeth was told he should beware of Macduff. This prophecy was "fulfilled," in a sense. He was told that "none of woman born" could harm him, and none did, for Macduff was ripped from his mother's womb before birth (we would call it Caesarean section). And he was told that he would not be defeated till Birnam wood moved to Dunsinane. The wood did move to Dunsinane, as the soldiers carried trees for camouflage. Note that the prophecies come true in reverse order.

4. How do Macbeth's better qualities—such as courage and humaneness—show themselves during this act? Does this make *Macbeth* a greater and more interesting play than if Shakespeare had let Macbeth become nothing else but a villain who is out of control? Macbeth's courage is shown in several places, especially when he meets the invaders; it is most notable in his final fight—against Macduff and fate. Macbeth is decidedly *in*humane in his treatment of most of the characters in this act, but there are touches of humaneness here and there, especially in his brief discussion with Seyton in Scene 5 and in his concern for Lady Macbeth. A poet of Shakespeare's ability can make virtually any subject great and interesting, even villainy—consider Iago and King Richard III. Still, one could agree that, on the whole, readers prefer characters who have varied personal qualities, rather than one-dimensional personalities. The play could therefore be said to be greater and more interesting because Macbeth is not made entirely villainous.

5. With what change of mood does the play end? What indications are there of the kind of king Malcolm will be? The play ends on a note of great hope for the future and for the healing of Scotland's wounds. In his final speech, Malcolm reveals himself as a compassionate, thoughtful, and "democratic" king. He is concerned with rewarding those who fought with him, and he says nothing against those who opposed him, with the exception of Macbeth and Lady Macbeth.

WORDS

A. Students are to use context clues to infer the meanings of these words. Answers will vary slightly.

1. **bodements** (p. 209, l. 96)—prophecies
2. **antic** (p. 210, l. 130)—grotesque
3. **pernicious** (p.210, l. 132)—wicked
4. **abjure** (p. 217, l. 123)—renounce

B. Learning the meanings of the words listed from Act IV, Scene 1, is not of primary importance. A knowledge of their meanings, however, would help to reveal the noxious nature of the witches and lead to an understanding of the chilling effect that the daughters of darkness had upon the typical Shakespearean audience.

C. Students are to explain selected expressions.

1. **lies**—tells an untruth
2. **grace**—charm; beauty
3. **grafted**—joined together
4. **forge**—fashion
5. **dam**—mother
6. **strokes**—blows
7. **start**—surprise
8. **course**—bout
9. **score**—debt
10. **ministers**—servants

USING THE STUDY NOTES

PAGE 232

I. TRAGEDY OF AMBITION

Under this heading, students are asked to discuss the following:

1. Trace some of the choices made by characters in *Macbeth* and show the consequences that sprang from them. If you have been using the Study Notes that follow each act, your students will already have discussed the major choices and consequences of Macbeth and Lady Macbeth. In that case, focus on some of the choices made by other characters. Duncan, Banquo, Malcolm, Macduff, and others made some choices that have fateful and far-reaching consequences.

2. Discuss *Macbeth* as a tragedy. Base your discussion on the description of tragedy on pages 4–5. We have listed below the statements about tragedy given on pages 4 and 5 of the text and discussed *Macbeth* under these headings. Reference is occasionally made to Aristotle's theory, but it should not be assumed that all the points mentioned are Aristotelian. Aristotle says nothing, for instance, about the third point.

a. Tragedy arouses the emotions of pity and fear, wonder and awe. Students may have difficulty in seeing that Macbeth is to be pitied and that his fate is one that can happen to any of us. Macbeth is a person of great potential whose desire to get ahead, an ambition that is certainly generally admired in American society, becomes so strong that it blinds him to moral considerations. Thus the emotion of pity springs from our watching the dissipation of Macbeth's human potential because of the inner drives of his own personality.

Certainly wonder and awe are inspired by the supernatural aspects of the play. An Elizabethan audience would be even more responsive than we are to the appearance of the witches, the dagger, and the mysterious voices that cry out.

b. A tragic hero must be a man or woman capable of great suffering. The main point here is that the tragic hero must be above the ordinary in sensitivity. The murders that Macbeth plots and the ways in which he treats most persons at the end of the play may cause students to think of him as insensitive. But these actions are offset to some extent by moments in which Macbeth seems very sensitive indeed. In his "Tomorrow, and tomorrow" speech, for instance, he shows a deeply poetic appreciation of the plight of human life.

c. Tragedy explores the question of the ways of God to Mortals. God must be interpreted here as a collection of supernatural forces rather than as the personalized entity of the Judeo-Christian tradition. Certainly there are mysterious forces that influence the characters. However, the play suggests, if anything, that Mortals can easily be lured into bringing about their own downfall.

d. Tragedy purifies the emotions. There is no general agreement as to what Aristotle meant by his theory of catharsis; nevertheless, it is broadly true that Greek and Shakespearean tragedies most often leave one feeling elevated rather than depressed, in spite of the suffering that they depict. There are many possible explanations of this paradox. One explanation may be the poetry. Another may be that tragic heroes often gain insight into themselves through their suffering—Oedipus is a good example. Also, although individual suffering and, commonly, death occur in classical tragedies, they often conclude with the restoration of order in the larger human community. With such restoration, audiences may conclude that, in spite of their own chaotic worlds, there is order, purpose, and justice in the universe.

e. Tragedy shows how the hero is brought to disaster by a single flaw in character. It is highly probable that Aristotle did not wish us to seek a *single* flaw in the nature of tragic heroes. In any case, Macbeth suffers from more than one character fault. It is often said that Macbeth's flaw was ambition, but clearly it is not ambition alone that causes him to pursue the course that he does. In the first act he specifically says that he wishes to retain his newly won reputation and not to seek greater things. And when Lady Macbeth tries to move him from this resolve, it is not primarily to his ambition that she speaks, but to his fear of appearing cowardly. Thus we could say that another major flaw in his character is his insecurity. Macbeth has other flaws as well: a quick temper and hypocrisy are two of them.

II. IMPLICATIONS

A. Students are asked to tell if they find any valid meaning today in the following quotations from the play:

1. But 'tis strange:
And oftentimes, to win us to our harm,
The instruments of darkness tell us truths,
Win us with honest trifles, to betray's
In deepest consequence.

We might observe first of all that "instruments of darkness" may be interpreted broadly. It could indicate the evil side of our own natures—whatever their sources. Or it may indicate outside sources—the arguments of persons who wish us to join with them in evil acts. In such cases it is clearly true that such forces may lure us with bits of truth. A politician or general, for instance, could prove that a given foreign power wants to do us some harm in order to convince us that the use of thermonuclear bombs is the best method of subduing our enemies.

2. False face must hide what the false heart doth know.

Obviously, people with false hearts still try to conceal them with false faces. Shakespeare's phrase says this very well, very memorably. It is notable not so much for what it says, but for how it says it. This is true of several of the other quotations as well.

3. Words to the heat of deeds too cold breath gives.

Putting this in a modern idiom, we could say that talking about things does not help to get them done and may even inhibit their being done. There is probably not a person alive who does not feel the sting of this remark; most of us tend to do more talking than doing. Specifically, some writers have often observed that if they talk too much about work in progress, they never get around to "writing it out."

4. To show an unfelt sorrow is an office
Which the false man does easy.

All of us have encountered the type of hypocrite referred to in this quotation; it often seems the falser the person, the easier is the expression of hypocritical sorrow—or of any emotion, for that matter.

5. Naught's had, all's spent,
Where our desire is got without content.

If we reach our goals but are not content, we have spent everything to get nothing. Some students may think that this idea should be qualified. There is probably no desire that when achieved produces complete content. Having achieved a particular goal, most of us set still higher goals for the future.

6. 'Tis safer to be that which we destroy
Than by destruction dwell in doubtful joy.

Lady Macbeth fears so strongly the consequences of being discovered that she claims it is better, "safer," to be destroyed oneself than to live under suspicion that one is guilty of murder. Under such circumstances one is continually under the threat of death, and one is pricked by conscience. Death itself may well be preferable—and safer.

7. Things without all remedy
Should be done without regard: what's done is done.

This speech is highly ironic in context, for the play underscores the theme that we cannot simply forget about acts that we have committed; they have consequences, whether they can be remedied or not, and the consequences may trouble us long after the original deeds have been done. We have many ways of saying that we should not worry about the past, but the past, too, has many ways of intruding itself into the present. Indeed, what is conscience but the power of the past exerted on the present?

8. They say, blood will have blood.

"They" said it in Shakespeare's time; "they" say it still.

B. Students are asked to determine whether the following statements are true or false and to support their opinions by citing specific references from the play.

1. Macbeth was led into evil almost solely because of Lady Macbeth's determination. This is false. We can tell from Macbeth's reaction to the witches that he harbored evil ideas before Lady Macbeth began to influence him. Of course, it is also true that he had resolved to do nothing immediately about his ambitions, but it is probably pointless to argue over what would have happened if Lady Macbeth had not been so determined.

2. Macbeth's indecision to commit the murder shows only that he is weak. Macbeth's indecision shows primarily that he has a conscience, that he is able to tell right from wrong. Later, when he has "murdered" his conscience, he is not indecisive at all.

3. The murder actually drives Macbeth and Lady Macbeth apart. In general, Macbeth grows more and more self-absorbed, and in that way it may be true to say that the murder drives the couple apart. But we find no deep chasm between them in other respects; on the contrary, there seems to be a good deal of tenderness and solicitude between them in Act III: See, for instance, the conclusion of Scene 4, which is the last time we see them together.

4. Once the first murder is committed, the other murders are inevitable. This is not true. There is nothing inevitable about the murder of Lady Macduff and the children.

5. Macbeth could have been a force for great and positive good. The picture that we get of Macbeth early in the play—and in some later scenes as well—makes it clear that this is true. He had a noble nature.

6. This play demonstrates that a move in the wrong direction must be followed by acts leading in the same direction. The word *must* is too strong. We could say that the play demonstrates that a move in the wrong direction may be, or is likely to be, followed by acts leading in the same direction. One should not generalize from a single instance.

7. Shakespeare wanted his audience to feel sympathy with Macbeth. The earliest scenes of the play help to make the audience sympathetic toward Macbeth. If Shakespeare had not intended to arouse our sympathies, he would not have begun the play as he did. There was also no reason for portraying the better sides of Macbeth's character in the last act if Shakespeare had not wanted his audience to feel sympathy toward his hero.

8. If tragedy shows characters experiencing great anguish of spirit which gives a feeling of release and purification to the beholder, then *Macbeth* is not tragedy. There are certainly characters who experience great anguish of spirit in *Macbeth.* Whether this leads to a feeling of release and purification in the beholder is a moot point; it may also be quite subjective—some beholders may feel purified; others may not. Plato—you may recall—decided that all tragic poets would have to be banished from his perfect state because they aroused weak emotions like pity and fear in the citizens; in short, Aristotle's tutor did not share his pupil's view of the releasing and the purifying powers of tragedy.

9. Unlike the tragic Creon, Macbeth never really repents his actions. Macbeth does not openly repent his actions, but in the sickness of heart that he confesses to Seyton and in the world-weariness that he expresses in his "Tomorrow, and tomorrow" speech, we may very well be moved to sorrow for him. We may also feel that he is sorry for what he has done.

III. TECHNIQUES

Character Development

For further discussion of the distinction between flat and round characters, you may want to consult Chapter 4 of E. M. Forster's *Aspects of the Novel.*

The following questions are asked of students:

1. What in Macbeth's character makes him susceptible to the witches' prophecies? Macbeth is ambitious, and the witches promise him that he will "get ahead." It is thus natural for him to be susceptible to their prophecies. Also, recall that the "thane of Cawdor" prediction comes to pass shortly after the witches make it.

2. Read the following lines. Write on a sheet of paper a word or two to tell what each succeeding quotation reveals or reinforces about Macbeth's character.

a. Bravery

b. Nobility of character

c. Kindness or gentleness of disposition; lack of wickedness ("without / The illness"); ambition

d. Ambition but also unwillingness to do evil

e. Timidity, perhaps, but more important, moral scruples

f. Conscience; guilt

g. Concern (at having done wrong) and fear of a sort

h. Conscience

i. Evil nature

j. Evil nature

k. A kind of gullibility or foolish fearlessness

l. Sympathetic concern and perhaps stoicism

m. Courage; fearlessness

3. Do Macbeth's actions spring from his personality or are they seemingly unrelated? How many different methods has Shakespeare used to reveal Macbeth's character? Notice that although Macbeth's character is many faceted, the dominant trait is ambition—the drive toward power. It is this characteristic that moves the action of the play, beginning with Macbeth's determination to kill the king, to his carrying out of the murder, to the later black deeds that he commits in order to retain the power that he has seized. Minor incidents in the play are often the outgrowth of other aspects of his character. For example, the fact that he has a conscience is evidenced by his sleeplessness and by the dagger that only he can see. In the last act, he gives evidence of his courage by his determination to fight in spite of the witches' prophecies. Shakespeare also reveals Macbeth's character by what others say about him; e.g., the sergeant who reports the battle and the king himself. Lady Macbeth also analyzes him in Act I. Macbeth reveals his character in his interactions with his wife, servants, and others. And, of course, he shows his inner feelings in his soliloquies.

4. Reread Scenes 5 and 7 in Act I, and Scenes 1 and 2 in Act II. From these write a paragraph giving your impressions of Lady Macbeth. Share these descriptions in class. Considering the general class picture of Lady Macbeth, do you think Shakespeare prepared you for Lady Macbeth's madness at the end of the play? Students may conclude that there is not much preparation in the early acts, but much depends upon how one defines the term *preparation.* Certainly there is a marked contrast between the Lady Macbeth that we first see and the one that we see some months after the murder; this in itself should suggest that something further may happen to her—one's character does not normally alter so radically in so short a time without further consequences. The increase in the number and the wantonness of the murders would also suggest that change will come. Finally, there are some direct indications of the possibility of change. In particular one might call attention to the following quotation from Act II, Scene 2: "These deeds must not be thought / After these ways; so, it will make us mad." Attentive readers will find a good deal of foreshadowing that prepares them for the later madness. As A. C. Bradley points out, the remark "A little water clears us of this deed" is later answered by "Will these hands ne'er be clean?" And the commonplace "What's done is done" is later answered by "What's done cannot be undone."

In short, there is considerable preparation, although much of it is rather subtle.

5. Do you think Shakespeare made the following characters round or flat?

a. Banquo

b. Malcolm

c. Macduff

Forster points out that the really flat character is constructed around a single quality or idea that can be described in one sentence. All the characters named above are more complex than that, and all should be considered round. To be sure, there are degrees of roundness, and none of these characters is as round, as fully known, as Macbeth or Lady Macbeth. But none is as flat as the porter, the witches, or Donalbain.

Imagery

Students are asked to discuss what picture, emotion, and mood each of the following images generates and how effective they find each.

1. The earth hath bubbles, as the water has,
And these are of them.

Banquo is comparing the witches to bubbles that burst easily. The image is appropriate, for it creates the same effect as does the suddenness of the witches' disappearance.

2. Sleep that knits up the raveled sleave of
care....

Care is like a tangled floss ("raveled sleave"), and sleep may bring a knitting or an ordering of the floss by giving a respite from care. The image is appropriate because one usually thinks of a knitter as a calm person; here sleep is pictured as the knitter.

3. There's daggers in men's smiles....

The contrast between a dagger and a smile makes this a good image. The idea here, of course, is that when a person smiles, one cannot tell whether the smile signifies good or evil.

4. We have scotched the snake, not killed it.

Scotched means "injured," and *the snake* represents the threat to Macbeth's position, especially the threat posed by Banquo. *Snake* is a good symbol for harm, and of course there is some irony in the remark because it is usually Macbeth who is referred to as the snake.

5. look like the innocent flower,
But be the serpent under't.

The image of a snake hiding under a flower is a simple but effective one for conveying the idea of putting on a false front.

6. Macbeth is ripe for shaking....

Macbeth is compared to a tree whose fruit is so ripe that mere shaking will bring it down. Perhaps the comparison to a tree in fall laden with dead leaves is a slightly better comparison because it suggests that Macbeth is in the late autumn of his life.

7. My way of life
Is fallen into the sere, the yellow leaf....

Here Macbeth compares himself to a withered leaf. The image evokes not only a picture, but also an emotion, a certain autumnal sadness. Note, by the way, that *leaf* is singular and thus suggests loneliness in addition to age and approaching death.

8. Out, out, brief candle!
Life's but a walking shadow, a poor player,
That struts and frets his hour upon the stage
And then is heard no more. It is a tale
Told by an idiot, full of sound and fury,
Signifying nothing.

The candle, the shadow, the poor actor are all images that conspire to make us realize the brevity and the meaninglessness of life on earth. The idiot's tale is the capping image, suggesting as it does irrationality and total incoherence.

Witness to the Truth: Socrates

PAGE 236

Edith Hamilton

Glossary Words

millenniums (page 236, col. 1) Periods of a thousand years each

anathemas (page 238, col. 2) Denunciations of persons or things as evil. Also, solemn curses

urbane (page 238, col. 2) Courteous, refined or elegant; polite; well-mannered

profusion (page 238, col. 2) Great abundance; lavishness

pretentious (page 238, col. 2) Making claims to excellence or importance

gadfly (page 239, col. 1) Person who goads others to action by irritating or annoying remarks

exhorting (page 239, col. 1) Urging strongly; advising or warning earnestly

dogmatic (page 239, col. 1) Positive and emphatic in asserting opinions; stubborn

fundamental (page 240, col. 1) Of or forming a foundation or basis; essential; basic

dogma (page 240, col. 2) Any system of principles; doctrine

Handbook

abstract terms, characterization, imagery, metaphor

***Check Test 23** (for "Witness to the Truth: Socrates" and "The Death of Socrates")*

INTRODUCTION

The body of this article is an appreciation of Socrates, the moralist and teacher. Miss Hamilton discusses the core of his teachings and then concludes by showing how he defended his principles and lived by them, even though the consequence of his choice was certain death.

Ideally, this selection should prompt students to ask themselves about the foundations of their own lives and to see that the unexamined life is indeed not worth living. Moreover they should see that the choices that one makes ought to emanate from the principles that one lives by. Then, the consequences of such choices can be faced realistically, and life will be worth living and worth dying for.

Students should be told that this selection is not a story. Tell them to read it carefully and slowly. Ask them to take notes while they read and to read the selection more than once. Perhaps you will want them to sum up the selection in their own words. To ensure that they will get the most from their reading, have them write their summaries and read them in class.

An alternative might be to ask students to state and support *one* characteristic of Socrates as described by Hamilton. You may want to assign at least two students to work together.

To ease the students into reading, ask them what they already know about Socrates. If they have little or no knowledge, perhaps you could spend a few moments outlining his life and his ideas.

USING THE STUDY NOTES

PAGE 241

I. IS AN IDEA WORTH DYING FOR?

Students are asked how the following statements of philosophy from Socrates' biography might apply to modern life.

1. Goodness has a most real and actual existence. In our nonabsolutist, relativistic age it is not easy to agree that goodness can be an absolute quality; yet it seems to us that the popular mind tends on the whole to think this way still. And as Greece had a Socrates, who personified this point, so have we had a well-known figure or two—Albert Schweitzer, for instance—who have helped us to see that "goodness has a most real and actual existence."

2. What a lot of things there are a man can do without. In our country today there are probably more things a person can do without than in any previous place or time. But we do not very often do without them; somehow it seems that even the poorer members of our society manage to own cars and television sets. Of course, Socrates' point is still relevant—the implication is that we would be better off, better able to concentrate on what really counts, if we did without a lot of things.

3. Happiness is activity of soul. Perhaps the modern student would prefer to rephrase this statement: Happiness comes from using oneself creatively. At any rate, the quotation clearly does apply to modern life; indeed, one can readily classify it as a timeless truth.

4. The unexamined life is not worth living. Human beings are distinguished from the animals by the fact that they not only act and feel but also possess the capacity for knowing *why* they act and feel. If they do not use their reason, human beings may be said to live an animal life, the kind of life that Socrates would say is not worth living. An "examined life" is of course also a principled, moral life. We certainly hope that students would agree that the unexamined life remains a life not worth living.

5. . . . goodness and truth are the fundamental realities and every human has the ability to attain to them. Even in a high school classroom, one ought to be able to debate this statement for hours. How can *goodness* and *truth* be defined? Are they really absolutes, as Socrates seemed to think, or are they relative, as most modern American philosophers from James on seem to think? Are these terms limited to *moral* goodness and truth, or should we think of them more broadly? If the latter, how can we say that everyone has the ability to attain them? For instance, can a person who cannot read expect to attain truth as readily as one who can? These questions are merely samples of the kinds of questions one may ask in trying to determine whether this statement applies to modern life.

6. The false and the trivial pass away. Let us take some examples. There is a good deal that is both false and trivial in Aristotle's works. Much of it—although not all—has "passed away," but it lived for close to twenty centuries. Again, the falser Ptolemaic system gave way to the truer Copernican system, but that took nearly fifteen centuries. And so it goes. The false and the trivial may indeed pass away—if one can wait long enough. And even at that, one sometimes wonders if what the "false" has been replaced by is any less false and trivial. In short, the statement, while comforting, is rather glib and overgeneralized.

7. Men have the highest destiny. They can know the truth. Statements about *the* truth may set off relativists; still, many persons would accept this statement in one form or another. A great number of us are believers in "the truth" where morals are concerned, for instance. Also, most people accept the notion that it is possible to learn "the truth" about yourself—with or without the aid of a psychiatrist. Knowing truths of this sort is generally considered a very high destiny.

8. No one may do wrong intentionally. This statement does not mean that it is impossible to do wrong intentionally, but rather that one must not (or ought not to) do wrong intentionally. In the *Crito,* Socrates is trying to persuade Crito that he (Socrates) ought not to do wrong even though wrong has been done to him, that he should remain in prison and take the hemlock rather than break the law by trying to escape. Obviously, the idea that one should not do wrong intentionally is still widely held today.

II. IMPLICATIONS

Students are asked whether they agree or disagree with the following and to support their view by examples from the selection.

1. Socrates' choice (to die) was based solely on logic . . . conscience and emotion played no part in it. Conscience was clearly the key element in Socrates' decision; indeed, Socrates specifically refers to an inner voice as he concludes his argument with Crito.

2. Socrates' teachings are not for the ordinary person. In the third paragraph of the selection, the author clearly implies that Socrates was concerned with ordinary people. Later, she makes it plain that Socrates' teachings were for everybody: "All men had within them a guide, a spark of the true light . . ."; and "Philosophy . . . must come down and live with mankind. . . ." In spite of these statements, it is also true that Socrates—at least Plato's Socrates—often speaks disparagingly of "the opinion of the many"; and it is also true that ordinary people put Socrates to death for his teachings.

3. Socrates' death demonstrates his credo that it is better to undergo evil than to perform it. It is clear from the penultimate paragraph of the selection that this proposition is essentially correct. Socrates regarded bribing his way out of prison as wrong and therefore would not do it. He chose instead to undergo the evil of unjust condemnation.

4. It took tremendous courage to "choose" to die. One would think that it would. Yet there is no emphasis on courage in the selection or in the Platonic dialogues dealing with the death of Socrates.

III. TECHNIQUES

Character Development

Students are asked to write down everything that they know about Socrates' personality and character. Then they are to review the reading and see how many different devices Hamilton used to convey the portrait.

Hamilton's portrait is formed largely by her descriptions of Socrates, although she includes a good many quotations from Socrates himself—or, more accurately, from Plato's Socrates. Describing others is a device used more rarely, but sometimes it is used quite effectively, as when Alcibiades speaks of Socrates' effect on him and when Phaedo speaks of the feelings that he had as he observed Socrates near death.

Imagery

Students are asked how the following metaphors help to make Socrates' ideas clear and vivid.

1. I think I am that gadfly. A gadfly is a fly that bites cattle. Socrates saw his mission as one of pricking the consciences of Athens' citizens, who, without such a gadfly, might have been all too ready to become morally sluggish, like cattle. The metaphor thus vividly depicts both Socrates and his "victims."

2. The mighty stranger, death. . . . On first glance this may seem to be a simple and even ineffective metaphor. What we like about it on second glance is the understatement. Making death a stranger—even a mighty one—renders death much less fearful than most other metaphors do; it also accomplishes this effect without turning away from the idea of death, for "mighty" suggests that death will prevail in all encounters. In short, the image does help to clarify Socrates' ideas on death.

3. And like the bee, leave my sting in you before I die. . . . Socrates was not interested in constructing a philosophical system but rather in urging people to live good lives, stinging them to act morally. Like a bee, he gave his life for this purpose, for the state clearly put him to death because he stirred the citizens into thinking for themselves.

The Death of Socrates

PAGE 243

Plato

Glossary Words

bereaved (page 244, col. 1) Being left alone and desolate; deprived

forfeit (page 244, col. 2) Lost or given up as a penalty

Handbook

characterization

Check Test 23 (for "The Death of Socrates" and "Witness to the Truth: Socrates")

INTRODUCTION

This selection is related very closely to the previous selection; indeed, it is little more than a full rendering of the death of Socrates, which Hamilton treats in summary fashion at the end of her article. The complete *Phaedo* is quite a long dialogue in which Socrates discusses death, the immortality of the soul, Plato's theory of ideas, his doctrine of recollection, and other matters. Our excerpt—a part near the beginning of the dialogue and its last nine paragraphs—is the core of the dialogue concerning Socrates' death. It is a simple, yet very moving, tale that is told—from the point of view of Phaedo—by a man who was not only a great philosopher, but also a great writer, Plato. From the point of view of the theme of this unit, the tale is especially valuable as an illustration of a person who, having made a choice, bravely faces the direst consequence.

If students have read the previous selection, no special introduction to this selection should be necessary. Merely ask students to read the headnote in the text, page 243.

USING THE STUDY NOTES PAGE 246

I. "WE WERE LAUGHING AND WEEPING BY TURNS"

As the commentary in the text indicates, one of the things that make the selection great is the contrast between the way that Socrates faces his own death and the way that his death sentence is taken by his friends and relatives. What makes Socrates so calm is his steady perception that the human spirit is of far greater consequence than the human body. This is a hard truth for his friends—for any of us—to accept.

Students are asked to tell what is revealed about the speakers of the following words:

1. . . . we were about to pass the rest of our lives as orphans. (Phaedo)

The statement is a measure of the depth of Phaedo's affection for Socrates. (And of course he is speaking for all of Socrates' friends.) He regards the old philosopher not only as a leader, but also as a parent.

2. I do not think that I should gain anything by drinking the poison a little later. (Socrates)

Most of us would cling to every half-second of life and do all that we could to prolong it; Socrates thus shows almost superhuman courage or fearlessness in facing death. Of course the statement shows other things as well—Socrates' willingness to see "justice" done, for instance. We would also hope that students will see that underlying the statement is Socrates' conviction that the spiritual life counts for more than the material.

3. Crito, I owe a cock to Asclepius; will you remember to pay the debt? (Socrates)

This statement clearly shows Socrates' great concern for justice; it is especially noteworthy that these were the last words that he spoke and that he spoke them when already half dead. By the way, it may be worth observing that Socrates was not certain that there was an afterlife; thus he is not necessarily asking that the debt be paid in order that his way to heaven should be clear. We have observed that it was largely with the spiritual in this life that he was concerned, but he did not live his life well simply because he hoped for later reward. He lived it well for its own sake.

II. IMPLICATIONS

Students are asked for their reactions to the following statements. They are to say whether they agree or disagree with them.

1. Once a choice is made, it is best to accept the consequences immediately. We assume that the consequences referred to are inevitable. Granting this, it seems to us that little is gained by delay that could damage one's integrity, perhaps by appearing a coward. Further, the time "bought" by putting off the consequences is very likely to be filled with anxiety.

2. If Socrates had chosen to give up his teaching in order to save his life, he would have discredited his own ideas and probably would not be remembered today. This proposition is impossible to settle definitively. What can be said, however, is that the Socrates who is universally admired would probably not be revered today. Of course, if we assume that Plato would still have written his dialogues, we would also have to assume that Socrates would be remembered, at least as a practitioner of the famous Socratic method. And of course we would still remember the Socrates of Aristophanes's *Clouds;* indeed this unflattering portrait might have become the "official portrait" if Socrates had given up his teaching.

III. TECHNIQUES

Character Development

Students are asked to discuss these questions:

1. Are there any new aspects of Socrates' character that you find in this section from the *Phaedo* which you did not find in Edith Hamilton's biography? The main new aspect would be the picture of Socrates as husband and father, although this is rather sketchily drawn. We get a clearer picture of the relationship between Socrates and his pupils. Finally, this selection shows something more than Edith Hamilton revealed about Socrates' relation to the ordinary person. We refer specifically to the brief exchange between Socrates and the jailer. In general, this is a more fully rendered portrait of Socrates the human being as opposed to Socrates the moralist.

2. How does Plato create a sense of Socrates' personality in the scene? Plato does this largely by noting how Socrates acts and by quoting him directly. Much is also contributed by the reactions of Phaedo and others.

IV. WORDS

A. Students are to find the meanings of these words, using context clues or a dictionary as needed. Answers may vary.

1. **millenniums**—thousand-year periods
2. **verity**—truth
3. **amoral**—neither moral nor immoral
4. **indictment**—charge
5. **anathemas**—vigorous denunciations
6. **urbane**—notably polite
7. **profusion**—abundance

B. Students are to explain each of the following names and, where possible, to give adjectives that have been derived from the proper names.

Plato—Greek philosopher and disciple of Socrates (platonic)

Athens—the ancient Greek city-state and the capital of modern Greece

Thucydides—a Greek historian ranked as the greatest of antiquity

Homer—the Greek epic poet who wrote the *Iliad* and the *Odyssey* (Homeric)

St. Paul—the apostle of Jesus to the Gentiles (Pauline)

Isaiah—one of the major Hebrew prophets

Jeremiah—a major Hebrew prophet whose writings are recorded in the Old Testament books of *Jeremiah* and *Lamentations*

Pericles—an Athenian statesman who labored to make his city the center of art and culture

Alcibiades—an Athenian general and politician who was a friend of Socrates

Aristotle—a Greek philosopher who is considered the father of classical logic

Goethe—a German philosopher and poet who is the author of the epic poem *Faust*

St. Augustine—an ancient church father and theologian, famous as the author of *The Confessions* and *The City of God*

C. The connotations of words are as follows:

ordered suggests "logical"
futile suggests "hopeless"
instinct suggests "automatic"
passionate suggests "unreasonable"
witness suggests "supporter"
homely suggests "commonplace"
formula suggests "rigid"

The Hint of an Explanation

PAGE 247

Graham Greene

Glossary Words

omnipotent (page 247, col. 2) Having all power; almighty

omniscient (page 247, col. 2) Knowing everything; having complete or infinite knowledge

anthropomorphic (page 248, col. 2) Attributing human form or qualities to gods, animals, or things

enmity (page 249, col. 1) Hostility or hatred; ill will

supercilious (page 249, col. 2) Haughty, proud, and contemptuous; disdainful; showing scorn because of feeling oneself superior

shackled (page 249, col. 2) Enslaved; held fast; restrained

subservience (page 250, col. 1) Slavish politeness and obedience

paradox (page 250, col. 1) Person or thing that seems to be full of contradictions

covetousness (page 252, col. 1) Desiring things that belong to others

wheedle (page 253, col. 2) Coax; persuade by pleasant words, flattery, or false promises

Handbook

characterization, imagery, metaphor, prose style

Check Test 24

INTRODUCTION

The narrator of the story, who is an agnostic, happens to sit next to a Catholic on a train. A friendly discussion between them climaxes with a discussion of God. When the narrator speaks of the evils that God "allows," the Catholic responds at first by saying that the view of mortals is limited, but then he adds that there are "hints." He proceeds to tell a story about his own childhood, one that illustrates the fact that there are indeed "hints."

At the age of ten, the Catholic (David Martin) was an altar boy in a town most of whose inhabitants were non-Catholic. One was a freethinker named Blacker, who had a special hatred of Catholics. Blacker lured the young Martin to the parlor behind his shop by giving him a cake; then he showed him a small electric railway and allowed him to play with it. Soon David was coming every day during his school holiday to play with the railway. (At several points the older Martin hints that Blacker is the servant of the devil.)

Near the end of the holiday, Blacker proposed to give the train to the boy if the boy in turn would get him a consecrated Communion wafer. Blacker says that he wants to know "what your God tastes like." He suggests that David hide the wafer in his mouth, then leave the altar and hide it somewhere else until the Mass is over. David is shaken by this suggestion, but he wants the train very much; furthermore, Blacker also suggests that if David does not get him the wafer, he will "bleed" him with a razor.

At mass the next Sunday, David—with Blacker watching from the rear of the church—hides a Communion wafer under his tongue and later transfers it to a piece of newspaper. That night Blacker appears below the boy's bedroom window and asks where the wafer is. Frightened as he is of Blacker's razor, David nevertheless swallows the wafer, newspaper and all, and tells Blacker to go away. The latter weeps in response, and the older Martin comments that he now fancies that the weeper was the devil himself, who had tried to use the youth as a weapon.

When Martin concludes his story, the narrator still doesn't quite understand what Martin means by "hints." But he feels that he does know after he discovers that Martin is a priest. In the last two lines Martin admits that he owes a lot to Blacker and says that he is a very happy person.

The story shows how an incident of decision in childhood can shape a person's whole future, for it is clear the boy's decision to deny Blacker the wafer has led to his state of priesthood and happiness. Of course, the story also conveys other values. Especially interesting is its view that the devil dwells among us, as it were, and that he, not God, is responsible for the evil in this life—he and the human beings who are given the choice between acquiescence and resistance.

Perhaps you will want to note beforehand that this is a story within a story. For slower classes you may also want to mark off the places where the narrator shifts from one character to the other and back again.

If your class is not familiar with the Communion service, you may want to say a few words about it. The story will have much less impact on students who do not realize that Catholics believe that the Communion wafer is literally the body of Christ.

USING THE STUDY NOTES PAGE 254

I. THE POWER OF DARKNESS

A good discussion of this story can begin by focusing upon its title, "The Hint of an Explanation." The chief questions would be *explanation of what?* and *what are the hints?* Essentially, the *what* is asked by the narrator, who wants to know how belief in God can be reconciled with the existence of evil in the world. Hints that the devil is real are scattered throughout the story. And it is the devil, of course, that explains the existence of evil.

Students who do not accept the reality of the devil should not therefore dismiss the story. They need only accept the reality of evil and see that Blacker is its representative. One of Greene's major triumphs here is to make evil real.

II. IMPLICATIONS

Students are asked to discuss the implications of the following quotations from the story:

1. "You can't imagine how seriously religion can be taken in a small town, if only for social reasons." Whether students will be able to imagine this will depend upon their own experiences. Certainly it is not true that religion is "taken seriously" (in the sense intended here) only in small towns. On the other hand, there are city and suburban communities in which social class divisions are not made on religious grounds.

One can perhaps best appreciate the quotation by considering how religious differences can easily divide people, underscore other differences, and disturb feelings of security. And recall that religion is something given at a very young age by one's parents. It may become as much a part of us as our own names. A threat to one's religious beliefs may be viewed as a threat to one's personality.

2. "Was it perhaps that the poor man was all the time seeking something incorruptible?" Blacker seems unhappy because David has taken the wafer, suggesting that he didn't really want this to happen, that he was perhaps truly hoping to find the boy incorruptible. Students must ask themselves why Blacker might have wanted this. It seems to us that there is no certain answer. Perhaps Blacker was once a good person—as Satan was a good angel—and he unconsciously yearns to return to this time. Perhaps the evil in him feeds on evil and would starve—thus restoring his good nature—upon meeting an incorruptible person. Perhaps Blacker realizes that good will destroy him and seeks unconsciously his own destruction.

3. "When I think of it now, it's almost as if I had seen that Thing weeping for its inevitable defeat." (What does the priest mean by "that Thing"?) "That Thing" is evil, evil personified. Its defeat is inevitable. That good will prevail over evil is Greene's belief as well as that of most religions.

III. TECHNIQUES

Character Development

These questions are to be considered and discussed.

1. What do you know about the narrator of the story—that is, the man to whom the priest is telling his tale? Actually, we know very little about him, except that he is an agnostic. And we know at least one important reason why he is an agnostic—he cannot reconcile belief in God with his perception of evil in the world. A key purpose of the story is to persuade the agnostic that this is a poor reason for not believing in God. Perhaps this is *the* key purpose. At any rate, it would help to explain why we know so little about the narrator: More knowledge would distract one from discerning the key intention.

2. Why does the narrator withhold the fact that the man in the railroad carriage is a priest until the end of the story? Would your impression of the story have been different if you had known he was a priest at the beginning? If we knew at the beginning of the story that David Martin was a priest, we might still be interested in why he entered the priesthood. That is, the story would still have interest, impact, and suspense. But knowing that Martin is a priest could make some readers less attentive to what he has to say. They might even discount what he has to say on the belief that priests are biased in certain ways. The extent that "The Hint of an Explanation" is a didactic story—as its title, among other things, suggests—the foreknowledge of Martin's being a priest could be counterproductive.

Imagery

Students are asked how effective the following metaphors are and whether the ideas could have been better expressed in "straight" prose. Students should be asked to try to express the same ideas without using either metaphor or simile. Have them observe whether their rephrased expressions are wordier.

1. ...our thoughts were huddled as closely as ourselves for warmth.

2. "He was very ugly to look at, with one wall-eye and a head the shape of a turnip...."

3. "...he had sowed the longing, the idea of a possibility...."

Consider the first and the third items. Thoughts do not "huddle" and longings cannot be "sowed." Nevertheless, the two images are quite effective, more effective than literal language would be. This is partly true because they are more vivid than literal language, but even more important because they are more precise. *Huddled,* for instance, connotes just the right degree of intimacy, and the communication of this degree of intimacy is of the greatest importance. Similarly, *sowed* implies the essential meaning that Greene has in mind: the conscious design on the part of the sower, the hope of reaping a harvest, the patience to wait for that harvest, the virtual—but not quite total—certainty that those who sow shall reap. It would be impossible to get all the meaning—denotative and connotative—of these images in "straight" language containing any number of words.

The second image is primarily descriptive and creates an impression of greater vividness than literal language could. Nonmetaphorical language in this case would be likely to be "scientific" language. Thus the turnip-shaped head would have to be measured. Obviously, this would require more words than does the figurative language used by Greene.

The Stamp Collection

PAGE 255

Karel Čapek

Glossary Words

venerated (page 255, col. 2) Respected highly

excavations (page 257, col. 1) Places uncovered by digging, especially ancient places

estranged (page 257, col. 2) Being turned from affection for a person to indifference, dislike, or hatred; keeping apart from a person

desecrated (page 257, col. 2) Being treated with scorn and disrespect; ruined

punctilious (page 257, col. 2) Very careful and exact; paying strict attention to details of conduct

cantankerous (page 257, col. 2) Hard to get along with because of a nature that is ready to make trouble and oppose anything suggested; headstrong; quarrelsome

exemplary (page 258, col. 1) Worth imitating; admirable; serving as a model or pattern

confiscated (page 258, col. 1) Took and kept

Handbook

characterization, first person narrative, imagery

Check Test 25

INTRODUCTION

Cast in the form of an extended story told by an old man to a priest, "The Stamp Collection" tells of a turning point in the narrator's life. As a child, Karas had been an avid stamp collector, an enthusiasm shared by his only friend Lojzik, the son of a drunken organ grinder. After an extended illness, Karas finds his stamp collection missing and jumps to the conclusion that only a lower class person like Lojzik would steal the stamps. At this moment Karas loses his state of social innocence and begins to draw a line between one person and another. As he grows older, he learns how to hate and devotes his whole life to duty. After his wife's death, he rummages through family keepsakes and comes across a box stamped with his father's seal. Inside is his stamp collection. It is only then that he realizes how unhappy his life has become because of one wrong choice that turned him away from people and toward self-sufficiency.

In introducing the story, point out the use of quotation marks. Be sure that students understand that Karas is telling his story to someone. You may wish to have them turn to the ending (the last two paragraphs), where the listener is identified. Suggest that, as they read, they try to decide what kind of man Karas has become.

USING THE STUDY NOTES

PAGE 258

I. CAN THE NARRATOR BE TRUSTED?

Discuss the Implications first, because students' opinions about these statements may give them insight into their judgments about the narrator.

II. IMPLICATIONS

1. The friendship between boys of such different backgrounds would have broken up sooner or later. Children are nonjudgmental in their friendships. As Karas and Lojzik matured, it is likely that the difference in backgrounds would begin to turn their interests toward separate goals and values. Such a separation does not always occur, but it seems to be the usual pattern.

2. Modern communications methods have made the world so small that names of distant places no longer evoke the emotions that are recorded in this story. Before discussing this question, have your students list the names of places that sound mysterious or exciting. From the responses that you get, you can tell whether this statement seems true or false to individual students.

3. A single traumatic experience can radically change one's personality. This statement should lead to a discussion of whether people can change radically or whether the seeds of change are inherent in the personality. Some students may provide illustrations—from the news, from sports, or from the world of politics—of individuals who have changed. Ask the class if the story convinced them that Karas's change was the result of one experience.

4. **Karas says that we all could lead many different lives. At some point, though—whether by chance or by inclination—we choose one way of life. Still, the others are never entirely dead.** Most students may believe that early choices will not trap them in the way that Karas thinks he has been trapped. Suggest that they are about to make very important choices in the coming year—what to do after graduation. Have they considered how these decisions will affect the rest of their lives?

5. **Karas says that the shock of Lojzik's supposed betrayal caused him to lose his social innocence, but this loss is something that everyone experiences in growing up.** See if students can define the phrase "social innocence." Things such as where the family lives, the parents' jobs, the way that they speak, their nationality, their race, their income level, the way that they dress—combine to give an impression of an individual's place in the social stratum. Children have little sense of such social order. Although most people lose "social innocence," others ignore social levels and treat everyone as equals.

III. TECHNIQUES

Characterization

1. **List the things that Karas tells you about himself, past and present.** Romantic as a child; disciplined by a stern, demanding father; admired Lojzik; came to hate and despise people; never had another friend; thought nobody liked him; was cantankerous and harsh toward those under him; didn't love the woman that he married and raised children to obey and fear him; gained a reputation by his industry and his sense of duty; and regretted that he had lived his life as he had.

2. **What do his voice and his manner of telling the story add to the picture?** Karas sounds mellow and emotional. Note his involvement with stamps and with his friend. Also call to students' attention the number of philosophical generalizations that are continually woven into the narration. What Karas says he is like does not fit his manner of telling the tale.

Imagery

In the following excerpts, Čapek has created vivid images. What is unusual in the combination of words or items that he puts together?

1. **"...why the thrill I had was perfectly agonizing—every vast happiness has a sweet pang about it."** Notice the pairing of contradictory words; *perfectly* and *agonizing, sweet* and *pang.*

2. **"Everybody ought to seek something: if not stamps then truth or golden ferns or at least stone arrow-heads and ash-trays."** The list of collections moves from the abstract to the concrete, from the moral and the romantic to the mundane.

3. **"...I rummaged about among all sorts of family keepsakes which had been left by my father and mother; photographs, letters, my old school exercise books...."** What is unusual in this list is the exercise books. It gives Karas a hint about his father's love for him. Call attention to the use of the word *rummaged* and the way in which it catches the quality of thumbing through memorabilia.

The Little Bouilloux Girl

PAGE 260

Colette

Glossary Words

prodigious (page 261, col. 1) Enormous; monstrous; marvelous; wonderful

chignon (page 261, col. 2) A large knot or roll of hair worn at the back of the head by women

malodorous (page 262, col. 2) Smelling bad

importunities (page 263, col. 2) Acts of asking again and again

Handbook

characterization, imagery, irony, narrator

Check Test 26

INTRODUCTION

Nana Bouilloux is a startlingly beautiful child with curly blond hair, a lovely complexion, and long lashes that flutter over great, dark eyes. Coming from the lower class, the little Bouilloux girl is apprenticed to a seamstress when she is thirteen. The narrator envies the trappings of Nana's business: a long dress, a black alpaca apron, a chignon, and high-heeled shoes. The beauty of the Bouilloux girl continues to increase; always there is a swarm of males around her. At a summer fête, when Nana is eighteen, an elegant young Parisian in a white suit dances with her. From then on she turns away from all the males of the community, apparently waiting for "the prince without a name." But he never comes. When the narrator is thirty-eight, she returns to her village and notices an older woman who appears to be about forty-five. But no, it is Nana Bouilloux who crosses in front of the car, erect, indifferent, a bitter look upon her face.

It is important that the class be able to pronounce the name, (bwē yü′). Repeat it in chorus several times until students feel comfortable with it. This is a story in which envy plays a major role. Provoke a discussion about envy. What people do your students envy? What is there about such people that seems so desirable? You may want to read Shakespeare's Sonnet 29 ("When, in disgrace with fortune and men's eyes,") and discuss what the speaker envies in others. Then end with the question: "If you could, would you actually take on another's life and everything that goes with it?"

USING THE STUDY NOTES PAGE 264

I. CHOICES AND TURNING POINTS

The commentary suggests that the narrator might have made Nana's choice a more definite one than the girl herself realized. But do people on the outside often see another's life more clearly than does the individual involved? The ability to help a reader to see others' lives is, of course, a major part of good story telling.

II. IMPLICATIONS

Give your reaction to the following statements:

1. Nana's beauty is really a curse. If Nana had been of ordinary appearance, would she perhaps have married a local boy and been content with the quality of her life? Or was she better off hoping although never achieving her dream? The story suggests that her beauty isolated her from friendship.

2. People usually resent a person who is too physically attractive. Often we are somewhat in awe before unusual beauty. We may think that a person who has unusual physical beauty is vain, arrogant, and remote, but that judgment may well be unfair. There is no suggestion in the story that Nana made overtures of friendship to other girls, but it should be remembered that she was from a lower social class than were the narrator and her friends and may have been reluctant to attempt friendship.

3. Nana chooses the impossible dream over humdrum reality. This is what the narrator is saying in the story. But we never see into Nana's mind nor hear her speak. Perhaps she really likes her life and her independence.

4. We tend to think the worst of those we envy. This is true in Nana's case. There are continual rumors about her. There is gossip about her drinking a half pint at the *Café du Commerce* with her father after vespers on the day of her first communion. When she is fifteen and sixteen, she is reported to laugh too freely on Sunday, and a few years later people whisper about her wandering in the lanes with a man whose arm is wrapped around her. And they all watch her waist.

Obviously, many people hope that a person that they envy will come to a bad end.

5. The mother says, "You can't have the hair-do without the rest of the costume. . . . It is just a matter of choice." The mother is speaking symbolically. What she is telling her daughter is that you can't have only a part of another person's life, the part that you covet. Faced with the choice, most of us would prefer our own familiar complications and problems to those of another person. Actually, at the proper time, the narrator would be able to wear her hair in a chignon.

III. TECHNIQUES

Characterization

Nana changes in the course of the story. Are the changes convincing? The picture developed of Nana from childhood on is of someone who is more or less passive. She lets others do things to her. She does not seem to take the initiative until she refuses her suitor. This same passivity could account for the fact that as an older person she is still in the same job, waiting for a glamorous suitor to rescue her. There is some suggestion that she is not overly bright, a characteristic that sometimes leads to passivity. In general, the changes that occur in Nana could be seen to be convincing because they are in keeping with her character.

Imagery

Reread the first paragraph. What are the images used to communicate the unusual beauty of the little Bouilloux girl? A yellow tea rose, a red flowering cactus, an Azure Blue butterfly trustfully asleep, hair golden as a half-ripe chestnut.

Throughout the story, only certain features of Nana are mentioned. Which ones can you recall without looking back at the selection? Most students will probably mention her curly golden hair, incredible lashes, great dark eyes, perfect teeth, complexion like a peach, and figure.

IV. WORDS

Prodigious and *arrogant* are discussed because of the interesting ways in which these words are used.

To Please His Wife

PAGE 270

Thomas Hardy

Glossary Words

agape (page 271, col. 1) Open-mouthed with wonder or surprise

renunciation (page 272, col. 2) A giving up entirely of something; a declaring that one gives up something; a rejection

scrupulous (page 274, col. 1) Very careful to do what is right; conscientious

attenuated (page 274, col. 2) Weakened or reduced

acquiescence (page 275, col. 1) Consent given without making objections; agreement

desultorily (page 276, col. 2) In a manner lacking aim or method; aimlessly

quondam (page 278, col. 2) Former; that once was

hallucination (page 279, col. 1) Momentarily seeing or hearing things that exist only in one's imagination; an imaginary thing seen or heard

purgation (page 279, col 1) Suffering or punishment

fervor (page 280, col. 1) Enthusiasm or earnestness; intense emotion

Handbook

atmosphere, characterization, imagery, mood

Check Test 27

INTRODUCTION

Shadrach Jolliffe has returned to his home town of Havenpool after several years away at sea. Upon leaving church, he meets Emily Hanning and Joanna Phippard, two eligible young women, and in a week or two there is "a tender understanding" between him and Emily. Shortly thereafter, however, he meets Joanna again by chance, is attracted to her, and becomes engaged to her. Joanna realizes, however, that she is not really in love with him and, further, that he is socially beneath her. Consequently, she writes a letter of renunciation with the intention of sending it if Emily should show that she really wants the sailor.

Joanna observes a scene in which Jolliffe tells Emily that he really loves her and that he and Joanna are not deeply in love. He feels that Joanna will release him from the engagement. He embraces and kisses the willing Emily, as Joanna looks on.

Joanna is green with envy, and out of pure covetousness she reverses her resolution. Eventually, Jolliffe concludes that he has misunderstood Joanna's feelings. Being a person of his word, he marries her in spite of the fact that he prefers Emily.

A month after the marriage, Joanna's mother dies, and Jolliffe, not wanting to leave his wife alone, goes into the grocery business rather than back to sea. He and Joanna run the business for years without great success. Emily marries a thriving merchant, who makes her very happy. She lives in a mansion directly across from the Jolliffe's grocery.

This twist of fate deeply upsets Joanna, who mistakenly feels that Emily assumes patronizing airs. Joanna is also concerned for her two sons, whom she loves "to idolatry." Emily is so wealthy that her children will be able to go to college, but Joanna is so poor that her children will have to go the parish school.

As a result of all this, and at Joanna's urging, Jolliffe goes back to sea. But upon his return, he brings only "hundreds" in profit, whereas Emily counts her fortune in "thousands." The only remedy is for Jolliffe to go to sea again and to take his two sons with him. Joanna does not want her sons to go, but seeing no alternative way of making much more money, she finally gives her consent.

The men do not return, yet Joanna retains the hope that they will. Reluctantly, she accepts Emily's offer to live in the mansion. She does not accept her friendship though and eventually wastes away. When, six years later, Joanna has a premonition that her husband and sons have returned, she rushes out of Emily's house and across the street to the grocery. But her question to the man who owns the store—"Has anybody come?"—is met with the answer—"No: nobody has come."

The selection is reminiscent of *Macbeth* because the choice is determined by unworthy motives and its consequences are disastrous. In this story, however, fate plays a larger role than in *Macbeth.* Also, the main character gains no insight, nor are there noble qualities that partially redeem her.

The story is divided into three sections of approximately equal length. The first concludes with the marriage of Shadrach and Joanna; the second ends as the Jolliffe men are about to sail away. If the chief interest of the story lies in Joanna's act and its consequences, the sections are roughly comparable to exposition, complication, and denouement. Or one may label them motives, complications, and consequences.

At any rate, the tripartite division suggests that the story be read in sections. Part I can be assigned for homework and discussed briefly the next day in class, focusing upon the roles of fate and human motivation. The second part could then be read in class, and perhaps this reading could be followed by a "guessing session," in which students try to predict the outcome of the story. Such a session could be very valuable. You may discover which students tend to project their own values onto the literature that they read and which let the literature influence them. The latter should be able to foresee the conclusion, for the tone established from the first paragraph of the story makes any other conclusion impossible.

After the third section is read—for homework—the discussion could focus, for one thing, on the "happy ending complex." Make the point that a story must be true to itself as well as true to life; it must be true to the author's perception of reality, too. By being true to itself, we mean that the ending of a story must follow from its beginning and its middle. That is, the story should be an organic whole.

USING THE STUDY NOTES PAGE 280

I. A DOMESTIC TRAGEDY

Students are asked if either of the following statements is a fair summary of "To Please His Wife."

1. People create their own "heaven" or "hell" in life. Joanna is largely responsible for creating her own "hell" in life, as is Shadrach, whose character traits lead him to make his disastrous choices. The couple's sons seem the victims of fate. But in any case, this statement is not a summary of the story as a whole.

2. We are powerless before the impassive, crushing movement of fate. Hardy himself believed that fate played a dominant role in a person's life. Certainly the final consequences visited upon Joanna were controlled by fate. The idea that human beings have no control over their own lives is not a popular one today, and the story itself does not present only this idea. Through discussion students should come to the conclusion that a summary of the story is best expressed by a combination of this statement and the first.

II. IMPLICATIONS

Students are asked to tell their reactions to the following statements; they are also asked to tell whether the story proves or disproves each statement.

1. The fatal choice of Joanna's life came at the moment when she decided to marry Jolliffe out of jealousy. Certainly her marriage is a necessary and sufficient cause of her fate. The other choices are all consequences of this key cause.

2. The happiness or unhappiness resulting from any action is in direct proportion to the good and evil of the motive that sets the action in motion. Make certain that students are not deceived by the fact that the statement seems to hold true for Joanna, for it certainly does not hold true in general. There was nothing unworthy in the motive that propelled the two Jolliffe boys to go to sea, for instance; yet, they died.

3. Joanna's madness is caused by the same pressures as was Lady Macbeth's. There are certainly some important similarities. Both women suffer from the belief that it was they who were responsible for the misfortunes that befell their husbands; both feel guilty because they know that they have succumbed to evil desires.

4. This is a moral story intended to teach a lesson more than to amuse or give pleasure. Students will undoubtedly agree with this statement; however, some should be able to see that a moral story can also give pleasure. In fact, this may well be a good definition of a mature reader: one who can gain pleasure from reading a moral story.

5. **Hardy's pessimism shows through the story.** It does, indeed, in many ways. Note, for instance, that the story opens in winter, that clouds are making the day dark, that the parson has his face buried in his hands, and that the congregation is sighing. Although these are only details, they nevertheless set the mood—one of grieving. You may want to point to such ironic statements as "God was good" and "Heaven was merciful" at the end of the story as instances of pessimism showing through.

III. TECHNIQUES

Character Development

These questions are to be discussed:

1. **Give the incidents in which Hardy builds a picture of Joanna.** There is a slight reference to Joanna after the church incident, but the major incidents that build Joanna's picture in the early part of the story are the chance encounter between her and Jolliffe on the moonlit night and the incident in Emily's shop. In Part II, the main incidents are the conversation between Joanna and Shadrach before and then after his first sailing and the conversation between them relating to the second sailing. In the third part, it is all Joanna—from the sad, brief incident involving the chalking on the bureau to the "nobody has come" incident at the end. The Emily encounters are, of course, especially revealing of Joanna in Part III.

2. **How does Hardy use Emily to accentuate Joanna's personality?** Emily accentuates Joanna chiefly through contrast. Notice that they contrast even physically, Emily being "a slight and gentle creature," whereas Joanna is "a tall, large-framed, deliberative girl." Emily is also simple, shy, loving, and unambitious; all of these qualities are in contrast to Joanna's.

3. **What is your impression of Jolliffe in the scene with Emily in the store? Does the rest of the story reinforce or change this impression?** There are likely to be differences of opinion on this question. In general Jolliffe may seem more passionate and more aggressive in the store scene than in later scenes. The change can perhaps be attributed to the fact that he married Joanna, who possesses the same qualities to a greater extent and thus tends to submerge them in her husband. And of course there is the fact that they are not in love. On a more positive side, Jolliffe appears as a simple, sincere person in the store scene, and the rest of the story reinforces this impression.

Imagery

Students are asked to study the last scene, beginning on page 279, and to select from it the phrases that convey (1) the quality of the night, (2) the street scene, and (3) Joanna's appearance.

For the quality of the night there are the following: "damp and dark," and "sea wind" that brings a "fishy mist" that mops the face "like moist flannel"; and there is a later reference to the mist, which was "...blowing up the street from the quay" and which prevented Joanna from seeing the shop.

The street scene is characterized as lonely. For one thing, the mist is so thick that one cannot see very far. The phrase "nobody stood there" and the knocking at the door by Joanna "with all her might" also suggest loneliness.

Joanna is dressed in "dragged-on" clothing, she wears no shoes or stockings, and she looks like "the skeleton of something human."

The Duchess and the Jeweller

PAGE 281

Virginia Woolf

Glossary Words

coronets (page 283, col. 1) Small crowns, especially those worn by nobility below the rank of king

obsequiously (page 283, col. 1) Flatteringly; servilely

shagreen (page 283, col. 2) Kind of untanned leather having a granular surface and usually dyed green

parasol (page 284, col. 1) A light umbrella used as a protection from the sun

flounces (page 284, col. 1) Wide ruffles

lustrous (page 284, col. 1) Shiny; glossy; radiant

cincture (page 284, col. 2) An encircling band of some sort such as a necklace or belt

Handbook

characterization, imagery, metaphor, stream of consciousness

Check Test 28

INTRODUCTION

The action in this story is slight. The Duchess of Lambourne visits a jeweller, Oliver Bacon, offering to sell him ten pearls for twenty thousand pounds. He is suspicious of their authenticity, and he is about to check when she invites him to her home for a long weekend. Other guests will be the Prime Minister, His Royal Highness, and Diana, the daughter of the Duchess, whom Oliver loves. Upon receiving this invitation, the jeweller writes the check. Then after escorting the Duchess out, he discovers that the pearls are indeed false.

Beneath this slight plot lies a great deal. Woolf manages to tell a powerful tale of an insecure status seeker. She does this through her intense focus on Oliver Bacon and through stream-of-consciousness techniques—notably through Oliver's "dismantlings" (imaginary returns to his childhood). From these dismantlings we learn that Oliver was extremely poor as a youth. Yet he has worked himself up to a position of considerable eminence; he is the wealthiest jeweller in England. Nevertheless, he cannot entirely rid himself of his feelings of inferiority. They are the root of his need for status and the root of his downfall. Along with his greed, they also help to account for the fact that he is a dissatisfied person who must always have more. In its probing of the factors upon which Oliver's choice—signing the check—depends, the story is most brilliant.

Some discussion of the importance of social class in England will be a useful preliminary. Unless students have a fairly keen awareness of the importance of status to the hero, it will be difficult for them to accept as realistic Oliver's decision to give the Duchess the check before checking on the authenticity of the pearls. It may be that you will want to discuss the third item in the Implications section before assigning the story.

You may also wish to note that twenty thousand pounds was worth about eighty thousand dollars at the time the story was published. Even for the wealthiest jeweller in England, this was presumably no small sum.

USING THE STUDY NOTES PAGE 285

I. "FORGIVE ME, OH, MY MOTHER"

Students are asked to discuss what the story implies about each of the following:

a. Human greed. Greed is certainly a drive primarily responsible for Oliver's fate, a fact that is underscored by the comparison between him and a giant hog (p. 282). His greed, however, is not so much for wealth, as it is for power and status.

b. The falseness of society. There is much emphasis on appearance rather than on reality; note, for instance, Oliver's concern with social trappings in the opening of the story. But perhaps the falseness of society is best reflected by the Duchess, who is false to the jeweller. Indeed, she is nearly all "show." Though appearing wealthy, she is actually destitute—not only materially but also spiritually. She fritters away her life in social nonsense and gambling.

c. Status-seeking. The need for status is the leading cause of Oliver's indiscretion. It is also a primary cause of other aspects of his behavior. Thus he keeps his mother's picture nearby, no doubt largely as a continual reminder that he has risen in status from such a lowly beginning. Also observe his treatment of his employees: He acknowledges their existence only by the slightest movement of a finger. His need to keep the Duchess waiting is yet another indication of his desperate need to feel that he has status.

d. Our inability to be satisfied. Oliver is indeed a dissatisfied person—partly (as we have indicated above) because his humble beginnings have engendered a sense of inferiority that cannot quite be overcome in a society in which so much depends upon one's birth. Naturally, however, not all human beings are dissatisfied for the same reasons, the students should realize that dissatisfaction is not necessarily a curse. There is a productive, creative sort of dissatisfaction that stimulates people to reach for greater heights rather than rest with past successes. One of the reasons why we admire an artist like Picasso, for instance, is that he did not find a success formula and then continue to repeat himself: instead, he continued to strike out in new directions, to invent new styles.

II. IMPLICATIONS

Students are asked to react to the following statements and to tell whether they are true, false, or neither with respect to the story.

1. Bacon deceived himself about the pearls' being real because he was a status seeker. Bacon is about to check on the authenticity of the pearls when the Duchess appeals to his status-seeking impulses by inviting him on the long weekend. This leads directly to his signing the check; therefore, we would consider the statement true. Some students, however, may want to argue about whether he was truly deceived. Perhaps one could say, "...allowed himself to be deceived about...."

2. Bacon knows that the pearls are false before he makes out the check. Bacon suspects that the pearls may be false, but we can find no positive evidence that he was completely certain they were false.

3. Status is more important that money. It certainly seems to be more important than money to Bacon. In general the relative value of the two depends upon the individual and social structure. Here in America, money itself tends to confer status. The majority of Americans, if confronted by a choice, would probably choose money. In England—especially in "old" England—it may well be the other way around.

Of course, these are only generalizations. Many Americans remain in high-status positions despite the fact that they could earn much more money in other occupations.

III. TECHNIQUES

Characterization

1. Students are asked to consider Bacon's character from the point of view of the following questions:

a. What are the reactions of other people toward him? The reaction of his employees is envy and, perhaps, a little fear. The reaction of the Duchess is rather complex. It is detailed in the first paragraph of page 284.

b. What do Bacon's thoughts about his childhood reveal about his drives and interests? They reveal that he was ambitious and that he was a status seeker. Selling dogs, for instance, put him in contact with the noble and the wealthy.

c. Is he round or flat as a character? The reader comes to know Bacon quite well, and although he is a person of rather limited appeal and interests, he would have to be called round.

2. Students are asked to describe the Duchess and to tell how the author has conveyed her character.

There is a magnificent description of the Duchess in the last paragraph on page 283. It shows her to be proud and "showy." We also know from her actions, as well as from Bacon's thoughts about her, that she is a liar and a cheat. Finally, we know from her behavior that she possesses shrewdness and a great sense of timing. And she is an actress of middling ability.

Imagery

Students are asked the following questions:

1. What does the use of animals in describing Oliver Bacon seem to say about him? Obviously, it seems to suggest that he is an animal. And he is, largely, as one can readily see by asking which of the pecularily human qualities he posesses. The answer seems to be none.

2. Consider the images used to describe the jewels as Bacon views them. How does this use of imagery expand your awareness of the inner person? The images referred to are "tears" for pearls, "heart's blood" for rubies, and "gunpowder" for diamonds. All the images involve "hurts" of some sort, and they reveal an underlying aggressiveness. They suggest that Bacon has suffered and that he will make others suffer in return. The gunpowder image is especially revealing, for immediately after Bacon mentions it, he says, "Gunpowder enough to blow Mayfair—sky high, high, high!" The implication is that he would like to rid the world of all those born with high status.

3. The entrance and exit of the Duchess are rich with imagery. Reread these descriptions and list the metaphors used. What kind of feeling do you get from these images? The Duchess is compared to a wave, swollen and breaking; to an army; to a parasol; and to a peacock. One feels from the descriptions that she is something immense, formidable, showy, and proud.

The Guest

PAGE 286

Albert Camus

Glossary Words

plateau (page 286, col. 1) A large, high plain in the mountains or at a height considerably above sea level; a tableland

estuaries (page 286, col. 2) The mouth of a river

interrogation (page 291, col. 1) A questioning
coagulate (page 291, col. 2) Become more dense; thicken
vulnerable (page 292, col. 1) Defenseless; open to attack

Handbook

characterization, identification, imagery

Check Test 29

INTRODUCTION

The story takes place in Algeria at a time when it was still a French colony and when the struggle for self-government was just beginning. Balducci, a French colonial gendarme, brings an Arab prisoner—a man who has murdered a cousin—to Daru, the hero of the story. Daru is a schoolmaster of French extraction, but he is also a native Algerian. Balducci turns his prisoner over to Daru, asking him to take the Arab to the proper authorities. Daru refuses to do this—he feels that it would be "contrary to honor." But Balducci leaves the prisoner with Daru anyway.

The Arab remains with Daru overnight, and a rather reserved sort of friendship grows between them. Daru hopes that the Arab will try to escape during the night, thus relieving his dilemma, but the prisoner stays. The next day Daru walks some distance with his "guest." Then he points out two roads: a road to the east, which leads to the administration and the police, and a road to the south, which leads to freedom among the nomads. Then Daru leaves.

When he reaches the top of the hill, Daru turns and sees the Arab walking slowly on the road to prison. Then Daru returns to his schoolhouse and finds chalked on the blackboard the words "You handed over our brother. You will pay for this." He feels alone.

The story has meaning on several levels, but what concerns us most is what it says about choice and consequence. Daru clearly does not want to make the choice between setting the Arab free and letting him go. Indeed, he lives the life of a hermit, and he would prefer to avoid choices of every sort. But although he has retired from the world, the world will not allow his retirement. In the end, through choosing not to choose (which is itself a choice), he finds that he has alienated all sides. He must face the consequence of his "choice"—aloneness—even in the landscape that he had loved so much. The story says, then, that choice and its consequences are inescapable.

A little historical background will help to make this story more meaningful. Algeria was a French colony for well over a hundred years; it was dominated by people of French extraction, many of whom, like Daru and Camus himself, were born and raised in Algeria. After World War II, however, the Algerian Moslems began to agitate for independence. This story takes place presumably at the beginning of that agitation.

Balducci is typical of the colonialists; he represents the French administration (although actually he comes from Corsica). Like Balducci, Daru is French, but like the Arab, he is a native of Algeria and he loves the land: "Everywhere else, he felt exiled." The fact that Daru felt Algeria to be his home is important—without this understanding, the end of the story loses its impact.

USING THE STUDY NOTES PAGE 294

I. FREEDOM IS RESPONSIBILITY

Daru is very much alone at the end of the story. He has lost the respect of the French community by refusing to turn the Arab in. He has become the enemy of the Arab community because he did not set the Arab free. And he has lost the friendship of the Arab himself.

If the story contains a moral, it seems to be that one cannot live happily on a hilltop isolated from other human beings. One must interact with other people; one cannot avoid making judgments. For, as Camus has said elsewhere, "To breathe is to judge."

II. IMPLICATIONS

Students are asked if they agree with the following statements; they are to defend their answers by reference to the story.

1. A good citizen would have handed over the prisoner as requested. A person who gives his allegiance to a particular state should abide by the laws of that state, and in this sense it is true that a "good citizen" would have handed over the prisoner. But there are complications in the story. For one thing, the implicit ownership of the state by the native Arabs contends with the ownership expressed by the occupying French. (The native Arabs did not want the prisoner handed over; they had protected him and had tried to keep the police from arresting him.) Daru has a problem because he was born in this Arab land and yet he is French "by blood." Another complication is the allegiance owed to what one may call the human community. This allegiance could cause one to ask whether it is honorable to turn over a fellow human being to the state. Daru is presumably thinking of this human bond when he says that turning the Arab over is "contrary to honor."

2. **An individual is always alone in the world.** Individuals are a part of those persons and things with which they identify. Although he is comparatively isolated, even Daru is not alone as long as he can identify with the land. And he is able to make this identification—until the concluding section of the story.

3. **Many people like to avoid responsibility. It requires courage to act freely and according to your beliefs.** It is easy to nod agreement to these statements. To appreciate the second, however, is not so easy. Perhaps it would be well to ask students to relate illustrations of the second statement from their own lives.

4. **The Arab's reasons for choosing the road to prison are clear.** We are not confident that we know all the reasons. It does seem likely, however, that the Arab may be trying to please Daru, who has been so good to him.

5. **Daru suffers the consequences of the Arab's choice.** The message chalked on the board makes it clear that Daru will indeed suffer the consequences of the Arab's choosing to go to the police.

III. TECHNIQUES

Characterization

Students are asked what the following details reveal about Daru:

1. **His mode of life and the kind of clothes he wears.** These suggest that he is a simple person, even a meditative one, who, like a monk, has reduced personal needs to the bare minimum. His room, for instance, resembles a monk's cell.

2. **His untying the Arab's hands and giving him tea.** This shows kindness, sympathy, and a willingness to treat the Arab humanely. Contrast Daru's behavior toward the Arab with Balducci's.

3. **His handling of the revolver.** At first he forgets that he has it; then he takes it with him rather than leave it with the Arab. Later, however, he puts it in a desk drawer and forgets about it. Daru seems uncomfortable with the weapon; he would prefer to rely on his faith in humanity for "protection"—at least in this case.

4. **His waiting when the Arab arises during the night.** This shows a number of things. First, an instinctive moment of fear and mistrust gives way to one of calmness and trust—trust that the Arab will do him no harm. More interesting is Daru's attitude toward the Arab's escape. When he thinks that the Arab is running away, his reaction on one level is "Good riddance!" On a deeper level, however, he is not happy, and it is only when the Arab is once again in bed that Daru finds it possible to get to sleep. On this deep level, he does not want his guest to leave. He does not want the Arab to treat him the way he treated Balducci; he feels a certain affection for the Arab as a person, a feeling that he would like to have reciprocated.

5. **The choice he gives to the prisoner.** It shows above all perhaps that he does not wish to judge his fellow human beings. Other things could be mentioned, too—passivity, perhaps, and certainly sympathy for the Arab and opposition to the Balducci position.

6. **His feeling for the landscape.** As mentioned previously, Daru is very much attached to the landscape. It is the nearest thing that he has to a mother or a home, to something with which he can identify.

Imagery

Answers will vary.

How Much Land Does A Man Need?

PAGE 295

Leo Tolstoy

Glossary Words

disparaging (page 296, col. 1) Speaking slightingly of; belittling

arable (page 298, col. 2) Suitable for producing crops which require plowing and tillage

fallow (page 298, col. 2) Plowed and left unseeded for a season or more

commiseration (page 303, col. 2) An expression of sorrow for another's suffering or trouble; sympathy for (something)

Handbook

characterization, flat character, imagery, metaphor, simile

Check Test 30

INTRODUCTION

The devil overhears Pakhom, a Russian peasant, saying that the only thing wrong with the life of a peasant is that one does not have enough land, that he would not fear the devil himself if he had all the land he wanted. The devil resolves to give him plenty of land and then to "get him" through his land.

Soon thereafter a woman living next to Pakhom's peasant commune sells her 325-acre estate, and Pakhom buys 40 acres of it. He farms his own land and at first is vastly pleased both spiritually and materially. But peasants begin to trespass on his land, and one even cuts down some of his trees. Pakhom takes an individual to court because of this incident, but he loses the case. He then curses the elder and the judges and gets into further difficulties. Ultimately he sells everything and moves to a new community. In his new community he has three times as large a farm as he had formerly.

Again, things go well at first. But difficulties arise later. Pakhom is able to rent a good deal of land, but he decides that he must have land that he can own permanently. As he is about to make a deal, he happens to meet a merchant returning from Bashkir country. This merchant tells a tale of limitless amounts of land that can be purchased quite inexpensively. Pakhom resolves to make the journey to this country and to buy all the land that he can get.

In talking to the Bashkir elder, Pakhom learns that one can have as much land as can be walked around in a single day for only 1000 rubles. There is only one problem: The potential buyer must return to the starting point by sunset or forfeit the entire sum.

Pakhom begins his walk early in the morning. Although he tries to keep his wits about him, he is so greedy that he walks a great distance from the assembled Bashkirs. Seeing that he will have difficulty returning by sunset, Pakhom starts to run very fast. At the end of his run, he drops dead. His laborer digs a grave just long enough to hold his body and buries him.

This story is from Tolstoy's later, "religious," period. It is a kind of parable, or moral tract, intended to show the consequences of greed. It is also an entertaining tale, especially the last part. Pakhom's "race" is so vividly rendered that the reader almost runs with the hero as he tries to beat the setting sun. The story suggests that in a race between a person and a natural process, such as the sun's setting, the person is bound to be the loser. This leads to the perception that it is greedy to want more land (or more of anything) than you need. A single acre more is too much. Less than one acre cost Pakhom his life. In the end Pakhom "needs" only enough land for a grave.

To help orient students to the story, you may wish to read the first small section in class and then ask students what kind of story they expect from this beginning. The headnote in the text will also help. You may also wish to point out that stories primarily aimed at teaching need not necessarily be dull. Remind students that this story ends with a section as exciting as any adventure tale.

In some cases you may wish to discuss the questions concerning the Russian land system and the Russian peasant *before* rather than after reading.

USING THE STUDY NOTES PAGE 303

I. ARE WE OUR OWN EXECUTIONERS?

Pakhom is indeed his own executioner in this tale. Especially supporting this point of view is the fact that Pakhom ignored the dream that he had (section 7, page 301)—a dream that one can infer was sent to him by God or by some spiritual force trying to help him.

Students are asked to tell what they know about the following items from reading the story.

1. The Russian land system of that day. Land was held in common by a community. This land could be rented to individuals inside or outside the community. There was also freehold land, land that could be bought and owned by individuals rather than by groups of individuals.

2. The spirit and mind of the Russian peasant. The peasants lived in communes and were apparently relatively content. They did do a good deal of quarreling, though, mainly because they were often crowded. Their lives seem to have been relatively stable—although this is not true of the greedy Pakhom—and they were very independent in spirit.

II. IMPLICATIONS

Students are asked to discuss the following statements, telling whether they agree or disagree with them.

1. It was Pakhom's motive, not the fact of his owning land, that was bad. It is Pakhom's greed, his need to own a great deal of land, that leads to his death, not the mere fact of ownership. Still there is some suggestion that ownership itself leads to possessiveness and the desire for more property. Pakhom's troubles begin when he first becomes an owner rather than a renter.

2. This story directly contradicts the premise that one should never be satisfied: that to be satisfied is to die. Yes, it does seem to contradict that premise. Tolstoy seems to believe that both inner and outer peace require that people be content with what they have and that each person should have a roughly equal share.

III. TECHNIQUES

Character Development

Students are asked what they know about Pakhom through the following specific incidents:

1. His behavior toward his family when he had to pay fines. Recall that Pakhom would "curse and beat his family." In short, he was a mean person who would take out his frustrations on those "beneath" him.

2. His reactions toward his first piece of property bought from the old woman. The emphasis in the story is on his possessiveness. See, for instance, the repetition of the word *own* in the last paragraph of section 2, page 297.

3. His relations with the peasants whose animals trespassed on his land. In spite of the fact that he understands the causes of the trespassing, he does not remain tolerant long. He sets himself apart from and above the peasants; he fines them and takes one to court. In short, he becomes a typical capitalist landowner.

4. His change in attitude from the period when he buys into the new commune until he decides he must buy land permanently. The point is that he becomes more and more greedy and more and more determined to have things "easy." For instance, even though he is doing quite well for himself, he resents the fact that he has to cart his grain ten miles, and he envies those who are richer than he.

5. His decision to go to the Bashkirs and try to buy 13,000 acres instead of 1,350. His greed is beginning to pass all bounds. We see this clearly in his decision to increase the amount of land that he wants to buy.

6. His attitudes as he is hiking to buy his "one" day of land. Here, his greed does pass all bounds, and he dies from its excess.

Would you call this a flat or a round picture of Pakhom? Characters in moral tracts often tend to be flat, and if forced to make a decision, we would have to say that Pakhom is a relatively flat character. He can be summed up in a single sentence, "I must have more land." Of course, this does not necessarily mean that he is a poorly drawn character or that Tolstoy—who was a master of the round character—has failed. On the contrary, there is every reason to think that he has created in Pakhom precisely the character that he wanted to create.

Imagery

1. Students are asked to recall what they remember about five incidents in the story. Answers will vary. There are no right or wrong responses.

2. One of the effects Tolstoy creates is the vision of the land. Discuss briefly:

a. The first piece of land Pakhom owns. It was 40 acres including a woods. It is fertile land, and it brings him joy at first.

b. The peasant's description of the commune land. Examples are given to indicate how fertile the land is. "...the land is so good...that they sowed rye, and you couldn't see a horse in the stalks, it was so high; and so thick, that five handfuls made a sheaf."

c. Pakhom's view of the Bashkir's land just before he begins his walk. Similes and specific examples indicate the value of the land. "It was all grassland, level as the palm of the hand, black as poppy seed, and wherever there was a hollow, there was grass growing chest high."

d. The overall image of the Russian landscape. It is a picture of rich, fertile land, unpolluted by commercialization and dense population.

IV. WORDS

A. The answers will of course vary. Many students will no doubt think that the last story is the easiest to read. The moral nature of the piece tends to foster simplicity of statement. In addition to vocabulary, students will find difficulties in all four stories. The setting of each is unfamiliar to most students. Although the language of the last is perhaps easier, understanding of the story demands some orientation to prerevolutionary Russia.

B. The *nave* of a church is the long, narrow central hall that rises (to the altar) higher than the aisles flanking it.

Chancel-steps are the steps leading to the choir and the sanctuary of a church.

A *coasting-ketch* is a fore-and-aft-rigged ship used for coastal trade. A *brig* is a two-masted, square-rigged ship.

Sovereigns were gold coins of Great Britain worth 1 pound. *Guineas* were English gold coins worth 21 shillings (1 pound and 1 shilling). Sovereigns, in various forms, were minted from 1503 to 1917. Guineas were minted from 1663 to 1813.

Hardy's place names are descriptive—Havenpool Town and Sloop Lane, for example.

Piccadilly is a street that runs through the center of London. The word suggests "wealth."

Savile Row suggests "taste in clothing."

Whitechapel was—and to a certain extent still is—a poor section of London. The word suggests "poverty."

Richmond and *Mayfair* are both fashionable suburbs of London. The words connote "wealth."

Bond Street is a fashionable shopping center of London. The name suggests "high fashion."

Students are also asked to explain the meaning of the following:

dress circle—the first or lowest curved tier of seats in a theater

stalls—front orchestra seats in a theater

sword of Agincourt—The Duchess defeats the jeweller just as Henry V with his smaller army defeated the French at Agincourt.

viscountess—a member of the peerage in Great Britain ranking below an earl and above a baron

tiara—a jewelled or flowered headband

coronet—an ornamental wreath or headband worn by women on formal occasions

obsequiously—with servile attentiveness

graved—carved or cut into a hard surface

astute—shrewd

lissome—easily flexed

shagreen—untanned leather covered with small, round granulations

cincture—an encircling area

Students are to find the meanings of the following foreign terms from the selections:

gendarme—French police officer

kilometer—unit of distance equal to approximately 0.62 mile

department—a territorial division

commune—a rural agricultural community organized on a communal basis

steppe—a level, treeless expanse in Russia

verst—a Russian unit of distance equal to 0.6629 mile

ruble—a Russian monetary unit

kumiss—a fermented beverage made from mare's milk

The use of local color words and references makes the writing seem more realistic.

C. The best way to answer the first question would be to discuss metaphors beforehand and then to ask students as they read the selections to note examples of verbs used metaphorically.

The dialogue of the characters in "To Please His Wife" is conspicuously plain and straightforward. Shadrach uses figurative language only once, and then he uses the commonplace simile "blind as a bat." The two female characters do not speak figuratively. Hardy avoids figurative language in the dialogue because he wishes his characters to emerge as people who possess easily identifiable characteristics.

SUMMING UP: CHOICE AND CONSEQUENCE

THEME

Students are asked to consider the following propositions in the light of the selections that they have read in this unit.

1. For the sake of drama, writers often present life as something that comes in sections which are hinged together like a screen. Actually, life has no clear-cut divisions, but unrolls like a continuous bolt of fabric. How writers present their material depends to a great extent on how much of life or of *a* life they are trying to present. When it is important for a long span of time to pass—as in the selections by Hardy and Tolstoy, for example—divisions seem necessary, and there may be "hinging." This technique is dramatically necessary—one could hardly expect Hardy to include every dreary moment of Joanna's married life, for instance. In many of the selections, however, there is no such hinging: Camus's "The Guest," for example, is all of a piece.

Whether real life "unrolls like a continuous bolt of fabric" depends upon one's perspective. In one sense, it does. In another sense, it can be viewed as Hardy views Joanna's life—a few high points "hinged together like a screen."

2. Which of the characters in these selections are completely aware of the fact that they are making important choices? Which characters make choices without being aware of the importance these decisions can have for their lives? Macbeth, Lady Macbeth, Socrates, Oliver in "The Duchess and the Jeweller," and the schoolmaster in "The Guest" are quite aware of the importance of their choices. The priest in the Greene story, Joanna in the Hardy tale, Pakhom in the Tolstoy piece, Karas in the Čapek selection, and Nana in the Colette story are unaware of the importance of a particular decision.

3. In which selections did the choices bring

about *expected* consequences? In which were the characters surprised by the results of their choices? Only in the Socrates selections does the chief character get exactly what he expected. There is at least some element of surprise in all the other cases.

4. Do any of the writers imply that Fate sends humans consequences which are unfair or unjust? Which consequences are portrayed as just rewards for strengths or for flaws of character? In response to the first question, students may list Joanna's sons, for they were largely victims of their mother's envy and ambition and their father's indecisiveness. Camus's Daru can also be cited as one treated unjustly by Fate, for seemingly he tried to do the best that he could in a very difficult situation. Banquo and Lady Macduff are also unjustly treated by Fate.

Concerning the second question, one could list Macbeth, Lady Macbeth, Joanna, Shadrach, the jeweller, Pakhom, Karas, and Nana as suffering consequences that were just rewards for their flaws of character. Conversely, those rewarded for strength of character are Greene's priest and Socrates. In the latter case, students may hesitate to think of death as "reward"; nevertheless, it was—under the circumstances—what Socrates himself wanted.

5. Moments of choice bring out the strength or weakness in a person's character. This statement holds true throughout the selections. You may wish to assign individual selections to individual students or to groups of students, asking them to cite evidence of the truth of this statement. And perhaps you will want them to include some of the minor characters. (In our comments on these propositions, we have noted mainly the major characters. In some cases, you may want to ask students to think of characters other than the major ones.)

TECHNIQUES

Character Development

Students are to discuss these statements or to answer the questions:

1. In which selections do the authors pass judgments on their characters directly? In which do they give their views indirectly by letting the reader build a picture of the characters? In many of the selections there is much slanting that makes certain judgments virtually inescapable. Thus, for instance, there is little doubt in the reader's mind concerning what Tolstoy thinks about Pakhom, Woolf's judgment of Oliver Bacon, and Colette's attitude toward Nana. But the writers in this unit are so skilled in their craft that they would never make out-and-out expressions of judgment. Hardy, Greene, Camus, Capek, and the greatest of them all, Shakespeare, do masterful jobs of letting readers build their own pictures of characters a little bit at a time.

2. Choose one or two characters in this unit who seemed real and convincing to you. In a short essay, try to explain the literary means by which the author was successful in presenting the characters. Or reverse the problem—tell why you think one of these authors has *failed* with the characters. You are likely to get more interesting results with this question if you limit the students' choices in some way. For instance, you could require that half of the class write about characters that seemed real and convincing and half write about characters that did not seem real. Another approach is to divide the class into three groups, each with only three selections to choose from. With this arrangement, some students will probably choose the same character to comment upon, one in a negative way and another in a positive way. You may also want to discuss the question of how important it is for characters to be real and convincing. The characters from selections such as "Witness to the Truth" and "How Much Land Does a Man Need?" offer some problems in this respect.

3. For each of these characters, select what you think to be his or her major moment of choice. What motives made them choose the way they did? Did the actions spring from their characters as portrayed by the author?

a. Macbeth
b. Socrates
c. The priest ("The Hint of an Explanation")
d. Karas
e. Nana
f. Joanna
g. Daru
h. Pakhom

This question can be used in either of two ways. As a review of the entire unit, you may want students to write relatively brief comments on each of the characters and have a comparatively full discussion in class. On the other hand, the question could be used to probe specific selections in depth. In this case, you could ask students to select only one or two characters, for which they would prepare comparatively extensive expositions of their situations and motives. Let students try to spell out just how the choice does or does not spring from the character as presented by the author.

Imagery

When readers have finished a story, poem, or play, it should leave them with a definite impression. Take each selection in this unit and find one or two adjectives that best describe its effect on you. Then share these answers in a class discussion. Students could find the use of single adjectives rather limiting. If so, allow them the option of using phrases or even a sentence or two. Adjectives, however, can be useful and effective summaries of fundamental impressions. Some such adjectives are *gloomy, rich, romantic, realistic, subtle, philosophical,* and *didactic.*

UNIT TEST

There are several options for testing your students' grasp of the unit. You may use the Summing Up section in the pupils' anthology—either whole or in part—as the unit test. For a second approach, you may select questions at random from the Study Notes at the end of each selection as a basis for constructing a final examination covering the complete unit. For a third option, you may choose to use the comprehensive unit test prepared on blackline masters available in a separate test booklet, ISBN 0-07-009823-9.

RELATING COMPOSITION TO THE UNIT

SUGGESTED ACTIVITIES

1. Describe an incident from your own life that illustrates the theme CHOICE AND CONSEQUENCE.

2. Find a newspaper story about a choice that brings about unexpected consequences. Write the news story as a short story.

3. Seen from one perspective, much of the history of civilization is a recording of choices that have had enduring consequences. The future, too, will be filled with choices, some of which will be made by individuals and others by people as a whole. In an essay, discuss one of the choices that will confront us in the immediate future. (For example: Should we continue to build up massive defenses against the threat of attack by foreign powers?) Discuss the different choices and the different consequences that are possible. Discuss the choice that you yourself endorse.

4. Select the paintings or works of sculpture that you feel best express the unit theme, CHOICE AND CONSEQUENCE, and write a short paper (one page or less) explaining the reason for your choice.

5. Write a character sketch of a classmate using some of the methods suggested in the study materials. Read your sketch out loud in order to see whether your classmates can guess the subject of the sketch.

RELATING THE GALLERY TO THE UNIT

PAGE 265

1. Writers use five basic techniques to inform readers about a character. They may tell readers:
   a. What the character looks like.
   b. What the character says and thinks.
   c. What others say and think about the character.
   d. The way the character acts in a given situation.
   e. The way others act toward the character.

Look at the galleries of fine art. Which of these techniques of revealing character do the painters have at their disposal? What advantages in revealing character do the writers have? What advantages do the painters have?

2. Legends form the basis for Dürer's "The Prodigal Son" (page 266) and Rembrandt's "Faust in His Study Watching a Magic Disk" (page 267). These two engravings may serve as a springboard for discussing the role of legends as literary and artistic sources. Parallels can be drawn between the literary and the artistic representation of legends: As the writer selects incidents from the legend, the artist selects images; as the writer adds a personal dimension of interpretation, so does the artist; as a legend may be recreated in various contexts by a writer, so the artist is free to interpret it in a multiplicity of ways. You may then wish to explore interpretations of the prodigal son legend—Debussy's "The Prodigal Son," for instance. Some interpretations of the Faust legend to explore are Goethe's *Faust* and Ingmar Bergman's *The Seventh Seal.* As a follow-up exercise, direct students to write a précis of a modern story that uses as background either the prodigal son or the Faust legend.

3. The paintings "Columbus and His Son at La Ribida" by Delacroix (page 265) and "The Lictors Bring Home to Brutus the Bodies of His Sons" by David (page 267) chronicle two personal but little known events in the lives of well-known people. Ask students the following questions: What seems to be the artist's purpose in choosing a little known event to depict? What dimension is this event designed to give to the famous person's life and personality? Why the choice of a personal, family incident? In which case does the choice seem to have the most effect and consequence? How can you tell? (Obviously the David canvas conveys this through the agonized poses of mother and daughters.) Why does each artist place the central subject in shadow?

4. The choice of emigration is captured in a stylized Victorian way by Ford Madox Brown in "The Last of England" (page 268). The *consequences* of this choice of emigration are shown dramatically in photographer Jacob Riis's collection of studies of immigrants, *How the Other Half Lives.* Examining this volume in conjunction with the Brown painting should complete a picture of choice and consequence. If you cannot obtain Riis's book, a discussion of the painting as foreshadowing will serve as an alternative

approach. In either case, the following questions should illuminate the situation: Is there any evidence in the stance and facial expressions of the immigrants in the painting that foreshadows the possible consequences of their choice? What messages can you read from these facial expressions? What information do the background details provide? In real life, how much do we know about the consequences of our choices when we make them? As a follow-up assignment, direct students to write an inner monologue for one of the characters that expresses satisfaction with or misgivings over the decision to emigrate. You might also suggest that students draw on their own families' experiences in emigrating.

5. Rodin's "The Burghers of Calais" (page 268) uses textural elements and mass to convey the agony of decision and the acceptance of its consequences. The incident that serves as the basis for the sculpture is, of course, important, and its parallel in World War II Europe is worth noting. The decision to give up one's own life to save the lives of others is a worthwhile discussion topic suggested by the sculpture. How has he avoided hackneyed stoicism? Although linked in their basic form and in their garments, each of Rodin's burghers is a definite individual. Ask students the following questions: How has Rodin accomplished this distinction? What of the deliberate textural roughness of the sculpture? Why does Rodin fail to smooth and finish his marble as the Greek sculptors in the previous gallery did? (By depicting the truth, Rodin achieves a more substantial heroism than orthodox sculptors would.) Does this statue commemorate a foolhardy act? Are there times when you would give up your life for others? When? Which of the sculpted figures expresses how you yourself could feel between making the decision and accepting its consequences? As a follow-up exercise, direct some of your more willing students to improvise a dramatic scene that recreates the last conversation of these burghers before their execution.

6. The choice made by Edouard Manet in "The Dead Toreador" (page 269) to paint his fallen toreador with stark simplicity should be examined thoroughly.

Ask students the following questions: Why is the dead man pictured in isolation rather than in the midst of thousands in a bull ring, where he realistically should be? Why is the consequence of a violent confrontation shown with such peace and calm? Why does the figure of the dead man fill the canvas so that there is no room for any other detail? Why is there not more terrible detail of the goring, as there would be, for instance, in a Sam Peckinpah film? Why is the small pool of blood so subtle? Why does Manet pick such somber colors? What does Manet's picture say to you about choice and consequence?

THE EXPANDED EXPERIENCE: RELATING THE HUMANITIES TO THE UNIT

1. Disciplines: E, SS. Skills: Rd, Wr, Org.

Read James Joyce's *Portrait of the Artist as a Young Man* or Antoine de St. Exupery's *Night Flight.* Each work chronicles the consequences of making a career decision that results in a life of comparative loneliness. Transform excerpts from either book into a journal that deals with loneliness as an acceptable form of consequence. Then, in a parallel journal, place yourself in a similar situation, and decide if, knowing the consequences, you would make the same decision. Analyze the results in terms of your own willingness and/or ability to accept isolation.

2. Disciplines: E, A, M, TA. Skills: Rd, Wr, PS, Org.

Ernest Hemingway's novella *The Old Man and the Sea* deals with—among other things—decisions and their consequences. Read the book, and then excerpt several monologues of the old man speculating about his decision to "go out too far" and its consequences for him and for the fish. (As you do this, you should realize that this tale is a parable about decisions, about our ability to reach for things beyond our capabilities, and about the consequences of that overextension.) Record these excerpts, using Joaquin Rodrigo's "Fantasia para un gentilhombre for Guitar" as background music. For illustrations, make slides of sea scenes by Turner and Delacroix. Present this slide and sound representation to illustrate a certain kind of choice and consequence.

3. Disciplines: E, M. Skills: PS, Rd.

Write on the board the names of several of the characters from the stories in the unit—for example, Macduff from *Macbeth*, the Duchess of Lambourne from "The Duchess and the Jeweller," and Nana from "The Little Bouilloux Girl." Ask students what kinds of music they would use to convey what each of these characters is like. Discuss why a particular music selection seems to convey a particular character. Students might also wish to see what types of music they would choose to convey the characters of their classmates.

4. Disciplines: TA, M. Skills: PS, Rd.

Suggest to students that they make a tape recording of *Macbeth* as a radio play. Usually a radio performance cuts some of the scenes and lines to make the performance fit a particular time slot. It is best that the teacher do this cutting beforehand. Then assign some students speaking parts and put others in charge of sound effects and background music.

5. Disciplines: E, SS. Skills: Wr, Org, Log.

Bearing the responsibility for your own actions

is considered a mark of maturity. Thus, in accepting the consequences of your own choices, you are asserting your own coming of age. Keep a log of the decisions that you make—both large and small—within a two-week period. Note the decision made, the degree to which you have been willing to accept responsibility for your action, and the consequence of that action (if it is known). Assess your log in the following ways: How many decisions need revision? Why? With how many decisions am I satisfied? What characteristics do these decisions possess that make me satisfied with them? What percentage of the decisions resulted in positive consequences? What does my log tell me about myself? Collect this information in an essay that can become a partial self-portrait.

RELATING ADDITIONAL READING TO THE UNIT

SUGGESTED BOOKS

Breck, Vivian. *Maggie*
Chekhov, Anton. *The Cherry Orchard*
Conrad, Joseph. *Lord Jim*
Dostoyevsky, Fyodor. *Crime and Punishment*
Faulkner, William. *Light in August*
Fitzgerald, F. Scott. *Tender Is the Night*
Freedman, Nancy and Benedict. *Mrs. Mike*
Godden, Rumer. *The River*
Greene, Graham. *The Power and the Glory*
Hardy, Thomas. *The Mayor of Casterbridge*
________. *Tess of the d'Urbervilles*
Hawthorne, Nathaniel. *The Scarlet Letter*
Head, Ann. *Mr. and Mrs. Bo Jo Jones*
Hemingway, Ernest. *Death in the Afternoon*
________. *The Old Man and the Sea*
James, Henry. *Daisy Miller*
________. *The Portrait of a Lady*
Malamud, Bernard. *A New Life*
Miller, Arthur. *Death of a Salesman*
Molnar, Ferenc. *Liliom*
Odets, Clifford. *Golden Boy*
Paton, Alan. *Cry, the Beloved Country*
Saint-Exupéry, Antoine de. *Night Flight*
Shakespeare, William. *Julius Caesar*
Sophocles. *Oedipus*
Steinbeck, John. *Of Mice and Men*

SEVENTEENTH- AND EIGHTEENTH-CENTURY BRITISH POETRY: An Age of Contradictions

This section contains poems by John Donne, Ben Jonson, George Herbert, Robert Herrick, Richard Lovelace, Andrew Marvell, John Milton, John Dryden, Alexander Pope, and Thomas Gray. The notes on individual poets suggest connections and relationships between the poems, and certainly many more can be found.

Following the chronological arrangements in the text will enable you to stress certain developments in thought and in poetic form. Students will be able to see how the sonnet, which was used for love poems in the first poetry section, has been turned toward religious themes. The development of the couplet as a major poetic form, starting with Jonson's tetrameter couplets, moving through Marvell's more fluid use of the same form, and then turning toward the heroic couplet (pentameter) of Dryden and Pope, is well illustrated in this section. Students may also be interested in the use of blank verse, especially after reading *Macbeth* and then turning to the excerpts from *Paradise Lost.*

Another change that you may want to stress is the movement toward public poetry. We are accustomed to thinking of poetry as personal, even private, and the lyrics of the first section are, for the most part, couched in personal terms. Students may be surprised by the more formal tone of Ben Jonson, even when he deals with his son's death, and certainly by the urbane public manner of a Dryden poem or a Pope satire. The nineteenth century returns to the more emphatic use of the personal voice, and students will have a better understanding of what the Romantic poets were doing if they can understand what the eighteenth-century poets valued.

Length of assignments will vary according to individual classes. You may want to take one or two poets a day, or you may want to pair some poems. A poet like Donne, however, could take two class sessions to cover. Students should be reminded that word meanings have sometimes changed and that any word that seems to be used differently should probably be checked in a dictionary. (If you have not already done so, you may wish to introduce your students to the *Oxford English Dictionary* (O.E.D.), so that they can see how words have changed their meanings and connotations throughout history.)

As you come to the end of this section, you will see how the concerns of Dryden and Pope lead easily to the satire of Molière's comedy and the central concerns of the next theme, FOIBLES. The best visual representation of this spirit can be found in the engravings of William Hogarth (available in a Dover paperback edition). John Gay's *The Beggar's Opera,* which some students may recognize in its modern version, Brecht and Weill's *The Threepenny Opera,* is a cheerful, delightful satire on corruption in government and society as well as on musical tastes. And, of course, the comedies of Etherege *(The Man of Mode),* Wycherley *(The Country Wife),* Congreve *(The Way of the World),* Farquhar *(The Recruiting Officer, The Beaux' Stratagem),* as well as the later comedies of Goldsmith *(She Stoops to Conquer)* and Sheridan *(The Rivals, The School for Scandal),* are works that can be read either to supplement this section or to introduce the next one.

NOTE: For reference sources, see the bibliography in the introduction to the first poetry unit.

Poems by John Donne

PAGE 308

Glossary Word

loath (page 308) Unwilling or reluctant

Handbook

rhyme scheme, sonnet, stanza

Check Test 31

INTRODUCTION

The poems chosen suggest the range of Donne's style and interests. "The Bait" is, of course, a love poem and represents the earlier Donne, whose poems of love and seduction still surprise us with their extravagant metaphors and assertions. In "The Bait," Donne uses conventional metaphors, then his own bold statements ("Gladder to catch thee, than thou him"), and finally a somewhat ironic conclusion, "That fish, that is not catch'd thereby, / Alas, is wiser far than I" to indicate his complex attitude towards the woman. A rereading of "The Passionate Shepherd to His Love" (page 149) and "The Nymph's Reply to the Shepherd" (page 150) should prepare students for "The Bait." The last study question suggests a useful way of structuring discussion of these three poems, not only to reflect differences in tone but to perceive the change between the centuries. Donne's view of himself as a trapped fish is much less romantic than Marlowe's entreaty or even Raleigh's rejection. Other love poems of Donne which students might enjoy are "The Good-Morrow," in which he asserts, "If ever any beauty I did see, / Which I desired and got, 'twas but a dream of thee" and "The Flea," which cunningly blends satire and seduction. "The Bait" might also be compared to Marvell's "To His Coy Mistress," another famous poem about a lover and his somewhat distant lady.

"Death, Be Not Proud" (from *Holy Sonnets)* offers a good opportunity to review the sonnet form and to observe how Donne's religious poetry is vigorous and immediate, with its direct address to Death and its defiant boldness. "Death, Be Not Proud" could be taught with Jonson's "On My First Son," which offers a more personal view of death.

Similarly, "A Hymn to God the Father" shows us Donne confronting death, but this time it is his own death and his fear of damnation that obsess him. He regrets the sins of his life from original sin (ll. 1, 2), to his earlier misdeeds (second stanza) to the final sin (stanza three), which is his despairing of God's mercy. Yet, the tone of the poem is obstinately cheerful, partially because of the repeated rhymes (there are only two rhymes in the poem) and because of the pun on "done" and "Donne," as if the poet is saying to God, "when you have finished, you still don't have me, John Donne, because I have more sins." But the final pun "Son" and "sun" makes possible the poet's change from "For I have more" to "I fear no more."

USING THE STUDY QUESTIONS PAGE 310

THE BAIT

1. What is "the bait"? Literally, it is the lure for catching fish—metaphorically, the woman.

2. What is the difference in fishing as an activity suggested by stanzas 1 and 2 and by stanzas 5 and 6? How does the language imply the difference? At the beginning of the poem, fishing is a pleasant, beautiful occupation that takes place near "golden sands" in "crystal brooks." Fish are not really hurt, not by "silken lines" or "silver hooks"; they are "enamour'd" fish that ask to be caught. But in stanza 5 the weather turns cold, the fisher's legs get cut, the fish are "strangled" by the net, the nest is "slimy," and the idea of "treason" occurs (both in lines 19 and 23).

3. What does the last stanza tell you about the poet's attitude? The last line reveals that the poet, like the fish, is caught by the woman. And by finding the fish "wiser," he suggests his own chagrin at being trapped.

4. What changes in attitude toward the woman can you find when you look at this poem in comparison with Marlowe's "The Passionate Shepherd"? (page 149) In Marlowe's poem, all the images suggest that love is beautiful, pleasant, rich, delightful. By casting the woman as "the bait" and by changing the connotations of fishing as the poem develops, Donne implies that love is a trap for the unwary. His attitude is noticeably more cynical than Raleigh's in "The Nymph's Reply to the Shepherd." Raleigh argues that the beauties of the world are only transient. Donne goes further by suggesting that they are like "traitors," bewitching and betraying men.

DEATH, BE NOT PROUD

1. What relationship is implied between the speaker and death? The direct address to death, as if it were a person, implies equality. "Poor" death (line 4) suggests an attitude of condescension or pity.

2. What reasons does the speaker give for not being afraid of death? The speaker connects death to "rest" and "sleep," which are not only images of death but pleasurable. He argues (in lines 4, 8, and 13) that death is only the beginning of eternal life. The repetition of this argument—its final, clearest statement appears in line 13—makes it the most important of Donne's reasons. He also shows how death is subject to mortals and their doings (line 9) rather than a force in itself.

3. How does the speaker persuade you (or himself) of the truth of the last four words? Here we have the religious conviction that if humans are to "wake eternally" through God's mercy, then death is defeated. The last four words ("death, thou shalt die") depend on the acceptance of the Christian perspective that salvation is possible for all people.

A HYMN TO GOD THE FATHER

1. What are the major puns used in the poem? The word "done," meaning both "finished" and "achieved," is also a pun on the poet's name, "Donne." Thus, "When Thou hast done, Thou hast not done," really implies that although God has forgiven the poet's sin, He still hasn't completely grasped the man, Donne, who finds himself unable to accept that forgiveness. The "Son" is Jesus Christ, but also the sun of God's forgiveness and mercy, shining on the dying man.

2. The occasion on which the poem was written and the subject suggest a serious poem. Do the puns support or contradict the seriousness? Students may have different reactions to Donne's punning humor. Some may feel that he's making a joke on a serious subject and therefore can't be taken seriously. Others may see the puns as a kind of "gallows humor," suggesting that Donne is desperately serious and is pushed by his fear of rejection/damnation into his defiant punning. When this poem is read together with "Death, Be Not Proud," an equally defiant poem, although different in tone, the notion of Donne's seriousness may be easier to defend.

3. Both "Death, Be Not Proud" and "A Hymn to God the Father" concern themselves with death. What differences in attitude do you find in the poems? Though Donne is defiant in both poems, his attitude is noticeably different. "Death, Be Not Proud," addresses Death as an equal while the addressee, God, in the second poem is clearly superior to the speaker. Donne challenges Death's power in the first poem, while in the second he questions God's willingness to forgive a miserable sinner such as himself. The speaker of the first poem is confident, the second speaker is scared; the speaker of the first seems to welcome Death as a release, while the speaker of the second is so aware of his own sinfulness (he keeps repeating "For I have more") that he sounds desperately guilty. The first poem asserts, the second questions.

Poems by Ben Jonson

PAGE 311

Handbook

balanced sentences, metaphor, satire

Check Test 32

INTRODUCTION

Because Jonson is a less personal poet than Donne, you may find that students respond less well to him. One way to get students to appreciate his craft is to ask them to try to do some of the same kinds of writing. You could, for example, ask them to write two four-line epigrams, one on a serious subject and one on a comic subject. That exercise would show students how difficult it is to express enough meaning in such a brief space, and it would also serve as a useful introduction to "On Court-Worm." "Still to Be Neat" is a brilliant poem that works beautifully when taught with Herrick's "Delight in Disorder." Both poems are about the same subject, the preference for naturalness as opposed to artifice, but they develop that subject rather differently.

USING THE STUDY QUESTIONS PAGE 316

ON COURT-WORM

1. How does Jonson connect the metaphor to his real subject? What words are appropriate for both? Jonson begins by announcing boldly that "all men are worms" and then suggests what seems to be a paradox, "but this no man." The implication is that a "court-worm" is less than a man. The word "silk" refers to both the cocoon and the courtier's clothes. "Wrapped" reminds us again of the cocoon and of a baby's blankets, whereas "white as milk" reinforces the image of the baby. "Butterfly" means both the insect and a brilliantly dressed, social butterfly, whereas "caterpillar" suggests someone who crawls around, possibly currying favor with those deemed important.

2. What change does Jonson make in the natural cycle? Why? By putting the caterpillar last, he emphasizes his disgust for the courtier as worm.

STILL TO BE NEAT

1. What is the attitude toward beauty expressed here? What words best show the poet's real feelings? The poet dislikes the artificial beauty created by overfastidious dressing, by powder (which can conceal blemishes), and by perfume (which can hide unpleasant odors). The word "art" takes on negative connotations from the imagery of makeup suggested in the first stanza. The phrase "adulteries of art," which connects art with the corruption of sex, makes his dislike even clearer.

2. Look at the balanced phrases in the poem. How is the last one different from the others? Why? Lines 1, 3, 6, 7, and 9 are balanced by syntactical likeness and sometimes joined by alliteration (lines 3, 6, and 9). The last line finally changes the balance by making the second half of the line negative, thus revealing the failure of "artful" artifice. We expect the balance to continue as it has in the poem and are thus more forcibly struck by the surprise when the balance changes.

ON MY FIRST SON

1. What reasons does Jonson use to comfort himself for the loss of his son? What development is there in these reasons? He argues that the boy was only lent to him (line 3) and must be paid back, like a loan (line 4); that death is not lamentable but enviable because it takes one out of the misery of the world (lines 6–7); and that old age, although inevitable, is likewise a sad time (line 8). He moves then from a rationalization about his son to an implied justification of his own (approaching) death.

2. The last two lines are difficult to understand, but somewhat easier if you add the suppressed "he" to the last line: "As what he loves (he) may never like too much." Can you see a connection between this line and line 2? What is the speaker's final attitude? In line 2, Jonson feels that "too much hope" may somehow have harmed his loved child. Thus, he seems to be wishing that he may not again love and hope so much for anyone, thereby avoiding the pain that comes with loss.

THOUGH I AM YOUNG AND CANNOT TELL

1. What are the similarities between Love and Death in this poem? Both Love and Death can be fatal or painful ("bear darts"); both have overpowering effects on the heart; both are extreme.

2. What are the differences between the two? What is the most important difference? The effect of death is to chill, of love to heat. But love is so powerful that it can actually arrest cold and, therefore, death.

Poems by George Herbert

PAGE 313

Handbook
rhyme scheme, symbolism

Check Test 33

INTRODUCTION

Herbert's poems express a fervent belief in God and a delight in language—commitments that may seem strange to students today. He was a private poet; his poems were not published until after his death. Herbert was probably as deeply religious as any English poet has been—and yet he struggled continuously, dissatisfied with himself and his relationship to God. In the four poems presented here, that struggle is expressed in the metaphor of "Easter Wings"; in the internal conflicts of "The Collar"; in the almost ironic vision of God as a designer of human restlessness in "The Pulley"; and in the diffident, shy, guilt-dusty traveler of "Love (III)," who feels himself unworthy to accept God's love.

A good way to teach "The Collar," the most complicated of the four poems, is to ask several students to read the poem together, each reading one of the different arguments. "Easter Wings," based on the old idea of shaped poem, draws on the tradition of *emblem poetry* (poems explaining a symbolic picture) by carrying the picture idea into the poem itself. The poem is also connected to contemporary *concrete poetry*. You may wish to ask students to try writing shaped poems, or you could show them some modern versions of concrete poems. "Love (III)," as a dialogue, would also become clearer if read aloud.

USING THE STUDY NOTES

PAGE 316

EASTER WINGS

1. What connections can you find between the shape of the poem and the subject? Students should notice the typography, the way in which the lines narrow and then branch out again. The center lines, appropriately, are marked by the speaker's sense of his inadequacy ("Most poor" and "Most thin") and then by his communion with God ("With thee"). The shape literally shows human decay (line 3) caused by sin and then the ability to rise through faith in God.

2. Why are "wings" an appropriate image? Easter is the celebration of the Resurrection, which was followed by Christ's ascension into heaven. Therefore, the idea of flight, of rising, and of conquering space is suggested by "wings." They refer simultaneously to Christ's rising and to the possibility of human salvation through that event.

THE COLLAR

1. What is the speaker rebelling against? Discipline is the problem. The speaker seems to feel confined by his role as a priest. He strikes the board (line 1), rejecting his function as a giver of communion. He asks, "Shall I be still in suit?" suggesting the double meaning of wearing the priest's "suit" and of waging an unsuccessful suit for God's grace. And he feels himself inside a cage of religious regulations.

2. The speaker seems to be conducting an argument with himself. What are the major divisions—the problems and the potential solutions—of this argument? The first problem (lines 1-9) is the speaker's expressed desire to escape from a life that he sees as confining and deadening. The religious life, with its emphasis on repentance, seems to be killing him. The answer (lines 10-12) implies that he himself, not the religious life, is responsible for the deadening effect. He reminds himself, "Sure there was wine" and "there was corn"—abundance was there before he "dried" and "drowned" it with his self-pity.

The argument begins again (lines 13-16), as he sees himself living a wasted life, unnoticed and unhappy. Again, there is an answer (lines 17-26), this time a longer, more emphatic one. (Note that the complaining gets shorter and the answering gets longer, thereby suggesting the progress of the speaker toward realization.) It is the speaker's own "petty thoughts" that have made his "cage." He has not found in God's laws "Good cable to enforce and draw." And so the problem is really self-created.

The argument recurs, with an almost petulant, "Away! take heed; / I will abroad." This warning turns into raving as the poet calls for a "death's head," a *memento mori,* a reminder that all creatures must die. And then suddenly the final answer comes, not from himself, but from God.

3. How do the last four lines, through meaning and rhythm, work to resolve the poem? The poet's internal struggle is expressed through his arguments (see question 2). It is reflected in the varying length of the lines and in the seemingly haphazard rhyme scheme. But the intense argument suddenly stops in the last four lines as the speaker experiences a moment of self-perception. This change is reflected formally in the change to a noticeably ordered quatrain, *abab.* The resolution actually occurs in the last two words, when the speaker stops arguing and accepts the presence of God.

THE PULLEY

1. What are the good things God gave to humankind? The good things referred to are strength, beauty, wisdom, honor, and pleasure.

2. What is the one thing God withheld? Why? Rest (in the sense of repose) is the one jewel that God has withheld. Without rest, human beings cannot be completely satisfied; therefore, they must return to God for fulfillment.

3. What is the significance of the title? The relationship between humans and God is implicit in the title. God has sent human beings down a pulley, and they will pull themselves back up, seeking their final rest in God. Their motivations will reflect either goodness or weariness. One can view a pulley as having one side going down as the other goes up. Similarly, God gives humans gifts but withholds the one gift that will enable them to enjoy the other gifts.

4. *Rest* is a word with two meanings: "remainder" and "repose." How does Herbert use both of these meanings? In line 10, *rest* means "repose"; in line 16, it means "remainder" (the rest of the gifts). Both meanings seem to operate in the verb in line 14, in which God imagines humans both resting and remaining in nature. The pun suggests the problem involved in rest, namely, that humans may become unaware of God. The cure involves another pun, "Restlessness," the opposite of rest.

LOVE (III)

1. What is the dramatic situation implied in the poem? How would you characterize the speaker? The situation involves a traveler who is being welcomed to dinner by a gracious host. The speaker is shy (his soul draws back, line 1). He feels dirty, both from the road and from his sins committed on the road of life. Further, he feels unworthy to be welcomed and is aware of his own part in God's misery.

2. What details in the poem lead you to identify "Love" and "The Lord"? The use of "soul" in line 1 should alert us to a possible religious context. The first major clue is in line 12, in which Love is revealed as the creator. The identification is made positive in line 13, in which the speaker addresses Love as "Lord." Further evidence is found in line 15, in which Love speaks of bearing the blame.

What is gained by using "Love" throughout? By delaying the identification of "Love," Herbert can use human attributes, reminding us that God became a human being. The revelation that Love is the Lord does not destroy the warm, loving relationship but simply expands the sense that love is the Lord's most important characteristic.

3. Why is the speaker so reluctant to accept Love's welcome? Why does he change his mind? The speaker's sense of his own unworthiness is increased by the friendliness of Love's welcome. The change of mind occurs in the last stanza in which Love reminds the speaker that the Lord (as Christ) assumed the sins of the human race and that the speaker is therefore forgiven. There is a final attempt at evasion, when the speaker offers to act as the servant (line 16). That attempt is foiled, however, by the act of communion, which is the symbol of the Crucifixion and therefore a reenactment of Christ's sacrifice for humanity. Given the enormous significance of that act, the speaker can argue no longer.

4. This poem is the last one in the collection of Herbert's poems called *The Temple.* What makes it seem a concluding poem? In the other poems we can see Herbert's struggle to find acceptance by God. In this poem, which ends with the symbol of communion, that acceptance is finally understood by the poet.

IMPLICATIONS (GEORGE HERBERT)

Consider the following statements. What does the poet think? What do you think?

1. The way to find salvation involves much painful struggle. Herbert would agree with this statement. In "Easter Wings," the speaker must become "most thin" before ascending to God. The last line of that poem, "Affliction shall advance the flight in me," also indicates Herbert's belief that pain helps humans to understand God better. In "The Pulley," the restlessness and weariness that God creates are also manifestations of that painful struggle. Students may want to discuss the relationship between this statement and the one that follows.

2. The way to find salvation involves simple acceptance of God's love. Herbert would agree with this statement also, particularly in "The Collar" and in "Love (III)." But "simple" acceptance is not easy to achieve. Is God there? How do we know? And if we feel sinful and unworthy, how can we accept forgiveness? The emotional difficulty of accepting love—whether it is God's love or that of another person—could be discussed here.

3. Playing games with words is a form of praising God. Once again, Herbert would agree with this statement. The shaped poem; the puns in "The Pulley"; the images implied in "The Collar" and "The Pully;" and the intricate varying of lines and rhymes in "The Collar" all suggest that Herbert was very fond of this craft. But a religious significance is also implied: Finding intricate ways of writing a poem is the poet's equivalent of creating a beautiful object; it is the poet's version of a cathedral adorned with intricate carvings and designs. Students should think about whether doing something as well as one can—whether that effort results in a very simple poem or in a more complicated one—is in itself a form of praising God.

Poems by Robert Herrick

PAGE 316

Glossary Word

stomacher (page 317) An ornamental covering for the stomach and bodice, formerly worn by a woman under the lacing of the bodice

Handbook

alliteration, atmosphere

***Check Test 34** (also for Lovelace and Marvell poetry)*

INTRODUCTION

Herrick, because of his surface simplicity, is sometimes quite tricky to teach; that is, it is difficult to get students to understand how good he is because his poetry seems so simple. Trying to write a list poem may help students to understand the problems involved in creating a poem like "The Argument of His Book." Another interesting exercise would be to try to rewrite the poem to see if other words can be substituted. "Delight in Disorder" can be taught with Jonson's "Still to Be Neat"; the similarities and the differences lead easily into a discussion. Herrick can also be taught with Lovelace and Marvell. Herrick's work offers a change of pace after the difficulties of Donne and Herbert.

USING THE STUDY NOTES

PAGE 319

THE ARGUMENT OF HIS BOOK

1. Herrick is making a list of various subjects he will write about. How random is his order? Can you detect any structure in his list? Any progression? Why does he begin where he does and

end where he does? A number of possible structures can be found in this short poem, and students should be encouraged to look for a variety of them. One could argue that the poem begins with natural objects (lines 1–2), moves to social celebrations (lines 3–4), and then to more abstract subjects (lines 5–6). The cycle starts again in lines 7–8, but these natural objects are noticeably less tangible than those in lines 1–2. The poem becomes increasingly removed from the real world in its reference to "times trans-shifting," and the transformation image takes us into the flower's color and then into fairy realms. Finally, the poem moves to completely spiritual and religious matters, marking a progression from an emphasis on this world to an emphasis on the next world. One can also note the structures created by individual lines: alliteration in lines 1 and 4, the progress of the seasons in line 2, the repetition of variant terms in line 8, and so on.

2. The poem is noticeable for its great number of nouns and small number of adjectives. What effect is gained by using so many nouns? Obviously, the poet cannot include every item that he is going to write about, but by accumulating nouns, he creates the illusion of completeness. He does not describe the items in this poem—that is, after all, the purpose of the poems to come. But by naming the subjects, he celebrates their existence; in a sense, they do not need description but are worthy of poetry because they are named.

DELIGHT IN DISORDER

1. Again, the question of order becomes important. Why does the speaker list the details in the order he does? The traditional way of describing a person is from head to toe. (In medieval lyrics, this was called the *blazon.)* Therefore, it is important that Herrick list the details of dress in that order. In this poem, the reader also gets the impression that the lady is being poetically undressed.

2. What words suggest "delight" on the part of the speaker? Unlike the first poem, the adjectives and verbs here are of crucial importance in creating the atmosphere of delight—"sweet," "fine," "winning." The verbs, equally important, suggest entrapment—"kindles," "enthralls," "bewitch." The contradictory phrase, "wild civility," echoes the central paradox of the poem.

3. What sense do you get of the personality of the woman described? Although she never speaks, the adjectives and verbs that describe her clothes are so personal that we transfer those qualities to the woman herself. She is, we infer, "sweet"; possibly wanton; distracting; "erring"; capable of producing confusion; "winning"; "deserving note"; "tempestuous" (she probably has a temper!); and, finally, bewitching.

4. Look back at Jonson's "Still to Be Neat" (p. 311). How would you distinguish the two poets' views on the subject of careful art and neglected beauty? This is not a "which is better?" question but rather an attempt to get students to understand how two poems that express fairly similar ideas are quite different. Jonson sounds more detached but seems to be making a judgment about the issue. The word "adulteries" is a strong one; he uses it so late in the poem that we take it as Jonson's final view. Herrick is more involved with the woman, and although he also uses a strong word, "wantonness," at the outset, he seems to qualify or moderate it in subsequent stanzas. In Jonson's poem the speaker *states* that his heart is stirred by careless beauty. Herrick's poem, by contrast, *illustrates* the speaker's rapture with the woman.

Poem by Richard Lovelace

PAGE 318

Check Test 34 (also for Herrick and Marvell poetry)

INTRODUCTION

Lovelace's lyric, "To Lucasta, On Going to the Wars," with one or two other poems ("To Althea, from Prison," "To Amarantha, That She Would Dishevel Her Hair") have earned him a place in English literature. The poem is direct, appealing, and sincere. The question that one could put to students after discussing the poem is the extent to which the poet's answer is true today. One thinks of the Vietnam War, a war that many people found dishonorable. Could a soldier going off to that war say the sorts of things that Lovelace says? One could also ask students if the notion of commitment to an ideal—be it political, social, philosophical, or religious—makes any sense to them. Do they think, instead, that personal commitments have the highest value? Although the poem can be appreciated on its own terms, you can use it in this way as a catalyst for a discussion of values. In another approach, you could teach it along with some of the modern poems about war (see Twentieth-Century Poetry).

USING THE STUDY NOTES PAGE 319

TO LUCASTA, ON GOING TO THE WARS

1. What has Lucasta said to the poet to evoke the answer that forms this poem? Is the answer the complete answer, or is the speaker really motivated by other desires as well? Lucasta has said that the poet is unkind to forsake her in order to go to war. The speaker is evidently enthusiastic about the prospect of encountering the foe, which he calls a "new mistress," but this does not mean that his answer to Lucasta is incomplete. Whether or not the speaker has given a complete answer to Lucasta can only be speculated about. Students may wish to debate the motivations other than honor that the speaker might have. (The use of the word "nunnery" as an image for Lucasta's presence and the reference to her "quiet mind" may imply that he is restless for some kind of action. Note the use of the verbs "chase" and "embrace" in the second stanza.)

2. To some, this poem might imply that women think of the immediate, while men think of life on a larger scale. To others, it might imply that men tend to falsely equate war with honor, while women are more concerned with more important human values. Do you agree with either of these views? This question may generate a good deal of debate among students. There is some truth to each view and the poem supports both views. To those who argue that Lucasta is concerned only with her own immediate loss, we counter that the speaker would not be addressing her in such a manner if he believed that were true.

3. The pattern of the poem is logical argument. How is this pattern achieved? One could think of the first two stanzas as premises and the last stanza as the conclusion. The argument begins with a statement of the allegation, followed by a concession (stanza 2) that in turn leads to the conclusion. The conclusion answers the allegation by asserting that love and honor are mutually supportive.

Poem by Andrew Marvell PAGE 320

***Check Test 34** (also for Herrick and Lovelace poetry)*

INTRODUCTION

"To His Coy Mistress" is one of the great poems in the English language, a triumph both of tradition and of individual talent. If you want students to read this poem in the context of *carpe diem* (seize the day) poems, you could also look at Catullus's "Come Lesbia, let us live and love"; Ben Jonson's song from *Volpone,* "Come my Celia, let us prove"; and Herrick's "Corinna's Going A-Maying" and "To the Virgins, to Make Much of Time." The last study question suggests a possible writing assignment that could also serve as an introduction to the poem; you could read the poem and then ask students to write responses (in tetrameter couplets, if you prefer). Then build a class discussion around whether or not the woman would say yes. Which arguments do students think are most convincing?

Another good way to work with this poem and to approach the difficult matter of tone is to ask a student to read the poem aloud with no expression whatsoever, making everything deliberately flat. This is bound to sound very funny. Then ask the student to read again—this time emphasizing feelings and attitudes—and encourage the class to suggest other readings. A class could easily spend ten minutes arguing about the interpretation of "lady" in the second line: Does the poet use that term courteously or sarcastically? The poem is obviously an invitation to seduction, couched in a mock-serious tone. It is also a frankly sexual poem, and you will want to decide, in terms of the individual class involved, how many of the sexual allusions should be explained. One could note that the "rubies" in line 6 are traditional talismans to preserve virginity. The last six lines are understandable on the level of "let us get what pleasure we may while we can," but they also have more explicit sexual connotations.

USING THE STUDY NOTES PAGE 324

TO HIS COY MISTRESS

1. The poem is written in three verse paragraphs. What is the central point of each one? The speaker is constructing an argument in favor of physical love. In the first twenty lines he suggests that if time were not an issue, he would be able to praise and court the lady as she deserves. His enumeration of the length of time needed to pay her proper homage is the skilled strategist's way of flattering her. In lines 21–32, he argues both that they do not have time (because death will come to them) and that virginity is of no advantage when one is dead. The final verse paragraph is a frank invitation to sex that argues essentially "let us sport us while we may" and builds on the sense of urgency created in the second paragraph.

2. List the hyperboles in the first twenty lines. What do they tell us about the speaker and his attitude toward the lady? "I would/ Love you ten years before the flood" implies that his love is older (and therefore more enduring) than the time of the flood. Her refusal, "Till the conversion of the Jews," would at least consume an equally long time. His love "should grow/ Vaster than empires," a clear exaggeration. The time that would be needed to praise the woman, culminating in "An age at least to every part," suggests that she is so beautiful that the speaker could spend eternity praising her. Yet the accumulation of hyperboles may seem *too* much; we begin to wonder if she really is all that beautiful or whether he is merely flattering her. The last line of the verse paragraph, with its connotations of monetary trade, "Nor would I love at lesser *rate,*" may subtly undercut all the praise if, after all, he sees her as someone he can buy with flattery.

3. What does the word *coy* mean? What sense do you get of the lady's interest (or lack of interest) in the speaker? *Coy* means displaying shyness or reserve. However, the connotation (both in Marvell's time and in our own) is that the display is more real than the shyness; coyness functions to attract through pretending to hold back. In the last verse paragraph, the speaker describes the woman as having a "willing soul," which may imply that she is really quite ready to accept his invitation. But it may indicate, instead, wishful thinking on the speaker's part.

4. How seriously do you think we should take this poem? Why? This is an opinion question that may well be answered by the tone exercise suggested earlier (reading the poem with no expression and then with as much expression as possible). Students could recognize that the poet is both serious and not serious. That is, he exaggerates his praise of the woman to provoke a receptive frame of mind. Even his description of death is not morbid but is rather gruesome as well as funny, what we would call grotesque. The tetrameter couplets, which trip lightly along, also make the poem sound less serious. On the other hand, Marvell uses death precisely because it is inevitable (as well as being an Elizabethan pun for sexual consummation) and because he is aware that time destroys power. The metaphors of "Time's winged chariot" and "Deserts of vast eternity" suggest that he is aware that if he is to find love, he must do so quickly. The poet is serious in another sense; he does indeed want to make love to the woman even if he sounds somewhat flippant about it.

5. Consider the following statements. Which do you find strongest evidence for:

a. The poet is an old man who is afraid of death and who is deeply in love with a young woman.

b. The poet is a young man who uses the inevitability of death to scare the girl into responding to him.

Students could well read the poet's emphasis on time as proof of his old age, especially lines 21–22. The woman's youthfulness is suggested in lines 33–34. The fear of death is expressed in the metaphors of the second verse paragraph.

The second statement seems truer to the tone of the poem than does the first. It can be resolved in terms of the previous question about tone and in terms of the students' reactions to the speaker's attitude. If they envision him as a man who consciously flatters the woman, knowing all the time that she has a "willing soul," then they will read the second verse paragraph as a somewhat lighthearted attempt to remind her that love (or lust) means nothing in the grave. The answer to whether he is trying to scare her should again be based on tone. Students should be encouraged to experiment with readings that would support either interpretation.

Poems by John Milton

PAGE 321

Glossary Words

ethereal (page 322) Light; airy; delicate; also, heavenly
obdurate (page 322) Stubborn or unyielding; obstinate
celestial (page 323) Having to do with the heavens; heavenly
sovereign (page 323) Person having the greatest rank or power
chide (page 323) Reproach or blame; scold

Handbook

epic, sonnet

Check Test 35

INTRODUCTION

Paradise Lost is both famous and widely unread. It has the reputation of being difficult, for people often think that they need a lot of background in order to understand the poem or to cope with Milton's grand style. If you are knowledgeable about the poem, the problem may be the reverse: You may feel tempted to tell students a great deal about the poem, and they may feel lost in dealing with only a small section of it.

The two excerpts from Book I come early in the poem and therefore do not require much background information. If your students are not familiar with the story of Satan's revolt against God, you might explain that incident. According to Biblical tradition, Satan was an angel. He became the leader of a small group of angels who denied God's wishes and in fact rebelled against God's commands. These angels were punished by being cast into Hell. Satan thus became the leader in Hell and the enemy of God as well as of humankind.

We would not recommend extensive background reading or the expositions of major critics, who tend to get involved in highly complex matters. Instead, we suggest working with the passages themselves and confronting the difficulties of style directly. Help students to see why the long words, the inverted sentence structure, and the run-on lines are components of the total effect.

The questions about Satan focus on his arguments and rationalizations and may well suggest a parallel with Macbeth. Macbeth, like Satan, consciously chooses the wrong way and later tries to rationalize it (see *Macbeth,* III:3). You could also have students compare the way that Shakespeare creates his "moral" landscape (the imagery of II:1, lines 49-60 and II:4, lines 1-20) with the way that Milton creates his. Later in the anthology, William Sansom's short story "The Long Sheet" presents a modern hell; students may also be interested in comparing Milton and Sansom. The sonnet on Milton's blindness also offers possibilities for discussion, particularly if you compare the attitude expressed in the last line of the sonnet (Milton's growing acceptance of his fate) with Satan's resentment and rationalizations. One final note: Gray's *Ode* also presents "poetic" language in a high style but for comic effect. Get students to see how Milton employs unusual words to create a solemn and even tragic setting. You will then be able to set up the comparison with Gray, who uses some of Milton's Latinate terms but with a very different purpose.

USING THE STUDY NOTES

PAGE 324

from PARADISE LOST

Paradise Lost, excerpts from Book I: (In the poem these are lines 44–74 and 242–263).

1. What are the major oppositions Milton sets up in these passages? The most striking is the opposition between light and dark, expressed in lines 1–31 through the continuous use of "fire" and "fiery" and the repetition of "darkness." The emphasis on light continues in the second excerpt in which Satan contrasts the "mournful gloom" of his new home with heaven's "celestial light." Other oppositions are those between "ethereal" and "adamantine," between "affliction and dismay," and between "pride and hate." There is a paradox, too—Satan is "Confounded though immortal." Note how Milton reminds us of what is lacking in hell: lines 22–24 stress peace and rest and hope, which will never come.

2. In lines 1–31, what words are particularly important for creating hell in a physical sense? In a moral sense? Physical details are not as important to the description as might be imagined. Hell is a place of "ruin"; it is "bottomless," "fiery," "waste and wild"; it is called a "dungeon" and a "prison" with a "great furnace"; and there is a smell of "sulphur." The moral universe is stressed far more by expressions such as "hideous," "perdition," "horrid crew," "confounded," "wrath," "lost happiness," "lasting pain," "torments," "baleful," "huge affliction and dismay," "obdurate pride and steadfast hate," "dismal," "horrible," "sights of woe," "torture," "unconsumed," and "rebellious." Milton emphasizes the emotions unleashed by hell to give us a sense of what Satan is feeling. Thus Satan's boast in the next passage that the mind can "make a heaven of hell, a hell of heaven" is ironically true.

3. In lines 32–53, we hear Satan talking to Beelzebub, another fallen angel. What arguments does Satan use to convince Beelzebub (and himself) that the demons are not really defeated? At first, there is an acceptance that God has won (lines 35–37), but this acceptance immediately turns into a statement that it is better to be as far away from God as possible (line 37). Satan argues that he cannot be influenced by "place or time," that he is his own master because he governs his own mind, and that he can make hell into heaven or the reverse through the power of his mind. Satan's final argument to Beelzebub (lines 48 ff.) asserts that they are actually freer in hell because God will not try to drive them out of so horrible a place. He ends with a summation that restates the previous arguments, "Better to reign in hell than serve in heaven."

4. What do you think of Satan's arguments? Are they convincing? Can you find any evidence that he is just rationalizing and trying to make the best of a bad situation? Students will probably find Satan's arguments attractive (so did William Blake who wrote that Milton was "of the Devil's party without knowing it"). There is something heroic in Satan's refusal to accept defeat, in his ability to turn banishment and imprisonment into a new kind of freedom, and, most of all, in his assertion that individual will is of supreme importance. Satan believes that humans (or a devil) can create their personal reality through the power of their minds. The problem with all of these arguments lies in the situation: Satan is, after all, in hell. He recognizes in the first part of the second excerpt that he is defeated, and so the claim in line 51 that it is his "choice" to be in hell rings false. He also notes the contrast between heaven's "happy fields" and hell's "horrors." In short, Satan's speech repeatedly reveals the weaknesses of his situation as well as the assertions of individual will and strength. Students should be encouraged to see both sides.

ON HIS BLINDNESS

1. This sonnet takes the form of an internal conversation. The speaker also asks himself a question and then answers it. In what mood does he ask the question? In what mood does he answer it? He asks the question in a "murmuring" mood (line 9), one could say; that is, in a mood of some resentment and perhaps of some despair. His answer is stated in a mood of hopeful resignation.

2. *Talent* is a word with two meanings: the modern meaning of "ability" and the Biblical meaning of "a coin." The Biblical story tells of a servant who was given money (a talent) to keep for his master and who buried the money for safekeeping. His master scolded him for not investing it so that its value would increase. In this sonnet is *talent* used in both the Biblical and modern sense? What was Milton's "one talent"? Why would it be "death" to hide it? "Talent" is supposed to put the reader on the Biblical track, and it clearly has the meaning of "ability," but of course Milton is not talking about coins or payment of money in his own case. Milton's "one talent" was presumably his creative ability. To hide this talent would be death because artists die in mind and spirit if they cannot express themselves in their art. It is also "death to hide," perhaps, because God expects persons given "talents" to use them and they "die" in God's graces if they do not.

3. How does Patience describe those who best serve God? Those "who best/Bear his mild yoke" are those who best serve God—that is, those who follow the commandments and accept and make the best of their abilities.

4. Does the last line imply that the best way to live would be to cease all activity? The last line does not offer any *general* advice on ways to live. It implies that people do not have to be intensely active in order to serve God well. They also serve who accept the station in life that they are given.

Poems by John Dryden

PAGE 324

Glossary Words

succession (page 325) Order or arrangement of persons having the right to take the place of another

deviates (page 325) Turns aside

lucid (page 325) Clear in intellect; rational; sane

Handbook

alliteration, allusion, assonance, balanced sentence, couplet, metaphor, satire

Check Test 36

INTRODUCTION

The selections by Dryden should appeal to students in several ways. First, they are satirical portraits, one quite obvious, the other a bit more subtle. As such, they can be compared with Chaucer's portraits in the Prologue. Second, you could ask students to compare Satan to Achitophel because both are characters who impress us in some ways and horrify us in others. However, the most important factor to stress is how Dryden so neatly seizes on the devastating things about a person and how he traps both the language and the object satirized in a couplet. We have previously suggested that students try to write their own versions of various poems as a way of appreciating them. In this case, invite students to turn loose their imaginations and their sarcasm on any contemporary person or cause—and to do it in rhymed iambic pentameter couplets. We think that they will enjoy the exercise and will more readily appreciate Dryden's skill.

The *MacFlecknoe* excerpt consists of the first twenty-eight lines of the poem. It begins with a neutral, almost reflective, attitude in the first two lines. But as soon as Flecknoe and Augustus are compared, we know that the objectivity of the opening lines is only a mask—a mask that Dryden slips on and off for the rest of the poem.

Dryden's feelings are less masked but more complicated in the description of Achitophel (lines 150–182 in the full poem). He is much more open about Achitophel's evil. But Dryden seems to experience a moment of partial sympathy for him when, in lines 13–20, he raises the possibility that Shaftesbury's behavior may be the result of madness rather than of evil. But as the description continues, Dryden's hatred returns. And yet a sense of Shaftesbury's strength (like Samson he shakes pillars) remains.

USING THE STUDY NOTES

PAGE 331

from MACFLECKNOE

1. What is the major metaphor developed in these twenty-eight lines? Why is it useful for Dryden's satiric purpose? The major metaphor begins in line 2 with the word *monarchs.* From then on, Dryden develops the idea of a monarch passing on the throne to an heir. References to monarchy recur throughout: "empire," "governed," "realms," "prince," "succession of the state," "reign," "rule," "majesty." The adoption of a lofty central metaphor and an implied plot is useful because it enables Dryden to accumulate compliments and then deflate them. In this manner, he ennobles the playwright by imagining him as a prince and then reminds us repeatedly of how unprincely he really is.

2. How would you describe Dryden's satiric strategy in lines 15–28? The basic technique used here resembles that of blowing up a balloon and then puncturing it neatly. Notice how line 15, for example, seems to set up a compliment ("my perfect image bears") and how line 16 completes the couplet and destroys the compliment. We see the same structure in lines 17–18, lines 19–20, and, in an extended vein, in lines 21–24 and lines 25–28. The compliments begin to corrode as the poem continues. In line 23, for example, it is "night" that is "genuine," already anticipating the "fogs" of line 24. And in line 26, the "majesty" is "thoughtless," a metaphor to be expanded in line 27. Then, in line 28, with the pun on "supinely" enhanced by the alliteration on *s,* the "majesty" is deflated.

from ABSALOM AND ACHITOPHEL

1. What details show Dryden's hatred of Achitophel? The adjectives carry the primary attack: "false," "cursed," "crooked," "turbulent," "restless," "unfixed in principles," "false," "implacable." We also observe a contempt for the body: "pygmy," "tenement of clay." The last nine lines contain attacks centered on Achitophel's public behavior rather than on his character. The verbs become central: "resolved to ruin or to rule," "broke," "shook," "seized," "affecting," "usurped." The balance in the last line sums up the entire attack: "public zeal" (shown in the last nine lines) and "private crimes" (detailed in the first twelve lines).

2. What details suggest his possible sympathy for or understanding of Achitophel? Even the attack of the first twelve lines contains words and descriptions capable of implying some admiration for the man: He is "sagacious," "bold," a "fiery soul," and "a daring pilot." He is not afraid, although that may be because he is too arrogant to appreciate fear. Then in lines 13–14 there is a curious shift away from direct attack to a philosophic musing by Dryden. It is as if the poet wished to divert our attention and perhaps even to offer an excuse: Maybe the man is mad. Lines 15–21 reinforce this idea: He must be mad, otherwise why would he destroy himself in this way? The description of the son, "that unfeathered two-legged thing," "a shapeless lump," may create sympathy for the father.

3. How would you distinguish between the satire of *MacFlecknoe* and that of *Absalom and Achitophel?* Do you think that Dryden is using the same techniques in both poems? In many ways, of course, the poems are alike: the couplets, the balanced phrases, the use of alliteration and assonance. But the tone seems very different, and students should be encouraged to define the difference. In part the different tone can be attributed to the blowing-up-and-deflating technique of *MacFlecknoe,* which creates a much funnier tone than the more direct attack of *Absalom and Achitophel.* There is also the difference in surface metaphor. *MacFlecknoe* presents a primarily secular, pagan monarchy; biblical reference predominates in *Absalom and Achitophel,* which may give the poem a more grave and important tone. In the first poem, the problems are those of writers, whereas in the second, the fate of a government (and thus of a country) is implied.

Poems by Alexander Pope

PAGE 328

Glossary Word

culls (page 329) Selects; picks out

Handbook

alliteration, couplet, irony, metaphor, mock-heroic, satire

Check Test 37 (also for Gray poetry)

INTRODUCTION

The excerpts from Pope have been chosen to give students another example of the satiric mode in eighteenth-century poetry. The two excerpts are replete with details that reveal Pope's attitude toward the society that he is describing. There are, of course, many possibilities for further work with Pope. *The Rape of the Lock* in its entirety is not really that long, and some students may want to read the complete poem. If students are familiar with one of the major epics, such as the *Iliad* or the *Odyssey,* they will relish the card-game in Canto III or the descent into the underworld in Canto IV. And Pope's couplets are so subtle and sprightly that if you have a class that is interested in formal problems, you can spend some time analyzing the structure of the couplet, the variations in tone, the skillful use of alliteration, and so on. However, the primary approach may well be through satire, as the study questions suggest.

The first excerpt is concerned with the idea of cosmetic beauty once again. The poems by Jonson and Herrick may well be compared with Pope's truly devastating (because overblown) description of the process of making up one's face. The whole idea behind the mock-heroic technique—taking something trivial and enlarging it with appropriate allusions, language, and images—is a technique that could be applied to current events, everyday objects, or familiar figures. Perhaps an exercise in which students try to create a mock-heroic description would prepare them for Pope's work in this style.

USING THE STUDY NOTES

PAGE 331

from THE RAPE OF THE LOCK
BELINDA GETS DRESSED

1. What is the central metaphor of this passage? The central metaphor is that of a religious ceremony, complete with altar, priestess, and ritual objects. There are many words that imply the religious aura: "mystic," "adores," "heavenly," "priestess," "altar," "sacred rites," and "goddess."

2. What details indicate that Pope is satirizing the involved makeup and dressing process? The combination of religious words and articles for dressing produces the satiric effect. "Toilet" in its earlier meaning of "dressing table and equipment" still seems a common word, especially when compared with "mystic order." We note that the nymph doing the worshipful adoring (line 3) is actually looking at herself! And the description of Belinda's combs, jewelry, and perfumes is introduced with the equivocal term "glittering spoil"—shining, yet somehow corrupt. The most famous line in this passage, line 18, is a masterpiece of condensed irony: The alliteration of "puffs, powders, patches," leads us smoothly on. We are thus startled to find "Bibles" thrown in casually, as casually as Belinda must have thrown the Bible onto her dressing table. And then the alliteration carries us forward again into "billet-doux." The absence of comment becomes the ironic comment.

AT HAMPTON COURT

1. What values of the society are revealed in this description? This is a society that values sociability and wit above all things. The queen herself seems to find counsel as easy to take as a cup of tea, which may mean that the counsel gets precisely that much attention. It is a society in which gossip, gaiety, flirtation, and cheerful conversation abound (lines 10–16). It is also a society run by the rich and the powerful (the judges, the merchants) and by the glamorous who spend their time at "the long labors of the toilet."

2. What is Pope's attitude toward these values? How do you know? Pope attacks not in a direct way but with sarcasm, faintly concealed. The balance of the couplet allows him to relate things that are morally unequal but that seem to be valued as equal by the people involved and as reflected in the rhythm of the line. Thus the fall in line 5 represents that of "foreign tyrants" and of "nymphs at home," the implication being that political campaigns are considered on the same level with sexual intrigue. Queen Anne's counsel and her tea receive the same ironic treatment. The gossip in the second verse paragraph is given the ironic description of "instructive hours" —a description that we may take seriously until we hear what the talk is about. And, of course, "heros" and "nymphs" become ironic terms for the gossiping society people. Pope's real bitterness becomes apparent in the last six lines that refer to actual death (as opposed to the death of a reputation). The wretches who hang, Pope concludes, are guilty in reality of keeping the judges and the jury from their dinners. That couplet, sandwiched between two others, reveals the hollowness of the society. But, as with the Bibles in Canto I, the couplet is not expanded upon. The lack of overt comment provokes us to supply the moral outrage ourselves.

A Poem by Thomas Gray

PAGE 330

Glossary Words

pensive (page 330, col. 1) Thoughtful in a serious or sad way

vies (page 330, col. 1) Contends in rivalry; competes

averse (page 330, col. 1) Opposed; having a strong or fixed dislike

presumptuous (page 330, col. 2) Too bold; forward; acting without permission or right

Handbook

alliteration, allusion, mock-heroic, ode, personification

***Check Test 37** (also for Pope poetry)*

INTRODUCTION

Gray's "Ode," although certainly less well known than his famous "Elegy," is such a delightful poem that students will enjoy it. And they should also be able to see how the mock-heroic style works. Gray takes a trivial episode with less than human characters and evokes an aura of great beauty, drama, emotional conflict, and even death. Note the various techniques that Gray uses: He presents an elaborate description of the cat; he personifies her; he turns goldfish into "the genii of the stream"; he adds a few classical allusions; and, finally, he interjects an unimpeachable but ridiculous moral. The effect of all this is to make the death of the cat memorable and funny at the same time. Students should enjoy seeing how Gray uses "heavy" language and how he always manages to undercut it. The use of rhyme is important, as are the short third and sixth lines, which act as stops, and so tend to slow down the flow of the lines. The discrepancy between the reality involved and the language employed is obvious.

USING THE STUDY NOTES PAGE 331

ODE (ON THE DEATH OF A FAVORITE CAT. . .)

1. What picture of the cat is created in the first two stanzas? The first three lines, although not directly about the cat, imply an atmosphere of grace and delicacy that is transferred to the cat. The cat herself is named ("Selima"); she is personified ("demurest," "pensive"); she is mythicized through the use of a mock-heroic phrase ("the tabby kind," as if she were not an ordinary cat but a member of a great race of cats); and she is adorned with compliments ("conscious tail," "fair round face," "snowy beard," "ears of jet" and "emerald eyes"). She is of a fairly common color (tortoiseshell), but that information is conveyed in complimentary terms. However, we must remember that the poem is about a cat. "Tabby" is a homely word. Her paws may be velvet, but they are "paws" nevertheless. And, like all other cats, she purrs. These reminders are few but carefully spaced.

2. What details in stanzas 3–6 contribute to the "grand" style? What details remind us of the less grand reality? The fish are made grand through being called "two angel forms," "the genii of the stream," and of "Tyrian hue" (the classical imperial purple). The cat is called a "nymph" and is threatened by none other than "Malignant Fate"—the classical world is thus invoked. The allusions in stanza 6 to the dolphin that saved Arion and to the Nereids reinforce the classical style, as does the reference to "every watery god." The reality of the event is evoked through words such as "whisker," "claw," "slippery," "tumbled" (hardly an heroic action!), and "mewed" and through the reference to the cat's nine lives. The most important line is "What cat's averse to fish?"—a question that underscores the reality of the cat's nature.

3. How seriously are we meant to take the last stanza? On one level, the last stanza is full of sound principles that are expressed in clichés. Gray's obvious use of cliché, especially in the last line (reinforced by alliteration), tends to undercut seriousness. And when we remember that the "beauty" is a cat and that the "gold" that shines is that of a goldfish, we sense that Gray is mocking the moral of the ode as well as the event itself.

UNIT TEST

You may select questions at random from the Study Notes at the end of each selection as a basis for constructing a final examination covering the unit Seventeenth- and Eighteenth-Century British Poetry. You may also choose to use the comprehensive unit test prepared on blackline masters available in a separate test booklet, ISBN 0-07-009823-9.

Foibles

Webster's Third Unabridged Dictionary defines a foible as a "harmless, and usually amiable, weakness or failing." In general, that description fits the foibles studied in this unit. It fits, for instance, the foibles of the persons Johnson meets in his stagecoach journey. But harmless as foibles usually are, they can lead to serious consequences if excessively indulged. Thus, we may sympathize with the natural and apparently harmless foible of Strindberg's Gustave, who wishes to provide luxuries like partridges and strawberries for his young wife—*until* his foible leads to ruin.

Occasionally, students may be able to identify some of their own foibles in these selections. When they can, the effect may be quite salutary, although self-awareness is not the only benefit that students may derive from a unit such as this. A foible has also been defined as something that none of us has yet all of us see everywhere around us—in others. That is perhaps why it is so easy to laugh at the exposure of human failings: We are normally quite sure that they have nothing to do with us. Indeed, the effect of the exposure may serve to make us feel superior. This reaction need not be altogether bad. Most of us occasionally have feelings of inadequacy, and it helps to be able to see that others, too, have their weaknesses.

OBJECTIVES

1. To help students to see that to have foibles is to be human.
2. To stimulate students to recognize their own weaknesses.
3. To encourage toleration for the foibles of others.
4. To study comedy as "the fine art of disillusion."
5. To expose students to literature that is fundamentally for fun.
6. To expose some of the more unpleasant follies of humankind.
7. To study the importance of setting and prose style in literature.
8. To develop vocabulary.

MOTIVATING THE UNIT

The following are some suggestions for opening this unit. You may wish to try more than one of them if you are teaching several classes.

Pattern I Ask students to study the pictures in the Gallery (pages 410–414 in the text) and the single picture that opens the unit (page 332). Suggest that they study the pictures closely, paying special attention to the faces and the numbers of people. Then ask them to select one or more of the pictures and write a brief essay on human foibles as depicted in art. Read and discuss some of the more perceptive of these essays in class.

Pattern II Write on the board the word "Foibles," and ask students to write whatever comes to mind when they think of this word. After five or ten minutes, collect the papers and read and discuss some of the more interesting ones. Then, assign the introduction in the text or the first selection or both.

Pattern III Ask students to make up two lists (or to write two themes). In the first list, ask them to name (or describe) some of the foibles that they have seen in the world. In the second, they should name (or describe) some of their own foibles. Discuss which of the lists (or descriptions) was easier to do and why.

Something similar may be done with some of the better-humored students in your class: ask Student X to list personal foibles and the foibles of Student Y, and ask Student Y to list personal foibles and those of Student X. Then compare the two lists and discuss the foibles of each student. Also discuss the problems caused by the fact that we often see ourselves differently than others see us.

Pattern IV In a class of less able students you will probably find many who do not know what the word *foibles* means. In that case, define the term for them and then read aloud the introduction on pages 332–33, pausing after each paragraph to ask for questions or to explain difficult points. Probably you will also want to page through the Gallery with students,

Foibles: Scope and Sequence

Selection	Language/Vocabulary	Comprehension	Critical/Literary	Composition
THE MISER	language style, levels of meaning, context	details, inferences, cause and effect, conclusions, classifying	farce, complications, characterization, prose style, conflict, climax, theme	exposition*
"The Influence of the Aristocracy on Snobs"		details, inferences, summarizing, conclusions	essay, setting, prose style, irony	exposition*
"A Journey in a Stage-Coach"		details, inferences	essay, setting, prose style	exposition*
"Love and Bread"	context, definition, metaphor	details, inferences, main idea	setting, prose style, irony, metaphor, simile	exposition*
"Jeannot and Colin"	context, definition, metaphor	details, inferences	setting, prose style, irony, exemplum, satire	exposition*, description, satire
"Dissecting of a Beau's Head"		details, inferences, supporting conclusions	essay, satire, prose style, stock characters	exposition*
"The Coquette's Heart"		details, inferences, conclusions, comparing/contrasting	essay, satire, prose style, stock characters	exposition*
"A Trip with Obstacles"		details, inferences, conclusions	setting, prose style, folk tale, characterization	exposition*
"How to Buy a House"	context, definition figures of speech	details, inferences	setting, prose style, autobiography	exposition*
from *The Decameron*		details, inferences	setting, prose style, tale	exposition*
"The Bound Man"	verb choice	details, inferences	setting, prose style, parable, symbol	exposition*
"A Man by the Name of Ziegler"		details, inferences, conclusions	setting, prose style, theme, characterization	exposition*
Summing Up		details, conclusions, comparing/contrasting	setting, prose style	exposition*
Relating Composition, the Gallery, and Humanities	definition	details, comparing/contrasting	characterization, diction, prose style, setting, satire	essay, vignette, dialogue, monologue, satire

Nineteenth-Century British Poetry

Selection	Language/Vocabulary	Comprehension	Critical/Literary	Composition
Blake, Wordsworth, Coleridge, Byron, Shelley, Keats Poems	definition, sensory images, coined words, archaic words, imagery	comparing/contrasting, details, inferences, conclusions	allusion, mood, sonnet, caesura, tone, ballad, ode, personification	
Tennyson, R. Browning, E. Browning, Arnold, Housman Poems		details, inference, conclusions, comparing/contrasting	dramatic monologue, allusion, irony, tone, sonnet, theme	

*Teachers can use the Implications in the study notes as writing assignments.

encouraging them to discuss how the pictures reveal human foibles.

Pattern V Tell students that George Bernard Shaw once defined comedy as "the fine art of disillusion." Ask them to discuss the meaning of this phrase. Specifically, in what sense may a disillusioning experience be regarded as comic? In what sense can the act of disillusioning be called an art? What are some differences between artistic disillusionment and psychological disillusionment? Are all kinds of illusions, or only some, fair game for the writer of comedy?

The Miser

PAGE 336

Molière

The Miser combines comedy and insight—clever theatrical craft and thought-provoking characterizations. Students should have no real difficulty with the play; the only formal convention that may seem strange is the scene division, which is explained in the Introduction. The play reads quickly and is easily stageable in short units. Scenes such as Harpagon searching La Flèche (I:3), Valère and Harpagon arguing about Élise's marriage (I:5), and the two famous misunderstanding scenes (III:7 and V:3) certainly lead themselves to reading and acting by the class. Indeed, the vitality of the characters becomes evident as soon as the lines are read.

Although *The Miser* is set in seventeenth-century Paris, the generational conflicts presented and the foibles of Harpagon are timeless human concerns. Students may recognize that the play resembles Thornton Wilder's *The Matchmaker* and the musical comedy *Hello Dolly!* Frosine, the intriguing matchmaker of Molière's comedy, is transformed into Dolly Levi; in fact, the description of "Ernestina Simple," the imaginary girl that she invents for Horace Vandergelder, is based directly on Frosine's account of Marianne's simple and thrifty habits.

The major objection that students may raise to this play is that it is not realistic. Compared with *Macbeth,* for example, which offers profound psychological insights into why human beings act as they do, *The Miser* may indeed seem shallow. To offset students' objections, it will be helpful to discuss with them how comedy and, especially, farce work as literary forms. The following discussion of farce may be used in several ways. You may want to offer some of the definitions of farce to your students and ask them to see how the play exemplifies the definitions. Or you may prefer to discuss the play and then examine the definitions to see if they fit the play. The second method allows students to respond to the play first, without having to fit it into a particular category; they then will have the pleasure of defining a farce from their own experience with the play.

A Handbook to Literature (Thrall, Hibbard, Holman) offers the following explanation of farce:

> The word developed from late Latin *farsus,* connected with a verb meaning "to stuff." Thus an expansion or amplification in the church liturgy was called a *farce.* Later, in France, *farce* meant any sort of extemporaneous addition in a play, especially comic jokes or "gags," the clownish actors speaking "more than was set down" for them. In the late seventeenth century *farce* was used in England to mean any short humorous play, as distinguished from regular five-act comedy. The development in these plays of certain elements of low comedy is responsible for the usual modern meaning of *farce:* a dramatic piece intended to excite laughter and depending less on plot and character than on exaggerated, improbable situations, the humor arising from gross incongruities, coarse wit, or horseplay. *Farce* merges into *comedy* and the same play (e.g. Shakespeare's *The Taming of the Shrew)* may be called by some a *farce,* by others a *comedy.*

The last sentence above illustrates the problem of definition, which is why this section on farce occurs here rather than in the student text. Surely *The Miser* grows out of both "plot and character" and "exaggerated, improbable situations." In fact, one could even argue that because the character of Harpagon creates the exaggerated situations, they are not improbable if we accept his existence.

Penelope Gilliatt, discussing the plays of Feydeau, the great nineteenth-century *farceur,* offers a more complex view of the relationship between farce and reality:

> People who dislike farce will often say that their reason for hating it is that the characters are inhuman, making the form unfunny and frivolous. I think 'inhuman' is the wrong word. The people in classic farce... are not so much inhuman as partially human, men with half their characteristics cut away.
>
> Characters in farce undergo the most severe moral stylization in all drama, because everything admirable

> about humanity is absent in them and everything superficial is uncompromisingly isolated. Far from being responsible for making the form unfunny or frivolous, it seems to me that it is exactly this process that can make farce hilarious and serious.

Penelope Gilliatt's ideas (found in her collection of reviews, *Unholy Fools)* are extremely helpful in dealing with the problem of whether the characters in *The Miser* are realistic. In one sense, they are supremely realistic, for their wants, their desires, and their failings are ones that we all share. But Molière strips away from Harpagon any redeeming humanity. He isolates his characters' foibles and so makes them both funny and extremely visible. The characters thus look like people in distorted mirrors, both real and surreal.

One more comment on farce may be helpful, this one from Robert Heilman's discussion of Shakespeare's *The Taming of the Shrew* (found in his introduction to the Signet Classic edition of the play). Note Heilman's emphasis on the "mechanical" nature of characters in farce and on our pleasure in escaping complexity:

> The essential procedure of farce is to deal with people as if they lack, largely or totally, the physical, emotional, intellectual, and moral sensitivity that we think of as 'normal.' The enormous popularity of farce for several thousand years indicates that, though 'farce' is often a term of disparagement, a great many people, no doubt all of us at times, take pleasure in seeing human beings acting as if they were very limited human beings. Farce offers a spectacle that resembles daily actuality but lets us participate without feeling the responsibilities and liabilities that the situation would normally evoke. Perhaps we feel superior to the diminished men and women in the plot; perhaps we harmlessly work off aggressions (since verbal and physical assaults are frequent in farce). Participation in farce is easy on us; in it we escape the full complexity of our own natures and cut up without physical or moral penalties. Farce is the realm without pain or conscience.... In farce the human personality is without depth. Hence action is not slowed down by thought or by the friction of competing motives.... These people rarely think, hesitate, deliberate, or choose; they act just as quickly and unambiguously as if someone had pressed a control button.

These discussions of farce may be helpful in getting students to understand the artistic choices that Molière has made in presenting a subject that is, after all, a serious one. Farce creates a certain world and because that world is heightened (exaggerated, if you will) it is supervisible. Because it is simplified, it is more recognizable. Because it is mechanical, it is funny. We are seduced into laughter by farce, yet we must not forget that we are laughing at people like ourselves.

ACT I

PAGE 336

Glossary Words

forebodings (page 337, col. 1) Feelings that something bad is going to happen

solicitude (page 337, col. 1) Anxious care; anxiety; concern

unremitting (page 337, col. 1) Never stopping; not slackening; maintained steadily

adroitness (page 337, col. 2) Resourcefulness in reaching one's objective; skillfulness

ingratiate (page 337, col. 2) Bring oneself into favor; make oneself acceptable

vouchsafe (page 339, col. 1) Be willing to grant or give

sumptuous (page 341, col. 1) Lavish and costly; magnificent; rich

flaunt (page 341, col. 1) Show off to impress others; display in such a way as to attract notice

disparity (page 343, col. 2) Lack of equality; the difference

Handbook

abstract terms, characterization, exposition

Check Test 38 (for Act I)

Check Tests for each selection—in the form of blackline masters—are available in a separate test booklet, ISBN 0-07-009823-9. Each test is titled and numbered for easy filing after use.

Give the Check Test after students have read the selection(s) and before you begin the discussion of the work(s).

USING THE STUDY NOTES

ACT I PAGE 344

EXPOSITION AND CHARACTERIZATION

1. What information about the Valère/Élise relationship is set up in Act I, Scene I? We learn that these two young people are in love. Élise is worried, however, that they will never be married, both because of her father's behavior and because she fears that Valère may stop loving her. We also find out that the two met in a most romantic way, when Valère rescued Élise from drowning. Furthermore, Valère is only masquerading as a servant in order to be near his beloved.

2. What do we learn about Valère's character and background in the first scene? Do later events in this act modify this impression of Valère? The facts, alluded to by Élise, seem to be as follows: Valère is of noble birth and is "stooping" by being a servant to Harpagon. We know that he has parents, although their whereabouts seem to be unknown. Valère himself tells us that he is playing a role in two ways: first, as a servant, and, more importantly, as a person who agrees with Harpagon's feelings. Thus, in Scene 5, when he agrees with Harpagon about a daughter's duty to obey her father, he is masking his true feelings. Students may note, however, that Élise worries whether he will always love her. Is that fear a commentary on Élise or on Valère? And even though Valère tells Élise that he agrees with Harpagon only to gain his confidence, students may find this behavior too hypocritical.

3. What do we learn about Cléante's character and situation in Scene 2? Cléante, like Élise, is also in love with someone of whom his father is unlikely to approve. Although he recognizes that his sister has problems, his love for Marianne and his preoccupation with his need for money make him essentially oblivious to anyone else's feelings. Thus the audience finds his comment, "You know nothing of the power of the tender passion over the hearts of us lovers," rather funny, because we have just watched the love scene between Élise and Valère.

4. What indications are there about Harpagon's character in the first two scenes? It seems that Harpagon is not a person, but a monster, if we take the views of these observers (who, admittedly, are not without prejudice). We hear in Scene 1 of his anger, his avarice, his mistreatment of his children, and his susceptibility to flattery. In Scene 2, Cléante calls his father "cruel" and "unnatural" in his stinginess. We do have a slight hint of Harpagon's humanity when Cléante says that he will try to talk to his father about the situation, thereby implying that his father *can* be talked to. But the scene ends with yet another attack on his "tyranny," his "obduracy," and his domination of children who have no mother to intercede for them.

5. Harpagon, the main character, does not appear until Scene 3. What effects does this postponed entrance have? Delaying the entrance of the main character allows a playwright time to create a number of impressions of that character, impressions that the entrance will either support or contradict. You might want to remind students of the way in which Shakespeare tells us a number of things about Macbeth before bringing him onstage. In the first two scenes Molière attacks Harpagon violently, through the speeches of Valère, Élise, and Cléante, thus whetting our appetites to see this paragon of avarice. When Harpagon enters, we are struck at once by his energy. Even though that energy is directed toward silly ends (questioning and searching La Flèche), the play really comes alive with Harpagon's entrance. He is, as La Flèche puts it, "possessed of a devil." Yet that possession, that obsession with his money, makes him the most interesting character seen on stage so far. And the vigor of his speech contrasts favorably with the pompous phrases of the young lovers.

6. Scene 3 is not an expository scene in the same way that Scenes 1 and 2 are. What, then, does it contribute to the play? We find out nothing in Scene 3 that we have not heard before, and so one could argue that it does not serve to move the plot forward. But it does *dramatize* Harpagon's stinginess, and, most importantly, it is the first major comic scene of the play. The first two expository scenes provide essential background information. But the third scene begins to *show* us, rather than *tell* us, what it means to be a miser. The persistence of Harpagon's questions, his extreme concern with his money, his almost unbelievable ability to find something suspicious in every remark and every item of clothing—all of these behaviors must be shown if we are to understand Molière's intention.

7. In Scene 4, we see the family together for the first time. How would you describe the relationship between the father and his children? The first thing we note is that any natural relationship has been overshadowed by Harpagon's suspicions. His first words to Élise and Cléante are "What is it?" and "Have you been here long?" We could understand that a master might suspect a servant of stealing, but when he treats his children in the same way, we become aware of just how obsessive his greed has become. And Harpagon's attempts to conceal the fact that he is wealthy are funny, though pathetic, because they only reinforce the notion that he is rich. Students may feel that the portrait has some realistic features, especially when Harpagon starts to attack the way that his children spend money. But this attack should be seen in the context of his obsession. Therefore it is difficult to know whether Cléante really is overdressed or whether the ribbons that cover him from "head to foot" actually consist of only one ribbon. (Of course, in viewing a production of the play, Cléante's dress would be apparent.) The major impression of the scene is probably the conflict that we see between father and son and between father and daughter. When Harpagon reveals that he is going to marry Marianne, Cléante walks offstage, thereby avoiding a confrontation. Élise, unexpectedly, reveals some assertiveness and argues that she would rather die than marry Anselme.

8. How is Harpagon's miserliness exhibited in his conversation with Valère in Scene 5? Scene 5 is referred to in French as the "sans dot" scene—the "without dowry" scene. We notice how Molière manages to use this phrase over and over again for comic effect; no matter what Valère says, Harpagon responds with the words "without dowry." A good actor can make the repetition of this line extremely funny. Perhaps Valère can even get a laugh by mouthing the line along with him, as he comes to realize that no argument will change Harpagon's mind. What makes the scene powerful, in addition to this comic device, is the contrast between Valère's sensible arguments and Harpagon's inability to hear any of these arguments so that he responds automatically, "without dowry." More than any other scene in this act, Scene 5 shows us the mechanical creature that Harpagon has become because of his avarice. His obsession has deprived him of reason, of the power to listen, and perhaps even of the power to speak.

9. What major plot complications are set up by the end of this act? These plot complications, expressed in the form of soap-opera questions, would be as follows: Will Valère and Élise get married? Will Harpagon marry Marianne, thus thwarting Cléante's happiness? Or will Cléante be able to stop him? Minor issues are also raised, such as the question of Valère's true identity, Harpagon's fear for his ten thousand crowns, La Flèche's resentment of Harpagon, and Cléante's need to get money for Marianne.

WORDS

A. Because students may find the style of language in the first two scenes of the play somewhat forbidding and cold, the questions in the student text are designed to suggest that dramatic purpose motivated Molière's choice of style. The difference between the language in the scenes with the young people who talk about love and the language in Harpagon's scene is quite noticeable. One begins to feel that Molière is deliberately using formal language to indicate the conventionality and even pretentiousness of the lovers. In this way the style serves to manipulate our feelings, to keep the play from being completely one sided. If the lovers were sympathetic both morally and theatrically, then Harpagon would seem a vicious and unlikable monster. But because his style is so alive and energetic and theirs is so pompous, we get an interesting balance. We find Harpagon interesting and funny, and we find the lovers somewhat wooden. We find him misguided and obsessive, but they sound priggish. We can't choose easily—and that is probably Molière's intention.

B. The two speeches mentioned, Valère's on page 337 and Harpagon's on page 341, are good examples of the differences in the kinds of words used by the two men. Valère continually talks in abstractions ("deeds," "love," "suspicions,") and even in exaggerations ("a thousand proofs"). Harpagon's speech is specific ("ribbons," "half a dozen pins," "wig,") and, of course, references to money. Valère deals with ideas/ideals whereas Harpagon deals with objects.

ACT II

PAGE 345

Glossary Words

usury (page 347, col. 1) An extremely high or unlawful rate of interest

niggardliness (page 347, col. 1) Stinginess; miserliness

insatiable (page 348, col. 1) Never satisfied; extremely greedy

extorts (page 348, col. 1) Obtains by threats, force, fraud, or illegal use of authority

adamant (page 349, col. 1) Firm and unyielding; immovable

fops (page 351, col. 1) Vain men who are very fond of fine clothes and have affected manners; dandies

Handbook

conflict

Check Test 39 (for Act II)

USING THE STUDY NOTES

ACT II PAGE 352

COMPLICATION: HARPAGON VERSUS CLÉANTE, FROSINE VERSUS HARPAGON

1. Act I focuses on two romantic problems. The reader might expect the second act to continue with these problems. Instead, Act II, Scene 1 concentrates on a different situation. What is it? Why does Molière take the play in this direction? A good playwright is predictable, but not completely so; surprise delights the audience. Act II opens by reminding us of the father/son conflict over Marianne, but it soon turns to the problem of Cléante's need for money. La Flèche describes in detail the contract that the lender has stipulated, thus building up our interest in the arrival of the agent, Master Simon, and the moneylender himself. The entrance of Harpagon and our sudden realization that *he* is the moneylender is thus even funnier because of the buildup to his entrance. On one level we are surprised that the lender is Harpagon; on a deeper level, we are not, because the scene fits with what we know of his character. The conflict between father and son now exists in two separate situations.

2. Frosine is a new character in the play. What do we find out about her in Scenes 4 and 5? Does she resemble anyone else in the play? What makes her different? Frosine depends on her wits to make her living, as her speech that begins "Following my usual occupation" reveals. Like Valère, she believes in the power of flattery ("As if I don't know how to get round men!") and trusts in her ability to manipulate Harpagon. What makes her especially interesting is her ability to find precisely the right thing to say at every moment. Frosine also has a wonderful imagination and is able to invent details about Marianne designed to convince Harpagon that she will be the perfect wife for him. Possessing special characteristics, she is unlike any other person in the play. Students may want to speculate about Frosine's age; it seems likely that she is close to Harpagon in age, a fact that would make him more likely to trust her.

3. In what ways does the second act increase the tension in the father/son conflict? In the first act, we see father and son competing for the same woman. In the second act, they appear in new and equally unsuitable roles, as moneylender and borrower. There would seem to be no chance for reconciliation and no hope that Cléante, having so angered Harpagon, will ever get his father's permission to marry Marianne.

4. What does Molière do to make Frosine's deception of Harpagon believable? What techniques does she employ? First, Molière creates Harpagon as a character susceptible to flattery. Like Valère, Frosine knows that Harpagon likes to be agreed with. (An interesting point of discussion would be the possible relationship between Harpagon's desire to control everything and everybody and his need to be appreciated and loved. Consider also the factor of age.) Note that Frosine begins the meeting with small talk that flatters Harpagon, telling him how well he looks and how long he will live. Rather than introduce the subject herself, she makes him ask, "And how is our little business getting on?" And when she describes Marianne, she does so in concrete detail—the very way to appeal to a man whose speech is so full of details. She does not talk in generalities, as Valère does, but lists the money that Marianne will *not* spend. She invents the detail of the fifty-six-year-old man whom Marianne refused to marry. Always she speaks in terms that Harpagon understands, even launching an attack on young people, an attack that we have heard from Harpagon in the first act.

What difference does it make that Scene 5 comes after Harpagon's confrontation with Cléante? After the confrontation with Cléante, which angers Harpagon extremely, he is perhaps even more susceptible to flattery by Frosine. Because he is preoccupied with thoughts of revenge on his son, he is probably less careful about choosing a wife than he would ordinarily be. One might also wonder if, in spite of his disclaimer of shame in Scene 5, he may not be a little embarrassed; after all, trying to lend money at exorbitant prices to one's own son is shameful. The emotions of anger, revenge, and shame cloud his thinking and thus make him especially vulnerable to Frosine's clever manipulation.

ACT III PAGE 352

Glossary Words

veritable (page 353, col. 2) True; real; actual; genuine; authentic

frugality (page 353, col. 2) Avoidance of waste; thrift; economy

precept (page 354, col. 1) Rule of action or behavior; a maxim

firmament (page 356, col. 2) The heavens; the sky

repugnant (page 357, col. 1) Disagreeable or offensive; distasteful; objectionable

dilemma (page 357, col. 1) A difficult choice; a predicament; also, a situation requiring a choice between two alternatives, which are or appear equally unfavorable

Handbook

climax, conflict, plot

***Check Test 40** (for Act III)*

USING THE STUDY NOTES

ACT III PAGE 359

COMPLICATION: HARPAGON AS LOVER

1. At the beginning of Act III, we suddenly find many people on stage—more than we have seen before (or will see, until the end of the play). What are the theatrical effects thus achieved? What does Scene 1 add to the portrait of the miser? So far, the play has progressed primarily through scenes involving only a few characters. If students look back at the first two acts, they will see that usually there are two or sometimes three characters talking to each other but rarely more. By suddenly bringing in additional characters, all of them comic and stupid servants, Molière changes the pace of the play and the tempo of the action. Students should consider whether it is believable for Harpagon to have so many servants. Point out the dramatic advantage of having many servants: A large household gives a stingy man more things to worry about. Molière, having shown us how Harpagon's greed affects his relationship with his children, now shows us, again through dramatic detail, how it colors even the most trivial of incidents. All the specific ways in which Harpagon tries to save money increase our sense of his obsession—and show us its pettiness at the same time.

2. What new plot complication is introduced in the first two scenes? Does it seem extraneous or can you imagine how it will be connected to the other major plot conflicts? At the end of the first scene and in the second scene, Molière develops the antagonism between Master Jacques, who doubles as cook and coachdriver (another sign of Harpagon's stinginess) and Valère, the steward. On first reading, this conflict may seem merely an extra detail, but students should be encouraged to see its importance. First, because the two opening acts have focused almost entirely on the problems of Cléante, it is now time for Valère's love affair and *his* problems to be dramatized. Rather than repeat the conflict that we have seen between the young lover and the older man, Molière creates a different kind of antagonist for Valère in Master Jacques. Second, Master Jacques's objections to Valère as flatterer (see p. 354) may mirror our own and thus deflect them; because Master Jacques objects for biased reasons to Valère's behavior, Valère may look better to us. Third, this conflict reinforces our sense of Valère as a force in the play, as someone to be interested in. And the argument here will be remembered when students come to the fifth act and the loss of the cashbox.

3. The climax of the act is the meeting of Harpagon, Marianne, and Cléante. How has Molière created anticipation for this scene? Students will be interested in seeing Marianne, if only to discover what she is like, especially after having heard her described by Cléante, Harpagon, and Frosine. We should note that Molière cleverly creates a situation in which Marianne does not know who Cléante is (Scene 4). Thus, in addition to wondering how Harpagon will react to Marianne and how Harpagon and Cléante will respond to each other after their argument, there is the delight of wondering what Marianne will do when she finds out that the "very attractive" young man whom she is in love with is the son of the man whom she is supposed to marry.

WORDS

This question of subtext deals with Scene 7 in which Marianne and Cléante address one another. Consider the double levels working through the language. Cléante manages first to let Marianne know that he is shocked at the embarrassing situation. She lets him know that she is similarly unhappily surprised. Their first two speeches sound to Harpagon, however, as if they are merely being formal. Cléante reassures Marianne of his love for her in the speech beginning, "Truly, madam, my father could have made no better choice." Yet, because of the previous conflict with his father, this speech may sound to Harpagon as if he is insulting Marianne. And Marianne can compliment Cléante, "I value such an avowal coming from him," letting him know that she understands his vow of constancy and yet sounding as if she is being polite to her fiancé's son. Cléante's second tactic in the scene is to switch from his position of being "difficult" to being superfriendly. He thus expresses his own feelings of love to Marianne while covering them with the excuse, "I am addressing the lady on your behalf." Still pleading politeness and accord with his father, Cléante can ask for refreshments to be brought in and even get the diamond ring from his father's hand—all as a way of showing his "affection" for his new stepmother-to-be. The change from "insult" to "affection" is cleverly managed; under either guise, he can let Marianne know what he feels and still keep his father unaware of his true feelings.

This would be a marvelous scene for students to stage in order to dramatize how beautifully the double meanings work.

ACT IV

PAGE 359

Glossary Words (for Act IV)

propriety (page 359, col. 2) Proper behavior; seemliness

irresistible (page 360, col. 2) Too great to be withstood; overwhelming

coquette (page 361, col. 1) A woman who tries to attract men merely to please her vanity; a flirt

audacity (page 362, col. 1) Rude boldness; impudence

Handbook

conflict, stage action

Check Test 41 (for Act IV)

USING THE STUDY NOTES

ACT IV

PAGE 365

COMPLICATON: CLÉANTE LOSES MARIANNE AND HARPAGON LOSES HIS CASHBOX

1. What are the possible solutions offered to Cléante's and Marianne's problems in Scene 1? How successful do you think they might be? Two solutions are suggested: *(a)* that Marianne persuade her mother to let her marry Cléante; *(b)* that Frosine find an elderly woman to impersonate a wealthy member of the nobility who wants to marry Harpagon, the assumption being that he, impressed by her "wealth," would break his engagement to Marianne. The first suggestion, it is implied, may succeed because Marianne's mother "isn't altogether unreasonable." The second sounds more complicated but possible because we have already seen that Harpagon is susceptible to flattery and, as Frosine says to Marianne, ". . . though I know he loves you very much, he loves money better."

2. Most of the act focuses on the Harpagon/Cléante conflict (Scenes 3, 4, and 5). What are the stages of this conflict? Why is it different from their previous arguments? The problems begin when Harpagon sees Cléante kissing Marianne's hand; his suspicions are aroused, and he decides to try to find out "Is there more in this than meets the eye?" In Scene 3 Harpagon cunningly leads Cléante to avow his love for Marianne, resulting in a violent dispute between father and son. Scene 4 sees them reconciled—but falsely so because the reconciliation was brought about through lies told by Master Jacques. In Scene 5 there is a bitter dispute once again. The arguments in Act IV are the longest and the most bitter thus far in the play. Because Harpagon has lured Cléante into revealing his true feelings, the son is more vulnerable to his father. Thus, when Cléante finds out that he cannot have Marianne, he is truly angry; he seems to have no other power, no hidden knowledge that he can use.

3. Consider Scene 4, involving Harpagon, Cléante, and Master Jacques. To what extent does the scene depend on visualizing the stage and the space separating Harpagon and Cléante? What kinds of comic devices are used in this scene? Clearly this scene must be imagined, preferably even staged. We need to see Harpagon and Cléante physically separated, just as they are mentally and emotionally opposed. And we need to see Master Jacques trotting back and forth between the two. Molière is using the device of comic repetition, the back-and-forth movement, together with the buildup of misunderstanding. The act ends on a note of deception: Harpagon tells Master Jacques that he deserves a reward, reaches into his pocket, and comes out with a handkerchief!

4. What has Molière done to prepare us for La Flèche's entrance with the money? What has he done to distract us from that possibility so that it comes as a surprise? From the first mention of money in Act I, when La Flèche asks if Harpagon has hidden money and Harpagon's obsession with money is established, we know that the buried money may be stolen. La Flèche's irritation with Harpagon is also suggested in the first act when Harpagon searches him, so that we can expect La Flèche to want to "get back at" his master. Molière drops the hints of a La Flèche/Harpagon conflict early in the play and then distracts us from thinking about it with the other conflicts. We fit the details about the money into the pattern of Harpagon's general obsession. Because so much of the play focuses on the love relationships and the problems stemming from them, we tend to forget about the buried money. Thus we are surprised, as is Harpagon, when the money is taken—and yet we feel that "we knew it all along."

5. Look at Harpagon's speech in the last scene of this act. How does this speech exemplify Harpagon's obsession? Does it make the audience at all sympathetic toward him, or does it just make him seem ridiculous? Harpagon's extreme reactions, including his feeling that he has been murdered, for he equates robbery with murder, accords with his behavior throughout the play. He feels more emotion for his money than for Marianne, and he speaks of the money as if it were a woman, "Oh dear, my dear, darling money, my beloved, they've taken you away from me and now you are gone I have lost my strength, my joy and my consolation." He seems ridiculous as he grabs his own arm in his excitement, threatening to hang himself if the money is not returned.

But there is something else in this scene, too, beginning with the second part of the speech, "What a crowd in here!" On one level, the character could be hallucinating, and we feel sorry that his loss has driven him to such extremes. On another level, Molière is playing a game with the audience, for Harpagon is clearly looking at the audience ("the crowd"), referring to their reactions ("What's that noise up there?" "They are all looking at me." "Now they are laughing."), and imploring them/us for help ("Please, I implore you, tell me if you know anything about him!"). As he says, we are "beyond question, all involved in the robbery." This direct reference to the audience works in at least two ways. First, his speaking of the "crowd" and our realization that he refers both to his hallucination and to the real audience is funny—a kind of language joke. It also makes us figures in the play—people who are being spoken to, who are imagined as responding; we are no longer merely spectators, and so we feel that we inhabit Harpagon's world and therefore can have some sympathy for this driven man.

ACT V — PAGE 365

Glossary Words (for Act V)

dastardly (page 367, col. 1) Mean and cowardly; sneaking

effrontery (page 370, col. 1) Shameless boldness; impudence; insolence

remnants (page 370, col. 2) Small parts that are left; fragments

depositions (page 370, col. 2) Sworn statements in writing

Handbook

plot, stage action, theme

Check Test 42 (for Act V)

USING THE STUDY NOTES

ACT V — PAGE 372

RESOLUTION

1. Act V, Scene 3 is a scene constructed almost solely on a single misunderstanding. What is that misunderstanding? How does it relate to a major theme of the play? When Harpagon accuses Valère of "the foulest, most dastardly crime that was ever committed," Harpagon is referring to the theft of the money, but Valère thinks that Harpagon is referring to the love affair between himself and Élise.

Their talking at cross purposes creates a very amusing dialogue. It is significant that the whole conversation, which revolves around Valère's love, can be so misunderstood by Harpagon because it shows us again the way in which all of his affection has been transferred from what should be its natural objects, other people, to his money.

2. The stage becomes progressively filled with people as the act continues; no one leaves and more people enter. What is the theatrical effect of the increasing number of people on stage? Students may want to compare this act to the finale of a symphony, when the music often picks up in intensity and the entire orchestra frequently plays. Here we have the sense that everyone concerned with events is coming on stage so that all misunderstandings will finally be cleared up. The visual impact conveys the impression that Harpagon, who has dominated the stage until now, will no longer be able to make his obsessions prevail.

3. Anselme's appearance is necessary to resolve a number of plot complications. How has his appearance been prepared for? Does it seem believable? If not, does it seem appropriate for the play? Anselme's appearance (hinted at in Act I:1 by Valère's account of his background and in Act I:5 by Anselme's indentification as Élise's suitor) has sometimes been criticized as a kind of *deus ex machina* resolution of the plot, as if Molière had written himself into a corner. Students may remember that a happy ending has been suggested in the first scene in Act IV, in which Frosine, Marianne, and Cléante devise several strategems. But Molière does not use these. Instead, he deliberately creates, through the presence of one man, a multiple resolution: Anselme finds that he is Valère's father and therefore will not compete for Élise's favors; he is also Marianne's father and therefore can give his consent to her marriage with Cléante; he can rescue Marianne's mother, his long-lost wife. from poverty; and he reveals that Valère is wealthy and wellborn rather than a steward. Students may find the "happiness" of this happy ending unbelievable in its specifics — but it is appropriate in the way that the ending of a fairy tale is appropriate. This play, although dealing with the real world, has continuously given us an exaggerated picture — as a fairy tale does — and thus it is appropriate that the ending be as extreme as the actions of Harpagon have been.

4. Do you see any changes in Harpagon in the last scene? To balance the unreality of Anselme, Molière shows us that Harpagon does not really change. He is still haggling about money, worrying about who will pay the dowries, who will buy new clothes for the wedding, who will pay the officer for his time; he is still the same obsessed person. And while the lovers are planning marriage and Anselme is planning to see his wife again, Harpagon's reunion will be with his "beloved cashbox."

USING THE STUDY NOTES PAGE 372

I. LAUGHTER AND SERIOUS IDEAS

In this section students are asked to relate the ideas of *The Miser* to the problems presented in *Antigone* and *Macbeth.* Students may have felt very involved in the conflict of wills expressed in those two plays, but Molière—unlike Sophocles and Shakespeare—makes the conflict in *The Miser* funny rather than serious. He does this by moving Harpagon into direct competition with Cléante, so that in addition to all the *normal* conflicts of a father/son relationship (spending money, buying expensive clothes, not following a parent's wishes), there is the *abnormal* conflict of a parent competing with his child for the love of a young woman. That one change moves the conflict from the familiar into the extreme—and because Harpagon is so unlikely a suitor, the situation becomes funny. If we believed that Harpagon might actually marry Marianne, the conflict would have tragic overtones; but because the proposed marriage seems so improbable, we cannot imagine that it will ever take place. Moreover, the presence of Frosine, a clever woman who helps the lovers, reassures us that everything will turn out all right in the end.

The ambition that drives Macbeth and the avarice that drives Harpagon are similar quests for power, but their actions are not completely alike. One difference lies in the reasons behind their drives for power: Macbeth wants the throne, not because he values the crown as a physical object, but because he wants the power that the crown conveys. Harpagon, although wanting power, really is in love with physical objects (the golden coins stored in his buried cashbox). The major difference, however, lies in the range of feelings that we perceive in Macbeth: his own awareness of his behavior and his horror at what he plans to do, his capability for goodness, which is turned into evil, and his deep concern for spiritual values. Harpagon, as Penelope Gilliatt's excerpt suggests, has been stripped of all admirable characteristics. We note that his wife, the mother of Cléante and Élise, is dead. Surely, this fact is not only a convenience for the plot. It is a necessary subtraction, for the presence of a wife would make us feel that Harpagon is capable of loving and of being loved. Molière wants us to infer that he is not. By taking away from Harpagon any display of reasonable behavior, by adding a large dose of suspicion and gullibility to his avaricious nature, by making him respond immediately to whatever anyone says (rather than resorting to soliloquy as Macbeth often does), Molière turns the desire for money and power into a comic rather than a tragic failing.

II. IMPLICATIONS

1. Discuss the following quotations from the play. They were written more than 300 years ago, but are they still true today?

a. Valère: "The best way to win people's favor is to pretend to agree with them, to fall in with their precepts, encourage their foibles and applaud whatever they do." Valère himself uses all parts of this formula to curry favor with Harpagon. He agrees with Harpagon that children must obey their parents. He applauds his cleverness in getting Élise married without dowry and insists that guests should be served a frugal supper. He flatters Harpagon by always taking his side, no matter what the issue. Some students may think that this kind of pretense is a poor way to get what one wants, that sooner or later such deception will boomerang. Others may insist that the method is acceptable in certain situations.

b. Cléante: "What use will money be to us if it only comes when we are too old to enjoy it?" The reactions of students will probably vary. There may be many who side with Cléante. It is a characteristic aspect of the generation gap for young people to feel that they can get more enjoyment out of having money than can older people. To bring the point home, change *money* to *sports car* and see the reaction. There may be other students who will argue that Cléante ought to earn his own money instead of trying to wangle money from his father. Be sure that the class considers the period in which this play was written. In that era wealthy young men were expected to pursue arts and culture rather than money. Is the situation much different today?

c. Valère: "Yes, money is the most precious thing in all the world." Valère makes this statement as part of his campaign to ingratiate himself with Harpagon. Because he professes to be so much in love with Élise that he took the low-paying job of steward in her father's household to be near her, it would seem unlikely that he really believes what he says. What about the contemporary world? Where does money stand in the scale of importance? How would the class rank money on a list of most precious things?

d. Valère: "One should eat to live and not live to eat." It is surprising to have this statement expressed in a play hundreds of years old because nutritionists are using exactly the same motto today. Ask the class to consider "junk foods" (potato chips, soda pop, and so on). Is there anything wrong in enjoying the taste and the texture of certain foods even though they give little nourishment? Consider also the importance of food in connection with holidays, Thanksgiving for example. Could moderation be the answer?

e. Harpagon: "Would you mind telling me what people say about me?" Master Jacques: "...you'll be angry." Harpagon: "On the contrary, I shall enjoy it. I like to know what people are saying about me." Note what happens in the play. Harpagon claims to be eager to hear what people are saying about him, but when Master Jacques reveals that their remarks are deprecating, nasty, almost libelous, he beats his servant. When we say that we want to know what others have said about us, most of us only want to hear favorable remarks. A member of the class may have read about (or heard of) someone who asked for the truth and, although it was unpalatable, acted upon the information in order to change himself or herself. How individual students react should engender a lively discussion.

f. Master Jacques: "I suspect him on the grounds—that I suspect him." The law in the United States mandates that a person shall be assumed innocent until proved guilty. But in our everyday personal relations do we ever make judgments about others without much evidence for doing so? Karas in "The Stamp Collection" suspects Lojzik of stealing his stamps and breaks off their friendship. Students may offer examples of other instances in which an individual succumbs to this human foible of condemning another person on suspicion only.

2. Consider the following characters and discuss whom each is trying to manipulate, why, and how. Does the manipulator play on the other person's foibles?

Harpagon tries to manipulate almost everyone whom he comes in contact with. His approach is head-on, not subtle. He orders Élise to marry Anselme and Cléante to marry an old widow. He no longer wants to support his children, and he wants them out of his house because of his plan to marry Marianne. He orders his servants to do impossible things, simply because of his miserliness. Only once does he use artifice: in the scene when he manipulates Cléante to confess his love for Marianne.

Valère is trying to manipulate Harpagon in order to gain his permission to marry Élise. He does this by using each of the methods that he, himself, suggests (see question 1a). He certainly plays on each of Harpagon's foibles, including the most important one—his greed.

Cléante is trying to get his father to let him marry Marianne. Harpagon creates a terrible problem for his son when he announces that he himself intends to marry her. In the scene in which Harpagon introduces Cléante and Marianne, Cléante certainly employs subtlety in telling Marianne of his love for her. He inveigles her into taking his father's diamond ring, perhaps hoping to make his father angry with her. Cléante tries to get Frosine to help him to marry Marianne, but he asks for her help in a very straightforward fashion.

Master Jacques's first attempt at manipulation occurs when he is asked to decide whether Harpagon or Cléante should marry Marianne. By lying to each of them, he gives each the impression that the other has agreed to withdraw and let him marry the young woman. Thus, Master Jacques gets himself out of a sticky situation. In attempting to get back at Valère for beating him, Master Jacques suggests to Harpagon and the officer that it is Valère who has stolen the cashbox, hoping that Valère will go to prison.

Frosine is trying to maneuver Harpagon into giving her some money for her services as a go-between in his proposed marriage to Marianne. She flatters him by praising his pinned-up breaches, by telling him that he is quite irresistible, and by admiring his old-fashioned ruff. She lies to him in saying that Marianne adores old men and that she finds Harpagon's glasses attractive. Frosine attempts to manipulate Marianne into marrying Harpagon by telling her that it is better to marry an old man with plenty of money than a young man who is poor. She also tells Marianne that Harpagon will probably die within three months of the wedding.

3. Consider the following relationships in the play. Who wins out? With whom do you sympathize? This is a question for which there is no right or wrong answer. The following ideas suggest possible reactions:

a. Father/son. Most students will side with the son in the dispute over who should marry Marianne. Had Harpagon won, the end could have been tragic. Again, most students will probably want Élise to marry Valère rather than his father. Even Anselme seemed happy at this ending.

b. Master/servant. La Flèche finds exactly the right method to get back at Harpagon for his ridiculous suspicions. He steals his cashbox. Most students will be on his side. Master Jacques seems always to do or to say the wrong thing and is consequently often in trouble. He is the typical dullard whom writers use as a comic foil. Few readers will feel much sympathy for him.

c. Schemer/victim. Valère is the schemer and Harpagon the victim in the young man's campaign to flatter Harpagon in order to win Élise. Valère wins out, but not because of his obsequious behavior; chance rewards him. Some students may sympathize with Harpagon because of Valère's deception. Frosine schemes to get a marriage fee from Harpagon, but when she realizes that her chances of doing so are slight, she decides to try to get a fee from Marianne's mother. When she discovers that Cléante and Marianne are in love, she devises a new scheme: She will get an older woman to impersonate a rich member of the nobility and pretend love for Harpagon in the hope that he will break his engagement to Marianne. In the end, everyone seems to win but Frosine. Some students may feel sorry for her.

4. Students are asked to give their reactions to each of the following statements:

a. Valère is just as wily as Harpagon. Although Valère is young and attractive, the means that he uses to try to attain his ends show him to be as wily as Harpagon. The difference in their maneuverings is that Valère's is done for love and Harpagon's for greed. Valère's actions generally hurt no one, but some of Harpagon's schemes could be called unethical (lending money at exorbitant rates, for example). That one kind of maneuvering may be worse than another is a matter of opinion.

b. Molière seems to be saying that people do not change; they continuously repeat the same follies and foibles. When you look at the cast of characters, no change is evident. At the end of the play, they are basically the same people that they were at the beginning.

c. Harpagon's foibles make him suspicious of everyone else. This is a true picture of how our faults cause us to misjudge other people. Students may feel that they themselves are very fair in their judgments of others. If there have been any recent events in the community or at school in which someone has been wrongly accused, it would be good to analyze the circumstances of the accusation. Remind students of the misjudgments made by characters in "To Please His Wife," "The Stamp Collection," and possibly "The Guest." When we misjudge others, it is often because of some weakness in our own character: for example, jumping to conclusions, being too lazy to investigate facts, letting fear rule reason.

d. The play implies that you can get what you want by flattery. The play does show people trying to get what they want through flattery, but it is not flattery that eventually leads to success. Valère, Jacques, and Frosine all try flattery on Harpagon and fail. Of these three, only Valère succeeds in getting what he wants (Élise's hand), and he does that because of the chance appearance of Anselme.

e. Harpagon's final speech at the end of Act IV can be delivered in such a manner that it elicits the audience's sympathy, not laughter. Ask students to volunteer to give this speech, some trying for comic effects, others trying to gain sympathy. The really great actors who have played the part of Harpagon have usually attempted to broaden the character of Harpagon by showing him to be a somewhat pathetic creature.

III. TECHNIQUES

Characterization

1. How would you define each of the major characters in the play? For each, think of (1) an adjective that describes the character and (2) an objective that the character wants. Do you see any distinct categories emerging? How does Harpagon fit into these categories?

Valère: cunning, smooth, hypocritical, masked, persuasive. Objective: to marry Élise.

Élise: timid, defiant. Objective: to marry Valère.

Cléante: extravagant, sentimental, foolish. Objective: to marry Marianne.

Marianne: graceful, malleable, polite. Objective: to marry Cléante.

Frosine: clever, scheming, manipulative. Objectives: to deceive Harpagon, to make money, to help Cléante and Élise.

La Flèche: resentful, moderately clever. Objective: to get back at Harpagon.

Master Jacques: pompous, irritable, resentful. Objective: to get back at Valère.

Harpagon: suspicious, greedy, susceptible to flattery. Objectives: to keep money and power, to marry Marianne, to control his children.

Students may find other adjectives and objectives for some of the characters. The noticeable thing is that the characters can be classified into two broad groups, those who want to get married and those who want to deceive, control, or get revenge on another person. Harpagon fits both of these categories; although he is the most unrealistic character in the play, he is also the most inclusive one.

2. How are flat characters useful in creating comic situations? What makes them successful as comic characters? Comedy usually occurs when the audience feels intellectually ahead of what is happening on stage, when they know something that a character does not know and which that character will subsequently be embarrassed by not knowing. Thus characters with limited perceptions set up these comic situations—Cléante's being deceived by Harpagon's "kindness" in Act IV, or Valère's not understanding the "crime" that Harpagon is talking about in Act V. Throughout the play, the limitation of vision grows directly out of the character's mental and moral qualities: Because Harpagon wants to get married, he fails to see that Frosine is lying to him; because Cléante wants to marry Marianne, he does not see Harpagon's trap; because Master Jacque's feelings have been hurt by Valère's interference, Master Jacques is willing to make ridiculous statements to implicate Valère in the stealing of the money.

3. What is our relationship to these characters? How involved do we become (or can we become) with their problems? Laughter almost always implies detachment; if our feelings are deeply concerned, we do not laugh at someone in a difficult situation. The play continuously demands objectivity; it asks us to look *at* the problems, to be amused, and not to become emotionally involved with the characters. Because we see so many characters pursuing the same kinds of goals, we tend to see them as interchangeable and thus are not individually involved with Cléante, Élise, Valère, or Marianne—although we may be generally sympathetic to the idea of young lovers. One could argue that the attempt to make these characters flat is a deliberate one, so that we will laugh instead of cry, so that we will find Harpagon's behavior ridiculous rather than horrifying. If Harpagon really threatened either the characters on the stage or us, he would be an actual monster; as it is, he is a comic character.

The Multiple Plot

1. How many separate plots can you find in this play? Valère and Élise want to get married. Cléante and Marianne want to get married. Harpagon wants to get married and employs the services of Frosine. La Flèche steals Harpagon's money. As a minor plot, Master Jacques wants to get revenge on Valère.

2. How would we feel if there were only one story, for example, Harpagon's attempt to marry Marianne? What would happen to our feelings about the characters? If there were only one story, the characters would have to be more complicated individuals (round rather than flat) in order to sustain the audience's interest. Having a number of stories makes it possible to present a variety of plot incidents that grow out of the various stories rather than out of the depth of characterization. If the play dealt only with Harpagon's attempt to marry Marianne, the threat that Harpagon *would* marry Marianne (and thus eliminate Cléante's chances for happiness) would become stronger, and the play would probably become a melodrama rather than a comedy. By giving us a number of stories, Molière compartmentalizes our interest and asks us to consider a number of characters. We therefore have less time to get involved with any one character and can more easily remain detached. This is a general principle in comedy, which usually offers us at least two pairs of lovers (think of Shakespeare's *A Midsummer Night's Dream* or *Twelfth Night).* Comedy is thus opposed to tragedy, which usually focuses on the problems of a single individual. In the case of *The Miser,* Harpagon is the title character but not as an individual; he is a type, a representative of human greed.

3. How do the multiple plots expand the thematic range of the play? Each of the major characters in this play is involved in trying to get something or someone. This is not merely a play about a miser but about what the desire to control people does to everyone. Valère is forced to turn into a toadying servant, Marianne and Cléante learn to deceive Harpagon, La Flèche lies and steals—no one is completely innocent. Harpagon, of course, is the major offender, and it can be argued that his actions cause these other acts. But by showing us a world in which people are motivated by self-interest and by showing us how self-interest interacts in a number of stories, Molière is inviting us to express our laughter and to extend our perceptions to a variety of people.

Organization of Incidents

1. What incidents does Molière choose to leave offstage? Why? We hear about but do not see the incidents of Valère saving Élise from drowning, of Cléante meeting Marianne, of La Flèche meeting Master Simon to arrange the loan, of the stealing of the money, and of Marianne's convincing her mother to let her marry Cléante. The first two incidents would be rather sentimental scenes that could involve us too much in the problems of the lovers as lovers. The meeting of La Flèche and Master Simon is a necessary incident, but it is probably more effective and more humorous to hear about it and simultaneously to see Cléante's reaction to it; thus Molière gives us the information and compresses two scenes (the setting up of the contract and Cléante's hearing about it) into one. The stealing of the cashbox is meant to come as a surprise and therefore needs to be offstage. Marianne's appeal to her mother could be another sentimental scene that would slow down the action just when the play is moving toward its conclusion. It is thus better kept offstage.

2. What scenes function as "set-up" scenes? Do they have any other function (such as giving time for other plots to develop or preventing the situation on-stage from getting too serious)? In addition to the first two scenes, which set up the general background of the play, Molière deliberately uses certain scenes to create comedy and to provide change. Act I, Scene 3, introduces Harpagon, sets up the Harpagon/La Flèche conflict (which will lead to the stealing of the money), and prevents the play from turning into a sloshy romantic comedy. The broad physical comedy involved in Harpagon's searching of La Flèche is part of the mechanism at work here. In Act II, Scene 5, Frosine's setup of Harpagon for his meeting with Marianne relieves the tension after the father/son confrontation. Act III, Scene 1 is a broadly comic scene that sets up the events of the third act and also creates the conflict between Master Jacques and Valère. Scene 2, in which Valère and Master Jacques chase each other across the stage, continues the physical comedy and serves as a relief for the entrance of Marianne. In Act IV, Scene 4, Master Jacques's "reconciliation" of father and son is a deliberately created comic routine, designed to relieve the pressure of their apparently unsolvable argument. Act V, Scenes 1 and 2 set up the misunderstanding of Scene 3: Without them that long stretch of double meanings in the conversation between Harpagon and Valère would have been impossible.

3. How would you justify the placement of the scene in which the money is stolen? Could it come earlier in the play or not? As soon as we hear about the buried money, we should suspect that it will be stolen. However, if the money had been stolen early in the play, Harpagon would not have been able to think of anything else. The theft of the money must occur later in the play to give Harpagon time to imagine himself as Marianne's suitor and to concentrate on wooing her. Because money is so central to Harpagon's thinking, the theft is the real shock; by positioning the theft late in the play, Molière saves it for the climactic event that will force the various plot strands to come together.

IV. WORDS

A. Words in context. All of the words should be understandable in context. Short definitions follow:

foreboding (I:1): fearful suspicion
solicitude (I:1): careful attention
unremitting (I:1): unceasing
subservience (I:1): slavish obedience
ingratiate (I:1): make agreeable
arbiters (I:2): decision makers; judges
vouchsafe (I:2): give; allow
sumptuous (I:4): rich, elegant
precipitate (I:5): hurried
disparity (I:5): difference
usury (II:2): moneylending, usually for exorbitant interest
insatiable (II:2): unable to be satisfied
adamant (II:4): hard-hearted; immovable
frugality (III:1): careful thrift
irresistible (IV:1): impossible to turn down
epithets (V:3): names

B. Master Jacques's speech (pp. 354-355) is believable primarily because it is a collection of specific details. In addition, these details correspond to events that we have already seen. Asking the cook to prepare a dinner for eight people that will serve ten people happens onstage earlier in this act and thus connects with the detail of the special calendar printed with extra fast days. Ignoring Frosine's request for money at the end of Act II justifies the line about Harpagon's picking a quarrel with servants when they are owed presents or are leaving. The detail about stealing oats from his own horse reminds us of the complaint that the horses and the servants get very little to eat—and foreshadows Harpagon's threat at the end of Act IV to arrest and hang himself because the cashbox has been stolen. The strategy of Master Jacques's speech is twofold:

It creates a very specific picture through the use of details, and those details are believable because they are similar to actions that we have already seen on stage.

The Influence of the Aristocracy on Snobs PAGE 375

William Makepeace Thackeray

Glossary Words

orthodoxy (page 375, col. 1) The holding of correct or generally accepted religious beliefs; also, conforming to established customs and traditions

truckling (page 375, col. 1) Cringing; submitting tamely

prodigious (page 376, col. 2) Enormous; monstrous; marvelous; wonderful

perpetuated (page 376, col. 2) Preserved forever; caused to be continuous

Handbook

irony, prose style, setting

Check Test 43

INTRODUCTION

Thackeray's main point is that society in England is so structured that snobbery is inescapable—"it is impossible. . . not to be sometimes a Snob." In particular it is the creation of a class, the peerage, that is responsible for increasing, encouraging, and maintaining snobbery. How can Lords and Ladies not think themselves superior to ordinary people when everyone treats them as though they were and when the peerage is treated like a sacred institution in England? In this essay, Thackeray supports his anti-snobbery position with many well-chosen and specific instances of snobbery.

There are two problems that you may have in teaching this essay. One is that students may not see how the essay is relevant to life in America. The other problem is that students not familiar with English society may have some difficulty understanding the essay.

The first problem is addressed in the Study Notes. Also, you could suggest to students that they think about the "peerage" that exists in the United States.

The second problem can be eased by providing some background for the students. In particular, they should understand what Thackeray means by the peerage. In England, a peer is a person who has a title: Duke, Duchess; Marquis, Marchioness; Earl, Countess; Viscount, Viscountess; Baron, Baroness—in descending order. Any person who possesses one of these titles may serve in the House of Lords of the English Parliament, although in Thackeray's day only men did so.

One may gain a title in various ways—Thackeray lists some of the ways on page 376. In his time, once a title was conferred, it was passed on through the eldest son. The younger sons were not given titles freely, but, as Thackeray notes, they were likely to be showered with all sorts of preferments. (Recently, however, the hereditary peerage was abolished.)

Finally, it may be advisable to define *snob* or to have your students look it up. They should know that the term refers both to people who consider themselves superior and refuse to associate with those below themselves *and* to people who seek association with their superiors and idolize and imitate them.

USING THE STUDY NOTES PAGE 379

I. ARE WE ALL SNOBS?

Students are asked which of the following statements best sums up this essay:

1. Thackeray is attacking the aristocrats for their foolish assumption that their rank makes them great and noble, deserving of adulation.

2. Thackeray is attacking the "little people" who by their worship make aristocrats arrogant and overbearing.

Thackeray is obviously attacking both types of people; they represent the two sides of snobbery. He seems to be saying that people of the second type are the main cause of the first. It is mainly against the first type that he launches specific attacks, but he also disparages the second type. In the case of the Marchioness of ———, for instance, he attacks her—or lets her attack herself—by quoting her. But he also notes that she would not have said what she did out of her "natural heart." It was the habit of "trucking and cringing" on the part of those around her that was indirectly responsible for her attitude.

This question should help students to see the two sides of snobbery very clearly, especially if there are some students who cite statement 1 and others who cite statement 2. Have them present their differing points of view so that the proponents of each can see the other side.

II. IMPLICATIONS

Students are asked to react to the following statements, justifying their opinions by examples.

1. There are as many snobs today as in Thackeray's time, but they worship money, fame, science, athletics, and celebrities, instead of the nobility. Students should have no difficulty seeing this similarity, and they should also note that it is not merely a matter of worshiping these *things* but also involves worshiping the *people* who have money and fame.

Advertisers frequently resort to snobbery to appeal to much of our society that is concerned with what and who is "in" or "out." It would be very difficult, indeed, to prove that there are fewer snobs in the United States today than there were in Thackeray's England.

2. It is a foible in human nature that people need to stand in awe of somebody. This statement seems true. In looking for reasons, however, students may be less successful than in finding "institutions" that provide objects that people can stand in awe of: kings and nobles, popes and priests, executives and boards—everywhere in life there seem to be such objects.

One of the sources of our need for awe-inspiring objects may be the early parent/child relationship—a relationship in which the child stands in awe of the parent.

3. A person must be little in soul and mind to be a snob. What is meant here is the fawning, imitative type of snob. The fact that a person feels others to be superior suggests some kind of littleness in that person's character. People with "big" characters do not need to fawn and imitate.

4. The amount of space devoted in American newspapers to the doings of European royalty shows that Thackeray's point of view is true for our time as well as for his. There does seem to be much space devoted to European royalty, but students may also note the amount of space given to those contemporary American "peers," the so-called jet set. Thackeray's point of view is doubtlessly valid today.

III. TECHNIQUES

Setting

Students are asked to reflect on the essay and to try to remember "scenes." Then they are asked what impressions they have of the background or the setting. Finally, they should reread these scenes to discover how many details were actually given and how many they supplied with their own imaginations.

The answers to this question are certain to vary widely. Some students may not be able to recall any scenes, whereas others may well fill in Thackeray's scenes with all sorts of rich details.

Thackeray is very sparing with details, *but* he does use proper names that are very likely to provoke the reader's imagination. Consider the following, for instance: Grand Cairo, European Royal Prince, Indiawards—all of which are used to introduce the episode of the young prince—and Brussels, Hotel de Belle Vue, Hotel de France, Mission, the Rocher at Paris, and a *diner en gourmand*—all of which are used in the last episode of the essay.

Prose Style

Students are asked to answer the following questions after listening to the sound quality, the flow, and the arrangement of words in paragraph two of the selection.

1. Could this selection possibly have been written in the twentieth century? Remind students that they are not supposed to answer the question by judging the selection of the words but rather by analyzing their flow and arrangement. The middle of the paragraph seems somewhat "foreign" to most twentieth-century prose, and students will probably sense this.

2. What would you imagine to be some qualities of the period in which this was written? Among the upper classes in that period, there prevailed a certain elegance and sophistication that are reflected in Thackeray's prose style. Among the lower classes there existed, of course, great hardship and poverty. Thackeray's England was very far from being a "democratic society" as we know the meaning of that phrase.

3. Is the writer serious or merely mock serious? If students read the paragraph aloud and catch the tone properly—perhaps you could read it to them—they should be able to discern that the writer is quite serious. He is mocking the snob, perhaps, but he is also passionately serious about attacking snobbery.

4. What kind of person might be writing in this kind of language? Students should be able to see that the writer must be an angry person as well as a person of considerable sophistication, someone who is able to use a certain style of writing to create a specific effect and to convey certain ideas.

5. What peculiarities of language structure or arrangement gave you clues for answering the above? The touch of irony at the end of the second paragraph, which is communicated partly by putting "priceless services" in quotation marks, is a key to Thackeray's sophistication. His seriousness may be seen in the lack of transitions in the middle part of the paragraph and by the sudden shifting from question to exclamation to statement. Both the use of the dash before the *And* and the use of the colon in the first sentence are the kinds of punctuation that one would rarely find in contemporary prose. (We are not implying that the dash and the colon are rare today, but that they are not used in the *way* that Thackeray uses them.) Some of the capital letters, too, are less frequently used in contemporary prose than they were in Victorian prose. Capital letters tend to give a certain weight and emphasis to the words.

A Journey in a Stage-Coach

PAGE 380

Samuel Johnson

Glossary Words

servility (page 381, col. 1) Attitude or behavior fit for a slave; base obedience

parsimonious (page 381, col. 1) Too economical; stingy; miserly

abstinent (page 381, col. 1) Very plain; restricted

supercilious (page 381, col. 2) Haughty, proud, and contemptuous; disdainful; showing scorn because of feeling oneself superior

corpulent (page 381, col. 2) Large or bulky of body; fat

emulation (page 383, col. 1) A copying or imitating in order to equal or excel; act of trying to equal or excel; competition; rivalry

latent (page 383, col. 2) Hidden; concealed; not developed

Handbook

essay, prose style, setting

Check Test 44

INTRODUCTION

This narrative essay begins by attacking the thesis that England has a greater variety of characters than do other nations because its liberty allows for greater individual differences and frees people from "the necessity of hypocrisy or the servility of imitation." Johnson disputes the idea that there are in fact more types of characters in England than elsewhere, and he believes even more strongly that liberty enough to develop character is not any more evident in England than in other governments, whether they be under "the many or the few, in monarchies or in commonwealths."

The narrative of the stagecoach journey is then used to prove the point by example. All of the characters on the coach—with the exception of Johnson himself and one woman—try to represent themselves as worth more than they are. They do this, Johnson points out, because of the great degree of liberty that they have on the stagecoach ride. But the deception does not work; each person sees that the other is trying to impose false appearances. Each continues to be haughty and grows more sullen because of the lack of effect that he or she is having.

At the end of the ride, Johnson discovers what each person really is. Then in his last paragraph, he generalizes the point, indicating that we deceive ourselves in order to try to deceive others.

The essay, on the whole, is a beautifully structured exposé of the human desire to think well of ourselves and to elevate ourselves in the eyes of others; at the same time it exposes the tendency of a nation (England) to do the same thing.

Your students may have difficulty with Johnson's style. There are two ways that you can help them. One possibility is to summarize the material in the first three or four paragraphs. This is the difficult part of the selection; the remainder should go smoothly. The other possibility is to ask students to read the entire essay but to show them beforehand the structure of the work. The first paragraph states a thesis; the second disputes this thesis; the third and fourth form a transition from the abstractness of the first two paragraphs to the concreteness of the middle ten paragraphs; the next-to-last paragraph philosophizes on the story; and the final paragraph generalizes on the folly of humankind.

If you have a very good class, you may wish to challenge them to discover this structure on their own.

USING THE STUDY NOTES PAGE 384

I. A CROSS SECTION OF HUMANITY

Students are asked to decide whether Johnson's evaluations of people are still valid today by thinking about the following statements from the essay:

1. . . . as all think themselves secure from detection, all assume that character of which they are most desirous. . . . Students may be somewhat limited in the amount of experience of this kind that they have had. However, there may be some students who have traveled and have fallen into conversations with "assuming" characters—perhaps on buses or airplanes. People today try to impress one another with how widely traveled they are, how influential they are, what important people they know, and what connoisseurs of food, of cars, or of clothing they are.

2. . . . the longer talk has been suspended, the more difficult it is to find anything to say. Here again students may not have had much experience, but it should be obvious that a long suspension of talk does not make it any easier to find things to say. Students may have had some embarrassing experiences in trying to carry on conversations, particularly with members of the opposite sex, but they may not be willing to talk about such experiences.

3. Every man deceives himself, while he thinks he is deceiving others. . . . People deceive themselves by lying to themselves and also, commonly, by thinking that they are deceiving others. The people on the stagecoach with Johnson were not deceived by one another's deceits.

Both these ideas are no doubt true today, although the ability to deceive others depends to some extent upon how good an actor one is and how gullible the other persons are.

II. IMPLICATIONS

Students are asked for their opinions of the following statements; they are told to base their answers on their own experience and the selection.

1. To assume a new face, a new personality, when among strangers is a common human foible.

2. People have always needed to hide what they are from others as well as from themselves.

3. Honesty is for fools and little children; adults are always "pretenders."

As far as the selection is concerned, it would be well to remember that there was one woman among the passengers whose silence was eloquent testimony to the fact that she felt no need to "pretend." Of course she would probably have agreed with Johnson that the need to assume a new personality is a common foible—common, but not necessarily universal. Much depends, it seems to us, upon what one is in the first place. One who is secure and has a firm sense of identity probably will not exhibit this foible.

III. TECHNIQUES

Setting

The following series of questions is asked of students:

How important is the setting in this essay? What do you know about a stagecoach trip after reading this selection? The kind of setting in which a number of different characters are forced to remain together in one place is a common device in fiction, plays, and films. Can you think of other examples of such a "closed" setting?

It is very important for the setting to be "closed," for Johnson is expressly concerned with people who are at liberty to behave as they wish; but Johnson makes virtually no attempt to make the readers feel as though they were experiencing a stagecoach ride. Still, one might feel the close quarters of the coach ride, and observant students will notice that such rides were apt to begin at very early hours: It is some time after they have begun their journey that one of the passengers remarks that it is after five o'clock. And Johnson notes that they left "in the twilight of the morning."

Students should be at no loss to cite examples of closed settings. From this text, they could cite the train in Greene's "The Hint of an Explanation." And of course they will have seen films and television plays in which the action is confined to a deserted island, an airplane, a train, and so on.

Prose Style

Students are asked to answer the following questions about Johnson's style in reference to the second and third paragraphs of this selection.

1. Is the language simple or does Johnson use long-winded, many-syllabled words? According to our count, there are eighteen words containing four or more syllables in a total of only six sentences. This seems to be a relatively high count, but we would not identify many of the words as "long-winded" in the sense of out-of-the-ordinary. In fact, there are hardly any words used that would not be in the vocabulary of an average high school student.

2. How many lines do the sentences tend to run? Do you think they are long or short, involved or simple, easy to read or difficult to understand? The average sentence length is about six lines, or roughly forty-eight words per sentence. This means that they are quite long, and they are certainly involved. The first sentence in the second paragraph, for instance, opens with a noun clause that is the object of the verb "satisfied." The second sentence opens with a very long infinitive phrase, which is used as the subject of the sentence; within that phrase the word *nearly* is used in the sense of "closely" or "intimately," rather than in the sense of "almost," which is the more common meaning today. In short, Johnson's prose is decidedly difficult to understand.

3. In paragraph two, Johnson balances comparisons with the word "or." Read them out loud. How does this use of "or" affect the rhythm of the prose? Students may say it is somewhat like a seesaw. They may also notice the way that the *or's* in the question tend to be balanced by the *or*'s in the answer.

Love and Bread

PAGE 385

August Strindberg

Glossary Words

egoists (page 388, col. 1) Persons who seek the welfare of themselves only; vain, selfish persons

demur (page 388, col. 1) Take exception; raise objections

prosaic (page 390, col. 1) Ordinary; not exciting; dull

surveillance (page 391, col. 1) Watch kept over a person

Handbook

colloquial, irony, setting, tone

Check Test 45

INTRODUCTION

"Love and Bread" is a short story that apparently intends to criticize the notion that love will solve all problems and to expose the foible of living beyond one's means. It is magnificently unified by the sustained irony of tone.

The story focuses mainly on Gustave Falk, the royal secretary; his young wife, Louisa; and the major, Louisa's father. The first scene is a dialogue between the two men, in which the secretary pleads for the daughter's hand on the ground that they are deeply in love, while the father repeatedly questions him about his income. It is, in short, a conflict between love and bread.

The father gives his consent, however, and soon the bride and the groom are out shopping for expensive furnishings and taking joy in spending more than they can afford. The glorious feast on their marriage morning is described in detail, while the wife hints at being concerned about her husband's prodigality. But he will hear of nothing but the best, and the first month of their marriage is consumed by "balls, companies, dinners, suppers, theatres."

Although Louisa makes an effort to live within their means, Gustave continues to buy expensive foods. Finally Louisa becomes pregnant, and Gustave resolves to do extra work in translating and proofreading. But work is hard to find, and his resolve is none too firm in the first place. Creditors start seeking him out, and the grocer, butcher, and others issue warnings.

When the baby is born, Gustave rushes to his father-in-law and exclaims that he is a father; the major replies, "Good! have you bread, too, for your child?" Although he resolves to help Gustave this time, he also makes it plain that it will be the last time. Gustave bemoans the "wretched times without any ideality," and continues to spend much more than he can afford.

Finally, Gustave is on the verge of bankruptcy. Everything is taken from the apartment. The major carries away his daughter and the child.

Gustave finally comes to see—but not to accept—the reality of the situation: It will take him twenty years to pay off his debts, even with his second job. And at that he will still be unable to provide for his wife and child. The story ends with his condemnation of life, which "cannot offer all men partridges and strawberries."

Although our society is more affluent than the one depicted in the story, students should have little difficulty identifying with the basic situation. The story really needs no introduction, but if you wish, you may refer to the title and ask students what it suggests to them about the theme of the story.

USING THE STUDY NOTES PAGE 391

I. DEATH ON THE INSTALLMENT PLAN

Students are asked what the story indicates about the following:

1. The elements in a society that put pressures on people to live beyond their incomes.

2. The weaknesses inside people that lead them to live beyond their incomes.

3. Where the blame rests when a couple lives beyond their means. Is the fault the husband's or the wife's? Or both?

The story emphasizes the second statement rather than the first—social pressures do not require that Gustave have partridges and strawberries for dinner. There is, however, some indication of social pressures; for instance, Gustave pays the nurse a hundred crowns because he doesn't want to give less than "others" do. Furthermore, the story notes that some people do not marry—Gustave's friend, the notary, for instance—because they realize that to do so would require a greater income than they have. In short, it is Gustave's own weaknesses that cause his downfall.

The answer to the third question would be different at the time of the story from what it would be today. Then the husband was usually much more authoritarian and made the major decisions, including how money was spent. Today, if a couple lives beyond their means, the wife is as likely as the husband to be at fault.

II. IMPLICATIONS

Students are asked for their opinions on the following statements:

1. It is a common foible of young people to believe that love will solve all their problems. We suspect that young people themselves will deny this assertion, largely because they feel the need to appear practical and realistic. Perhaps they feel the need so strongly because it *is* one of their weaknesses to think that love will solve all problems—or at least most of them. There may be some differences of opinion between those students whose parents will continue to support them for some time (pay college expenses, for example) and students who will be faced with the prospect of having to earn a living upon graduating from high school.

2. Living beyond one's income is a common fault of society in America today. Students who deny this statement will be hard pressed to provide their case. Much of American selling is based on the idea of "buy now—pay later." Banks run heavy advertising campaigns urging people to borrow money, and the government itself continues to raise the national debt ceiling.

3. It is the duty of a parent to prevent a child from making a disastrous marriage. The critical question here should be how one can know in advance that a marriage is going to be disastrous. Nobody wants to make a disastrous marriage, and in most cases if children were convinced that their parents knew positively that a marriage would turn out badly, they would probably agree that it was the parents' duty to try to prevent it. But who can be sure? Parenthood does not automatically give one foresight. These are some of the points that students will probably make in defending their right to make their own mistakes.

III. TECHNIQUES

Setting

Students are asked to name some of the details (like props) that are used to help to convey the meaning of the story. They are also asked how the setting itself becomes an important force in the story.

The main props would be the food (especially the

wines, the birds, and the strawberries) and the apartment with its furnishings.

The setting is an important force in the story because material goods provoke the ruin of the chief character. Notice that near the beginning of the story the apartment is filled and that it is empty near the end. And Gustave always seems to be either carrying or eating a bird; the story ends of course with a reference to partridges, although Gustave is neither carrying nor eating one on that occasion.

IV. WORDS

A. Students are to use context clues and a dictionary to find the meanings of these words:

1. **orthodoxy**—conventional belief or practice
   prodigious—enormous
   emulation—ambition (see footnote 3, page 376)
   victuals—supplies of food
2. **servility**—subservience
   supercilious—extremely proud
   corpulent—fat
   obdurate—inflexible
   pernicious—deadly
3. **gesticulate**—to make gestures while speaking
   egoist—a person who believes that self-interest is of primary importance
   demur—to object
   prosaic—commonplace; dull

B. Students will probably conclude that the Strindberg selection is easier reading, in terms of sentence structure and word choice, than the Thackeray and Johnson selections. Strindberg's vocabulary and prose style more closely parallel those of contemporary writers than do the vocabularies and the styles of Thackeray and Johnson.

C. Johnson compares the journey in the stagecoach to the journey through life.

Thackeray, too, speaks figuratively. People are not *literally* down on their knees, but in spirit they are. The second Thackeray quotation employs personification, for death is abstract but "vacating shoes" is a human act.

The two Strindberg figures mentioned are found in column 2, line 28, page 387 and in column 2, line 32, page 387. Students will be able to find other examples of comparisons, but Strindberg's writing does not attempt sustained simile.

Jeannot and Colin

PAGE 393

Voltaire

Glossary Words

patronizing (page 394, col. 1) Treating in a haughty, condescending manner
chaos (page 396, col. 2) Very great confusion; complete disorder
succor (page 399, col. 2) Help; aid
straits (page 399, col. 2) Difficulty; need; distress
rubicund (page 400, col. 1) Reddish; ruddy
paraphernalia (page 400, col. 2) Personal belongings

Handbook

prose style, satire, setting

Check Test 46

INTRODUCTION

Writing under the guise of telling a moral fable, Voltaire is actually satirizing foibles as prevalent in today's society as in eighteenth-century France. As the story begins, two young men from lower-class families are growing up in a provincial town. Jeannot's father, a dealer in mules, goes to Paris, strikes it rich, and sends for his son. The young man is to be made into an aristocrat. His nincompoop of a tutor and a court dandy deride the parents' notion that the boy should learn anything at all—certainly not Latin, geography, astronomy, history, or geometry. With such ignoramuses as advisors, the parents choose for Jeannot to learn to please people, to dance, and to sing. The young man succeeds wonderfully in these skills. He is about to marry a wealthy young widow when his father is jailed for going bankrupt and his mother beggared. The widow's ardor vanishes, and Jeannot's Paris friends reject him. Only Colin, who accidentally arrives at this time, stands by him. This old friend is now the owner of a factory and married to a wealthy tradesman's daughter. He offers Jeannot a chance to learn his business and own a part of it, gets his father released from prison, and takes them all back to Auvergne. Jeannot eventually marries Colin's sister and lives happily ever after. The moral as given: Vanity is no true source of happiness.

In introducing the selection, you might talk about the structure of this type of moral tale. You could use a familiar Aesop fable, such as "The Boy Who Cried Wolf," to demonstrate the framework of the moral tale: a few brief vivid scenes that highlight a moral. The moral is always put into precise words and carefully placed at the end to ensure that the reader grasps the intended meaning. Have the students look at the stated moral at the end of the story on p. 401. Read the brief biography of Voltaire aloud. Having read this information about Voltaire, ask students if they think the story may be something very different from a traditional moral tale.

USING THE STUDY NOTES

I. SATIRIC JABS AT PEOPLE'S FOIBLES

You may wish to discuss with the class the innuendos made in the statements given in this tale. Voltaire is saying that Auvergne is an unsophisticated rural spot where such diverse things as kettles and a college are both considered notable and the young bumpkins could not possibly be handsome. In the tutor's arguments, Voltaire is parodying the serious arguments scholars make for their subjects. At the same time he is laughing at the ignoramuses in society who can so twist words about that they convince the gullible. He is also criticizing country folk who think anyone who calls himself a tutor is knowledgeable. As for the Paris friends, Voltaire seems to suggest that they are shallow money-lovers and lack moral values.

II. IMPLICATIONS

Do you agree or disagree with the following statements?

1. Voltaire is actually satirizing the hypocrisy of people, not their vanity, in this story. Have the class look up *vanity* in the dictionary. It means excessive pride in one's appearance, conceit, and hollowness. In all these meanings Jeannot fits the word. Now consider the definition of *hypocrisy:* a semblance of having publicly approved attitudes, beliefs, principles but not actually possessing them. Jeannot's Paris friends are aptly described by this definition, especially the tutor, the courtier, and the widow. It would seem that Voltaire was satirizing both vanity and hypocrisy.

2. The attitudes presented in the quotations below are still in evidence today.

a. "The minds of children are smothered under a mass of useless knowledge. . . ." There are still people who believe that the majority of children need only a smattering of skills such as reading, writing, and math. These same people think that "frills" such as music, art, history, debate, sports, etc., are unnecessary for most youngsters.

b. "The marquis and his lady did not understand much of the meaning of what the tutor was saying; but they were quite of his way of thinking." How many of the students feel that if people use long words and involved sentences they must be educated people and know what they are talking about? Have they ever been in a situation with a scientist or doctor or artist or computer analyst where the vocabulary used was so unfamiliar to them that they found themselves agreeing although they weren't sure to what?

c. ". . . it is much better to patronize [the arts] than to practice them." The money-oriented students will look on the arts as nonlucrative for the majority of performers and hence to be avoided. There is also a snob appeal in being able to donate money to artists rather than being on the taking end. Other students may already have discovered the joys of creating something on their own. The point of view students support will depend on whether they are participants or viewers in life.

d. ". . . whatever becomes common loses its attraction." This seems to be a common truism today. Any fashion whether it is in language, clothes, hairstyle, etc., seems to die once it has become popular with the masses. There should be current examples that students can give to support the statement.

e. ". . . an army-hospital contractor . . . who could boast of having killed more soldiers in one year than the cannon had destroyed in ten." There should be current examples of contractors who have cheated on public contracts and made fortunes. But be sure the students realize that not everyone who works for the government is cheating.

III. TECHNIQUES

Setting

Students are to answer questions about the setting which is important although not specifically described.

1. **What are the two settings?** Auvergne and Paris.

2. **What is implied in the choice of these two places?** Since Auvergne is a rural town and Paris is a large city, the implication is that the former is simple, unsophisticated, and natural, while the latter is extravagant, sophisticated, and pretentious. Auvergne symbolizes what is right about Colin, and Paris what is wrong about Jeannot.

3. **If you were writing a similar story today, what two places might you pick for your settings?** Students will probably choose combinations of rural and metropolitan settings such as Plains, Georgia, with Chicago, Illinois.

4. **Would the story have had the same effect if it had taken place completely in Auvergne?** Probably not. The two sites are important and contribute to the total effect.

Prose Style

Look back at the first paragraph. Notice that the sentences immediately begin with the subject and the verb. Then there are a long series of phrases or clauses that comment by innuendo on the simple fact stated by the subject and verb. Check to see if this is a stylistic characteristic running through the story. Yes, it is.

IV. WORDS

A. Students are asked to use context and dictionaries to find the meanings of words in phrases from the story.

1. **ignoramus:** an ignorant person
2. **inextricable:** that one cannot get out of
3. **lineage:** ancestors, family
4. **prodigious:** great, wonderful
5. **stupefied:** overwhelmed
6. **countenance:** face, features

B. Students are asked to find other examples of metaphors in the story. Some of them are these: "When one is in the current of the stream, it is only necessary to let oneself drift...," "...dry up his brain...," "...whose charms had been her passport...," "...young lord should be able to shine," "...drained their purses...," "...dazzled with the splendor of the alliance... ."

V. COMPOSITION

Students are asked to write descriptions of possible actions or attitudes of a character in "Jeannot and Colin." You might want to take a few of the examples students write and have class discussion on the appropriateness and economy of word choices.

Dissecting of a Beau's Head

PAGE 403

Joseph Addison

Glossary Words

virtuosos (page 403, col. 1) Persons skilled in the techniques of a special art or profession

dissection (page 404, col. 1) Act of cutting apart an animal, plant, etc., in order to examine or study the structure

cursory (page 404, col. 1) Without attention to details; hasty and superficial

imperceptible (page 404, col. 2) That cannot be seen or felt; invisible

Handbook

essay, form, satire

***Check Test 47** (also for "The Coquette's Heart")*

INTRODUCTION

This and the following brief selection are satires on the beau and the coquette. The author claims to have had a dream in which he witnessed the dissection of the head of a particular beau and, as described in the next essay, of a certain coquette's heart. It is discovered that in the beau's head is not a real brain but cavities filled with strange materials. One gland is encompassed by little mirrors suggesting that the soul spent most of its time gazing at itself. Some of the cavities are filled with lace and embroidery and love letters and fancy powder. A cavity on the right filled with promises and flatteries is joined through the tongue with a cavity filled with oaths and curses. Other cavities that provided source material for the tongue were full of wind and nonsense. The observers saw the muscle that pulls the beau's nose upwards in contempt at what he did not understand. They also noticed that the ogling muscles of the eye were worn and decayed, but the "elevator," or muscle for turning the eye toward heaven, had hardly been used at all. The beau has been a man of no sense, concerned with fashions only.

The pleasure for students in reading this and the following essay should come from the connections it forces them to make between what is seen by the anatomists and what their discoveries signify. The ultimate aim of the essays is to satirize the foibles of these stock characters.

USING THE STUDY NOTES PAGE 406

I. LAUGHING AT STOCK CHARACTERS

Stock characters are explained and students are asked to consider Addison's satirizing of the beau.

In this essay he has made fun of the beau, or the dandy. He is a man of fashion, but what does Addison say he is when seen truly? Addison implies that among the qualities of the beau are that he is artificial, vain, untruthful, comtemptuous of anything he doesn't understand, and full of nonsense.

II. IMPLICATIONS

1. The framework for this satire is an imagined dissection of a head. What was your reaction to the device? Can you think of another framework that might work equally well? To some students, the idea may seem repulsive, but it is an attention-getter. Notice that since almost no physical details of knives, cutting, or blood are given, the scene is not a morbid one. Students may suggest the dissection of a heart might also work, and that is the subject of the next essay.

2. What details are given about the head? Thinking of the head as the center of reason, intelligence, and the soul, what foible does each detail highlight?

Detail	Foible
a. strong essence	**a.** pretentiousness
b. horny substance cut into mirrors	**b.** vanity
c. filled with lace, powder, love letters	**c.** false emotions; can act romantic on demand
d. flatteries on one side and oaths on the other joined to the tongue	**d.** intentional insincerity
e. bladders filled with wind or froth	**e.** unintelligent, meaningless, and endless conversation
f. thick skin of forehead incapable of blushing	**f.** not smart enough to be embarrassed by his own ignorance or mistakes
g. muscle that draws nose upwards	**g.** contemptuous
h. worn and decayed ogling muscle in eye	**h.** lecherous
i. unused elevator muscle that turns eye heavenward	**i.** consciously impious

There are, of course, many foibles that could be suggested by these details. Students' imaginations should be given a good workout. It might be wise to have someone record the ideas on the chalkboard for reference in answering the next question.

3. Which of the traits might be applied to a woman as well as to a man? Most of them could be a woman's foibles as well as a man's although perhaps less obviously displayed.

The Coquette's Heart

PAGE 407

Joseph Addison

Glossary Words

waived (page 407, col. 1) Given up; refused

labyrinths (page 407, col. 1) Many winding passages so arranged that it is hard to find one's way from point to point

orifice (page 407, col. 1) An opening or a hole

phenomenon (page 409, col. 1) A rare circumstance that can be observed; a marvel

Handbook

essay, form, prose style, satire

***Check Test 47** (also for "Dissecting of a Beau's Head")*

INTRODUCTION

In his dream, the author witnessed the dissection of the heart of a coquette. It was found that the pericardium of the heart had been scarred in many places but never pierced. The fluid of the pericardium is like mercury used in thermometers, but instead of reacting to weather, it reacts to people: It rises when a plume of feathers, an embroidered coat, a pair of fringed gloves, or laughter is present, but it falls in the presence of less fashionable clothing or a serious disposition.

The heart itself is like "a smooth piece of ice," and there is no connection between it and the tongue; further, the nerves that run from it are connected to the eye rather than to the brain. It is hollow inside, and there are no faces to be discovered in its foldings—until the center is reached. There is found the beau.

Finally, the heart is put in hot coals, but it does not burn; in fact it is not even singed by the flames. But suddenly it cracks and evaporates. The noise wakes up the dreamer and the essay ends.

USING THE STUDY NOTES

PAGE 409

I. LAUGHING AT STOCK CHARACTERS

Why did Addison choose the coquette's heart to dissect rather than the head as for the beau? What is he saying about the chief characteristic of the coquette's nature? Addison is suggesting that as the beau is supposed to be reasonable and intelligent but in fact is not, the coquette is supposed to be romantic and desirable but is really a sham. The head is said to be the source of reason and intelligence, and the heart is said to be the source of emotion.

II. IMPLICATIONS

Discuss the following questions:

1. The framework for this satire is an imagined dissection of a heart. What was your reaction to the device? To some students, the idea may seem repulsive, but it is an attention getter. Notice that almost no physical details are given: knives, cutting, blood. So the scene is not a morbid one. **Can you think of another framework that might work equally well?** Other possibilities are the objects in a coquette's closet or bathroom.

2. What details are given about the heart? Thinking of the heart as the center of emotions, what foible does each detail highlight?

Detail	Foible
a. many labyrinths and recesses	**a.** many twisted, hidden emotions that are hard to separate
b. slippery	**b.** emotions unpredictable, can't be pinned down
c. scarred with arrows, but none have penetrated	**c.** many encounters but none are real or deep

d. fluid like mercury in a thermometer	**d.** reacts to the externals of people such as clothes, laughter, empty chatter
e. cold	**e.** not a warm, loving human being
f. filled with twisted, knotted fibers	**f.** tied up in knots when an emotional reaction is demanded
g. no connection with the tongue	**g.** couldn't really communicate; just makes empty sounds
h. connected with eye, but not with brain	**h.** depended on eyes, not intelligence, in emotional situations
i. very light	**i.** no deep, real feelings
j. unburnable	**j.** could not be hurt by other's emotions
k. little figure of a man in the innermost recess	**k.** may be the ideal man she seeks, or a symbol for any man, just as many as possible

3. Which of the traits might be applied to a man as well as to a woman? Probably all of them, even *k,* if you substituted a woman's figure for that of the man.

III. TECHNIQUES

Prose style

The students are first asked to discuss the length of the sentences in the first three paragraphs of each of Addison's essays. They are also asked to tell if they find it easy to read them aloud.

The sentences in the first three paragraphs of both essays are long. The students will probably also find them difficult to read, although perhaps not as difficult as those of Johnson.

1. Can you find a good adjective to describe the personality of Addison's style? Students may very well choose such an adjective as *long-winded,* for the sentences are almost invariably above the medium length of most of the student-read prose being published today. *Stately* or *formal* are other possibilities that students might select. *Graceful, witty,* and *charming* are some that they probably will not pick.

In any case, you might ask students why Addison's style was so widely admired in his own day. They might find it difficult to answer this question, but thinking about it will—if nothing else—help to make them aware of how much tastes may change.

2. Look for examples of contrast and comparison. Are there many sentences in which Addison balances phrases and clauses against each other?

There are of course numerous examples. They are one of the chief reasons why Addison's style might be described as stately or formal. As the students should be able to tell from the fact that similar balances are plentiful in Johnson's style, this sort of thing was much more in fashion in the eighteenth century than it is today. It is one of the reasons why students find these writers difficult to read.

A Trip with Obstacles

PAGE 415

Juozas Grušas

Glossary Words

patriarch (page 416, col. 1) A church leader of high rank

havoc (page 418, col. 1) Very great destruction; ruin

obsequies (page 419, col. 2) Funeral rites or ceremonies

Handbook

flat character, prose style, satire, setting

Check Test 48

INTRODUCTION

"A Trip with Obstacles" satirizes the common human foible of being annoyed when things do not go as planned. An eighty-one year old farmer has announced repeatedly during the winter that he is dying. His wife, twenty years younger and a most practical woman, feels little sorrow and is mainly concerned that he should die at a time convenient for her and the neighbors. She buys a casket and has candles ready. When she is convinced that the time has come for him to die, she calls in the neighbors and instructs the servant to obtain supplies for the wake. There is a festive feeling about the coming death; the neighbors even wish the old man "a happy death." Then "the most vehement woman in the village" walks in and tells the old man to order the would-be mourners out of the house. He dismisses them, makes a miraculous recovery, and eats beet soup with sour cream. When the straw roof on the pantry catches fire, the old man walks out and directs the fire fighters. With delight he points out to a neighbor that the casket, which his wife had stored in the attic of the pantry, is in flames.

Read the first line of the story to the class: "Once there lived a farmer..." The word *once* immediately clues the reader to what type of story to expect. As in most folk tales, there is no specified time or place. The reader accepts the fact that this will not be a story about a real happening.

"A Trip with Obstacles" is an example of black humor, a term that may need definition. Generally, authors do not treat humorously subjects such as death, physical deformity, or natural disasters. It is only in black humor that such tragic subjects are portrayed with humor.

USING THE STUDY NOTES PAGE 421

I. A TRIP DISRUPTED

Is the author satirizing a common human foible of being annoyed when things do not go as planned, even when it is something as final as death? There are certainly indications that most people feel at least a twinge of annoyance when things do not go as expected. People may even be unhappy when death does not follow on schedule—for example, needy heirs waiting for the death of a rich person who has been given a limited time to live but who inexplicably lives on and on.

II. IMPLICATIONS

Discuss your reactions to the following statements:

1. Both Molière and Grušas, by highlighting only their characters' foibles, make them one-dimensional. In *The Miser* Molière has stripped away all of Harpagon's human characteristics except his greed. Grušas has emphasized only one outstanding trait for the farmer and one for his wife. Her practicality is emphasized, as is his need to do what is expected. Note how the husband tries to die when he is expected to die and how he orders the waiting mourners out of the house when Simkiene tells him to do so.

2. The neighbors' and friends' foibles are satirized as well as those of the principal characters. The story points out how much the neighbors and friends enjoy participating in deathbed scenes; such times are high points in their lives. The ceremony makes these events important, and perhaps they rejoice because they are still alive.

3. An individual is an emotional cripple if he or she is unable to feel sympathy for the plight of another. Ask students how they feel about the wife's reactions as her husband supposedly lies dying. Most will feel that she is a hard-hearted, cold, and calculating person. Such people tend to repel us. There is definitely a psychological or emotional lack in a person who cannot sympathize or empathize with another individual's feelings at a time of crisis.

III. TECHNIQUES

Setting

If you were staging this story as simply as possible, what would be the necessary props? A bed and a coffin are probably the only two essential props.

Prose Style

In the scene of the lighting of the candle, the author suddenly shifts tenses from the past to the present. Then he goes back to the past tense to tell the rest of the story. What could be the reason for this? Sheer accident is possible, but the author might have deliberately shifted to present tense to make this scene seem more urgent, more immediate. In English, a sustained use of the present tense, however, tends to seem pseudodramatic.

How to Buy a House

PAGE 422

Lawrence Durrell

Glossary Words

desiccated (page 422, col. 2) Shriveled and dried up

harangue (page 424, col. 1) A noisy, forceful speech

propitious (page 426, col. 2) Favorable

maundering (page 427, col. 2) Moving and acting in an aimless, confused manner

icons (page 429, col. 1) Pictures or images of Jesus, an angel, or a saint, usually painted on wood or ivory

paroxysm (page 432, col. 2) A sudden outburst of emotion

perorated (page 434, col. 2) Talked in a grand manner as if making a public speech

nonagenarian (page 435, col. 2) Person who is 90 years old or between 90 and 100 years old

execrations (page 436, col. 2) Curses; loud expressions of hatred

comestibles (page 437, col. 2) Things to eat

Handbook

autobiography, description, mood, prose style, setting

Check Test 49

INTRODUCTION

This autobiographical sketch is set in Cyprus, and its plot is essentially very simple. Durrell wants to buy a house inexpensively. He goes to a Turkish real estate agent, Sabri Tahir, and through a tactful speech becomes his friend. Sabri promises to do what he can to find a house at the proper price, but he points out that such things require time.

After some time has passed, Sabri comes to Durrell and tells him that he has a place for him to look at. Durrell is quite fond of the house, but Sabri cautions him against showing his feelings or discussing money. He must say that he does not want the house at all; "this will make the necessary despondence...."

Almost another week passes before the time to bargain comes. In the meantime, Sabri has discovered that Durrell will not have to pay for water rights because the government is planning to pipe water into the village, and a public pump will be right outside the door of the house. This is a stroke of good luck.

The highly amusing bargaining finally begins. Sabri and the woman who owns the house take turns banging the huge house key on his desk, claiming alternately that the wood of the house is or isn't rotten. After a certain amount of bargaining back and forth, the first round ends in a draw. The owner returns to her relatives, who are sitting across the street, and Sabri tells Durrell about his trump card: they will get the house cheap because the owner of the house does not know about the water. She will later try to "sting" them because of it. Thus, Sabri concludes, he must pretend to forget about the water. He also observes, however, that the deal must be consummated that day, for if she returns to her village, the gossips will talk her out of selling at the price.

After much more bargaining, Sabri gets the owner to admit that she wants the money, although she never quite says that she will sell the house. There remains the task of getting the papers from the widow Anthi's house. Durrell and Sabri drag the owner to a waiting cab and whisk her away. Her family follows in another cab, but Sabri has seen to it that the second cab will shortly have a puncture.

The deal is finally concluded, although not without some further difficulties, and everyone—the owner's family included—winds up in good humor. Sabri then takes Durrell to Kyrenia castle so that he may feel the *meltemi* wind. He tells Durrell that he will always be his friend, even if Durrell should cease being friendly toward him.

Durrell remarks on the fact that a Greek sent him to the Turkish Sabri and that now Sabri is sending him to a Greek for house alterations. Sabri laughs, "Cyprus is small . . . and we are all friends, though very different."

The story exposes a good many foibles, of both East and West, but perhaps its chief point is that human beings are essentially the same as long as one can penetrate the surface (cultural) differences.

You may want to begin by asking your students what they know about Cyprus. They should know at least where it is and that its population is a mixture of Turkish and Greek. The town in which most of the story takes place—Kyrenia—is a seaport on the northern coast, just above the capital city of Nicosia.

With the exception of *The Miser,* this selection is easily the longest in the unit, and the long descriptions may make it seem even longer than it is. It could therefore be broken into two assignments, perhaps at the point on page 431 where the bargaining is about to begin. This is just past the middle of the story.

Students who do not like descriptive writing may not care for the first half of the assignment, but it is hard to conceive of anyone's not liking the second half. Perhaps at the end of the first half you could summarize the main points so that students have them clearly in mind as they begin the second part of the assignment.

USING THE STUDY NOTES PAGE 437

I. "WE ARE ALL FRIENDS, THOUGH VERY DIFFERENT"

Students are asked to consider and discuss the following questions:

1. What are the foibles Durrell is exploring? Have each student make up a list, and then let the class combine the lists. By our count, there are at least a dozen foibles that students could pick up.

2. How are these foibles amusing? Troubling? Incomprehensible? Many of the foibles are amusing because they are so different from Western foibles. For instance, we are used to a certain amount of feigning in some business transactions, but the idea of a "*necessary* despondency" is not familiar and thus is likely to be amusing. Also likely to amuse us because of its unfamiliarity is the fact that the owner of the property has *no idea* of what the property is worth. Students will certainly be able to provide other examples from the story.

To what extent some of the foibles may be troubling will depend upon individual students. Many may be troubled by all the crying and fussing that goes on, but of course, if they are, they will have been drawn into the seller's trap. More troubling, perhaps, is the fact that the Turkish agent and Durrell are perfectly willing to let the owner think that she will be able to get more money later for the water rights. This foible, however, is not peculiar to the East, a fact emphasized by Durrell's going along with the idea without protest.

It is hard to say which foibles the students may consider "incomprehensible," although we shall suggest a couple. Family ownership of things such as trees and water rights is likely to strike some students as incomprehensible, particularly the idea that even idiots share in the ownership. It may also seem incomprehensible that one can make a lifelong friend by a single tactful speech and that this friend will always remain your friend, regardless of what you do.

3. How are Durrell's own foibles as an English citizen illuminated? They are generally illuminated by actions. One such foible is his saying that he has less money than he actually does. Another is his general impulsiveness, shown by his tendency to want to buy the first home that he sees. Also, in great contrast to the Turk, Durrell finds it very hard to suppress his real emotions.

II. IMPLICATIONS

Students are asked whether the story bears out or refutes the following statements. They are also asked how they themselves feel about the statements.

1. Bargaining is a part of everyone's life. The story bears out this statement. In Cyprus, the owner's entire family becomes involved in the bargaining process. In our country, there seems to be less bargaining, or, at any rate, its ritualistic character is less developed. However, bargaining is sometimes a characteristic of certain occupations—selling used cars, for example.

2. The haggling of the Cypriots is without lasting rancor because they accept and understand that it is the custom in business dealings. In our society, haggling in business dealings is considered undignified. The first part of the statement is certainly true; students who do not see that it is have missed something important in the story. In American society haggling seems to depend upon what one is buying and from whom. We assume that one does not haggle over the price of a diamond from Tiffany's. But Americans typically haggle over the prices of houses, for example.

3. Durrell is really amazed at the foibles of the Cypriots. Toward the end of the story, Durrell comments, "All this was purely gratuitous drama and could be taken lightly." This is hardly the remark of a person who is amazed. In general, Durrell takes the Cyprian foibles more or less in stride, although there is a point or two at which he is horrified (notably when Jamal's car almost runs over the grandfather).

4. "But we must take time. In Cyprus time is

everything," says Sabri. Do you think this attitude represents a foible or a virtue? Actually, the answer to this question depends upon one's point of view. Many students are likely to feel that the Cyrpriots take too much time—but that is to judge them by our standards. It seems that we are being asked to believe that all of the time that Sabri took was necessary. If so, one should probably not consider his attitude toward time a foible. On the contrary, it would be reasonable to count it a strength rather than a weakness, for Sabri won the "game."

III. TECHNIQUES

Setting

Students are asked what the setting does for the story and how necessary the details are to the story.

The setting makes the island, the towns, and the house that Durrell buys come alive; the descriptions are brilliant. However, some students may feel otherwise, and they are almost certain to say that the details are not necessary to the story. They are right if they define *story* as primarily a matter of action. In that case, the details are certainly excessive.

But Durrell wants to know the people, and he wants to feel at home in Cyprus; he presumably also wants the reader to share these feelings. If the story is to include these aspects, then the details are necessary. After all, one does not know people fully unless one knows their environments, and one cannot feel at home if one cannot "see" it. The descriptions, in short, are integral parts of the story. Try to get students to see this.

Students are also asked to tell everything that they know about:

1. Sabri's "godown." The "godown" (warehouse) is in the Turkish quarter of the city. It contains Sabri's office, which is described as cool, dark, and crowded. The godown is strategically situated on a junction of streets. It faces a Turkish shrine and beyond that a field and some shacks in which people are working.

2. The locale of Kyrenia. Students should remember particularly the castle and the fact that it is a seaport town as well as Sabri's "Empire." They may also recall that the city is near the capital, Nicosia, that one can see the Caramanian mountains of Turkey from the castle, and that one may feel the *meltemi* wind there.

3. Jamal's taxicab. It has no door handles, and so Jamal has to climb through the trunk to open it. Also, it has no wipers, and Jamal has to drive in the rain by sticking his head out the window. It is ancient, but it moves.

4. The town of Bellapaix. There is a long description of this town on page 427. Perhaps students will remember best the Tree of Idleness, the abundant roses, and the almond and peach blossoms. There is also a village coffee shop and a ruined Gothic monastery, in addition, of course, to Durrell's house.

Prose Style

Students are asked to answer the following questions after rereading the first four paragraphs of the story.

1. Are Durrell's sentences short or long? Or a mixture? How does this affect your ability to read the paragraphs? The sentences vary in length from sixty-one words to thirteen words. In short, there is considerable variety. Most students will not experience difficulty reading Durrell's prose, although it sometimes requires a certain amount of patience—the long descriptions, for example.

2. Consider the following adjectives. Which ones best describe the kinds of words Durrell uses? Are the words precise or vague? Are they ordinary or unusual? Elaborate or simple? Give examples to support your answers. The words that Durrell uses are quite precise. Some can be described as unusual —*godown, ex voto, carob, terrain vague,* and others. Perhaps a few are elaborate, in the sense that they are not the first words that pop into one's mind, but this does not necessarily mean that they are not simple. By any measure of simplicity *carob* is a very simple word. In short, the fact that students are unfamiliar with a word should not cause them to jump to the conclusion that the word is elaborate.

3. What mood do you feel Durrell is trying to create: comic, tragic, romantic, realistic? How does Durrell create the mood of the essay? The first four paragraphs are rendered with an explicitness that can only be described as "realistic." He creates this mood by precision of word choice and with many details. The essay as a whole is another matter. Students could justify it as comic, romantic, or realistic. Have them support their choices by referring to specific passages.

4. In these four paragraphs explain how Durrell balances the following opposites:

a. Action and inaction. Sabri himself is inactive; his workers are active. At the end of the fourth paragraph, we get an ironic picture of Sabri himself being at once active and inactive.

b. Light and dark. Sabri is sitting in the cool and dark interior; outside it is hot and light, as emphasized by the "sun-blistered" sign and the "dusty and desiccated" pepper tree.

c. Turks and Greeks. They are balanced in the opening quotation from the Bulgarian folk tale and later by the contrast between Sabri's *kayf* and the fidgety nature of Greeks.

In what way does this balancing contribute to the mood? How does it mark his style? The balancing shows Durrell's attempt to portray realistically the aspects of Cyprian life. Also, by setting up a series of contrasts, Durrell prepares the reader for the major East/West contrast.

IV. WORDS

A. Students are to use context clues and their dictionaries to find the meanings of these words.

disembodied—divested of necessary working parts
monolithic—exhibiting massive uniformity
harangue—a ranting speech
propitious—favorably disposed
maundering—wandering slowly and idly
icon—religious image venerated by members of Eastern Orthodox sects
paroxysm—convulsion
nonagenarian—a person in his or her nineties
execrations—curses
comestible—food

B. In Durrell's story, the condition of the sign is compared to skin blistered through too much exposure to the sun. The parts are compared to parts of the human anatomy separated from the body. Buses at a dump are compared to dead horses being used for glue. The effect of the saw is compared to the gnashing of teeth. The Turk is compared to an enormous stone that is usually in the form of an obelisk or a column. The price of land is compared to a rising airplane. The side of the castle is compared to the side of a lion.

The Decameron

PAGE 439

Giovanni Boccaccio

Glossary Words

penuriously (page 440, col. 2) In extreme want; in great poverty

straightened (page 442, col. 1) Impoverished; difficult

deigned (page 442, col. 1) Thought fit (to do something); stoop (to do something); lowered oneself

abate (page 442, col. 2) Put an end to; stop

Handbook

absurd, irony, prose style, setting

Check Test 50 (for "Federigo's Falcon" and "The One-Legged Crane")

FEDERIGO'S FALCON (FIFTH DAY, NINTH TALE)
THE ONE-LEGGED CRANE (SIXTH DAY, FOURTH TALE)

Each of the two stories from Boccaccio's *The Decameron* highlights the foibles of human beings in love. "Federigo's Falcon" tells of a man who cooks his prize falcon to serve to the woman he loves when she visits him unexpectedly. Ironically, her reason for coming was to beg the falcon from him as a gift for her sick child. This twist of plot is an early version of the one used in O'Henry's "Gift of the Magi," which many students will know. By the end of the story, however, the man and woman are married and, in fine fairy-tale fashion, live happily ever after.

In "The One-Legged Crane," a rougish cook named Chichibio gives a leg of the crane that he is cooking to the woman he loves. When he serves the one-legged crane, Chichibio attempts to pacify his angry master by telling him that cranes have only one leg. Forced on the next day to prove his point, the cook drives with his master to a riverbank where all the cranes are standing on one leg. The master shouts, "Ho! Ho!" and the cranes drop their other legs and fly off. Chichibio is dismayed but blurts out that if his master had only shouted "Ho! Ho!" the night before, the bird would have extended its other leg. Fortunately for Chichibio, the master has a sense of humor, and his anger changes to merriment and laughter.

To introduce the tales, you may wish to point out the structure of *The Decameron.* The framework is one that is used both in oriental and in medieval literature. Students should see the similarity of the tales in *The Decameron* and those in Chaucer's *The Canterbury Tales.* Also, have students read the headnote on Boccaccio in their texts. It describes the actual setting of the stories in *The Decameron.*

USING THE STUDY NOTES — PAGE 444

I. THE OUTWITTED AND THE WITTY

Most readers enjoy these stories simply because they are fun to read. The main incident in each—cooking the falcon, cutting off the crane's leg—has a certain intrinsic absurdity. Each incident could have happened but would be unlikely to happen, at least in today's society. In each story, too, an element of fantasy surrounds the happy ending. Despite their fairy-tale qualities, however, the stories do lend themselves to some serious discussions, as the questions and the implications reflect.

II. IMPLICATIONS

Students are asked to consider the following statements:

1. **According to *The Decameron,* to be truly noble, we must accept life as it is without bitterness; we must accept, above all, the consequences of our own actions, however contrary to expectation they may be. Such nobility is examined in both these tales.** "Federigo's Falcon" is a perfect example of this particular type of nobility. When Federigo loses all his wealth through his own extravagances, he retires to his farm and asks nothing of anyone, simply enduring his poverty with patience. It is his qualities of nobility and courtesy (exemplified by serving his treasured falcon) that capture Monna Giovanna's fancy and that win her to him. Little of this kind of nobility is demonstrated in "The One-Legged Crane," for the cook does not possess any. His master shows a certain kind of courtesy by giving the cook a chance to prove his story, although the master's motives spring from anger and the conviction that his lying servant will be trapped in his lie.

2. **We have a grudging admiration for an ingenious lie.** Currado does not seem enchanted by the cook's lie. In fact, rage prevents him from sleeping on the night of the dinner party at which the one-legged crane is served. But if one is not involved in the situation, the lie can become amusing. Most of us admire someone who is quick-witted enough to come up with a brilliant retort. Certainly Chichibio's comment at the end of the story is a masterpiece of quick thinking. Because there are liars' clubs and competitions for the best lie, one must assume that some people appreciate the ability to lie. And it does take imagination to tell a lie that fits a particular situation. Perhaps Chichibio is not as much a fool as the storyteller thinks.

3. **Love can cause a normally rational person to behave foolishly.** Yes, both Federigo and Chichibio do foolish things. Call to students' attention the fact that Federigo is noted for his courtesy and nobility. Wasting his entire estate in wooing a woman who showed no interest in him was a far more foolish act than killing the falcon, because courtesy demanded that he give his guest the best provisions that he could. Chichibio, on the other hand, is described as a bit of a fool, and so it is not surprising that he feels compelled to give Donna Brunetta the crane's leg.

III. TECHNIQUES

Setting

Like *The Canterbury Tales,* these two stories are placed in a framework. They are told by wealthy aristocrats who have fled to a country house to escape the plague. In what way does this setting add meaning to each of the stories? Because of their backgrounds the listeners would be aware of Federigo's foolishness in pursuing a woman who showed no interest in him and in wasting all his wealth on the project. They would also understand his killing the falcon to serve her, for the etiquette of that time would have demanded this action. In addition, they would admire his acceptance of life on the small farm.

Because the listeners are wealthy people with many servants, they sympathize wholeheartedly with the master's anger at his cook. At the same time, they would be amused that Chichibio could wiggle his way out of the situation; it is a kind of self-satire—to tell jokes on oneself.

Prose Style

Students are asked to look at paragraph four of "Federigo's Falcon," to pick out the subject and the predicate of each sentence, and to note how many modifiers surround these basic parts. There are only four sentences in this paragraph, but the number of modifiers is amazing. Would a story-teller use this extravagant flow of words today?

The Bound Man

PAGE 445

Ilse Aichinger

Glossary Words

weals (page 446, col. 1) Marks or ridges on the skin made by a stick or whip
superfluous (page 447, col. 2) Needless; unnecessary
proprietor (page 448, col. 1) An owner
sacked (page 448, col. 2) Dismissed from employment; fired

Handbook

prose style, setting, symbol

Check Test 51

INTRODUCTION

"The Bound Man" is a complex story that invites many interpretations. A nameless man is attacked, bound, and robbed. He manages to get to a traveling circus where the proprietor persuades him to appear as a new act. He becomes immensely popular, a bigger draw than any of the other acts. People delight in his freak act, and yet he always seems to be in danger from jealous performers and strangers. While bound, he kills an escaped wolf, but the audience at the performance that night is disbelieving and demands that he kill another one. After this demand is rejected by the circus proprietor, the mob storms the animal cages, forces the attendant to open a door, and watches as the Bound Man moves to the cage. At this moment the proprietor's wife cuts the ropes. Freed from his bonds, the Bound Man grabs a gun and shoots the wolf. The mob and the circus people pursue him, but he eludes them by hiding in a bush where he watches the moonlight on the meadow, the color of both growth and death.

This story is quite different from the others in the unit. Through the Bound Man's reactions to his bonds and through the responses of people to him, the story presents a catalog of human foibles.

The story has built-in shock value and therefore can be assigned with no introduction. But if you prefer, you may wish to launch a discussion about what makes a circus appealing. Why is it that people universally like to witness the bizarre, the dangerous, and the incredible?

USING THE STUDY NOTES

PAGE 452

I. WHY

This story confronts the reader with a number of unanswered questions about the Bound Man and about the meaning of the story. Students are directed to the Implications in order to find answers.

II. IMPLICATIONS

Reflect on what you have read and consider your own experiences in discussing the statements that follow.

1. All human beings are *bound*. You could begin by asking students whether there are limitations of movement in the lives of all human beings. Among possible limitations students may suggest are: body, mind, emotions, environment, family, nation, society, culture, and so on. We may be able to change some of the limitations, but there are some from which we can never escape. Point out that we can use mechanical devices (tools, for example) to extend the capabilities of our bodies and thus stretch some of our physical limitations a bit. Inventions such as planes and rockets have also helped humans to break through limitations. However, it can be argued that moving to another country or even going to outer space is merely exchanging one set or kind of limitations for another. The conclusion should be that we are truly bound.

2. The most important thing for people to learn is what they can do within their own limita-

tions. This is a good place to review the characters of Antigone and Macbeth. Both attempted to break out of their limitations. But, when Antigone exceeded her proper limitations as a citizen of Athens, she brought disaster on her whole family, and when Macbeth killed Duncan, he violated his society's precept of the sanctity of the king's person. Note that the Bound Man kept testing his bonds, but when he exceeded the limitations set by them, he was thrown down or injured.

3. The story is a comment on the restrictions of freedom in a totalitarian country. There may be differences of opinion in response to this statement. Most of the Jewish people in Nazi Germany could not escape death no matter how they tried to act within the limitations imposed on them. Many of those who did survive went into exile, thus trading the old set of national limitations for a new set (which was indisputably better). In a dictatorship, people can only survive by performing within the prescribed limitations. Going beyond these limitations is dangerous.

4. There are multiple explanations for why the people want to cut the rope. Jealousy, compassion, malice, daringness—these are some possible motivations. The most interesting motivations to consider are those of the proprietor's wife. Is she perhaps in love with the Bound Man, or is she merely protecting a valuable property? Does she deliberately wish to destroy him, or is she simply an impulsive person?

5. In the last sentences of the story, the linking together of growth, death, and memory is the key to the story's meaning. What a story means is largely subject to individual interpretation. However, the linking of growth, death, and memory does offer an interesting interpretation: Human beings grow by struggling against their bonds; when they have grown enough, death cuts the bonds and releases them. All memories are then obliterated.

III. TECHNIQUES

Setting

1. The principal setting is a traveling circus. Is the circus ever described? Not really. But details are interspersed throughout.

What details are given? Some of the specific details mentioned include the tent, the animal tamer, other performers, the audience, the master of ceremonies, the cages of wolves. The circus is set in a field near a town, and there is a river nearby with undergrowth on its banks.

Do these total up to a setting? For most readers, yes, because readers will probably bring their own images and experiences of a circus to the story.

2. What symbolic associations has the word *circus* garnered through its long existence? Some associations are a collection of the unusual in both people and animals, transitory glitter, the real hidden by the unreal, frivolity.

Prose Style

A writing style may be stripped down or rich, depending on the number of ideas and details that are put into a sentence or a paragraph. These qualities come through even in translation. How would you characterize the style of "The Bound Man"? The words that best describe the style of this story are rich, dense, and detailed. If your classes are familiar with transformational grammar, count how many kernel sentences are contained in the first sentence. Another approach could be to list actions and things mentioned in the sentence.

IV. WORDS

Have students find the sentences with the words listed and discuss the effect of the verbs chosen by the author.

A Man by the Name of Ziegler

PAGE 453

Hermann Hesse

Glossary Words

affectation (page 454, col. 1) Behavior that is not natural, but assumed to impress others; pretense

meticulous (page 454, col. 2) Extremely or excessively careful about small details

amulets (page 454, col. 2) Lockets, carved images, or other small objects worn as magic charms against evil, disease, etc.

succinct (page 456, col. 1) Expressed briefly and clearly; brief; concise

degenerate (page 456, col. 2) Showing a decline in physical, mental, or moral qualities

dissembling (page 456, col. 2) Hiding one's real feelings, thoughts, plans, etc.; pretending

Handbook

prose style, setting, theme

Check Test 52

INTRODUCTION

Hermann Hesse's novels have continued to be popular with young adults because they are not difficult to read and because they have fairly obvious themes. This is true of "A Man by the Name of Ziegler." Ziegler is portrayed as an ungifted, average person with many pretentions who governs his life less by his desires than by his fear of punishment. He takes particular pride in his clothing and has great faith in the power of money and in the power of science. Visiting an historical museum one Sunday afternoon, he wanders into a room displaying objects of medieval superstition. Absentmindedly, he picks up a small, dark-colored pellet. When another visitor enters the room, Ziegler puts the pellet into his pocket, for it is prohibited to touch the objects on display. While waiting for his lunch to be served, he satisfies an impulse to swallow the pellet. That afternoon, during a visit to the zoo, he discovers that he can understand the language of the animals. They discuss how stupid and contemptible he is. At the elk's cage he realizes that the animal thinks that his foppish clothes make him "an absurd and repulsive bug." After searching for and finding no comfort among human beings, he strips off his clothes, clings to the elk's cage, and sobs. He is taken away to an insane asylum.

Ziegler, of course, represents not one person but all persons. The animals' (and Hesse's) denunciation of him is, in effect, a denunciation of the whole human race.

Many of your students may have read Hesse's novels (*Demian* and *Steppenwolf* are especially popular). Ask those who have to give their opinions of Hesse's work. What type of stories do they expect from him? You may wish to point out that "A Man by the Name of Ziegler" was written in Germany before World War II. Suggest that students consider what young person today might be the model for Ziegler.

USING THE STUDY NOTES

PAGE 456

I. THE FOLLY OF PRETENTIONS

Students are asked to reread the first four paragraphs of the story and to list Ziegler's foibles.

1. loved money and pleasure
2. liked to dress well—beyond his means
3. somewhat cowardly
4. governed his life by prohibitions
5. thought his life was the center of the world
6. held tight to his prejudices although facts contradicted them
7. thought people of the middle ages were foolish to be superstitious

II. IMPLICATIONS

Reflect on the following quotations from the selection. What do they mean? Do you find them perceptive judgments of people in general?

1. "He was one of those people we see every day on the street, whose faces we can never really remember, because they all have the same face: a collective face." Individuals in a great mass of people are as indistinguishable from one another as is one animal from another in a herd of cattle. See if students think that they could accurately describe a person whom they met casually a week ago. Generally, looking at a group of people is similar to looking at a photograph of a mass of faces at a football game. Only rarely does any one individual stand out. Ask students if a group of people of another ethnic group tend initially to look alike.

2. ". . . like other men he regarded himself and his life as the center of the world." This statement is true of most human beings. We tend to see everything from our own egocentric views. We think of our town, our state, and our country as the center of the world. We must overcome this localism in order to become aware that others exist and to realize that we are only a small part of a large whole. This awareness is one of the major marks of maturity. One could say that Ziegler is really locked into childhood.

3. **"As a modern man, he had unlimited respect not only for money, but also for a second power: science."** Certainly many Americans hold both money and science in great esteem. There are very few people who are not impressed by money. Nor is Ziegler unique in his admiration of science. Although he actually knows little about science (he cannot even define it), he has great faith that science will solve the world's problems. Most people today feel the same way about science; we expect scientists to find new fuels, new heating designs, new pollution-control devices, better ways to extract salt from sea water, and so on.

III. TECHNIQUES

Setting

Since Hesse, too, is using nonhumans as commentators in this story, what other setting might he have used? Hesse might have used a pet shop, a livestock farm, a garden with rabbits, a home overrun by ants, a beehive located in a tree on a boulevard, and so on. Ask the class to suggest other settings.

What makes the zoo a particularly good choice? The animals in the zoo are from all over the world. Hence, their diverse speech seems to express opinions of human beings that are universally held by animals.

Prose Style

Read the second paragraph aloud. What positive comments does the narrator make about Ziegler? What negative ones? How are they arranged? What is the effect on the reader's feeling toward Ziegler?

Many readers will consider the following comments to be positive: Ziegler is not stupid. He loves money and pleasure and likes to dress well. He doesn't let his desires govern his life, he is gratifyingly normal, he regards himself as an individual who is at the center of the world.

Negative: He is not gifted, he is cowardly, and he governs his life by prohibitions and the fear of punishment. Hesse has listed the qualities so that the positive ones and the negative ones usually alternate. There will probably be some disagreement among students about whether or not the positive qualities listed above are actually good traits. In general, by listing the qualities and by the manner in which he lists them, Hesse is trying to establish Ziegler as an "every person." That designation will probably come through to most readers.

SUMMING UP: FOIBLES

THE WORLD OF COMEDY

Students are asked to discuss the following questions in terms of the selections they have read in this unit.

1. **How many of these employed humor?** There were elements of humor in all the selections except for "The Bound Man," "Jeannot and Colin," and possibly "A Man by the Name of Ziegler." Sometimes the humor was obvious, and sometimes it was the more subtle humor of irony as in "A Trip with Obstacles."

2. **Select the two characters with whom you felt the most sympathy and explain why.** Tell students that their replies should emphasize *why.* Permit them to pick only one character or to pick more than two if they have good reason for doing so. Perhaps an individual student can do an exceptional piece of work with only one character, and to add another would spoil the effect. On the other hand, some students could sympathize with three characters who have marked similarities and may want to discuss all of them.

3. **Do the authors seemingly agree in their attitudes toward human foibles or is there a wide difference of opinion?** It should be clear to students that there is a wide difference of opinion. Some of the authors tend to regard the foibles that they discussed as rather amiable weaknesses—Durrell and Johnson, for instance. Others, such as Thackeray and Voltaire, take an intermediate attitude. Still others, such as Aichinger and Strindberg, have very serious attitudes.

4. **What is the total effect of these selections, that is, what do they say to you about human foibles?** Students will probably recognize that they themselves as well as other human beings, have repertoires of foibles, that these little eccentricities in many cases make individuals more interesting, and that some of the foibles are amusing to read about but would be distressing to confront in another person. Answers will vary from class to class, depending, of course, on each individual's reaction to the selections.

IMPLICATIONS

1. **Open your book to the Table of Contents. For each selection in this unit, name the foible that is highlighted.**

The Miser: the rich fearing for the safety of their possessions; using flattery to gain one's ends; lying to get even with someone; letting love control one's actions

"The Influence of the Aristocracy on Snobs": snobbery itself; gaining status by association (attending the same church or shopping at the same stores)

"A Journey in a Stage-Coach": pretending to strangers to be something that you are not

"Love and Bread": living beyond one's means; extravagance; showing the depth of one's love by an ostentatious style of living

"Jeannot and Colin": pretentiousness, outward show, flattery

"Dissection of a Beau's Heart": artificiality, vanity, falseness

"The Coquette's Heart": shallowness, concern with outward show, frivolousness, flirtatiousness

"A Trip with Obstacles": living with practicality and order as one's guidelines

"How to Buy a House": play acting in a business deal; volubility

"Federigo's Falcon": excess courtesy; foolish action when in love

"The One-Legged Crane": lying to get out of trouble

"The Bound Man": delight in the abnormal; loving one's limitations; envy

"A Man by the Name of Ziegler": foppishness; pretentiousness

The above are not necessarily the only answers. What one sees in a story is, of course, largely an individual matter.

2. Do the selections in this unit confirm or contradict the ideas in the following statements? Use examples to support your opinions.

a. Foibles distort a person's behavior. "To twist out of shape" is the meaning of *distort* as it is used in this statement. Some of the more obvious examples of distorted behavior are found in "A Journey in a Stage-Coach," *The Miser,* and "The Bound Man." Students may make a case for distorted behavior in some of the other selections.

b. Foibles make a person interesting. This is not true in all cases, but certainly Harpagon, Chichibio, and the Bound Man fit this description. These people may be distressing to live with, but they are enjoyable to read about.

c. Most people are better known for their foibles than for their virtues. Have students think about the stories that they have read in this unit. Choose half a dozen characters, and, as you read the characters' names, ask students to jot down the trait of that character that first comes to their minds. Then choose a half dozen people who are well known to the students (both local and national figures) and do the same thing. Compile the results, which should show whether foibles or virtues stand out. What we remember about others depends on very personal judgments.

TECHNIQUES

Setting

1. In which selection is the setting most vivid? Durrell gives the most details of the setting, which plays an important part in his essay. Some students may choose "The Bound Man" as having the most vivid setting; should they do so, be sure to point out how much of the setting springs from their own imaginations. At the opposite extreme of vividness in setting is "A Journey in a Stage-Coach," in which few details are given. Also, there is not much elaboration in the description of settings in Boccaccio's tales. The extent to which students will remember details of setting will depend on how closely they read the selection and on the accuracy of their memories.

2. In which piece did the setting have the most effect on the plot? In the Johnson piece, the particular kind of setting was necessary to make the action plausible. In Hesse's story a zoo was needed in order to convey the message that animals around the world hold a low opinion of human beings. And only in a circus, an environment exhibiting the freakish and the bizarre in life, would the Bound Man have been prompted to stay tied by his ropes. Throughout the discussion help students to realize how very important setting is to the plot of a story.

3. Did any of the settings contribute to the mood of the story? Setting contributes a good deal to mood in "How to Buy a House," "Love and Bread," and "The Bound Man." Naturally, students may select stories other than these. In "Jeannot and Colin," the two settings of Auvergne and Paris affect both the mood and behavior of the Jeannots leading to success in the small town and failure in Paris. With each selection under discussion, have students attempt to analyze *how* the setting contributed to the mood.

4. Which selections used parts of the setting almost like props in a play? Perhaps the best nominees for this award would be "Love and Bread" and "A Man by the Name of Ziegler." "The One-Legged Crane" may be chosen by some students because the final setting of the cranes sleeping on the river bank actually triggers the ending.

Prose Style

1. How do the types of dialogue used by Strindberg and Johnson differ? How does the dialogue affect the movement or rhythm of these pieces of writing?

Johnson uses many-syllabled words and long sentences. Each of his characters talk in one uninterrupted, long speech, and there is no oral interaction among the persons in the coach. This type of dialogue gives a slow, somewhat ponderous and old-fashioned movement to the selection.

Strindberg, who was perhaps best noted for his play-writing, constructs his dialogue as if it were appearing in a drama, and the rhythm is that of natural conversation. He frequently omits, once the characters' personalities are established, who is speaking. The speed and complexity of his style contrast with Johnson's ponderous style.

2. Read several narrative passages from both "Federigo's Falcon" and "Love and Bread." Assuming that Boccaccio and Strindberg each used a style typical of his time, how has the style of writing changed over this 500-year period? Strindberg's sentences are far shorter than those of Boccaccio; they also are far less complicated and contain fewer modifying structures. At times, Boccaccio's sentences seem almost to twist and turn upon themselves.

UNIT TEST

There are several options for testing your students' grasp of the unit. You may use the Summing Up section in the pupil's anthology—either whole or in part—as the unit test. For a second approach, you may select questions at random from the Study Notes at the end of each selection as a basis for constructing a final examination covering the complete unit. For a third option you may choose to use the comprehensive unit test already prepared on blackline masters available in a separate test booklet, ISBN 0-07-009823-9.

RELATING COMPOSITION TO THE UNIT

1. Thackeray's essay is an attack on the snobs of his time. Write an essay that attacks the snobs of *your* time.

2. Write a vignette, a short literary sketch, in which you poke fun at one human foible. You may, for example, want to describe the comeuppance of a vain and arrogant individual.

3. Write a dialogue between two people in which one is trying to point out the other's foibles. ("Can't you see how you're behaving; it's ridiculous" could be an opening comment.)

4. Pick a character from one of the selections and write an interior monologue (what the character is thinking) for one of the scenes in the story. Be sure the language fits the character's personality, level of education, historical period, and so on.

RELATING THE GALLERY TO THE UNIT

PAGE 410

1. People caught with their dignity down is the subject matter of this gallery that examines some historical parries at human foibles by artists with clear eyes and sharp brushes. It is important to note that, although the costumes and the scenery may be several centuries old, the situations depicted and the satirical treatment rendered by the artists are timeless. The character and the universality of satire should be the dominant note of an introductory discussion of the gallery. Questions to ask include: What are the characteristics of satire? What parallels to literary satire does each of the artists in the gallery employ? What human foibles are ripe for satirizing in this gallery?

2. The age-old practice of the con game is captured vividly in Georges de La Tour's "The Fortune Teller" (page 410). Distracted by an appeal to his vanity, the young dandy is an easy mark for the fortune-teller's pickpocketing assistants. Questions to ask include: What do the facial expressions tell us about the satire that is being employed? If this were a contemporary fortune-teller, what sort of setting would probably be picked by the artist? What kind of person would become the butt of the joke?

3. Toulouse Lautrec was able to portray simply eccentric people who laugh at the conventional predictability of the world. Examine with the class his drawing of Yvette Guilbert on page 412. Notice how, with a few simple strokes, Lautrec gives Guilbert a definite facial expression that brims with a sort of superior humor. The regal pose of the body contributes to this impression, and the garishness of hair color and the starkness of makeup complete the picture. If possible, show students other examples of Lautrec's satirical portraits of nonconforming, antiestablishment Parisians. This exploration should trigger discussion of benign nonconformity as a form of satire. Lautrec was ostracized because of his habits and physical handicaps. Was it thus easier for him to satirize the establishment? What other qualities help people to place themselves outside of the establishment?

4. The political satire of Hogarth's "The Election—Chairing the Member" (page 414) has its direct counterpart in contemporary political cartoons. Showing a dignified man in an absurd situation at the moment of his greatest triumph trims him down to size and perhaps below it. The setting depicted pokes fun at the entire system that allows this absurdity to take place. Examine the painting with students, noting the individual facial expressions, the inclusion of satirical details such as the pigs, the violinist, and the bird poised above the official. Ask students how this painting could be revised as a modern political cartoon satirizing the overblown self-importance of political figures. As a follow-up assignment, direct students to bring to class political cartoons emloying some of the same elements of absurd juxtaposition and choice of incident that are apparent in Hogarth's painting. More artistically talented students may be directed to draw political cartoons that satirize the pomposity of a recognizable celebrity.

THE EXPANDED EXPERIENCE: RELATING THE HUMANITIES TO THE UNIT

1. Disciplines: E, SS, A, M, F. Skills: Rd, Wr, PS, LS, Org.

View the short film "Help, My Snowman's Burning Down," which is a satire on contemporary advertising techniques. Then, using the film as your model, create your own satire of advertising techniques, using magazine illustrations, television and radio commercials, and so on. Present this satire to the class.

2. Disciplines: E, A, SS, M, TA, F. Skills: LS, Rd, Wr, PS, Org.

Research the absurd, wild revolt against smugness that was called Dada. Collect some examples of Dada poetry by Tristan Tzara, Richard Hulsenbreck, and Hugo Ball as well as illustrations of the sculpture, paintings, posters, and films of Hans Arp, Marcel Janco, Marcel Duchamp, Francis Picabia and Man Ray. Conduct a Dada event resembling the events that were conducted in the early 1920s in Zurich and Paris. Involve other class members in some of the absurd displays of nonsense to which Dadaists subjected their audiences. After the presentation, discuss the healthy effect and the historical importance of this absurd revolt against entrenched smugness.

3. Disciplines: M, E. Skills: Rd, PS.

As we have seen, styles of writing and of painting are related to the historical period in which a work is written as well as to the peculiarities of the individual writer and artist. Music, too, expresses the spirit and mood of a historical period. Ask students who are interested in music to bring records of music composed in the fourteenth century (Boccaccio's *The Decameron),* the seventeenth century (Molière's *The Miser),* the 1920s (Hermann Hesse's "A Man by the Name of Ziegler"), and the 1950s (Ilse Aichinger's "The Bound Man.") Does the music echo or reinforce the mood and spirit of the stories? Do the writers and musicians seem to share similar concerns and tendencies of style in each period?

RELATING ADDITIONAL READING TO THE UNIT

Suggested Books

Austen, Jane. *Pride and Prejudice*
Bennett, Jack. *Mister Fisherman*
Brautigan, Richard. *Trout Fishing in America*
Brecht, Bertolt. *Threepenny Opera*
Caudel, Elizabeth. *Come Be My Guest*
Cervantes, Miguel de. *Don Quixote*
Davis, Valentine. *Miracle on Thirty-fourth Street*
Dennis, Patrick. *Auntie Mame*
Dickens, Charles. *David Copperfield*
Durrell, Gerald. *Rosie Is My Relative*
Flaubert, Gustave. *Madame Bovary*
Galsworthy, John. *The Forsyte Saga*
Gogol, Nikolai. *The Inspector General*
Goldsmith, Oliver. *She Stoops to Conquer*
Guareschi, Giovanni. *The Little World of Don Camillo*
Lewis, Sinclair. *Main Street*
Molière. *Tartuffe*
Pirandello, Luigi. *Six Characters in Search of an Author*
Pound, Richard. *Don Quixote U.S.A.*
Rostand, Edmond. *Cyrano de Bergerac*
Saroyan, William. *My Name Is Aram*
Shakespeare, William. *As You Like It*
———. *A Midsummer-Night's Dream*
———. *Twelfth Night*
Shaw, George Bernard. *Androcles and the Lion*
———. *Pygmalion*
Sheridan, Richard. *The Rivals*
Swift, Jonathan. *Gulliver's Travels*
Thackeray, William. *Vanity Fair*
Vonnegut, Kurt. *God Bless You, Mr. Rosewater*
West, Jessamyn. *Except for Me and Thee*
Wibberly, Leonard. *The Mouse That Roared*
Wilder, Thornton. *The Skin of Our Teeth*
Williams, Tennessee. *The Glass Menagerie*
Wilde, Oscar. *The Importance of Being Earnest*

NINETEENTH-CENTURY BRITISH POETRY: Revolution and Imagination

In this unit we come to poems that are likely to be more accessible to students and more familiar to teachers. The poems are less dependent on poetic conventions and are more clearly expressions of personal emotions. Getting the students to understand the poets' feelings is the major focus here. Although the language is not particularly difficult, you may need to help students to understand the signficance of the metaphors, whether expressed in one or two words (Blake) or whether extended through a whole stanza (Keats).

The poetry of the nineteenth century presents a great temptation to teach only "themes," because so many of the poets were passionately committed to various ideas that they expressed in their poems. Thus, Blake is sometimes reduced to a protest poet, Wordsworth to a nature poet, Coleridge to a poet of the imagination, and so on. By getting students to focus on the personal aspects of the poems and on the rich metaphoric qualities you should avoid this problem.

Because so many of these poems express individual feelings, this unit may offer opportunities to discuss the backgrounds of the poets. Students who have never seen the English lake district, either in actuality or in pictures, may have a hard time understanding Wordsworth's intense love for his boyhood home. Those who have never seen pictures of dirty, smoke-filled London may not understand why Blake and Wordsworth got so upset about the Industrial Revolution. The relationship between Wordsworth and Coleridge as friends and collaborators could also be explored. Or the story of Robert Browning and Elizabeth Barrett Browning could be discussed (perhaps through Besier's play *The Barretts of Wimpole Street).* Pictures of Renaissance Italy or of nineteenth-century Italy would also be helpful, the former for giving students some sense of the Italy that Robert Browning wrote about, the latter for showing students the sunny country that so many English poets (Shelley, Keats, the Brownings) fled to.

Another way to work with the poems in this unit is to refer to poems studied in previous units so that students can see both the similarities and the differences among them. "The Wanderer" could well be compared with Tennyson's "Ulysses"; the ballads with Keats's "La Belle Dame Sans Merci"; and the sonnets of Wordsworth and Keats with earlier sonnets. Or you could also take a general theme such as faith and look at the questioning attitudes revealed by Tennyson and Arnold as compared with the more secure faith of George Herbert or even of John Donne. The poets in the next unit (twentieth century) frequently address themselves to the same questions raised by nineteenth-century poets.

NOTE: For some suggested reference sources, see the bibliography in the introduction to the first poetry unit, pages 34-36 in this teacher's guide.

Poems by William Blake

PAGE 459

Glossary Words

symmetry (page 460) Pleasing proportions; harmony

manacles (page 460) Handcuffs; anything that chains or binds; restraints

Handbook

allusion, metaphor, personificaton, rhyme scheme, rhythm

Check Test 53

INTRODUCTION

Teaching Blake's poetry can be easy and difficult. For the most part, the poems are deceptively simple. The difficulty involves getting past the nursery-rhyme feeling to the power of the images and to the questions raised in each poem.

Our selection of Blake's poems focuses on the more accessible ones; none of the later, highly symbolic work is included. "The Lamb" and "The Tyger" form a natural teaching unit. In fact, "The Tyger" refers to "The Lamb," and the contrasting symbols should be discussed together. "London" and "The Garden of Love" may be taught together, for they are both poems about repression. Religion is the principal repressive force in "The Garden of Love," whereas "London" offers a broader picture of the society's evils.

USING THE STUDY NOTES PAGE 461

THE LAMB/THE TYGER

1. "The Lamb" is part of a collection of poems Blake called *Songs of Innocence* and "The Tyger" is a companion piece in a collection called *Songs of Experience*. What details in each poem would be associated with those two different qualities, innocence and experience? Students will probably have formed a number of associations for *lamb* and *tiger* quite apart from the poem and those could be discussed. In "The Lamb," Blake creates a pastoral world, "By the stream and o'er the mead." The lamb is personified in a gentle way, for example, by calling the lamb's fleece "clothing of delight" and "softest," "wooly bright." The "tender voice" that makes "all the vales rejoice" suggests an innocent, happy quality.

The tiger, on the other hand, is mysteriously "burning bright." Further, it is found, not in the innocent meadow, but in the forests "of the night"—forests that are dark and mysterious. The tiger is "fearful"—that is, not afraid but rather something to be feared. All the references to fire and blacksmithing create a sense of something being burned (by experience?) or being hammered into shape (again, by experience?).

2. Both poems begin with a question. How many questions are there in each poem? How many answers? In what ways is the difference important? There is only one question in "The Lamb," although it is repeated four times. But "The Tyger" is composed entirely of questions, fifteen in all. There is, fittingly enough, one answer in "The Lamb," preceded by the assurance of an answer, "Little Lamb I'll tell thee." This answer is not given in one word but is embodied in lines 13-18. And the implication of the last two lines is that "God" is the answer. But there are no answers at all in "The Tyger"; instead we return to the question with which we began. One can argue that when innocent, one believes in answers and believes that they actually exist, whereas the experienced person knows that there are no final answers. In this case, the difference between the poems derives from the different states of innocence and experience from which each poem springs. But perhaps there are no answers in "The Tyger" because the question is far more complicated and cannot be answered directly. The closest that we come to an answer is line 20, "Did he who made the Lamb make thee?" And that line, which implies the answer "yes," is, significantly, not a statement nor an assertion but another question.

3. In what ways are these poems concerned with a religious question? Can you state the question? What is the answer in "The Lamb"? What is the answer in "The Tyger"? "The Lamb" raises the question of creation: Who is responsible for the creation of nature? And the answer, simply stated, is that God, as Christ, is the creator. Christ is traditionally called the Lamb of God, who "became a little child" when incarnated as a human being. The adjectives *meek* and *mild* are often associated with Christ. "The Tyger" raises a much more complicated religious question that takes a long time to pose. At first the question seems to be how the tiger, a force of evil and destruction, came to exist in the world. But finally that question becomes one of whether or not God is responsible for creating both the lamb and the tiger, both good and evil, both salvation (as Christ became human to save humankind) and destruction. And the answer is not given directly. We infer the answer "yes" to the question "Did he who made the Lamb make thee?" because that question sounds like a concluding statement. (After that line, the poem returns to its opening question.)

4. In "The Tyger," what seems to be the central metaphor in stanzas 2-4? Why is this metaphor appropriate? The middle stanzas really depend on the word *frame* in the first stanza—a word that suggests control through framing or perhaps shaping. Stanza 2 contains two allusions, to Icarus ("On what wings dare he aspire?") and to Prometheus ("What the hand, dare seize the fire?"). Both are rebels; students may therefore infer that only someone as daring as these rebels could try to shape or control the forces of evil. Stanza 3 alludes to Vulcan, the smith of the gods, and here the metaphor of blacksmithing implied in "frame" becomes explicit. In stanzas 3 and 4, the fire that melted Icarus's wings and that Prometheus stole is now the furnace fire over which some heavenly blacksmith beats out the shape of the tiger. Blacksmithing is a forceful activity. It is hard work—hot, dirty, and brutal. Such an activity seems to be appropriate in order to create the tiger and its destructive power.

5. The first and last stanzas of "The Tyger" are identical, except for one word. How is the meaning altered by this word change? What is the effect of the repetition of the first stanza? The shift is from *could* to *dare.* The meaning shifts from "ability to do" to "courage to do"—that is, from who would have the ability to create a tiger to who would have the courage to create a tiger and to unleash it in the world. Thus we shift from God as creator (as in "The Lamb") to God as simultaneous creator/destroyer. The repetition of the first stanza, with this significant change, achieves closure. Otherwise, one thinks, the questions could go on forever, for the coexistence of good and evil in the world is one of those truly puzzling philosophical and moral questions. But because the first stanza is a question, the poem ends with a question rather than with a resolution. Blake, lover of opposites that he is, manages to have it both ways. He ends, but he does not end; he asserts, but he questions.

What is the effect of repetition in "The Lamb"? In "The Lamb," by contrast, the repetition suggests total closure: The lines of the second stanza are not the same as those of the first. We move from question to answer, from confusion to assurance, from uncertainty to blessing.

LONDON

1. Look up the possible meanings of *charter'd.* How many meanings seem relevant to the poem? The word *charter'd* suggests charted or mapped out. It also means "legally defined," as with a charter. And it means "constricted," "limited." These are the major meanings that seem relevant to the poem. London is a place that is geographically defined, placed on maps, bound by laws that may restrict or limit. Such restriction, found both in the streets (which we would expect) and in the river (which we probably do not expect), is what Blake finds unendurable.

2. Blake sets up a conflict between two groups in his society. What are these groups? By whom are they represented in the poem? Do you think Blake is fair to both groups? The conflict is between the oppressors and the oppressed. The oppressed are represented by the soldier, the chimney sweep, the harlot, and the infant—all those who have no choice about the direction of their lives. The oppressors are those who "charter" rivers and streets, those who represent the authority of the Church, those who live in palaces, and those who uphold institutions. Blake is not fair to either group. The speaker is making a protest and therefore shows the oppressors in a totally negative light.

3. Blake is describing eighteenth-century London. Is the description that he gives of a huge city still a valid one? How does the London of Blake's time differ from today's New York, Chicago, or Los Angeles? Blake's description of a huge city is still valid two hundred years later, with some qualifications. We still have slums and people who cannot move upward in society. Cities are still inhabited by large numbers of the lost, the lonely, and the poor; and the effects of city life can be seen on the faces of the people who live there. Differences between eighteenth-century London and modern cities do exist, however; for example, women who bear illegitimate children are not branded as harlots. One hopes that in the twentieth century the "mind-forg'd manacles" are not what they were two hundred years ago.

4. In lines 5-7, Blake repeats the words *in every.* How does this repetition affect the tone and meaning of the poem? The repetition of "in every" strengthens the tone of hopelessness because of its inclusiveness: there is no person, no voice, no infant, no cry, and no ban exempt from the terrible effects of oppression.

5. What are the sources of oppression suggested by the poem? Does Blake imply any solution? Some of the sources of oppression have been mentioned in question 2. They include the institutions of government, the church, the palace, and the military— all of which oppress others. But the phrase "mind-forg'd manacles" implies that slavery emanates from the mind's acceptance of society's restrictions. The poem is therefore extremely bleak, for only when human beings can throw off or unlock those "mind-forg'd manacles" will they be able to end society's oppression. And yet, as the last stanza implies, such change may not be possible—not if the "new born Infant" is "cursed" from the beginning and not if the marriage bed is so infected (with plagues) that it turns into the "Marriage hearse."

THE GARDEN OF LOVE

1. Try reading this poem aloud. Listen to the sound of the words, to the rhymes, and to the rhythm of the stanzas. Do you notice any difference in these elements as you read the three stanzas? How might this difference be connected to Blake's notions about freedom and repression? When students read the poem aloud, certain differences should become obvious. The first stanza is essentially regular in beat and in rhyme scheme. The second stanza contains some sudden rhythmical shifts ("Thou shalt not" interrupts the flow of line 6, and there is a similar irregularity in line 8). The third stanza has a beginning rhythm similar to that in the first two stanzas, but line 11 is noticeably different—there are ten syllables instead of eight, and there is an internal rhyme, "gowns" and "rounds." The same pattern—ten syllables and an internal rhyme ("briars" and "desires")—can be found in line 12. The change in rhythm in the second stanza, which interrupts the established order of the first stanza, could be compared to the effect of the prohibition "Thou shalt not." Any prohibition, Blake implies, is as restrictive, stifling, and uncomfortable as the lines suggest. And the third stanza amplifies the change— suddenly the order of the first stanza is transformed. Instead of the closure that we expect, we get internal rhymes that could be repeated indefinitely; that is, lines 11 and 12 create a new pattern that could be extended. There is no end, Blake implies. Just as the priests will continue to walk round and round, so the imprisonment of feeling by institutions will never cease.

2. What is the central image of the last stanza? How is it related to the image suggested by the phrase, "the Garden of Love"? In the last stanza there is a cemetery with "graves" and "tomb-stones." The garden has been transformed; it has changed from a place of love into a place of death. The image of the "briars" is particularly frightening; the "sweet flowers" of the second stanza now have thorns that are used to bind joys and desires. A potentially beautiful and happy symbol, the flowers, has been turned into something evil and destructive.

IMPLICATIONS (BLAKE)

Students are asked to consider the following statements, both in terms of Blake's ideas and in terms of their own feelings.

1. It is more important to raise questions than to have answers. Blake would probably agree with this statement, if agreement can be inferred from the example of "The Tyger." He questions the value of assertions, especially in the negative prohibition contained in "The Garden of Love." Students may disagree with this statement. They may assume that it is better to have answers. You may wish to ask if having answers is more important in some situations than in others. Certainly some situations are so complicated that any "answer" can only involve a simpleminded solution.

2. Religion is an institution that deadens rather than revives the soul. "The Garden of Love," in which the chapel destroys the garden, suggests that Blake would agree with this statement. And in "London," the church seems to be an agent of oppression. Yet religion, truly understood, offers humanity the vision of the heavenly city, Jerusalem, and Blake wants to establish such a city in England (see his poem "And Did Those Feet in Ancient Time"). Furthermore, his poems are informed by religious imagery. It would appear that, perhaps, the *institutionalizing* of religion causes the deadness. Students may want to bring their own experiences into the discussion. What may emerge is a sense that religion in itself is a powerful force that is not always served by its particular institutions.

3. A person's mind can act to enslave or to set free. Certainly Blake would agree with this statement. The human mind both forges the manacles and provokes "mental fight." It is important to note that Blake's vision, although often terrible and stern, does not despair. Students will also agree with this statement, which could lead to a discussion involving a number of texts. We recall, for example, that Antigone, defeated physically by Creon, triumphed through her will; or that Macbeth, seemingly pressured by the witches and Lady Macbeth, was actually the slave of his own will and his own desires.

Poems by William Wordsworth

PAGE 462

Glossary Words

ignoble (page 463) Dishonorable; disgraceful

reconciles (page 463) Brings into agreement or harmony

modes (page 465) The ways in which things are done; methods

Handbook

climax, imagery, sonnet, theme, tone

Check Test 54

INTRODUCTION

Wordsworth is a poet both familiar and strange. He is a figure around whom a number of clichés have been built, notably that he is a poet of nature. Unfortunately, his power as a philosopher/poet is sometimes dissipated in the popular notion of him as a man who wandered around looking at daffodils. Certainly Wordsworth celebrated nature and his relationship to the natural world, but what we should notice is that the relationship was not always a pretty one. The memories that seem to have the most power for Wordsworth are, in his own words, "fostered alike by beauty and by fear." Not only the loveliness of nature but its dreariness, its loneliness, and its awesomeness affected him most strongly.

The selection from *The Prelude* stresses two of Wordsworth's major themes: his sense of learning from nature and his awareness of fear as caused by his experiences. Wordsworth talks about his boyish pranks that have darker sides. We see him pilfering from other people's bird-snares and then imagining that "low breathings" follow him. He climbs up mountains to rob birds' nests and finds himself hanging alone on a windswept crag. And, in one of the most memorable passages of the poem, he steals a boat, rows it on the lake, and feels as though the surrounding mountain is moving after him. The passage thus concentrates on the concrete experiences of Wordsworth's childhood and on the potent memories of fear that they aroused in him.

The Prelude, as a whole, concerns Wordsworth's growing up, and the passage selected should appeal to your students who may well be encountering some of the same problems. Wordsworth's sense of being related to nature, even of being pursued by nature, may well tie in with experiences that they have had.

The sonnet "Composed upon Westminster Bridge" is a familiar one that is open to different interpretations. As the questions suggest, you may want to teach the sonnet with Blake's poem "London." And students may have different reactions to the sonnet as they try to explain Wordsworth's attitude. Is London beautiful to him because it is asleep? Would it be less beautiful if he were looking at the turmoil of the city's daily life? And does the last line imply that perhaps what he really likes is a dead London ("all that mighty heart is lying still!")?

USING THE STUDY NOTES PAGE 466

from THE PRELUDE, BOOK I

1. Wordsworth describes three different episodes in this section. What do they have in common? The episodes all involve stealing. Wordsworth is always alone; even in the second episode, when he seems to set out with others, he ends up hanging on the mountain by himself. Finally, Wordsworth is always scared.

2. Lines 340-344 talk about the "dark/Inscrutable workmanship that reconciles/Discordant elements." How does this generalization apply to the specific events described before and after these lines? Each one of the episodes described can be said to have "discordant elements," namely, those stirrings of fear and terror that make Wordsworth feel as if nature is somehow turning on him and punishing him for his behavior. But the fact that he remembers these episodes and uses them as the basis for his poetry suggests that a reconciliation has taken place. Now those moments function as harmony rather than as discord. One might also observe that Wordsworth's frightful perceptions that the hills are breathing, that the wind is talking, and that the mountain is moving after him serve to make him aware of nature as a living force. The fear is necessary to create that awareness, but the awareness itself is positive and thus is a part of the reconciliation process.

3. Why is the boat-stealing episode described in greater detail and placed after the other descriptions? What makes this episode particularly memorable, for Wordsworth and for us? Placing the episode last and setting it off through the device of inserting a paragraph of generalization about the meaning of these experiences is Wordsworth's artistic strategy. Because this moment is the most important one to him, he gives it the climactic place in this series. A principle of artistic economy is at work here; he describes two episodes rather briefly and so builds up to the longer one. What makes the episode especially powerful is the combination of beauty and fear, the two forces to which he refers at the beginning of the passage. The images contribute to our romantic impression of the scene—"Small circles glittering idly in the moon," "an elfin pinnace," "silent lake," the boat moves "like a swan." All of these images reveal a peaceful, almost fairy-tale quality. Then the poet recreates his surprise when he startles us with the changed atmosphere. As the mountain suddenly thrusts itself upon him, so does the word "Upreared," coming suddenly at the beginning of a line, jolt us. The lines beginning with "I struck and struck again" seem to gather speed; we sense that the boy is trying desperately to escape. Once again, the placement of words is crucial; at the beginning of line 385, "Strode after me" gives us the sense of the mountain's inescapable power.

Another source of power is the strong visual image that Wordsworth conveys. The other two episodes concerned sounds, but in this episode we are concerned with the sense of sight. Our ears may deceive us, but "seeing is believing." Wordsworth sees a fantastically frightening thing. We know that it must be his own guilty conscience, but it is surely an amazing thing that Wordsworth's conscience could conjure up a mountain coming after him.

COMPOSED UPON WESTMINSTER BRIDGE

1. Where is the poet standing? According to the poem's title, the poet is on Westminster Bridge. Judging from the poem itself, he must have a perspective that allows him to see a great part of the city; that is, he must be above the city.

What time of day is it? How is the time related to the mood of the poem? The phrase "The beauty of the morning" clearly reveals the time of day. And that particular time of day is essential for the mood of calmness, of solitude, that the poem communicates.

2. What lines convey the speaker's emotion? The chief emotion, perhaps, is the deep calm that is conveyed most directly in line 11. The same emotion is communicated in the last two lines as well. In addition to the feeling of deep calm, there is conveyed a sense of the emotion that one feels upon looking at any object of beauty. Indeed, we can say that the calm grows directly out of this perception of beauty.

3. Is this a poem about city life or nature? Students should define "city life." The phrase can be defined as "the city at work." But clearly, this is not a poem about city life, for the city is asleep. At this moment, the city is part of nature, not opposed to it. The air is "smokeless," and we feel the connection of "ships, towers, domes, theaters, and temples" with the "fields" and "the sky." On the other hand, so many of the places described are only city places—and Wordsworth seems to glory in them, in "majesty" related to the vastness of London.

4. How does Wordsworth's view of London differ from Blake's (see p. 460)? By choosing a sonnet, a form associated with love poetry, and by using words that suggest beauty ("fair," "touching," "majesty," "beauty of the morning," "bright," "glittering," "beautifully," "spendor," "sweet"), Wordsworth projects what is essentially a positive reaction to the city. The only reservation may be the one mentioned earlier, namely, whether that beauty is perceivable only when the city is asleep. Blake's London, as we have seen, is a terrifying place. His images are brutal, his tone is harsh, and his picture is savage. Wordsworth sees the city in relation to natural forces. Because he feels an intimate kinship with nature, he can relate to the city. Blake sees the city as a social construct. He is therefore appalled by what people have done to themselves. These different perspectives account in large measure for the different perceptions of the poets.

IMPLICATIONS (WORDSWORTH)

Students are asked to consider the following statements, both in terms of Wordsworth's ideas and in terms of their own feelings.

1. Pain and fear are necessary preliminaries to achieving a "calm existence." The passage from *The Prelude* clearly supports this view. Students may at first contend that pain and fear are emotions to shun. They may feel, as Lucy asserts in *Peanuts,* "Why can't I go from one up to another up to another up?" But they should realize that we learn from experience and that we must start learning how to cope with the unpleasant side of life at an early age. Facing separation or death or unhappiness is not easy. It is even harder if one has never had any experience, even in a small way, in coping with pain.

2. Nature will give us strength if we are able to understand its lessons. Again, Wordsworth would agree, and students will probably also agree. They should be encouraged to talk about experiences in which they have found some kind of peace or relaxation or restoration from being out of doors, from working in natural surroundings, from outdoor sports, and so on.

A Poem by Samuel Taylor Coleridge

PAGE 466

Glossary Words

decree (page 466) Command; order; decide

meandering (page 467) Following a winding course

Handbook

atmosphere, imagery, rhyme scheme, stanza

Check Test 55

INTRODUCTION

"Kubla Khan" can perhaps never be fully explained, either in terms of its source or of its meaning. Yet it is one of the great poems that celebrate the imagination, and as such it is central to an understanding of the poetry of the late eighteenth and early nineteenth century.

The poem begins with a description of a fantastic and exotic place. It contains a "sacred river," which may be one of the rivers flowing underground in paradise. There is an encircled spot that reminds us again of paradise. There are also "caverns measureless to man" and "a stately pleasure dome." As the description continues, the place seems to become more violent and "savage"; the relative calm of the first stanza is broken. This contrast is summed up in the final lines of the second stanza, that present a number of contradictions: a "mingled measure" and "a sunny pleasure dome with caves of ice." The place of refuge in the first stanza is now disturbed by voices prophesying war. The third stanza presents an abrupt change as a new vision is described. At first we may feel as if we are reading a different poem, but then the poet/ speaker tells of his desire to "build that dome in air." Can it be done? Is it an impossible dream? Or has the poet, in this poem, already achieved that vision, that contradictory harmony?

Students may find the poem both appealing and baffling. It appeals directly to the senses with its vivid images and lush diction, but the meaning is not at all clear. Perhaps meaning may not be pertinent here, although the poem is a fascinating one to try to fit together. (The study questions below offer some possible approaches to meaning.) What is really important, however, is the texture of the poem, the use of images, and the experience created. We may not be able to explain dreams, but they are vital to our lives.

USING THE STUDY NOTES PAGE 470

KUBLA KHAN

1. What atmosphere is created by the first stanza? How do the images and the rhythm of the lines contribute to that feeling? Students may have a number of answers to this question. There is a "stately" feeling, suggested by the proper names in the first three lines. A sense of majesty, a scene of an enclosed garden, is conveyed through the orderly scene described. The atmosphere is lush, as the words "fertile," "girdled," "bright," "sinuous," "blossomed," and "incense-bearing" imply. There is also a sense of movement, an expanding, a flowing like the river. Then, toward the end of the stanza, the lines begin to get longer, and the rhyme scheme becomes irregular. The undulating movement conveyed in the changing rhyme scheme may remind students of water's ebb and flow.

2. What changes do you find in the second stanza, both emotionally and rhythmically? The first two words "But oh!" give us the clue—things are becoming more agitated and there are more pauses (caesuras) in the middle of lines. There is a sense of things bursting from within. Instead of the relatively calm sound of the first stanza, words appear that suggest noise—"wailing," "seething," "pants," and "burst." The images are not just lush but violent: The place is "savage"; the hills in the first stanza are now broken by a "chasm"; and the river turns into rapids, with rocks being disgorged by some underground force. There is a moment of quiet near the end ("Then reached the caverns measureless to man,"), but then we move into a grimmer world. The ocean is "lifeless," and the world is full of "tumult." Kubla Khan is no longer only the builder of the "pleasure dome" but a person who listens to the prophecy of war.

3. Suddenly in the third stanza, a speaker ("I") enters the poem. How do you explain the speaker's appearance? Who is the speaker? How is the third stanza connected to the previous two stanzas? At first the speaker seems like an intruder. But the second line reassures us a little because he is also a visionary, like the dreamer of the first two stanzas. And when he explicitly connects the song of the damsel with a desire to build the pleasure dome himself, we may begin to see the connection between the first two stanzas and the last one. The first two describe the vision itself, with all its contradictions—the beauty and the violence, the music and the discord, the sense of paradise and the threats of war. The third stanza seems to be the poet's comment on his own activity. He is aware that he is creating a vision and he longs to be able to do it eternally. The only way to achieve that goal, however, seems to be through a mystical state, the kind described in the last five lines of the poem. We cannot be sure who the speaker is, but he seems to be the poet, the builder of imaginary pleasure domes through poetry, as Kubla

Khan is the builder of the physical pleasure dome.

4. In the subtitle, Coleridge calls this poem "a vision in a dream" and "a fragment." Do you agree with either or both of these descriptions? Why? Is this really an unfinished poem? Students are likely to agree with both of the descriptions. The dreamlike description is easy to defend if one looks at the fantastic images and the lack of explicit connection between them. Coleridge's prefatory note (see below) to the poem states that he never finished it, but one cannot assume that he is telling the truth—perhaps that note is also fiction, a made-up explanation that satisfied him as a rationalization. But to many readers the poem seems finished. Several details combine to bring the poem to a satisfying end: the entrance of the poet; the statement of his desire to build a pleasure dome, which takes us back to the opening of the poem and thus creates a kind of circular closure; and the mention of "Paradise" as the final word of the poem, evoking the world only alluded to in the first stanza. Some students may argue that the poem is a fragment, as Coleridge says. They may feel that the imagination could go on and on, creating new visions, new "pleasure domes."

Coleridge's Prefatory Note to "Kubla Khan"

In the summer of the year 1797, the author, then in ill health, had retired to a lonely farmhouse between Porlock and Linton, on the Exmoor confines of Somerset and Devonshire. In consequence of a slight indisposition, an anodyne had been prescribed, from the effects of which he fell asleep in his chair at the moment that he was reading the following sentence, or words of the same substance, in *Purchas's Pilgrimage:* "Here the Khan Kubla commanded a palace to be built, and a stately garden thereunto. And thus ten miles of fertile ground were inclosed with a wall." The author continued for about three hours in a profound sleep, at least of the external senses,[1] during which time he has the most vivid confidence that he could not have composed less than from two to three hundred lines; if that indeed can be called composition in which all the images rose up before him as *things,* with a parallel production of the correspondent expressions, without any sensation or consciousness of effort. On awaking, he appeared to himself to have a distinct recollection of the whole, and taking his pen, ink, and paper, instantly and eagerly wrote down the lines that are here preserved. At this moment he was unfortunately called out by a person on business from Porlock, and detained by him above an hour, and on his return to his room, found, to his no small surprise and mortification, that though he still retained some vague and dim recollection of the general purport of the vision, yet, with the exception of some eight or ten scattered lines and images, all the rest had passed away like the images on the surface of a stream into which a stone has been cast, but alas! without the after restoration of the latter!

[1]On a manuscript copy of "Kubla Khan," Coleridge gave a more precise account of the nature of this "sleep": "This fragment with a good deal more not recoverable, composed, in a sort of reverie brought on by two grains of opium, taken to check a dysentery. . . ."

Poems by George Gordon, Lord Byron and Percy Bysshe Shelley

PAGE 468

Glossary Words (for "On Fame" and "Ozymandias")

rummaging (page 469) Searching in a disorderly way; ransacking

colossal (page 469) Of huge size; gigantic; vast

Handbook

colloquial, imagery, symbol, theme, tone

Check Test 56

INTRODUCTION

"Ozymandias" and "On Fame" are easily taught together. The two poems also furnish a kind of capsule introduction to Byron and Shelley. If students are interested in these poets, you can certainly study them in greater depth. There are a number of delightful poems by Byron, especially "She Walks in Beauty"; the long satire, "Don Juan"; and his moving poem in the year of his death, "On This Day I Complete My Thirty-Sixth Year." Shelley's longer poems seem a bit pretentious, but you may wish to present the beautiful poems, "Ode to the West Wind" and "To A Skylark" as well as his moving elegy for Keats, "Adonais."

The study questions ask students to focus on both content and tone. They also emphasize the question of immortality and the attitudes with which the two poets face that question.

USING THE STUDY NOTES

PAGE 470

ON FAME

1. Consider and discuss the following propositions:

a. "Ozymandias" and "On Fame" make identical statements. Yes, the statements in both poems are the same.

b. The poems differ in tone. The tone differs radically. Byron's tone is intended to be humorous—consider the melodramatic, exaggerated question in line 1; the colloquial "it was just the thing" and "somebody or other rummaging"; the coined, awkward "burglariously"; the humorous rhyme of "hopes/Cheops"; and the phrase "pinch of dust," which is reminiscent of "pinch of salt." Shelley's tone is far more serious. Note the dark imagery created by phrases such as "shattered visage," "sneer of cold command," "these lifeless things." Note also the bitter irony of the last five lines.

2. What effect is created by the word *burglariously?* The humorous coinage "burglariously," composed of five syllables, echoes "hilariously" and thus reinforces the note of humor throughout.

OZYMANDIAS

Students are asked to consider and discuss these statements after they are sure that they understand the scene that Shelley is describing.

1. Everyone feels a need to be remembered in some way. It seems that it is very human to want to be remembered. Why this is so may serve as an interesting topic for discussion.

2. Ozymandias succeeded in being remembered for something quite different from what he had intended. Ozymandias wanted to be remembered as a powerful ruler and as a creator of great works. However, the only great work about Ozymandias that remains is part of one done by someone other than himself.

3. The most enduring things a person can achieve are the creations of art. Creations of art are among the things that people seem most likely to want to preserve, but they are not necessarily more enduring than some other things. Legal codes, ideas, objects of war, and so on also have endured for long periods of time. The poem, however, does imply that art is more likely to endure than other things. It would be interesting for students to speculate upon the timeless quality of art.

4. It is significant that the scene is laid in a desert. The desert is a symbol of waste and barrenness and thus is a fitting setting for the poem's theme.

Poems by John Keats

PAGE 470

Glossary Words

opiate (page 472) Medicine that soothes, dulls pain, induces sleep, etc., especially one containing opium

mellow (page 474) Soft and full-flavored from ripeness

winnowing (page 474) Blowing chaff from grain; sifting

Handbook

allusion, archaic, atmosphere, ballad, ode, personification

Check Test 57

INTRODUCTION

Keats is an immediately accessible poet, especially for students who are interested in and attuned to highly felt imagery. If there is a problem in teaching, it may be his frequent references to classical mythology. But students will probably see that for Keats the whole of past literature is part of the world that he tries to discover and to embrace. For each of these poems, lead students to focus on language.

"La Belle Dame sans Merci" is Keats's version of a medieval ballad. In addition to comparing it with earlier ballads, students may be interested to see Keats's revision of several points in the poem. The earlier version is given here because most critics think that it is the better one; students may want to study the differences.

We also include two of the great odes, "Ode To a Nightingale" and "To Autumn." The first is possibly the most dramatic of Keats's five odes. In it Keats, or the speaker, is heard expressing his longing to die, to join the nightingale that he imagines to be in a realm far removed from this ill and dusty world. The ode dramatizes in unforgettable language his evocation of that other realm (stanza 4), his consciousness of his present state (stanza 5), and the mental process by which he returns to an understanding of life rather than a longing for death. Although "To Autumn" is much less dramatic, it marks Keats's finest fusion of imagery and experience. This poem does not try to make a philosophic statement. But as it moves from a view of autumn as the season of "mellow fruitfulness" to a view of autumn as the time of the "soft-dying day," it enacts a vision of the cycle of the year and thus of the cycle of life. Death is present, but gently so, in the poem; we sense that gentleness in the final image of the swallows twittering in the skies. They are preparing to leave for the winter, the death of the year, yet their song is the music that will come again in spring.

USING THE STUDY NOTES PAGE 475

LA BELLE DAME SANS MERCI

1. **Who are the two speakers in the poem? Why are two speakers necessary? Why doesn't the poem return to the first speaker?** The first speaker is someone who seems to be part of the normal world and who wonders, rather compassionately, why the knight is alone and loitering by the lake. The second speaker is the knight himself, now returned from the immediate company of "La Belle Dame." One could guess that the speaker is necessary to connect the knight with the real world, to force him into an utterance. Otherwise, the knight might never speak or explain why he is behaving the way he does. The poem does not return to the first speaker because in some sense Keats wants us to remain with the knight, under the spell of "La Belle Dame." We cannot return to the first speaker, just as the knight cannot really escape from the lady.

2. **Keats is deliberately imitating an old form, the ballad, and he is purposely using old-fashioned language (as Spenser did). How does this poem remind you of the ballads in the first poetry section? What deliberately archaic words and phrases can you find? Why does Keats use them?** Like "Sir Patrick Spens" and "Edward," the story is told concisely, even elliptically. Events are described without much explanation or motivation. We do not even know whether the knight has died or if he is trapped in some kind of living death. Keats uses archaic words such as "thee," "sedge," "granary," "withereth," "Meads," "faery," "Zone," "grot," "latest," "hath," "thrall," and "sojourn." Like Spenser, he is trying to create a fairy-tale atmosphere for this poem. Therefore, he turns to an older form and language that suggests an ancient time. The poem thus has a "misty" quality about it that somehow makes it more frightening.

3. **Keats changes the ballad stanza in a significant way by shortening the fourth line of each quatrain. What effect does that change have on our experience of the poem?** If students count the syllables of the first three lines, they will find eight syllables per line. The expectation in this *abab* form is that the fourth line will also have eight syllables. Instead, it has only four. The effect of this shortening is to stop readers short, to disconcert them because they expect the line to be longer. The stanza seems cut off in a particularly harsh way, and that harshness of rhythm emphasizes the barren harshness of the landscape. The last lines of the quatrains often refer to that bleakness: "And no birds sing," "And the harvest's done," "Fast withereth too," "And her eyes were wild," "And made sweet moan." In this context, it is important that the woman's assertion "I love thee true" comes in that short, crisp fourth line. Perhaps, in a subtle way, her statement is part of the bleakness, part of the trap into which she is drawing the knight.

ODE TO A NIGHTINGALE

1. **What is the emotional condition of the speaker in stanza 1? How does the speaker connect that emotion to the nightingale's song?** The first four lines tell us how the speaker feels. He is sad ("my heart aches"), and he is sinking into a dull depression, expressed in the images of "drowsy numbness" and "dull opiate." He seems to be falling into a state of oblivion ("Lethe-wards") and yet is still in pain. He says that his feeling is not caused by envy but rather by a sense of the happiness of the

bird—as if the happiness expressed in lines 7–10 somehow causes him pain. We notice how the imagery of the last part of the stanza contrasts with the first half.

2. In the second stanza, the speaker asks for drink in order to "fade away" from the world. Why? Where does the speaker imagine the nightingale to be? For the speaker, the world is full of "weariness, the fever, and the fret." It's a world of age, of illness ("palsy"), and of death. It is a melancholy world ("full of sorrow/And leaden-eyed despairs"), and he wants to be free of it. In stanza 4, he imagines that through poetry he can reach the nightingale, who seems to be in heaven with the "Queen-Moon" and the stars. The contrast between that world and the sick world that he wants to leave is very clear.

3. What atmosphere is created by the images in stanza 5? Stanza 5 is the lushest, most "touchable" stanza in the poem. Note that the poet is not in heaven; the end of stanza 4 makes clear that he is in a place of "no light" except heavenly light that penetrates "through verdurous glooms and winding mossy ways." That last line of stanza 4 begins the imagery of touchable sight; that is, because the speaker cannot see with his eyes, he must see with his other senses. He feels that there are flowers at his feet; he smells the "soft incense" (and that phrase combines the scent of incense with a touch word, soft); he has to identify the flowers by smelling them.

What is the importance of this stanza to the poem? Stanza 5 seems to serve as a necessary transition. In the real world, back in stanza 1, the poet could feel nothing but dullness and melancholy. Now he is somewhere between the world and the heaven/death world of the nightingale—and what happens? He is keenly aware, and so therefore he is alive. It is the perception of all those flowers and the sensation of feeling them that may enable him to listen as he does in the next stanzas and to move back toward life and away from death.

4. In stanza 6, the speaker feels it "rich to die." What changes of thought occur in stanzas 6, 7, and 8 that keep the speaker from satisfying his death wish? A change first comes in line 59 when the speaker realizes that the nightingale's song will continue after he dies and that he will not be able to hear it. And that realization causes him to rethink his view of the nightingale. He sees, in stanza 7, that the bird is "immortal," and he remembers the fable of the emperor who heard the nightingale singing. (There is a wonderful version of this fable told by Hans Christian Andersen.) He can thus feel that the night is "passing" rather than eternal. He thinks of Ruth, a symbol of love and constancy in the Bible, and he imagines her listening to the nightingale for comfort, not for oblivion. And he returns to consciousness of himself (the opposite of forgetfulness) when he repeats his own word "Forlorn" and knows that he is alive and awake. Therefore, he says goodbye to the nightingale and to that image of death that he had imposed on it.

5. The poem ends with a question. How would you answer it? There is probably no right answer to this question. Sleep can be associated both with death and with the vision that the speaker has entered into. Similarly, waking can be seen as symbolic both of the real world that the speaker wants to escape and of the new understanding that he has achieved. Like the visionary in "Kubla Khan," the speaker knows that he has had a dream, a vision, and that is the important thing. And so he asks the unanswerable question, which suggests that he has come a long way emotionally from the drugged, drowsy speaker of the first stanza.

TO AUTUMN

1. What relationship and what feeling does Keats create by personifying Autumn? He creates a relationship of friendliness and a feeling of intimacy.

2. The meaning of the poem must be traced through its lush imagery. To what senses does the poet appeal in each stanza? What pictures are drawn in words? The first stanza is primarily visual; the second is also visual, but the sense of smell is also appealed to; the third stanza is very heavily auditory. Keats draws four word pictures of a personified Autumn in the second stanza. In the third stanza there is a word picture of a late autumn day.

3. What sound effects give this poem its solemn and stately movement? The solemn and stately effect comes from the pentameter lines, the long stanzas, the apostrophized Autumn, and the personification as well as from the tone quality. The tone is achieved through the use of open and sustained sounds in words. The words are ones to be rolled lushly off the tongue and slowly savored. Note the frequent *l's* and *m's*, the long vowel sounds, and the many words with *s* sounds. The sound effect is drowsy; the connotations are all warm, lush, and also drowsy. The discussion of the poem should end with a competent person, teacher or student, reading the poem aloud, giving full expression to these qualities. Poetry is meant to be heard.

4. What is the dominant impression of Autumn that this poem leaves with you? Answers to this question may vary. The first stanza leaves a strong impression of ripeness, the second of languor. Perhaps the only dominant impression for the whole poem is autumn's loveliness or beauty.

5. What patterns are repeated in each stanza? The rhyme patterns are very similar from stanza to stanza, and stanza length is identical. Iambic pentameter lines are used throughout.

Poem by Alfred, Lord Tennyson

PAGE 476

Glossary Words *(for "Ulysses," "My Last Duchess," and "Sonnets from the Portuguese")*

abides (page 478) Remains or stays

officious (page 479) Offering unwanted help; interfering; meddlesome

largesse (page 480) A generous giving

Handbook

allusion, dramatic monologue

Check Test 58 *(also for "My Last Duchess" and "Sonnets from the Portuguese")*

INTRODUCTION

"Ulysses," a dramatic monologue, could well be taught together with Browning's "My Last Duchess," although it is a much more straightforward poem. Another poem to look at again is "The Wanderer" (in the first section); there, too, is an old man, thinking back on his life, although his reaction to the journey is noticeably different from Ulysses's. When students look at the characters of Ulysses and the Wanderer together, they will be able to see the spirit of hope, of unquenchable energy, and of searching that characterizes Tennyson's speaker. That same spirit is one of the major ideals of the nineteenth century. Many of the lines in the poem lend themselves to discussion. You may want to talk about, for example, "I cannot rest from travel; I will drink/ Life to the lees" or "I am a part of all that I have met." Robert Kennedy, you may remember, used the following lines when he was campaigning for President: "Come, my friends,/ 'Tis not too late to seek a newer world." And the last line of the poem seems to sum up the indomitable spirit that kept the Victorians active in business, in travel, and in battle, though in doubt about religion, science, and industry: "To strive, to seek, to find, and not to yield." The study questions focus more closely on the development of Ulysses as a character and the foil relationship between Ulysses and his son Telemachus.

USING THE STUDY NOTES

PAGE 481

ULYSSES

1. **What different motives does Ulysses have for wanting to leave Ithaca? Which seem to be the most important?** Students may wish to begin with the strictly personal and emotional motives. For one, he feels "idle" and is tired of being with "an aged wife." For another, he does not like his "savage race" and is bored with sitting around, "rusting" unburnished. And so the immediate situation that he faces is not one that he finds gratifying. But there are other feelings, what we could call spiritual motives. Like Faust, Ulysses wants "to follow knowledge like a sinking star,/ Beyond the utmost bound of human thought." He wants more experience, even though he admits that he has had a lot. And he wants to be a hero again, to recapture "some work of noble note." One feels that after the Trojan War and the adventures of the ten-year return to Ithaca, he wants to become again a legendary figure.

2. **Why is Telemachus brought into the poem?** Telemachus becomes the foil to Ulysses; he is someone who is able to live in this ordinary world. Telemachus is "Most blameless" although he is probably not very interesting. He can work slowly in imposing law on people. By contrast, Ulysses seems too impatient. And Telemachus is content merely to worship the gods; he does not wish to be one.

3. **Is Ulysses looking for death (he speaks of touching the Happy Isles and of seeing Achilles)? If not, what is he looking for?** Students may make different responses to this question. Obviously, the death wish is not as clear as it is in Keats's "Ode to a Nightingale." However, the ship does set out on "the dark, broad seas." Ulysses says that the voyage will last "until I die," and he mentions the possibility of being at the Happy Isles. Moreover, his consciousness of his age is present at the end, "We are not now that strength which in old days/ Moved earth and

heaven." But students may also feel, and with some cause, that although this journey will certainly be Ulysses's last, it is really another voyage of discovery. He is looking for that "newer world." He knows that he does not have his former strength, but he is not ashamed: "that which we are, we are." And in the last lines, he asserts the supremacy of human will and spirit over the power of "time and fate." He believes that they will "strive" and "seek" and "find"—and he envisages no yielding, not even to death.

Poem by Robert Browning

PAGE 478

Handbook

couplet, dramatic monologue, irony, tone

***Check Test 58** (also for Tennyson and Elizabeth Barrett Browning poetry)*

INTRODUCTION

Robert Browning stands as one of the great Victorian poets, and "My Last Duchess" is probably his most teachable poem. The study questions are designed to lead students through the poem carefully, getting them to see its various ironies. Most readers never notice that this extremely subtle poem is written in couplets. After a discussion of the duke and his motives, you could ask students to consider Browning's choice of verse form and its effect on their experience of the poem. You might also want to discuss the conflicting reactions to the duke in the terms suggested by Robert Langbaum in his helpful study of the dramatic monologue, *The Poetry of Experience.* Langbaum argues that Browning creates "a tension between sympathy and judgment." That is, we are torn between, on the one hand, our attraction to the duke and our admiration for his brazen confidence and, on the other hand, our moral judgment of him for killing his wife. If your class expresses these reactions, you could then ask if the text contains other works in which we are pulled in contradictory directions. *Macbeth* comes to mind, as does *The Miser.*

USING THE STUDY NOTES

PAGE 481

MY LAST DUCHESS

1. What words immediately give you the clue to the identity of the speaker? Who is the listener? The words *my last Duchess* (line 1) tell the reader that the duke is speaking. The listener is a servant of a count; he is an envoy who has come to arrange a new marriage for the duke.

2. What do you learn about the duke from the words in parentheses in lines 9 and 10? We learn that he is a dictator in his own house.

3. What are the complaints that the duke had about his wife? He complains that she did not discriminate—that is, she did not treat him as the special individual that he thought he was.

4. What is implied by the words: "I gave commands; then all smiles stopped together"? What may have happened? Most will interpret this line to mean that the duke gave commands that the duchess be put to death, but he might also have had her shut up in a convent. The former would be the clearer reason for all smiles stopping and would justify the sentence that follows: "There she stands/ As if alive."

5. Since the envoy's master is wealthy, what is the effect of the duke's confession that the woman's "self" is his real object? The duke can afford to profess that the woman's "self" is his real object because he is rather sure of getting the money that he wants. He may feel that he will get still more money by pretending that his primary interest is in the woman.

6. What final bit of information do you gain about the duke through his pointing out the sculpture of Neptune and the sea horse? The information that paintings mean as much—or more—to him than people. We could say that he regards people as possessions, just as he regards paintings as possessions.

7. **What was most threatened in the duke: his pride or his faith in love?** His pride. Lines 22–45 indicate that what irritated the duke most was the lack of special respect that he expected to receive from the duchess.

8. **To what extent is this poem intended to reveal something about the individual personality?** Although both the setting and the style of life portrayed in the poem will be unfamiliar to most students, Browning nevertheless treats, in a dramatic fashion, traits of behavior that are common to most people. He shows our tendencies to be easily offended by the behavior of those close to us, to become suspicious, and to allow little annoyances to assume greater significance than they merit.

9. **The duke lists four things (besides the painter's remarks) which would bring to the duchess a blush of pleasure. What have they in common? What irony is there in the relation of the first of these to the other three?** One would expect a duchess to be pleased by experiences that are exclusive to the privileged; yet those that please this duchess are common experiences that could be enjoyed by anyone. The irony is that the first experience involved interpersonal relationships and could have produced the most pleasure; yet it met with no greater reaction than that produced by riding a mule, seeing a sunset, or receiving a bough of cherries.

10. **What tones of voice does the duke employ?** The duke's overall tone can be described as snobbish, but several variations are also apparent. From a tone of relative warmth, he moves toward disbelief, even outrage. He then shifts to a sternness of tone that quickly changes to matter-of-factness. This in turn gives way to a relatively informal—even chummy—tone that persists to the end of the poem, although a somewhat self-aggrandizing tone can be perceived in the concluding lines.

Poems by Elizabeth Barrett Browning

PAGE 480

Handbook

imagery, sonnet

Check Test 58 *(also for Tennyson and Robert Browning poetry)*

INTRODUCTION

As the pupil text mentions, Elizabeth Barrett Browning was for some time a more famous poet than was her husband Robert Browning. The two sonnets presented here from *Sonnets from the Portuguese* work nicely as a group. The first expresses the poet's sense of inadequacy. The second shows her acceptance of love and of life.

USING THE STUDY NOTES

PAGE 481

from SONNETS FROM THE PORTUGUESE

1. **What view of self is presented by the speaker of "Sonnet 8"? What view of the beloved? How is color imagery used in the poem?** The speaker of "Sonnet 8" sees herself as "poor," as open to the charge of being "cold," and essentially as unworthy of love. She continually puts herself down in this poem: "such as I," "so dead and pale a stuff." Her beloved, by contrast, is called "liberal/ And princely giver." And the colors that she associates with him are the royal colors, "gold and purple." Again, in contrast, her life is colorless.

2. **Assuming that the speaker of "Sonnet 23" is the same person, what change in attitude do you see? What has caused this change?** The new factor is a letter from the beloved that tells her, evidently in convincing language, how much she means to him. And that letter persuades her that she is worth something, that she must not allow herself to die (whether actually or figuratively by remaining single and in London). Her persistent sense of mortality had a real basis; if she had stayed in cold, damp London, it is

likely that she would have died much sooner. Of course, spiritual and emotional life is her subject here, but the physical and the spiritual are always connected.

Poem by Matthew Arnold

PAGE 482

Glossary Words (for Arnold and Housman poetry)

strand (page 482) Shore; land bordering a sea, lake, or river

furled (page 482) Rolled or folded up

certitude (page 483) Certainty; sureness

rue (page 483) Sorrow; regret

Handbook

metaphor, theme

Check Test 59 (also for Housman poetry)

INTRODUCTION

"Dover Beach" shows us the poet in a mood of questioning and doubt. Yet Arnold or the speaker does find some comfort in the presence of his beloved; he looks for support from love, from constancy, and from trust. What makes the poem especially moving is its evocation of several worlds. We begin in a real place, near the coast, and move into a metaphoric world. The sea (the English Channel) becomes the "Sea of Faith." The last stanza presents both the ideal and the real, the "land of dreams" and the "darkling plain." Arnold's ability to evoke both makes this poem unforgettable.

USING THE STUDY NOTES

PAGE 485

DOVER BEACH

1. **What starts the poet on his meditation?** His view of the tranquil sea and the clear moonlight.

2. **What does Arnold mean by the "Sea of Faith"? When was it at the full? What does he mean when he says it is withdrawing?** The sea of faith image is used to indicate a time when faith—perhaps, more narrowly, religious faith—was as universal as the sea. It would have been at its full presumably during the Middle Ages. When he says that it is withdrawing, he means simply that people no longer have faith—religious and possibly other kinds of faith as well. The cause is often taken to be the advances in science. (The poem was published in 1867.)

3. **State in your own words the human condition as Arnold describes it in this poem. What single positive value does he still cling to?** People find it difficult to distinguish between appearance and reality; they have lost faith and are confused by doubts; they are deeply insecure. The only positive value worth clinging to is love.

Poems by A. E. Housman

PAGE 483

Handbook

connotation, imagery, irony, rhyme scheme, rhythm, symbol, theme

Check Test 59 (also for Arnold poetry)

INTRODUCTION

At first glance, it may seem as if students will find it difficult to appreciate Housman's poetry. Many of his poems use death as their theme, and few students will have had personal experience with death. We have found, however, that high school students do respond to Housman, often quite deeply.

The reason, we think, is that the pervasive theme of Housman's poetry is better described as *loss* rather than death, and high school students, especially seniors, are in an excellent position to appreciate this theme. They have reached puberty and in so doing have lost much of the emotional security that childhood offered them. In addition, seniors face the prospect of losing still more security as the future beckons them into college or into the working world. Furthermore, many students will have had the experience of "losing" in love by the time that they have reached their senior year.

In class the best approach may be to read the poems aloud. Then perhaps students could discuss the propositions in small groups. Another approach is to ask students to select a favorite poem and to write an essay on its personal appeal. The solitary Housman might have preferred this approach.

USING THE STUDY NOTES PAGE 485

For each of the poems, the students are asked to think through and discuss the propositions.

WITH RUE MY HEART IS LADEN

1. The basic idea of the poem, "I am sad because so many of my friends are dead," is commonplace, but the poem makes it fresh. Actually, this idea is modified by the fact that the dead friends are so young. *Maiden, lad, boys, girls* emphasize—along with the adjectives used to describe them—the fact that youngsters have been cut down in their prime.

2. The only expression of emotion is in line 1. Students should see that line 1 is the only line in which the speaker expresses emotion *directly;* the remainder of the lines detail the cause of that emotion. Thus it is best to say that the poem *as a whole* expresses emotion, following a sort of cause-effect model, or perhaps an effect-cause model.

3. With the exception of line 1 and the last word of the poem, all of the words have good or pleasant connotations. Ask students to study the poem word by word. They will probably agree that nearly all the words do in fact have positive connotations, although they may well disagree about the word *laid* at the end of line 6. Like the word *sleeping,* *laid* may have positive connotations because it can be associated with the idea of rest. Here, however, it is connected by rhyme with the negative word *fade;* it is also connected by assonance and consonance with the negative word *laden* of line 1. It is in fact a pivotal word in the poem, holding within itself both positive and negative connotations.

4. The irony exists in the contrast between what is being said and the choice of words and rhythm in which it is being said. As the previous question suggested, there is much truth in this proposition. The ironic contrast is announced at the outset, in the first noun of the poem. Rue is an herb that is used in medicine but is best known for its bitterness.

The rhythm of the poem could be described as tripping, airy, or light. Yet the message is just the opposite, a fact that is emphasized by the heaviness of the rhyming words in the odd-numbered lines of the first stanza and the even-numbered lines of the second, especially the words *laden* and *fade* at the beginning and at the end of the poem.

LOVELIEST OF TREES

1. All the loveliness of spring is suggested by the description of only one object. The loveliness of spring is indeed suggested by only one object, the cherry tree. But the sound of the poem, not merely the visual imagery, is a very important part of the description. Ask students to tell why the cherry tree is such an excellent symbol of spring. They should see that it is not only the great beauty of the cherry but also the brevity of its beauty that makes it such an appropriate symbol.

2. The poem suggests the characteristic human restlessness during the spring that Chaucer suggested in the opening lines of the "Prologue" to *The Canterbury Tales*. Clearly, there is a restlessness in both poems. Ask students to compare the restlessness in both poems to the restlessness that they themselves have felt with the coming of spring. Ask them, too, what they think the root of that restlessness is. Finally, you could ask them to compare the restlessness in the two poems. In the one case, it seems as if the keynote is beauty; in the other, it seems to be connected with spiritual yearnings.

3. In spite of the joy in spring, the poem is tinged with melancholy. Ask students to try to discover the causes of the joy and the melancholy. The former may be found in the beauty of the season; the latter, in its brevity. Note, too, that the ironic contrast between the emotions of joy and of melancholy is not the only irony in the poem. Call attention to the words *only* and *little* in lines 8 and 10, and have students discuss why they are ironic. (Students must understand, of course, that the speaker is "only" twenty-one years old.)

4. Joy is enhanced by our knowledge that it cannot last. Ask students to think about this proposition in terms of joys that they themselves have known. Focus on the last line of the poem, in which the speaker says that the cherry tree is hung with "snow." It seems to us that the word is purposely ambiguous here: It suggests both literal snow and the snowlike appearance of the cherry blossoms. Thus the brevity and the beauty of the tree's bloom are united in a single image, for "snow" suggests both loveliness and death.

WHEN I WAS ONE-AND-TWENTY

1. The advice given in stanza 2 differs slightly in its content from that given in stanza 1. Obviously, the first stanza warns against giving the heart away, whereas the second speaks of the consequences of the giving. The stanzas are also linked, for the first tells of the material things that one may freely give away, whereas the second speaks of the nonmaterial costs that one must pay for the giving of affection.

2. The irony lies in the fact that the reader is led to expect that the speaker is an old person. There is certainly truth in this statement. When we hear people speak of advice they were given when only twenty-one, our natural expectation is that they are now considerably older. The speaker's comparative youth is emphasized in the last line of the first stanza: "No use to talk to me." The same line leads us to expect that the speaker has since aged a good deal. An "aging" has, of course, occurred at the end of the poem in the sense of becoming wiser through experience. But we do not expect to learn that the speaker is only twenty-two, merely a year older.

There is another irony in the phrase "in vain," for it leads us to expect that there will be some positive reward for the giving. But we soon learn that the reward is quite ironic.

TO AN ATHLETE DYING YOUNG

1. "Shoulder-high" has a different meaning in stanza 1 from that in stanza 2. In the second stanza *shoulder-high* refers to the way the athlete's coffin is being carried, whereas in the first stanza it obviously refers to the chair-lift ride that he was given by the townspeople after having won a race. The phrases "the road all runners come" and "a stiller town" should make it obvious to students that in the second stanza the athlete must be dead. They should see that there is a reason why the poet has used the same description—*shoulder-high*—in both the first and the second stanzas. He wishes us to think of the athlete as victorious in both stanzas. Thus, there is a kind of ambiguity in the second use of this key phrase.

2. The words "smart lad" are meant by the speaker as a sincere expression of admiration. Given Housman's point of view, there is no doubt that the words constitute a sincere expression of admiration, although the admiration is for what the athlete has accomplished—dying before his fame expired—rather than for what he might have consciously planned. (There is no indication in the poem that the athlete purposely chose to die.)

The idea of praising a person for dying young may impress some students as unpleasantly outlandish. If so, you could do two things. First, you could point out that the poem leaves the identity of the athlete unspecified; that is, the poem is not a personal elegy but an impersonal one. Second, you could try to get students to see Housman's deeper concerns. After they see that the poem is not a personal elegy, the next problem logically is to determine what the poem is about. (Incidentally, the chief evidence that the poem is not intended as a personal elegy is the fact that it does not contain a single personal reference.)

3. It is better to die young than to live to "see the record cut." One implication of the poem can be expressed this way: It is worth living only if one achieves some "honor" or "renown"; when this fades, it is better to be dead. Of course, it may be that most people do not accept that thesis. There are other things that students will want to say about this topic. They may point out, for instance, that athletic records are frequently broken today. However, many athletes become radio or television announcers who remind the public that "the game isn't what it used to be."

4. The poem implies that people who die in a moment of victory will be longer remembered than those who live out their lives. The poem does imply that the garland of victory is even briefer than a person's beauty. If people die young, they are in a sense spared the pain of this insight. There is no implication that they will be remembered any longer, however, than those who die long after their victories. Fame is equally fleeting in both cases.

If students think the proposition is true for the poem, ask them for evidence from the poem to prove it. The proposition may be true in life, but that is another matter.

UNIT TEST

You may select questions at random from the Study Notes at the end of each selection as a basis for constructing a final examination covering the unit Nineteenth-Century British Poetry. You may also choose to use the comprehensive unit test prepared on blackline masters available in a separate test booklet, ISBN 0-07-009823-9.

Critics of Society: Scope and Sequence

Selection	Language/Vocabulary	Comprehension	Critical/Literary	Composition
AN ENEMY OF THE PEOPLE	definition, etymology, context	details, supporting conclusions, inferences	drama, author's purpose, irony	exposition*, skits
"A Modest Proposal"		inferences, drawing conclusions, fact/opinion	essay, irony, satire, author's purpose	exposition*
"Quality"		details, inferences, drawing conclusions	tone, author's purpose, irony	exposition*
"Life of Ma Parker"		inferences, supporting conclusions	irony, author's purpose, flashback	exposition*
"Two Polish Tales"		inference, conclusions, comparing/contrasting	irony, satire, author's purpose, tone, setting	exposition*
"The Long Sheet"	context, definition	inference, supporting conclusions	symbols, author's purpose, irony	exposition*
"The Attack on the Mill"	metaphor	sequence, summarizing, cause/effect, comparing/contrasting	author's purpose, irony, setting	exposition*
"The Judgments of Shemyaka"		supporting conclusions, inference	folk story, hyperbole, characterization, author's purpose, irony	exposition*
"A Tale About Ak and Humanity"	definition, connotation, propaganda	details, inference, conclusions, fact/opinion	author's purpose, irony, satire	exposition*
Summing Up		summarizing, comparing/contrasting, fact/opinion	folktale, fantasy, essay, author's purpose, irony	exposition, research, essay, extended simile
Relating Composition, the Gallery, and Humanities		comparing/contrasting, drawing conclusions	satire	narrative

Twentieth-Century British Poetry

Selection	Language/Vocabulary	Comprehension	Critical/Literary	Composition
Hopkins, Yeats, Lawrence, Eliot Poems	imagery	comparing and contrasting, conclusions, cause and effect, inference, verifying	alliteration, assonance, imagery, meter, symbol, rhythm, allusion, balanced lines, personification, rhyme scheme, dramatic monologue, point of view	
Poetry and War Poems	imagery, metaphor, synonym	supporting conclusions, comparing/contrasting, verifying	irony, connotation, quatrain, rhyme scheme, allusion	
Some Modern Themes		supporting conclusions, comparing/contrasting, details, classifying	tone, form	

*Teachers can use the Implications in the study notes as writing assignments.

Critics of Society

The selections in this unit attack social ills or society generally. Galsworthy's "Quality," for instance, is a relatively limited attack on the tendency of present-day society to ignore quality in favor of mass-produced goods. Sansom's "The Long Sheet," on the other hand, is a broad attack on society that concludes with quite gloomy implications. Ibsen's *An Enemy of the People* falls somewhere in between these two selections, for though the drama is an attack on a particular community, Ibsen has singled out a problem that could appear in almost any community in the world; specifically, in a conflict between public welfare and money, it is money that seems almost always to win.

Most young people are in the process of developing a social consciousness. The selections in this unit are intended to provide stimuli for discussing students' own social ideas and to help them clarify their thinking.

OBJECTIVES

1. To illustrate the power of literature as a weapon in the protest against social injustices.
2. To encourage students to think about some of the flaws in the society in which they live.
3. To make students conscious of the contrast that frequently exists between individual welfare and social welfare.
4. To study the ways in which an author's purpose affects her or his writing.
5. To study the uses of irony.
6. To develop vocabulary.

MOTIVATING THE UNIT

If you have more than one class, you may wish to use more than one of the following patterns to open the unit.

Pattern I Ask students to think of a particularly serious fault of American society, of their school society, or of some other society that they would like to criticize. Then have them write essays discussing the fault, especially its causes, its effects, and some possible remedies. Finally, ask them to assume that their essays are to be read by someone in power in the establishment that they are attacking, and ask them to discuss how this fact may alter what they say or the way that they say it.

Read the best essays to the class, and discuss the whole matter of social ills, their correction, and the methods that can be used to attack them.

Pattern II Write on the board the phrase "Critics of Society" and/or the single word "Alienation." Ask students to write freely on either or both of these topics for ten or fifteen minutes; then collect the papers and read the most interesting ones to the class as a basis for a discussion leading to the first assignment.

Pattern III The gallery on this theme is especially suggestive. Have students page through it, looking at each of the pictures. Then ask them to write brief essays discussing one or more of the paintings in the light of the unit theme CRITICS OF SOCIETY.

Pattern IV Read aloud or have students read for themselves the Introduction in the text (pages 486-487). Be sure students understand what is being said, especially the four points made at the end of the Introduction. Ask them to keep these four points in mind as they read *An Enemy of the People.*

An Enemy of the People

PAGE 490

Henrik Johan Ibsen

ACT I

The scene is Dr. Thomas Stockmann's sitting room. It is evening. As the curtain rises, Mrs. Stockmann is in the dining room serving roast beef to Billing, the subeditor of the "People's Messenger." Peter Stockmann, the mayor of the town and Dr. Stockmann's elder brother, enters, closely followed by Hovstad, editor of the "People's Messenger." The two discuss the handsome new Baths that are such a boon to the town—they provide money for the business people and jobs and tax relief for the workers. When Hovstad credits the doctor with the idea, Peter takes exception to the statement, claiming that it was he who made the idea feasible. Mrs. Stockmann tries to soothe his feelings, but his irritation shows. After the mayor leaves, the group in the dining room—Captain Horster, Billing, Hovstad, and the Stockmann's two sons (Ejlif and Morten)—retire to the living room and discuss politics. The captain says that he pays little attention to such things and that people should keep out of things they know nothing about. At this point Petra, the Stockmann's daughter, returns from her teaching job and gives her father a letter. He disappears but in a few minutes returns to make a devastating announcement: The Baths, which were built for their medical value, are dangerous to the health of their users. The water is contaminated. A letter from the university has confirmed his suspicions. Dr. Stockmann sends his brother a report on the Baths and recommends that the problem be eliminated. The dumbfounded editors ask permission to publish the news and hail Dr. Stockmann as a savior of his town.

ACT II

It is morning at Dr. Stockmann's home. Peter Stockmann has returned the report on the Baths with a message that he will be stopping by. Morton Kiil, Dr. Stockmann's father-in-law, comes in elated. Angry at having been hounded out of the town council, he believes that the trouble at the Baths is what the town deserves. He further believes that the report is a scheme on Dr. Stockmann's part to discredit those in power. Hovstad returns to ask if he may publish the report. He is hoping that the town will cast out the people in power for having made such a drastic error. Dr. Stockmann is delighted to have the report published but for more altruistic reasons: he feels that he is saving the town. Aslaksen, a printer at the "People's Messenger" and head of the Householders' Association, announces that the doctor can be assured that the compact majority of shopkeepers, which he represents, will support him. He also suggests that a testimonial of some kind be held. The visitors leave, Peter arrives, and the picture changes. He informs the doctor that repairs will cost twenty thousand pounds and will take two years to complete. He wonders who will pay for it and how the town will survive in the meantime? But Peter has a plan. He suggests that the doctor should say that the situation is not as dangerous as he first thought and that the officials of the Baths will take care of it. Peter also warns his brother that, as an employee of the Baths, he has no right to an individual opinion. When the doctor staunchly refuses to change his position, the mayor announces that the Baths committee will have no alternative but to dismiss him. Mrs. Stockmann begs her husband to consider the family. Petra urges him to hold to his ideals. And Dr. Stockmann vows not to give in.

ACT III

The scene is the editorial office of the "People's Messenger," where everyone views the report on the Baths in a different light. Billing thinks of it as the first salvo in a war; Hovstad views it as a way to unseat the people in power; Aslaksen favors moderation. When Peter Stockmann tells them that he admires their willingness to sacrifice so much in order to have the Baths improved, they are startled. When he explains that the money must come from tax funds and that the Baths will be closed for two years, his listeners do an about-face. Suddenly it is Dr. Stockmann who is the enemy of the people. When the doctor comes in to check on the printing of the report, he at first attributes the change in attitude to their plans to honor him. Before anyone can tell him the truth, Mrs. Stockman comes in to beg Hovstad and Aslaksen not to print the article because her husband will lose his job if they do. At this moment Dr. Stockmann spies his brother's official hat and staff of office, which the mayor had left behind as he rushed through the door to avoid meeting the doctor. Once again Peter demands that Dr. Stockmann retract his statement about the Baths. The editors tell the doctor that they cannot publish the article. Mrs. Stockmann suddenly reverses her attitude and urges her husband not to give in. He now announces that he will not be silenced. Peter fears that his sister-in-law has lost her mind.

ACT IV

Dr. Stockmann has found a place to hold a meeting, a big old-fashioned room in Captain Horster's house. As the meeting begins, it is obvious that there is a conspiracy afoot to prevent the doctor from speaking. Peter suggests that Aslaksen chair the meeting. Then he petitions Aslaksen not to permit Dr. Stockmann to speak because Peter himself has already explained the whole situation in the "People's Messenger." Hovstad speaks next and deplores the doctor's lack of consideration for his wife and children. Finally, Aslaksen lets the doctor speak, and he quickly manages to insult everyone present: the community, by saying that it is built on falsehood; the authorities, by pointing out their colossal stupidity; his brother, by describing him as slow-witted and prejudiced; the compact majority, by calling it the most dangerous enemy of truth and freedom. The people are incensed, and everyone except one person, who is drunk, votes that Dr. Stockmann is an enemy of the people. As Dr. Stockmann leaves, he asks the captain if there is room on his ship sailing to the New World. As the family leaves the meeting, the mob follows, howling and hissing. There is irony in the last line when the freeloader Billing says, "Well, I'm hanged if I go and drink toddy with the Stockmanns tonight!"

ACT V

This scene takes place in Dr. Stockmann's study the next morning. The doctor is busy hunting for stones that the mob had tossed through his windows the night before. The family's situation is deteriorating, and they have been asked to leave by their landlord. Petra comes in to tell her parents that she has been fired from her teaching job. Captain Horster enters next with the news that his employer has fired him and that he cannot take them to the New World after all. Then Peter Stockmann comes in with the document dismissing the doctor from his post as medical officer of the Baths. But he has a suggestion: If the doctor will go away for six months and then write a letter acknowledging his error, the committee may reappoint him. He also drops the information that the doctor's father-in-law is very wealthy and that Mrs. Stockmann and the children will inherit the money. Dr. Stockmann's reaction to the news that his family will be provided for is one of sheer relief. And this makes Peter certain that his brother and Morton Kiil conspired to announce that the Baths were polluted so that they could buy up the stock cheaply. He retracts his offer and says that the dismissal is irrevocable. Next the doctor learns that Morton Kiil has been doing exactly what Peter Stockmann had deduced: He has been buying up shares in the Baths. But the poor doctor is even more shocked when Kiil tells him that he has used the money that his daughter and her children would some day inherit to buy these shares. And if Dr. Stockmann will not publicly announce that the filth coming from Kiil's tannery has nothing to do with the pollution, the shares will go to a charity. He gives the doctor until two o'clock to answer. The final visitors are Hovstad and Aslaksen, who berate the doctor for not telling them about the scheme to get control of the Baths. They offer to back Stockmann in return for his financial support of the paper. The doctor reacts violently, chasing them from his study. Then he writes three large "No's" on a piece of paper and sends it to Kiil. The die is cast. He now announces to his wife that they will remain in the town and fight. Captain Horster offers his house to them. Petra and the boys are enthusiastic about the decision. And the doctor's final pronouncement is that the strongest person in the world is the one who stands most alone.

INTRODUCING THE PLAY

It is important that students read through the play as quickly as possible. One way to accomplish this is to spend the first day reading Act 1 aloud, perhaps by assigning parts and having a spontaneous reading. Do not interrupt to explain or comment during this reading. Suggest that students answer for themselves the questions at the end of Act I. Assign Act II for home reading. Use the next day to read Act III aloud. Assign Act IV for home reading. Spend the third period reading Act V. Then, break the class into five groups and let each group select a director, cast characters, and appoint stagehands. Assign each group one act; ask them to select a part of the act for dramatization. Tell the groups to discuss thoroughly the interpretations of the characters in their segment before they begin to rehearse. Students will undoubtedly need a period or two to prepare their performance.

The productions should convey differing interpretations of the major characters and various feelings about the tonality of the play. These differences can serve as a springboard to discussion of the Study Notes.

A second kind of role-playing situation could be a court trial of Dr. Stockmann on the charge of libel. Appoint individuals to be the principal characters in the play. You will, of course, need a defense attorney, a prosecuting attorney, a judge, and a jury. Everything that is said or claimed must be verifiable in the play itself. In other words, students are not to let their imaginations run free. They will have to study the play carefully in order to participate.

A third kind of role-playing situation could be a hearing in an American town where a factory is being asked to close because its waste is polluting the local river and killing the game fish.

ACT I

Glossary Words

prolific (page 491, col. 1) Highly productive

indefatigable (page 492, col. 1) Never getting tired or giving up; tireless

mettle (page 492, col. 1) Quality of disposition or temperament

sepulcher (page 498, col. 2) Place of burial; tomb; grave

testimonial (page 499, col. 2) Gift, banquet, or the like, extended to someone as a token of esteem, admiration, gratitude, etc.

Check Test 60

Check Tests for each selection—in the form of blackline masters—are available in a separate test booklet, ISBN 0-07-009823-9. Each test is titled and numbered for easy filing after use.

Give the Check Test after students have read the selection(s) and before you begin the discussion of the work(s).

USING THE STUDY NOTES PAGE 500

1. What do you know about the following people?

a. Peter Stockmann. He is the mayor of the town and the head of the governing body of the Baths. He is set in his ideas—refusing, for example, to eat meat at night. Peter is also pompous: He does not like to eat with common people. He is irritated by his brother's spending habits and is jealous of his brother's part in planning the Baths. Peter, himself, wants full credit for the Baths. He also feels that everyone should support the Baths.

b. Dr. Stockmann. He is seemingly a jolly, generous person who thoroughly enjoys his new prosperity and revels in playing the generous host. He has a scientific mind that wants to know the truth. When his suspicions about the Baths are confirmed, he assumes that people will be delighted to hear this truth. He seems unable to foresee the effects of such news.

c. Mrs. Stockmann. She is a warm person, a gracious hostess, and she acts as a buffer between her husband and his brother. She shows motherly concern for her sons by trying to protect them from talk that she does not think they should hear.

d. Petra. She is energetic, outgoing, and enthusiastic, like her father, of whom she is very fond. She is a liberal and sees no reason why her younger brothers should not hear everything that is being said. She believes that society tells children too many lies.

2. How are the Baths important to the town's economy? Since the Baths have been operating, the town's economy has boomed. They literally provide the town's living.

3. To whom does Dr. Stockmann make the announcement that the Baths are polluted? What is their reaction? The group includes Mrs. Stockmann, Petra, Hovstad, Billing, and Horster. At first the group is shocked and disbelieving. Then Hovstad asks permission to publish the findings so that the town will know. Billing suggests that the town ought to give Dr. Stockmann some kind of testimonial. Petra is pleased that her father is right, wonders what Uncle Peter will say, and offers a toast to her father. Horster wishes him good luck. Mrs. Stockmann is supportive of her husband.

4. Why is Dr. Stockmann so pleased with his findings? He is sure that the townspeople will recognize him as a careful scientist who is pursuing the truth. He is sure that they will be grateful.

5. What two people does he single out to be notified immediately? Mrs. Stockmann's father, Morton Kiil; and Peter Stockmann, the mayor.

ACT II

Glossary Words

morass (page 502, col. 1) A piece of low, soft, wet ground; a swamp; a marsh

adherents (page 502, col. 1) Faithful supporters or followers; allies

vacillation (page 504, col. 2) A wavering in mind or opinion; uncertainty

imminent (page 507, col. 1) Likely to happen soon; about to occur

pugnacious (page 508, col. 1) Fond of fighting; quarrelsome

propensity (page 508, col. 1) A natural inclination; a tendency; a liking for something

cantankerous (page 508, col. 2) Hard to get along with because of a nature that is ready to make trouble and oppose anything suggested; head-strong; quarrelsome

opportune (page 508, col. 2) Timely; suitable; just right

askance (page 508, col. 2) With suspicion and disapproval

embellish (page 509, col. 1) Make more interesting by adding real or imaginary details

Check Test 61

USING THE STUDY NOTES PAGE 511

1. How long a period of time do you think has elapsed between Act I and the beginning of Act II? Probably one night, for that would give Peter Stockmann time to read the report and send it back. Remember that the play takes place before the days of the telephone. Because the doctor sent the report to his brother via the maid, it can be assumed that a servant also brought it back.

2. Throughout Act II a number of people react to the news in characteristic patterns. What is the reaction of each of the following? What does it reveal about them as people?

a. Morton Kiil. He is delighted because he sees it as a way to get even with the council, from which he has been ousted. He assumes that it is all a scheme on his son-in-law's part. Kiil seems self-seeking and crafty.

b. Hovstad. He has a chip on his shoulder toward members of the council, and he believes that the townspeople will now oust them. He has feelings of inferiority and considers himself an outstider because he was born to a poor farmer's family.

c. Aslaksen. Aslaksen supports Dr. Stockmann. Although he is well-intentioned, he evidences a certain political naiveté—for example, his suggestion that the townspeople give Dr. Stockmann a testimonial without offending the authorities.

d. Peter Stockmann. He is positive that the economy of the town is more important than the health of the people. He refuses to believe that things could possibly be as bad as his brother claims. He hints that the doctor's insinuations are made for some sinister reason and tries to get him to retract the report. He claims to have the best interests of the town at heart.

3. Do any of these people see the real issue? No. None of them does.

4. What arguments does Mrs. Stockmann use at the end of the act? She reminds her husband of what it was like to be poor and urges him to remember the welfare of the children, who still need protection and support.

5. Does anyone really seem to understand Dr. Stockmann? Yes. His daughter Petra does.

ACT III

Glossary Words

irreparable (page 514, col. 2) That cannot be repaired, put right, or made good

cursory (page 517, col. 2) Without attention to details; hasty and superficial

dupe (page 520, col. 1) One who is being deluded or tricked

arrant (page 522, col. 1) Thoroughgoing; downright; complete

Check Test 62

USING THE STUDY NOTES PAGE 522

1. Before Peter Stockmann arrives, how does each of the following react to Dr. Stockmann's article?

a. Billing, the assistant editor. He believes that the article is a step toward social revolution and that the doctor is a good friend of the people.

b. Hovstad, the editor. He feels that the doctor is striking a blow for the common people against the wealthy. He is glad that the article will discomfit the mayor. And he is sure that the article will rally all enlightened people to its cause, thus enhancing the importance of the "People's Messenger."

c. Aslaksen, the printer. He counsels moderation rather than hasty action. He believes that it is dangerous to tangle with local authority.

2. What job has Billing applied for? How does Billing explain this action? He has applied for the job of secretary to the bench. He claims that he wants to annoy the bigwigs.

3. Why does Hovstad continue to use Aslaksen as his printer when he does not agree with him politically? Aslaksen advanced Hovstad money for the newsprint and the printing bill.

4. Why does Petra refuse to translate the English story? She thinks that it teaches an unrealistic point of view about life, namely, that a supernatural power rewards the good and punishes the bad.

5. What reasons does Hovstad give for printing it? He thinks that on unimportant matters an editor must publish what the public really wants. It makes subscribers feel more secure and prompts them to read other articles, especially the political ones.

6. What is the real reason that Hovstad is supporting Dr. Stockmann? How does Petra react to this revelation? Hovstad is in love with Petra. But she feels that the editor has made a fool of both her and her father and vows never to forgive him.

7. What discouraging facts does the Mayor tell the newspaper editors? How does Aslaksen react? What is the crux of the Mayor's article? The Mayor tells them that to make the alterations that the doctor calls for will cost about twenty thousand pounds, a sum that will have to be paid by the town's taxes. Also, the Baths will have to be closed for at least two years, cutting off the people's incomes. Aslaksen is immediately aware that the householders will suffer terribly. Therefore, his support of the doctor's plan instantly dies. The Mayor's counterarticle is a résumé of the situation as it appears to a reasonable person and suggests certain possible defects that can be remedied without great cost.

8. Why does Mrs. Stockmann come to the newspaper office? What is her attitude toward her husband's article? She is eager to take her husband home. She believes that he is ruining the family for the sake of a cause.

9. In the confrontation between the Mayor and the Doctor, what does the Doctor find has happened to the editor's and the printer's support? What is Mrs. Stockmann's attitude now? Neither the editor nor the printer will now support the doctor. Seeing him stand alone, Mrs. Stockmann now comes to the support of her husband.

10. What is the final piece of bad news for the Doctor? No one will give him a hall for his lecture.

ACT IV

Glossary Words

tacit (page 526, col. 1) Implied or understood without being openly expressed

mandate (page 526, col. 1) An order or command; an instruction to act on behalf of another or others

assiduously (page 526, col. 1) Carefully and attentively; diligently

pestiferous (page 527, col. 1) Bringing disease or infection

scurvy (page 529, col. 1) A terrible disease due to lack of fresh vegetables

menagerie (page 530, col. 2) A collection of wild or strange animals; also, the place where such animals are kept

plebian (page 531, col. 1) Belonging or having to do with common people; common; vulgar

quagmire (page 531, col. 2) A difficult or precarious position; also, soft, muddy ground; a bog

blasphemous (page 533, col. 2) Saying or using mocking words about God or sacred things

Check Test 63

USING THE STUDY NOTES PAGE 533

1. Where does Dr. Stockmann hold his meeting? What do you learn from the crowd's comments before the meeting begins? The meeting is at Captain Horster's house. Because the crowd has no idea what the meeting is about, they decide to take their cues from Aslaksen.

2. How do the newspaper editors and the Mayor set out to muzzle the Doctor? First, although the meeting has been called by the doctor, the group insists on electing a chair. Aslaksen is selected. Following parliamentary procedure, he recognizes first Peter Stockmann, then Hovstad. Both downgrade the doctor and his report. They permit him to speak because he says that he is not going to talk about the Baths.

3. What is the gist of Dr. Stockmann's talk? His talk is a tirade against the rule of the majority. He says the intellectually superior should have the right to govern. He alienates everyone in the crowd.

4. How does the crowd react to the speech? They hiss and boo and call him an "enemy of the people."

5. What does Morton Kiil ask his son-in-law? Kiil asks if his own tannery is involved. Stockmann asserts that it is and that he will so indicate in his paper. Kiil says that this will cost Stockmann dearly.

6. How may the meeting affect Captain Horster? He may lose the command of his ship because the owner is so upset at Horster's permitting the meeting to be held in his house.

7. What request does Dr. Stockmann make of Horster? He wants to sail on the captain's ship to the New World.

8. How does Dr. Stockmann's departure from the meeting give you new insight about him? He refuses to slip out the back way and insists on using the front door, walking through the howling crowd. Thus we see him as a courageous person, willing to dare physical danger.

ACT V

Glossary Words

pilloried (page 534, col. 2) Exposed to public ridicule, contempt, or abuse

rampant (page 535, col. 1) Passing beyond restraint or usual limits; unchecked; widespread

mutable (page 538, col. 1) Capable of or liable to change; changeable

innocuous (page 540, col. 1) Not hurtful or injurious, harmless

finesse (page 541, col. 1) The skillful handling of a delicate situation to one's advantage; subtle or tactful strategy

invective (page 541, col. 2) A violent attack in words; verbal abuse

conduit (page 541, col. 2) A channel or pipe for carrying liquids long distances

insidious (page 543, col. 2) Secretly harmful; working secretly or subtly; seeking to entrap or ensnare

Check Test 64

USING THE STUDY NOTES PAGE 545

1. What actions have the townspeople taken against the Stockmanns? They have torn the doctor's trousers, thrown stones through the windows, evicted him from his home, fired Petra, and sent the sons home from school. Even the glazier has refused to come and repair the windows.

2. What is Mrs. Stockmann's attitude toward leaving the town? She is reluctant.

3. What does Dr. Stockmann anticipate he may find in the New World? He doubts that the free West will be much better. However, he says "...there things are done on the larger scale. They may kill you, but they won't put you to death by slow torture."

4. What news does Captain Horster bring? He has been fired and therefore cannot take the Stockmanns to the New World.

5. What is Peter Stockmann's mood when he first talks to his brother? What brings about a change in his attitude? At first Peter is conciliatory, suggesting that his brother go away until things settle down and then write acknowledging his error. When the doctor shows elation at hearing that his wife and children can expect a big inheritance from Morton

Kiil, his brother jumps to the conclusion that the doctor has conspired with Kiil to gain control of the Baths and to discredit the council. He states that now the doctor's dismissal is irrevocable.

6. What news does Morton Kiil give the doctor? What is his ultimatum? Kiil has taken all the money that would be left to Mrs. Stockmann and has bought stock in the Baths with it. He wants to be cleared of any accountability for the pollution of the Baths. And he gives the doctor until two o'clock to withdraw his charges.

7. What is Aslaksen's and Hovstad's conclusion about Kiil's buying of the stock? What is their proposition? How does the doctor react? They think the doctor and Kiil are scheming to make money, and they want to benefit. The doctor is so furious that he drives them from the room.

8. What help does Captain Horster offer the family? The captain offers them his house.

9. Whom does Dr. Stockmann now expect to treat medically in the town? What will his price be? He expects he will now be treating only those who cannot afford to pay. In return they must listen to his lectures.

10. Whom does Dr. Stockmann proclaim as the strongest man in the world? He proclaims himself because the strongest person is the one who stands most alone.

USING THE STUDY NOTES PAGE 545

I. THE KNIFE OF SATIRE

Considering their attitudes as presented in the play, how do you think Dr. Stockmann and his brother would react to each of the following statements? In your opinion, how would most people react to the statements today?

1. An employee should hold the same opinion as his or her employer. Peter Stockmann expresses this opinion when he tells his brother: "You have no right to express any opinion which runs contrary to that of your superiors." He asserts that the issue is not simply a scientific one; it has economic and technical overtones as well. Dr. Stockmann believes that he has the right—even more, the duty—to proclaim his private opinion on any subject. Students will have varied opinions about whether this attitude prevails today. Certain employees, because of their official capacities, are not permitted in their private lives to enter politics or to engage in any activity that may offend the public. Are others also restricted? How about teachers? Ministers?

2. The public should not be exposed to new ideas. The old ones are good enough. This, again, is Peter's opinion. He thinks that the old, established ideas are the best and the safest. His brother takes the opposite view. Students may cite adult reactions to new music, new dances, and so on, as evidence that middle-aged and older people are against new ideas. This could lead to an interesting discussion and also offers a possibility for a composition assignment. Students could be given the option of taking either side of the argument.

3. Too much culture demoralizes and destroys a people. Dr. Stockmann makes a somewhat similar statement but then asserts that ignorance and poverty do the devil's work. His brother is probably an adherent of the argument that education is bad for people. The way people today would react to the statement would depend upon their particular backgrounds and points of view. In this country a tradition holds that all children have a right to equal educational opportunities—but a gap does exist between the ideal and the reality.

4. Might is more important than right in an ideological struggle. Mrs. Stockmann belittles the effect of having right on one's side. Her husband is of the opinion that right is quite enough. His opinion reflects his irrepressible rashness and his lack of understanding of the public. By comparison, Peter Stockmann appreciates the necessity of having the press, business leaders, and people in general support his viewpoint. He is not much concerned with the rightness of his side. Students should be encouraged to discuss any ideological struggle, local or national, that involves the pollution of streams or of air, the destruction of national forests, the devastating results of strip mining, the treatment of minorities. Try to use current struggles so that students will have information on which to base their opinions.

5. To change a social situation, all that is necessary is to inform the public of the need for change. This is Dr. Stockmann's opinion. He even expects to be hailed as a hero for discovering that the Baths are polluted. Peter is realistic and realizes that anything that costs the people more money in taxes is sure to meet defeat. Today the majority would probably subscribe to Peter's attitude. Students may cite bond issues for new schools, roads, libraries, and so on, that have been defeated by taxpayers. As Peter Stockmann says, "The small taxpayers are the majority—here as everywhere else." His assessment of the public reaction to the doctor's news turns out to be correct.

II. IMPLICATIONS

Students are asked to react to a series of statements made by the characters in the play and to judge the validity of the statements in today's world. Ideally, these should be handled as composition topics. They can be used to help students work out themes using specific patterns of development. For example, you could ask them to explain in the first paragraph what has transpired in the play that has led the character to make this statement. In the next paragraphs, students should state whether they agree or disagree with the quotation and why. Instruct students to use illustrations from daily events (from school if possible) to support their conclusions. Have them write on specific quotations so that all the quotations will be covered.

III. TECHNIQUES

Author's Purpose

Students are asked to give their opinions about whether Ibsen avoided the pitfalls of social criticism in literature listed in the Introduction (page 487).

1. ***Sentimentality:*** **Are the following characters sentimentalized?** Does the writer attempt to arouse more emotion about the following people and their lives than the situation merits?

a. Mrs. Stockmann. She comes the closest to being sentimentalized. Mrs. Stockmann is portrayed as the loving, understanding wife and mother, ready to fight to protect her home. She does not really understand her husband's stand and yet blindly supports him. It is she who will suffer the most from this fight, for she will lose her inheritance and her security. She is, perhaps, unnecessarily pathetic, although this point is debatable.

b. Dr. Stockmann. If the doctor were sentimentalized, he would be the perfect "good guy" fighting evil. But he has human faults. He is naïve in thinking that if you tell the truth, people will do what is right. He is portrayed as rash and impulsive—his speech at the meeting supports this point. And he is an impractical dreamer, as seen in his assumption that the town would be willing to pay taxes to rebuild the Baths and to do without income for two years, in his plan to take off for the New World, and in his final scheme to start a school for street urchins. Because the doctor has faults as well as virtues, we react to him as a very real person.

c. Peter Stockmann, the mayor. Is he the stereotyped villain? Ask the class how they feel when he comes on stage. Do they want to hiss and boo or does he seem like all the others—a real person? See if they can identify redeeming traits that relieve the ugly side of his personality.

2. ***Oversimplification:*** **What is the problem presented in the play? Is one side totally right or wrong?** The problem is whether a town should sacrifice its economy for the sake of public health. At first the answer seems clear cut. Obviously, the Baths should be closed down, but little by little the repercussions of such a move are revealed. The issue is still clear cut, but the resolution is not so simple as it first appeared.

3. ***Didacticism:*** **Has Ibsen stopped the flow of action to preach?** Students may differ in opinion about this, but the action does seem to carry the story. Ibsen does not preach. Even at the town meeting at which there are long, preachy speeches, they constitute a natural and normal part of the story. Furthermore, the characters all speak within the limits of their stated natures, and so their ideas do not seem to be intrusions on the play.

Do you understand something after reading the play that you didn't grasp earlier? What will be a new idea for most students is that the majority is not necessarily right. In a democracy the majority wishes usually prevail, but this play takes quite a different position. The topic, whether or not the majority is right, can lead to a lively debate. To help in the discussion, have students list those areas of life where expert opinion rather than majority vote is to be trusted; for example, in the diagnosis and treatment of disease.

4. ***Too narrow or local a concern:*** **Is the problem presented here outmoded or contemporary? Is it local or of general human concern? Will the problem continue to be a human dilemma?** There should be little doubt here. It is startling that a play written almost a hundred years ago should be so contemporary. In fact it is probably even more pertinent today than when it was written. The problem of worldwide pollution versus human welfare is not only an ongoing but also an increasingly serious problem.

Irony

Students are asked to determine what is ironic about the following:

1. **Dr. Stockmann's feeling about his town?** He loves his town and its people and is eager to serve them. It is ironic that when his findings threaten the town's economy, the people stone him and want to drive him out.

2. **The doctor's expectations about the town's reaction to his news?** He expects that they will want to make a hero of him. Ironically, they declare him an "enemy of the people."

3. **Hovstad's reason for publishing the English novel?** Hovstad is willing to publish a novel that expresses an opinion that he believes is false. Yet he states that newspapers should be devoted to truth.

4. **Mrs. Stockmann's inheritance?** The doctor is delighted that his family will have financial security. Kiil's investing the money in the stock of the Baths makes him the instrument by which she will be denied the money.

5. **The doctor's brother being the Mayor?** It is an assumption that blood is thicker than water. Hence, the audience could expect Peter to support his brother. Ironically, he is the one who maneuvers to bring about the doctor's downfall.

6. **Horster's being fired?** The captain is seemingly the last friend that the family has in town. When he loses his ship, their escape is cut off.

IV. WORDS

A. Students are asked to define the following words:

1. **pestiferous**—producing or breeding infectious disease
2. **pugnacious**—eager to fight; having a quarrelsome disposition; belligerent
3. **morass**—an area of low-lying soggy ground; a bog or marsh (By extension, in a metaphorical sense, *morass* can be used to mean "any difficult or perplexing situation.")
4. **adherents**—supporters, as of a cause or an individual
5. **sepulcher**—a burial vault
6. **conduit**—a channel or pipe for conveying water or other fluids
7. **acquiesce**—to consent to or agree passively without protest
8. **invective**—a denunciatory or abusive expression

B. Students are asked to select the best definition for the italicized word in each sentence.

1. **arrest**—*b.* to stop or check the motion, course, or spread of
2. **body**—*c.* a group of persons considered together; a collection of persons or things; a body of troops
3. **conception**—*a.* a mental impression or image; general notion; concept
4. **conviction**—*c.* firm belief

A Modest Proposal

PAGE 548

Jonathan Swift

Glossary Words

importuning (page 548, col. 1) Asking urgently or repeatedly; asking again and again

rudiments (page 549, col. 2) Part to be learned first; the beginning; something in an early stage

probationers (page 549, col. 2) Persons who are learning a trade or profession; pupils

deference (page 550, col. 2) Great respect

encumbrance (page 552, col. 1) Hinderance; burden

digressed (page 552, col. 1) Turned aside from the main subject; wandered from

inducement (page 552, col. 2) Something that influences or persuades

emulation (page 552, col. 2) A copying or imitating in order to equal or excel; act of trying to equal or excel; competition; rivalry

enumerated (page 552, col. 2) Named one by one; listed

inclemencies (page 554, col. 1) Harshnesses; severities

Handbook

essay, irony, purpose, satire

Check Test 65

INTRODUCTION

Swift's simple proposal suggests doing something about those persons in Ireland who cannot support themselves and their children: Of the 120,000 children born every year to the poor, put aside 20,000 for breeding purposes and sell the remainder for food to persons of quality and fortune. Swift particularly recommends the children to landlords because they have already "devoured most of the parents." The price of the children is to be ten shillings each, which will give their parents an eight-shilling profit. The children are to be sold at the age of one year.

Some other suggestions are that the skin of the children be used to make gloves and summer boots and that it may be best to buy the children alive and dress them "hot from the knife."

A friend of Swift's has suggested that children from twelve to fourteen years of age could also be sold in order to take the place of the deer of Ireland, most of which have been shot. But Swift rejects this proposal on several grounds. An American friend has assured him that boys of this age are too tough; the girls are too close to being breeders. Besides, some persons could consider the practice cruel, and this "hath always been with me the strongest objection against any project, however so well intended." The implication here is clear—there is no cruelty in the proposal that Swift himself is making.

After some "digressions," Swift lists six great advantages of his proposal:

1. It would lessen the number of Papists, because they breed more actively than others.
2. The poorer tenants will have money of their own and thus will be able to pay their rents to the English landowners.
3. The nation's stock will be increased by 50,000 pounds per annum and there will be a new dish.
4. The poor will not only have their eight-shillings profit but will also be relieved of the burden of maintaining their children after the first year.
5. The business of taverns will be increased, thanks to the new dish.
6. There will be a greater inducement to marry, and husbands and wives should get along better. Parents will also become more caring, knowing that they will reap a profit for fat children.

Next, Swift says that he can think of no objection that could possibly be made to his proposal, except that the number of people will be lessened, but this is one of his principal designs. He also makes clear that the proposal is for Ireland alone, and he rejects a whole host of other expedients for improving life in Ireland, particularly because experience has shown that there is no hope of ever having them put into practice.

Swift asserts that another advantage of the proposal is that it will not disadvantage England, and although England would be glad to eat up the whole of Ireland, this plan will help prevent that.

Finally, Swift closes by asking his potential critics to consider how they would find food and clothing for 100,000 useless mouths and backs. Also, he asks them to ask the poor whether they themselves would not prefer a scheme such as he proposes over the life that they are living now. He professes that he will not personally gain from the scheme and that he has no motive other than the public good of his country.

This is the most bitter piece of prose in the unit. For some students, indeed, it may be too bitter to bear. Perhaps you could remind such students that there are occasions in life when great bitterness is called for. Furthermore, Swift's proposal is not entirely negative—a good number of serious, positive proposals are given near the end of the essay (page 553 in the text). The problem for Swift—and for Ireland—is that the kinds of positive proposals that he mentions here were never acted upon.

By the way, there should be nothing remote in this essay. The kind of bitterness that it illustrates may be found readily in modern literature, especially in modern theater.

You may also prefer to introduce the selection by outlining some of the conditions that existed in Ireland at the time that Swift wrote the essay. If so, see the discussion in the commentary that follows.

USING THE STUDY NOTES — PAGE 554

I. SAVAGE INDIGNATION

When Swift wrote "A Modest Proposal," Ireland was in effect being managed by English people for English interests. In particular, there was a system of absentee landlordism, through which more than four-fifths of the land was owned by English families who had never lived in Ireland. Many of them had never even been in Ireland or seen the land that they owned, but they charged crushingly high rents to the Irish who did live on the land. Catholics in particular were persecuted; they were barred from the trades and the professions, they could not vote, they could not hold office, and so on. In short, the extreme indignation of Swift must be measured against the extreme conditions that existed in the country of his birth. It should be clear, furthermore, that only something as shocking as "A Modest Proposal" would be likely to move the English people to do anything about such deplorable conditions, conditions that they themselves either through action or inaction had caused to exist.

Be sure that students discuss this point: The weapons that one uses depend upon the job that has to be done.

II. IMPLICATIONS

Students are asked whether they agree or disagree with the following statements:

1. **Swift's essay is so bitter that it loses its im-**

pact. Some students may agree with this; others may find it so bitter it only disgusts them. But the point to be made is that anything less than what Swift wrote would have had no impact at all. You may want to call attention to the first full paragraph in the right-hand column on page 553, in which Swift notes the impossibility of improving conditions by the means that he mentions in the previous paragraph. Note also the second full paragraph in the right-hand column.

2. There is enough common sense in this essay to make the "proposal" acceptable to some people. We trust that the proposal on the whole will be unacceptable to students, but perhaps some of the same students may be against such things as anti-poverty legislation, relief aid for the poor, and so on. Is this an inconsistency?

3. Swift is not so much concerned with the starving Irish as he is with attacking the British who rejected him. There is no doubt that Swift felt great bitterness toward "landlords," and most of the landlords were English. Students will be able to infer this from the fact that he repeatedly attacks both them and England. On the other hand, he indirectly attacks the Irish themselves (see especially left-column, page 553). Thus it seems to us that his chief concern *is* with the starving Irish, for he is willing to strike at any group that bears responsibility for their plight.

III. TECHNIQUES

Author's Purpose

Students are asked whether one of the following statements expresses their opinion of why Swift wrote the essay, whether a combination of statements best expresses his purpose, and whether they have other ideas about his purpose.

1. Swift wrote this as a protest against English absentee landlordism.

2. Swift wrote this to make the English aware of Ireland's terrible poverty.

3. Swift was crying out against the increase of Catholics in Ireland.

Students should have no difficulty in seeing that the first two statements represent Swift's purpose and that the third does not. Perhaps more important is the need for them to see that Swift also makes some positive proposals through which the Irish could help themselves. Essentially, he wanted something done to alleviate poverty in Ireland.

4. How well do you think Swift fulfilled his purpose? Find out if his bitter criticism led to any reform. Swift's criticism may have affected some individual attitudes, but widespread reforms were not realized until the 1870s and 1880s.

Irony

Students are first asked what irony they find in the title.

Modest should probably be interpreted as meaning "moderate," as well as "unassuming." In its formal meaning, it is clearly ironic, for there is nothing "moderate" in the proposal.

Students are also asked the following questions:

1. Are the last six points given by Swift as a reason for his proposal dramatic or verbal irony? If carried out, all the points would produce what they claim would be produced; for instance, if the proposal were carried out, it would reduce the number of Papists (point I). From the definitions in the text, the six points can be considered verbal irony, but there is some question about whether Swift really intends "the opposite" of what his words say.

2. In the following quotations, Swift is saying one thing, but you, the reader, know that what he says is not his real intent. He is saying it tongue-in-cheek, daring you to believe him. What makes the following statements ironic?

a. I have been assured by a very knowing American of my acquaintance in London, that a young healthy child well nursed is at a year old a most delicious, nourishing, and wholesome food. . . . This statement is made ironic because what Swift says is in contrast with what he intends. Specifically, he wants to shock his reader into some sort of action, and this is in contrast to his straightforward, matter-of-fact tone.

b. I grant this food will be somewhat dear, and therefore very proper for landlords, who, as they have already devoured most of the parents, seem to have the best title to the children. Here the intention is to criticize landlords for their treatment of the poor. There is an ironic contrast between the literal meaning and the figurative meaning of the phrase "they have already devoured most of the parents." But of course Swift does not literally intend to offer the children for devouring.

c. . . . the skin of which, artificially dressed, will make admirable gloves for ladies. . . . The irony here is the same as that in item *a*.

Quality

PAGE 555

John Galsworthy

Glossary Words

prototypes (page 555, col. 2) The first or primary types of anything; the originals or models

incarnating (page 555, col. 2) Putting into concrete form; personifying

sardonic (page 556, col. 2) Bitterly sarcastic, scornful, or mocking

rebuking (page 557, col. 1) Expressing disapproval of something

ingratiating (page 559, col. 1) Trying to make oneself acceptable

Handbook

dialogue, irony, narrator, purpose

Check Test 66

INTRODUCTION

The story concerns the "fall" of the Gessler brothers, a pair of old German bootmakers in London who made boots of great quality, boots that had something of "the Soul of Boot" in them.

The opening section tells about the Gessler shop—or shops, for they have two little shops merged into one. It also explains the art of bootmaking and the deep concern of the Gessler brothers for their trade and for their customers.

In the second section, the narrator describes four separate visits to the bootshop. On the first occasion, he complains that a pair of boots that he bought there creaks. The younger Gessler—who is the only brother that we actually meet—offers to look at them and not charge for the boots if the fault is his. On the second visit, the narrator is wearing a pair of boots that he had bought "in an emergency" at a large firm. The younger Gessler recognizes that the boots are not his, and he complains that he, who loves his boots, is losing customers to big firms that prosper not because they do good work but because they advertise.

On the third visit—two years after the second—the narrator discovers that one of the two Gessler shops is being rented by another bootmaker. The younger brother tells him that it was too expensive to have two shops. Finally, on the last visit, the narrator thinks that he is being served by the elder brother, but he soon discovers that it is the younger who has aged considerably. He also discovers that the elder brother died because he was disheartened about losing one of the shops.

More than a year later, the narrator returns to the shop to find that the surviving brother appears to have aged fifteen years. He has grown so feeble, indeed, that it is upsetting to watch him. Partly out of pity, the narrator buys four pairs of boots. When the boots finally arrive, he finds that they are the best he ever had, but he also finds a bill with them. This is most unusual, for the Gesslers normally bill only quarterly.

A week later, the narrator goes to the shop and finds that Mr. Gessler has died. A clerk from the shop next door—which has taken over both of the original Gessler shops—tells him that he died of "starvation." Till the last, all his energy went into bootmaking, and all his money went into rent and the best leather that money could buy. "He was a character," the clerk says. "But he made good boots."

As the title suggests, the story is not only a tale of the Gessler brothers. "Starvation" characterizes the dying of the "old world" concern for quality. Perhaps one should go a step further, for the Gesslers are also committed to a deep personal concern between buyer and seller. When the narrator returns to the shop for the last time, the clerk gives him "a strange, ingratiating look." It is the sort of look that he would never have had from the Gesslers. The story suggests that when quality dies, so do warmth and personality.

You may want to call attention to the title of the story. Ask students to think about the title as they read, and ask them at the end to consider why Galsworthy chose this title.

The story presents no special difficulties, except perhaps for the dialect of the bootmaker. If you think that your students may have trouble with this, suggest that they read the dialogue aloud. If they pronounce it just as it appears, they should have little difficulty. With poor readers, perhaps you will want to read some of the dialogue, as an example of how it should be read.

USING THE STUDY NOTES

PAGE 559

I. THE PASSING OF AN ERA

Students are asked what they have learned about the characters as well as people in general from the following lines:

1. The Gesslers:

a. For to make boots—such boots as he made—seemed to me then, and still seems to me, mysterious and wonderful. There are many things that students may say about this. One way to open up discussion would be to ask them to think of some sort of making that seems mysterious and wonderful to them. To us, it is always rather mysterious and wonderful to see anything beautiful made out of "nothing."

b. "Isn't it awfully hard to do, Mr. Gessler?" ..."Id is an Ardt!"

The statement of Mr. Gessler reveals a certain justified pride. He considers himself an artist, as opposed to, say, a tradesperson or plain "worker." Students may well discuss just what the term *art* means.

2. The narrator of the story:

a. ...some inkling haunted me of the dignity of himself and brother. This statement comes from the second paragraph of the story. It is apparent that the narrator is associating "dignity" with the ability to make something beautiful. It shows his concern for human dignity, a key concern of Galsworthy in this story and elsewhere. The narrator's use of the word *inkling* is explained by the fact that he is referring to a time when he was only fourteen. It is interesting that he should be concerned about dignity at so young an age.

b. I had, I do not know quite what feeling of being part, in his mind, of a conspiracy against him.... The quotation shows the narrator to have been quite sensitive and to have suffered perhaps from feelings of guilt. There is really little reason for his feeling guilt: Except for the one occasion when he bought boots in an emergency, all his boots were purchased from the Gesslers. Of course it is true that he is a comparatively young man and thus part of the "modern world," and it is this modern world that is, in a sense, conspiring against the Gesslers.

II. IMPLICATIONS

Students are to consider the selection and their own experiences and then to give their opinions of the following statements:

1. Society today is not interested in the quality of a product but only in cost and the speed of production. This is obviously implied by the selection. Whether it is true in general seems to be a moot point. There is a great deal in the very nature of a capitalistic society that would seem to point to the truth of the statement, but on the other hand, there is some evidence against it, too. Ask students to cite specific examples both for and against the proposition.

2. The Gessler brothers failed because of their inability to adapt and not because of any wrong on society's part. One could certainly argue that the Gesslers were unable to adapt, but the story is obviously not putting the blame on them. If any students think that such is the case, ask them to reread the last scene of the story. It should be clear that all the narrator's sympathies lie with the Gesslers, not with those who take over the shop or with society.

3. Justice does not play a part in an individual's success. In light of the selection, this proposition implies that it would be "just" if those who made the best products would have achieved success. That is, the Gesslers should have had success had there been justice in their society. Interpreted this way, the proposition is true for the story. As far as students' own experiences are concerned, it seems likely that they will find that justice prevails in some cases but not in others. Probably they will agree, however, that justice alone is not enough to guarantee success.

III. TECHNIQUES

Author's Purpose

Students are asked which of the following best expresses their ideas of Galsworthy's purpose; they are asked to find support in the story for their opinions.

1. His purpose is to criticize the Gesslers for not adapting to the times.

2. His purpose is to criticize society for not helping people of Gessler's ilk.

There is no word of criticism of the Gesslers for not adapting to the times, and so the first statement could hardly be the author's purpose. His attitude toward the Gesslers is one of admiration for their skill and regret for their passing. There is, on the other hand, some expression of criticism of society. We see it notably in the last scene in the comments made about and by the clerk. Also, the narrator himself does everything he can to help Gessler; presumably, then, he would have had others do the same.

Irony

Students are asked the following questions: **How does the ending demonstrate dramatic irony? Why is this ending appropriate?** It is noted (page 546) that dramatic irony occurs when events that evolve are entirely different from those expected or intended. In this story there is every reason to expect an unhappy ending, and that is why the ending is appropriate. The ending could be considered dramatic irony from the point of view of the narrator, however. He comes to the shop intending to tell Gessler how good his new boots are, and he finds that Gessler is dead.

What would be the effect on the story if it ended happily? If the story had ended happily, the ending would have contradicted the story's tone and its direction of movement.

Is there anything ironic in the statement—"not a man in London made a better boot!"—when you know that Mr. Gessler starved to death? Clearly there is. One's natural expectation is that the best bootmaker in London would at least be able to make a living. The contrast between this expectation and the fact that Mr. Gessler starved to death may be called ironic.

Life of Ma Parker

PAGE 560

Katherine Mansfield

Glossary Words

tomes (page 562, col. 1) Books, especially large, heavy books

vigilant (page 563, col. 1) Keeping steadily on the alert; watchful; wide-awake

Handbook

irony, purpose

Check Test 67

INTRODUCTION

As the title promises, the story deals with the life of Ma Parker. It opens with a view of her as a Tuesday maid of a "literary gentleman" and with the information that she has just buried her little grandson Lennie. This is followed by a brief flashback in which we see Lennie and her together.

After some further insights into the "literary gentleman's" character, including the knowledge that Ma Parker pities him for having no one to look after him (although he shows precious little pity for her), we again shift to the past, led there by the motif of Ma Parker's hard life. We learn that she has been on her own working as a maid since she was sixteen; that she married a baker and had thirteen children, seven of whom died; that her husband died when the surviving six children were still small; and that all the children left home after they were grown. The youngest daughter, Ethel, however, returned to live with Ma Parker after her husband's death; and she brought with her her child, Lennie.

While she is cleaning the apartment, Ma Parker's thoughts are occupied with Lennie's suffering and death. She does not understand why he had to suffer so much, and she continually wonders, "What have I done?" Her employer appears again, ready to go out. First, however, he speaks to her about some cocoa—a teaspoonful—that he believes she has stolen or thrown away. Although Ma Parker simply denies this and makes no comment upon it, the incident makes its subtle contribution to the reader's sense of Ma Parker's situation.

More miserable than she has ever been, Ma Parker simply walks out of the apartment "like a person in a dream." She is looking for a place to cry, but there is no place for her to go, no place where she can "keep herself to herself." It begins to rain.

The story generates a great deal of sympathy for Ma Parker and her hard life, especially because it is clear that fate is the cause of much of her trouble. Yet the story is not merely a slice of one person's life. It also explores the universal concerns of alienation and the indifference of human beings to one another.

A good question with which to introduce the story is this: How is this story an illustration of social criticism? If you ask students this question, you will prevent them from seeing the story only as a tale of individual misery.

Students often have a great deal of difficulty following stories that shift from the present to the past as often as this one does. Consequently, you may want to warn them in advance about these shifts. With weak readers, it is a good idea to show them the places where the story moves from the present to the past and back again. Probably nearly all students would profit from being told in advance that the author uses dots where these shifts occur; note that the shifts are especially frequent in the middle of the story.

USING THE STUDY NOTES PAGE 564

I. FOR THE DIGNITY OF THE INDIVIDUAL

When the commentary notes that Ma Parker is "interesting but unimportant," it is not suggesting, of course, that she is unimportant to the author or to the reader but rather unimportant in the social fabric and for the persons for whom she has worked. That is a "truth" of this story; it is also a "truth" that everyone ought to be important to everyone else.

II. IMPLICATIONS

Students are asked if the following statements are true, false, or something in between:

1. Most people are calloused and indifferent to anybody else's troubles. One can often find support for this assertion in newspapers. We refer to the reported cases of public indifference to beatings, rapes, murders, and so on. There seems to be very little sense of *community* in modern American life. At least, this is our impression. Students, of course, may disagree, and it is certainly true that the statement is a rather broad generalization. One could note, for instance, that most people are not calloused and indifferent to the troubles of those they love.

2. Poverty saps personal initiative and thus inhibits an individual from overcoming difficulties. It seems likely to us that reactions to this statement will vary a great deal, depending upon the kinds of experiences that students have had. Our own impression is that the truth or falsity of the statement depends a great deal upon the kind of poverty involved. If it is what one may call "hopeless" poverty, it may very well sap initiative; on the other hand, if it is not "hopeless," the opposite effect may be produced—it may actually stimulate initiative. (In this latter connection, one thinks of the impoverished immigrants who made their fortunes in America.)

3. The poor do not even have a place where they can grieve in private. Because the poor often live in crowded quarters of one sort or another and because they do not have money to move about, this may quite often be the case.

III. TECHNIQUES

Author's Purpose

Students are asked to give their reaction to the story and tell what social injustice it attacks.

The story mainly attacks the indifference of persons toward other human beings, but one could also see this as a case of "social injustice"—the indifference of the well-off for the impoverished. Note, for instance, that the literary gentleman refers to Ma Parker as his "hag."

The reactions of students will no doubt differ, but it is hoped that none of them will find the tale maudlin or sentimental.

Irony

Students are asked how the following are ironic:

1. Ma Parker's answer to the literary gentleman's question about Lennie. The question referred to is the literary gentleman's inquiry in the first paragraph, to which Ma Parker replies, "We buried 'im yesterday, sir." We can assume that her employer asked about Lennie without any true concern, and the contrast between his lack of feeling and the answer he got may be termed ironic—the question was "unreal," insincere; the answer was very real.

2. His asking her about the cocoa. This is ironic because he brings up a trivial matter like a spoonful of cocoa on the day after she has buried her grandson. It is also ironic, in a way, that he should care more about the cocoa than about her and her feelings.

3. Her finding herself walking aimlessly with no place to go and cry. It is ironically appropriate that at this key time of her life she should be able to find no place where she can "keep herself to herself," for she has lacked that all her life.

Two Polish Tales

PAGE 570

Slawomir Mrożek

Glossary Words

chaise (page 570, col. 1) A light, open carriage, usually with a folding top
verge (page 570, col. 2) The edge or border or shoulder of a road
elucidation (page 571, col. 1) An explanation; a making clear
impertinent (page 573, col. 2) Disrespectful and rude
libel (page 574, col. 1) Any false or damaging statement about a person; a slander

Handbook

absurd, irony, purpose, satire, tone

Check Test 68

INTRODUCTION

These two delightful stories, translated from the Polish, highlight the absurdities of society. "On a Journey" describes a telegraph system in which messages are relayed by people who are stationed within shouting distance of one another. As in "A Modest Proposal," all of the "obvious advantages" of such a system are delineated: Wires do not break in winter; the system provides employment; it saves timber.

In "Children," an ordinary snowfigure built by children is decried by several townspeople—a news agent, who sees its carrot nose as mocking his red, frostbitten nose; the manager of the cooperative, who thinks the three snow balls, one on top of the other, symbolize the cooperative as one thief sitting on top of another; and the president of the council, who feels that the row of buttons is lampooning his walking about his house with his fly undone. The next day, the children, now restricted to their yard decide to build three new snowfigures to represent exactly what each person accused them of.

The two stories are brief and simple. No introduction needs to be made. You may want to point out that both selections were written by a Polish writer who supported himself in his early writing career by working as a cartoonist, using both satire and humor as his tools. The same qualities are apparent in these short tales.

USING THE STUDY NOTES

PAGE 575

ON A JOURNEY
CHILDREN

I. TONGUE IN CHEEK

Satire can be placed on a line that ranges from very mild to very bitter, depending on the seriousness of the aspect of life being satirized and on the intent of the author (usually indicated by the tone of the language). The tone of these stories seems very lighthearted. You may wish to have students discuss whether the faults satirized here are more or less serious than the fault that Swift attacks in "A Modest Proposal." Or a discussion could center on whether students think that this amusing, gentle satire is as effective as Swift's bitter tone.

II. IMPLICATIONS

Students are asked to discuss the following statements:

1. Human power is preferable to mechanical power. This statement should lead to a good discussion. Should we go back to using more bicycles, to washing clothes by hand? Get the class to make a list of machines or gadgets that they would eliminate from our culture, such as the electric can opener, electric knives, hair dryers, clothes dryers. . . . See how far they are willing to go.

2. People tend to be unduly sensitive about their weaknesses and watch for anything that seems to make fun of them. Advertisers, con artists, and adventurers play on human weaknesses and fears. People fear obesity, unpopularity, aging, sexual inadequacy, and so on. The next time you watch television, observe how many commercials use fear of personal inadequacies as an approach to selling a product.

III. TECHNIQUES

Author's Purpose

Which of the following is Mrożek criticizing in "On a Journey"?

1. The absurd ways a government tries to save money.

2. Mechanization of the modern age.

3. Society's way of solving problems.

Mrożek seems to be gently criticizing all three. Get students to reflect on each one. Perhaps they can add to the list; for example, considering property (such as poles and wires) more important than human lives.

Irony

In "On a Journey," what is ironic about the coach driver's answer to the question of whether this kind of telegraph works? In the first two sentences of this paragraph, the driver says, "Why shouldn't it work? It works all right." He then proceeds to mention all the times and ways that the system does not work: Messages get twisted, more so when the workers are drunk; there are interruptions during the winter when the wolves evidently attack the workers.

What is ironic about the ending of "Children"? The children are going to build three snowfigures to mock the three adults who protested about the first one. The children would never have conceived this idea if the protestors had not suggested it.

The Long Sheet

PAGE 576

William Sansom

Glossary Words

furtive (page 576, col. 2) Secret; sly; stealthy

cubicle (page 576, col. 2) A very small room or apartment

eradicate (page 579, col. 1) Get rid of entirely; destroy completely; eliminate

envisage (page 580, col. 1) Form a mental picture of

implicit (page 580, col. 2) Meant, but not clearly expressed or distinctly stated

veneer (page 581, col. 1) Surface appearance or show

resilience (page 581, col. 1) Power of recovering readily; cheerfulness; springiness

approbation (page 581, col 2) Favorable opinion; approval

Handbook

atmosphere, irony, purpose, symbol

Check Test 69

INTRODUCTION

A group of twenty-two captives are put into a long steel box containing four rooms or cubicles. In order to earn their freedom, they must wring bone-dry a sheet that passes through the center of each cubicle three feet from the floor. The warders, who watch the captives from skylights, daily inject steam into the rooms so that for every ten drops that the captives wring from the sheet, seven new ones settle on it. Also, to make sure that the captives' lives do not become too ordered, the warders occasionally release squadrons of saturated birds.

Sansom details briefly how the captives in each of the rooms approached and dealt with the ordeal of gaining freedom. The captives in Room Three fail because they seek outside (themselves) for freedom; those in Room Two fail because they seek "in and out and around." The captives in Room Four never seek at all; thus they obviously fail. But the captives in Room One seek inside (themselves), and eventually they wring the sheet bone-dry—"dry as desert ivory, dry as marble dust"—and call on the guards to release them, to give them freedom. The guards then douse the sheet with water and reply that they already have their freedom, for it lies in the attitude of the spirit.

"The Long Sheet" succeeds very well in creating the atmosphere and the unenviable task of the captives, and students will probably respond to it emotionally even if they do not completely understand it. The steel box may be taken as a symbol for society, and the captives themselves suggest certain approaches to living. The fact that in the end even the successful group does not gain "freedom" (in the sense of release from the box) may suggest several things. For one, it seems to suggest that we normally misdefine "freedom." For another, it suggests that individuals must live in a society, and that they cannot achieve pure individuality.

USING THE STUDY NOTES PAGE 581

I. THE NIGHTMARE OF LIFE

Students are asked to comment upon the four groups listed below:

Room Three—Those Who Sought Outside.

It seems to us that the people in this group look outside themselves for "the good things." They are criticized for the value that they place on material things and for living a life of habit.

Room Two—Those Who Sought In and Out and Around.

Considerable detail is given about the individuals in this group, and so students should have little difficulty in identifying the specific character types being criticized. The second person of the group in a sense is not being criticized, but each of the others is—the first and the last are neurotics of a sort, the other two are goldbricker and fumbler, respectively. But perhaps the main point is that they cannot work together; they are asocial creatures. Sansom calls them "individualists," but it is clear that the word is not being used in its usual laudatory sense. Even the second person does not work with the others but makes an individual rather than a social contribution.

The title relating to those in Room Two could be explained as follows: Some seek *in* the task, but without the larger view; some seek *outside* the task; and some try to get *around* the task, to avoid it.

Room Four—Those Who Never Sought at All.

These are the "small" people, the people who don't care enough. The title explains itself.

Room One—Those Who Sought Inside.

We could say that these people seek inside themselves. But in seeking freedom there, they find that they have a common goal and they work together. They learn that no person is an island; they see that freedom is a spiritual thing. And in learning these truths, they learn all there is to know.

II. IMPLICATIONS

Students are asked for their opinions of the following statements:

1. The people who are seeking security, who are always looking after their own privileges, are the most to be pitied, for they are confined by their own weaknesses. Students will probably see that this best describes the group in Room Three. Whether they are to be pitied the most is debatable. The captives in all rooms except Room One were confined by their weaknesses.

2. Freedom means different things to different people. Students may well decide that freedom means something rather different to them from what it seems to mean to Sansom. Actually, the definition is often determined by the situation of the definer. Thus, those who are impoverished would probably define freedom quite differently from those who are wealthy. Students often tend to think of it as being able to do what one likes, free from restrictions. In part, this may be because their lives, since childhood, have been hedged by so many restrictions. The sort of spiritual freedom of which Sansom writes will probably be quite unfamiliar to them.

3. The organization of society is cruel, and real freedom is only for those in control. One could certainly argue from the story that the first clause is true enough—it is not an easy life, wringing that sheet all the time. The truth of the second clause is questionable as far as the story goes. Since we do not see the warders except when they are dealing with the captives, we perhaps should not generalize that they are free.

4. Most people live and die in cubicles of their own making, spending their lives doing things just as senseless as the wringing out of the sheet. As a generalization about life, this statement may be true enough. Sansom is saying that there really isn't much to do in life but wring that old sheet, and the only thing that really matters is how you do it—*if* you do it. But this does not necessarily imply that life is totally senseless; it isn't senseless if you achieve what you seek, as those in Room One do. On the other hand, the story does imply that progress is an illusion; in that sense, we may say that life is senseless.

5. Freedom of mind and spirit is the only real freedom. Students will probably agree with this, at least from the story's point of view. You may wish to ask them how they would explain this idea to people who do not know where their next meal is coming from or who are living in prisons or concentration camps.

III. TECHNIQUES

Author's Purpose

Students are asked to form their own interpretations of the story and then to compare their interpretations with the following. Note that this is not an easy story to interpret, and it may well be that more than one interpretation could fit the facts. Perhaps the main criterion for judging your students' interpretations should be whether or not they contain anything that is contradicted by the details of the story.

1. The warders represent the supreme authority. . . God; the cubicle is the world; the people represent the different segments of society. Students may have a little difficulty seeing that a group could represent God; yet it seems most likely that the warders do represent some sort of supreme authority. Not only do they control the lives of the people, but they also seem to possess final wisdom.

The cubicle could well be the world. Some students may object to the notion that the world holds so little, but note the somberness of the final insight that fits in with the somber picture of the world.

The people do not represent segments of society in the sense of upper class, middle class, lower class. Nor do they represent children, adolescents, adults. But they do represent different psychological makeups that lead people to make different compromises with life.

2. The warders represent the business leaders; the people are the workers in the cubicles; the cubicles are the classes of society. One could make a case for the idea that the warders exploit the people in the cubicles, *except* that we fail to see what the warders are getting out of their exploitation. The only answer that we can find is some sort of sadistic pleasure. As for the cubicles representing classes, one could say that Room Four contains the masses and Room Three, the bourgeoisie; but we do not see what classes are represented by Rooms One and Two.

3. The people in each cubicle are there through their own attitudes and abilities; the cubicle is devised in their own minds; the task is representative of the useless jobs we are forced to perform in life; the warders are our natures, which complicate the task. The captives in the cubicles seem to represent a cross section of all people; thus it seems unlikely that they are meant to symbolize people who have somehow condemned themselves through their attitudes and abilities. One may argue that the cubicles were devised in their own mind were it not for the fact that the warders are so real; and the warders put the people into the cubicles.

The task seems indeed to be useless, except that to perform it well yields a certain kind of freedom—or perhaps we should say insight. Finally, the warders do not merely complicate the task—they also give the final wisdom.

Irony

Students are asked the following question:

What would have been the effect if the tale had ended with the people in Room One gaining their freedom? The irony—or *one* irony—is that they *did* gain their freedom, and a major purpose of the story is to teach what freedom is. The story could not have made this point if the captives had gained their physical freedom. The effect would have been to tell a story different from the one Sansom wanted to tell.

IV. WORDS

A. Students are to use these words in their context clue and dictionary study.

1. **sustenance**—nourishment
   raiment—garments
   ragout—well-seasoned meat and vegetables cooked in a thick sauce
   scrupulous—strict; exact
   digress—turn aside from the main subject under discussion
   curate—an assistant to a church's pastor
2. **prototype**—model
   incarnate—invested with bodily (especially human) form

integument—something that covers or encloses

3. **tomes**—large or scholarly books
4. **furtive**—sly
lascivious—lewd; lustful
veneer—a superficial show
approbation—approval

B. In "A Modest Proposal," what do you understand by the following: Barbadoes, Formosa, Mandarin? *Barbadoes* and *Formosa* are places identified in the footnotes. A *Mandarin* was a high Chinese official.

What does Galsworthy mean by saying, "Nemesis fell"? The phrase *Nemesis fell* means that retribution arrived. Nemesis was the goddess of retribution.

The Attack on the Mill

PAGE 583

Émile Zola

Glossary Words

subterranean (page 584, col. 2) Underground

perpendicularly (page 584, col. 2) In an upright position; vertically

citadel (page 585, col. 1) A strongly fortified place; a fortress

taciturn (page 585, col. 2) Speaking very little; silent

fusillade (page 589, col. 1) A rapid or continuous discharge of many firearms at the same time

belligerents (page 592, col. 1) Persons engaged in waging war

stupefaction (page 593, col. 1) A dazed or senseless condition; overwhelming amazement, shock, etc.

anguish (page 596, col. 1) Extreme mental pain or suffering

accomplice (page 597, col. 1) A person who helps another in wrongdoing

lamentable (page 601, col. 1) To be regretted or pitied; deplorable

Handbook

exposition, irony, purpose, setting, symbol

Check Test 70

INTRODUCTION

The opening section of the story is largely descriptive. The setting is Rocreuse village and its environs in Lorraine, but most of the action focuses upon the old mill at the end of town, which is owned by old father Merlier, who has been the village mayor for twenty years. The description emphasizes peace and coolness, which are soon to contrast sharply with war and heat.

Merlier has an eighteen-year-old daughter, Françoise, soon to be married to a young man, Dominique, who lives just across the Moselle River from the mill. Originally, Dominique was thought to be lazy, and he was vaguely suspected of being a poacher. But after a three-hour talk with old Merlier, Dominique becomes a very hard worker.

At the opening of the story, old Merlier announces that his daughter will wed Dominique in a month. Shortly after this, we learn that France has declared war against Prussia and that most of the young men of the village have already gone to war. Dominique is a Belgian, however, and old Merlier is not worried about the war. The first section of the story closes with the words: "Never did a deeper peace rest upon a spot more blessed by nature."

The second section opens a month later, the day before the wedding is to take place. A detachment of

French soldiers comes to the village and prepares for battle; they are scattered in and around the mill. The Prussians attack at first from the other side of the river. The lovers—Dominique and Françoise—at first look on as spectators, but the first deaths affect them and a hail of bullets drives them indoors.

The situation becomes worse and worse for the French, who are trying to hold out only until six o'clock. Then Françoise is grazed by a bullet, and Dominique, who is a crack shot, begins to fire. He actually saves the day for the French, although he thinks only of defending Françoise. When six o'clock comes, the French retire; the captain tells old Merlier, "Amuse them! . . . We shall come back."

Dominique is so furious that he is unaware of the French retreat, and he continues firing, killing someone with every shot. But finally the Prussians come into the mill and capture him. The officer in charge says that Dominique will be shot in two hours.

In the third section of the story, the Prussian officer offers to spare Dominique if he will lead the troops through the Sauval forest, but Dominique refuses. He is then given till dawn to think it over and is imprisoned in a room just below Françoise's. After it is pitch-dark, she climbs down to her financé's room. She bids him escape and gives him a knife with which to defend himself against the one sentry that she has observed on the other side of the river. She is so desperate to have him escape that when he asks if the idea has her father's support, she lies that it was he who urged her to carry out the plan.

After Françoise returns to her room, Dominique escapes. In doing so, he kills the sentry on the other side of the river.

At the opening of the fourth section, the dead sentry is discovered, and shortly thereafter the Prussians also learn that Dominique has escaped. They assume that he killed the sentry and that old Merlier knows where he is hiding. Because Merlier says nothing in response to their request to give Dominique up, they prepare to shoot him. But then Françoise confesses that she helped her fiancé escape, and ultimately the officer decides to spare old Merlier for two hours while Françoise goes looking for Dominique. For Françoise, the situation is intolerable—she cannot bear to think of either old Merlier or Dominique dying.

She goes wandering off into the forest, full of mixed emotions, looking for Dominique. When they finally meet, her agitated condition reveals to him that something is wrong, but she refuses to tell him what it is. When she hears the steeple clock strike eleven, she realizes that her father's time is up, and she rushes back to the village, telling her fiancé that she will shake her handkerchief from her window if she needs him.

When she returns to the village, she meets Bontemps, a beggar, who reports that he has seen her father in the midst of Prussians. At the mill, Francoise, thinking that the French will be coming soon, begs the Prussians to give her father one more hour, but the officer refuses. Then suddenly Dominique appears. He has been told about the situation by Bontemps.

In the fifth and last section, Dominique is once again imprisoned and once again is offered freedom if he will guide the Prussians through the woods. But he refuses, and the officer decides that he must be shot. Just as they are about to shoot him, the French appear on the other side of the river. Françoise is ecstatic, but only for a moment, for the Prussian officer decides to dispose of Dominique before taking up the defense of the mill. Françoise is stunned; old Merlier is taken as a hostage.

The French have cannon this time, and in the ensuing battle the mill is destroyed. Old Merlier is killed by a spent bullet, but ultimately the French win the battle. The French captain has won his first campaign, and when he happily enters the yard, seeing Françoise between the corpses of her father and fiancé, he salutes her with his sword and cries, "Victory! victory!"

"The Attack on the Mill" is the sort of story that most students will enjoy a good deal, for it is full of action and suspense. Yet the rather long exposition at the beginning could prove a stumbling block. Perhaps the story should be broken into two assignments; the first or the first and second sections could be the first assignment. You may want to ask students to summarize the important facts before they go on to the second assignment. At the end of the story, you could return to the beginning and discuss why Zola spends so much time establishing the setting and the cool and tranquil atmosphere.

Although the last three or four sections of the story may seem relatively long, there is so much action and suspense that you will probably be safe in making a single assignment of them in most classes.

USING THE STUDY NOTES PAGE 601

I. A SENSELESS WASTE

There is no doubt that Zola wants his reader to feel that the war is a senseless waste. The irony of the ending surely indicates that intention. He is also showing individuals trapped by forces beyond their control; nevertheless, there is some indication that a person is not simply a pawn in the hands of fate. Twice Dominique could have escaped his fate if he had been willing to lead the Prussian soldiers through the forest. Although it is true that old Merlier, and presumably Dominique himself, would look upon such an act as cowardly, the possibility is not entirely closed. Indeed, Françoise at one point (page 600) tries to urge this action on her fiancé. Thus, even in Zola's naturalism, one senses that human choice has some influence upon human destiny.

II. IMPLICATIONS

Students are asked to consider what Zola's story implies about society. With these implications in mind they are to react to the following propositions:

1. In war the innocent inevitably suffer. Perhaps the best example of this is neither Françoise nor Dominique, for the latter does fire upon and kill Prussian soldiers and the former does help him to escape, but old Merlier, who does practically nothing that could be interpreted as directly hostile to either side.

2. It is impossible to make plans for the future. Zola certainly does imply that it is risky to plan for the future, even for those living in what seems to be an eminently secure and peaceful environment.

3. No matter how hard you work, you may lose everything because of things over which you have no control. Students will probably support the statement and see it as an important point in the story. It may be advisable to ask students to specify what some of these things are. In particular ask them to specify some *social* things.

4. Character is destiny. On the whole, of course, the story shows that destiny lies outside of character. But as we have noted previously, Dominique's character is partly responsible for determining his destiny. And his refusal to lead the Prussians through the forest is not the only example that could be given. Another is his decision to fire on the Prussians in the first place. Of course, fate placed him in the position in which he found himself, but it was his own nature, or character, that prompted him to take up arms. Someone else might have grabbed Françoise and cowered with her in the wine cellar.

5. Happiness is only an occasional interlude in a basic drama of pain. From the parts of the story that deal with the Franco-Prussian battle, one could legitimately come to this conclusion, but the early part of the story just as clearly suggests that life in Rocreuse village *had* been just the opposite for many years.

6. There is a parallel between the destruction of the mill and the destruction of the romance. The mill certainly has symbolic significance. Its chief parallel seems to be Merlier, for both of them are old and declining and are destroyed in the end. But students may find connections between the mill and the romance, too. A mill may be a symbol of romance. Recall that Françoise and Dominique had fallen in love "by dint of making eyes at each other over the mill-wheel."

III. TECHNIQUES

Author's Purpose

Students are asked to answer the following questions:

1. What aspects of the setting does Zola emphasize in the first section? How do these things contrast with what happens later in the story? In the first section, the chief emphasis seems to be on peace, beauty, and coolness in both the human and the natural spheres. There is a direct contrast between these aspects and the war, the ugliness, and the heat of later episodes.

2. How does Dominique change after his betrothal? How does this change in attitude affect the situation he eventually finds himself in? The change in Dominique occurs after he talks to old Merlier. Dominique's passivity shifts to activity, and the narrator tells us specifically, "There is nothing like love for giving courage to young folks." Without this courage, Dominique might never have fired at the Prussians in defense of Françoise; thus he would never have gotten into the situation that prevailed at the story's end.

3. What are the thoughts that Françoise has about the dead Prussian soldier? In what ways is he like her own sweetheart? The dead soldier looks like Françoise's sweetheart, and she fancies that he may have a loved one just like her back in Germany. She also feels responsible for his death because it is the knife that she gave Dominique that is protruding from his throat.

4. All in all, what would you say is the purpose of Zola in constructing the story as he did? All the points made above tend to show the unpredictability of human affairs; they show that what may seem to be good—the change in Dominique's attitude, Françoise's giving him a knife to defend himself—can lead to unforeseen and evil consequences. It looks as if this is a major purpose of the story—to show that human beings cannot fully control their destinies, that they are largely controlled by forces outside themselves.

Irony

Students are asked what is ironic about each of the following:

1. Dominique's change of character in which he settles down and becomes a hard-working young man. One could consider this ironic from several points of view. For one thing, his hard work is spent largely on the mill, and it of course is destroyed in the war. Also, he becomes hardworking for the sake of his coming marriage, and that never takes place because of the war. Again, his shift of character makes him courageous, and his courage leads almost directly to his death at the hands of the firing squad.

2. The fact that the attack on the mill takes place on the particular day it does. It occurs the day before the wedding; thus the contrast between the love and beauty of a wedding and the hatred and ugliness of war is made sharper.

3. Father Merlier's great care of the mill and the mill-wheel. The irony here is that the great tenderness and care that have gone on for such a long time can be wiped out in just a few moments. All Father Merlier's care went for nothing. Here also we see a human being who becomes a victim of outside forces.

4. The appearance of the man whom Dominique kills. One usually thinks of the enemy as different from oneself, preferably as not quite human. This expectation is sharply disappointed in this case, thus creating irony.

5. The kind of town and landscape in which the events take place. As we have already noted, the landscape is in direct contrast to the kind of place where one would expect a war to be waged. War is ugly and brutal; one can picture it being fought in a dirty city or perhaps in some sort of natural wasteland, not in a sleepy small town in a beautiful landscape.

6. Dominique's nationality. Dominique was Belgian—not French or Prussian. Thus, he was technically a noncombatant, and it is ironic that he should be virtually the very focus of the combat.

7. The final words of the story: "Victory! victory!" Perhaps the main ironic contrast here is that between the soldier who cries these words and Françoise. But there is also a larger irony, for the whole story causes us to ask just what has been won. In the "victory" everything that really mattered was destroyed.

IV. WORDS

A. Teachers may want to use this discussion as a springboard for reviewing activities.

B. Students will find the best examples of figurative speech in the opening section, which describes the town. Some passages are found on page 584, column 2, line 8; page 585, column 1, lines 5–8; page 586, column 1, lines 31–33; page 587, column 2, 23–29.

The Judgments of Shemyaka

PAGE 603

Anonymous

Glossary Words

upbraiding (page 603, col. 1) Finding fault with; scolding

maimed (page 603, col. 1) Disabled; crippled

plaintiffs (page 604, col. 2) Persons instituting a lawsuit

amity (page 604, col. 2) Peace and friendship; friendliness

Handbook

characterization, irony, purpose

Check Test 71

INTRODUCTION

"The Judgments of Shemyaka" is cast in the form of a folk story. As such, it is crowded with incidents and has little or no exposition. The two main characters are a rich brother and a poor brother. As in most folktales, you know that the poor brother will win out in the end. He has three misfortunes. First, he borrows his rich brother's horse, whose tail he accidentally pulls off. Then he falls off a balcony onto a cradle and kills a priest's baby. Last, in trying to commit suicide by jumping off a bridge, he lands on a sick man, killing the man. For each accident he is tried before Judge Shemyaka. Having nothing of value to give the judge, the defendant wraps a stone in his kerchief and puts it in his cap. Each time the judge asks him what he has to say for himself, he takes out the kerchief and silently holds it in front of him. Thinking that he is being offered a bag of gold, the judge hands down these verdicts: The horse is to stay with the poor brother until it has grown another tail; the priest's wife is to live with the poor brother until she conceives a child to replace the one who was killed; the son of the dead man is ordered to jump from the bridge and fall on the poor brother as he passes under it, thus killing him. In each case the wronged individual prefers to give the poor brother money, grain, and animals to escape the judgment. Thus the poor brother becomes wealthy. When the judge's servant comes to pick up the supposed bags of gold for Shemyaka, the poor brother takes out the kerchief and shows him the stone, with which, he says, he intended to hit the judge if his decisions went against him. Shemyaka is grateful that he handed down the right decisions.

To introduce this story, talk about the folktale and its function in the culture of a people. Folktales were originally oral and often expressed in a good-humored way the resentments of the common people against those in authority. Generally, folktales make use of hyperbole in the same way that children do—the "my father can whip your father" technique. Death is usually treated as an ordinary, casual happening. In the tale of little Red Riding Hood, for example, the wolf eats the grandmother and, in the original version, the girl as well. Such exaggeration served to underline the point of the story. Be sure that students understand that in the selection they are about to read they are entering a make-believe world.

USING THE STUDY NOTES

PAGE 605

I. THE RASCAL WINS OUT AGAIN

The brother in this story is poor, inept, and stupid. Why then is the reader amused by him? Perhaps it is because human beings in vicarious situations (such as reading), tend to side with the poor against the rich, with the clumsy against the clever, and with the persecuted against the persecutor, even though in real life their sympathies may not lie in this direction. In reading literature, we find ourselves imagining what our reactions would be if we were caught in a similar plight, and we want the assurance that by luck and pluck we will get out of the situation. Thus we enjoy seeing the wealthy, the clever, and the overrighteous defeated no matter what true justice demands. In this story, the reader is also delighted by the logical illogicalness of Shemyaka's judgments. He, too, is a rascal who wins. After all, he escaped from being hit by the accused's rock.

II. IMPLICATIONS

Students are asked to discuss the following:

1. Shemyaka follows the principle of making the punishment fit the crime. There is something peculiarly appropriate about Shemyaka's judgments, but they result in a strange kind of justice. It is the wronged person rather than the perpetrator who is punished. Get the class to decide what punishments would really fit the crimes. The obvious ones are for the poor brother to buy his sibling a new horse and to be crushed to death for his other crimes.

2. Consider the situations given below and decide what punishment Shemyaka would have meted out to the culprit. Inventing punishments should produce an interesting round of suggestions. The answers given below are, of course, not the only possibilities. It is the intent of this exercise to show how ingenious the author was in designing both the calamities and the judge's punishment for each.

a. Accidentally spilling a soft drink on a teacher's new cashmere sweater. The student has to wear the sweater until the spot vanishes.

b. Accidentally tripping your best friend and breaking his or her ankle. The friend must take the injured party home to live with him or her until the ankle heals.

c. While riding your three-speed bike you run into someone on a ten-speed bike. The other person's bike is slightly damaged. Yours is okay. Trade bikes.

III. TECHNIQUES

Author's Purpose

Students are asked to discuss the following statement:

Folk stories have no other purpose than to delight the reader. This statement is primarily true, but often such stories capture the fears or the resentments of people as well. In this story about Shemyaka, one feels sympathy for the poor brother as he triggers one calamity after another. But the judge is shown as a conniving soul, and his decisions are ridiculous. The storyteller is obviously amusing his listeners with this tale, but he is also highlighting the blindness of justice.

Irony

The punishments are all obviously ironic, but what is the final irony in the story? It is, of course, ironic that the punishments meted out to the poor brother really punish those whom he has injured. The final irony is that the judge would have been similarly influenced even if he had realized that the poor brother held a stone in his kerchief instead of a bag of gold.

The Tale About Ak and Humanity

PAGE 606

Yefim Zozulya

Glossary Words

azure (page 606, col. 1) The clear blue color of the unclouded sky

perturbation (page 607, col. 1) A thing, act, or event that causes disturbance or agitation; condition of being greatly disturbed; great distress; worry; anxiety

vainglorious (page 608, col. 1) Excessively proud or boastful; arrogant

profligates (page 608, col. 1) Very wicked or extravagant persons

decorum (page 608, col. 1) Proper behavior

partisans (page 609, col. 2) Supporters (whose support may be based on feeling rather than on reasoning) of a person, party, or cause

mediocre (page 610, col. 1) Neither good nor bad; of average quality; ordinary

proximity (page 611, col. 1) Nearness or closeness; the neighborhood

colloquies (page 613, col. 1) Conversations; a talking together

perturbed (page 613, col. 2) Greatly troubled; uneasy; distressed

Handbook

irony, purpose, satire

Check Test 72

INTRODUCTION

"A Tale about Ak and Humanity" takes place in an unnamed country that has a totalitarian government. (The author is Russian, and the story was translated from that language.) A decree is posted proclaiming that the Courts of the Higher Decisions will decide on a person's right to live and that all superfluous (unnecessary) people will be given twenty-four hours to depart from life. The placards announcing the new program throw the populace into a panic. Some people try to escape from the town but are turned back by guns and sticks. Records of the characteristics of those declared superfluous are kept in a gray cabinet. Things proceed smoothly until one day when Ak, the head of the courts, is found sitting in the Gray Cabinet. He claims to be learning about the strange life of human beings by sitting among the documents of destruction. Then without explanation, Ak vanishes. Chaos develops as rumors run rampant. Next, new pink placards are posted, announcing that all people are now to be allowed to live and that the name of the courts will be changed to the Courts of the Higher Delicacy. These new courts will appoint special commissions to visit all homes, to congratulate the occupants on being alive, and to keep records of each person's life. These Joyous Records are to be kept in a Rose-tinted Cabinet.

Ak reappears and sits in the Rose-tinted Cabinet from time to time. One day after screaming "It's necessary to kill them! To kill them! To kill them!" Ak disappears and is never seen again. Today people live as though there had been no Ak, as though no one had ever questioned their right to live.

The story is a satire on the nature of totalitarian government, but it is almost equally a satire on those aspects of human nature that make it seemingly impossible to reconstruct society for the greater happiness of all people. Be sure that the class understands the meaning of *superfluous* before they read the story.

To introduce the story, you may wish to refer to Shirley Jackson's "The Lottery." Many students will have read it, and once read, that story is seldom forgotten. Suggest that this selection may produce a similar impact on them. Or you may ask students to think of one change that they would propose to improve the quality of life today. Let each student contribute one idea. Then have the class turn to the story.

USING THE STUDY NOTES

PAGE 614

I. HOW AWFUL! HOW AWFUL!

This is both the readers' and the people's reaction to the edict. You may want to discuss the strange need of people from time immemorial to judge the worth of others. Physical strength, talent, productivity, beauty, and intelligence are only a few of the many criteria that different cultures have used to evaluate people. The ultimate impossibility of ranking people is expressed in the Bible: "Judge not lest you yourself be judged." This injunction is echoed in Shakespeare's *Hamlet* when the ghost advises Hamlet to "Leave her [his mother] to Heaven," indicating that only a god has the right to pass judgment. What then is Ak? Is he a human being, someone from another planet, or perhaps a god? Notice his attempts at understanding human beings. The story illustrates the inextricable mixture of good and bad, of worth and worthlessness in each person—a mixture that makes judgment impossible for another human being.

II. IMPLICATIONS

Students are asked to discuss their reactions to the following:

1. To determine the worth of a person's life, the Courts of the Higher Decisions ask not only the usual biographical information but also such questions as: What are your pleasures? Your loves? Your ambitions? Your relationships with others? The most memorable event in your life? Try answering these questions yourself. Do the answers give a fair picture of an individual's value? This exercise would make a good writing assignment. Suggest that students follow the pattern of the reports given in the story. On the basis of their written reports, they should decide whether they are useful or superfluous individuals. It should be interesting to see whether students think that the questions elicit sufficient material on which to base judgments. There could be pros and cons.

2. Define the human frailties epitomized in each of the four case studies.

Superfluous Male No. 14,741—loves to give advice; loves objects more than people; lazy; eating at a restaurant most exciting of his experiences.

Superfluous Male No. 14,623—dislikes his job; takes easy way out; fearful of everything; a hoarder during revolution; dull.

Superfluous Male No. 15,201—vain; overconfident; a gossip; indifferent to people and animals; joyless.

Superfluous Female No. 4,356—a scold; lacks interest in others; frivolous; capricious; hysterical; secret snacker.

3. React to Ak's statement: "When one examines the lives of the living, one arrives at the conclusion that three-fourths of them should be rooted out of existence. But when one examines those who have perished, a doubt comes. . . ." The discussion should lead students to see that every individual is infinitely complicated, neither all good nor all bad. When people are alive, we tend to see only their faults. After their deaths, we often forget their faults and emphasize their virtues.

4. Ak is really a great person. The story seems to support this statement. The people trust and respect Ak. When he disappears to meditate, the whole structure of the society is disturbed and chaos takes over. He is the only person who questions what is happening and who feels compassion and sadness for those whose lives have been sacrificed. It takes a strong person to admit a mistake and to reverse direction. As he sits in the Gray Cabinet and, later, in the Rose-tinted Cabinet, he evidences an ability to be personally moved. He sincerely wants to improve the lives of the people in his society. But when he realizes that he simply does not know how to do this, he vanishes.

III. TECHNIQUES

Author's Purpose

The author of this selection is Russian. Do you think he intends to criticize only Russian society or humankind in general? Those familiar with the Russian Revolution may be able to pinpoint parallel actions of Ak and Lenin. But the thrust of the story is to highlight the ambiguities within human beings. On the one hand, people are self-centered, delight in accusing one another, and lead mediocre lives; on the other hand, they exhibit personal dignity, kindness to one another, and love for their children.

Irony

What is ironic about the following situations?

1. The people have elected Ak and have great trust in him. The people trust and believe in Ak, and yet he is the instrument of their destruction.

2. The officials scorn primitive usefulness to a neighbor. The term *primitive usefulness* is defined as kindness or helpfulness. It is ironic to think that such qualities are not valued.

3. The Joyous Records are filled with complaints. People seem never to be satisfied. Ak expects the people to rejoice in being alive and to praise the wonder of life. Instead, they find their pleasure in acquiring possessions, in quarreling, and in complaining. It is ironic that they should do so because they could easily have been among those condemned to die.

4. In quarrels, the people say such things as: "It is evident that you're alive only because of

some mistake. The Courts of the Higher Decisions did their work carelessly.'' It is a primitive instinct in human beings to feel that they have been chosen because of superior qualities but that others have been chosen through error.

IV. WORDS

There is a tendency in officialdom to invent new phrases for things to make them acceptable to the populace. This practice is sometimes called ''double speak.'' What is the actual definition of the following?

1. Courts of the Higher Decisions	murder courts; inquisition courts; kangaroo courts
2. depart from life	kill yourself; commit suicide; die
3. human rubbish	the useless; the unfit; the inefficient; the incompetents
4. primitive usefulness	helpfulness; kindness
5. Courts of the Higher Delicacy	approbation board; commendatory commissions

SUMMING UP: CRITICS OF SOCIETY

THE WRITER AND THE STATE

Various assignments suggest themselves in connection with this final commentary. Perhaps the most general would be the assignment of essays on the topic of ''The Writer as Social Critic.'' It might be considerably better, however, to narrow the topic—for instance, ''Social Criticism in American Writing of the 1930s'' or ''Social Criticism in Lewis's *Main Street.*''

Oral reports on various writers who have felt pressured in one way or another by the state would be another good idea. A brief list of such writers is in the commentary in the text, but many other names will undoubtedly suggest themselves to you, such as Alexander Solzhenitsyn, Dalton Trumbo, John Steinbeck, George Orwell, and William Golding.

IMPLICATIONS

Students are asked to discuss the following:

1. For each selection in this unit, explain what the author was criticizing.

An Enemy of the People	self-interest; the welfare of business over the welfare of people; the compact majority
''A Modest Proposal''	the English people's treatment of the Irish; inhumanity of human beings to one another
''Quality''	society's neglect of excellence
''Life of Ma Parker''	society's indifference toward the poor
''On a Journey''	society's method of solving problems
''Children''	self-centered behavior of those in authority; treatment of children
''The Long Sheet''	the way people go about handling a job
''The Attack on the Mill''	the brutality of war
''The Judgments of Shemyaka''	justice
''A Tale about Ak and Humanity''	the value of a person's life; the nature of people; the futility of efforts made to improve other people's lives

2. Criticism is inherently ugly and produces bitter, depressing literature. To say that criticism is inherently ugly implies a preconceived opinion that we would hope few students would have. On the other hand, it is true that much—although by no means all—of the literature of criticism could be described as bitter. Certainly this is true of much of the literature in this unit. Depressing is a more subjective term. For instance, many students will feel depressed by the Sansom story. But for other students who may already feel that society is a prison, the ending will not be depressing.

3. Galsworthy is so involved with his theme of social justice that he has not made his portrayal of the old shoemaker a realistic one. The statement may be a bit difficult for students to judge, for the old shoemaker is not the sort of character who is easy to find in contemporary America. Stereotyped is perhaps a fair way to describe Galsworthy's portrayal of him, and such a standardized characterization does seem slightly unreal. It is probable that Galsworthy was more concerned with theme than with character.

4. Making fun of society is easy but does little to reform evils. Making fun of society in a way that stimulates reform is not easy. How much effect literature has as a tool of change would take extensive research; for instance, it would be easy to demonstrate that there were many reforms in England after Dickens's novels were published, but the novels did not necessarily cause the reforms.

In general, however, it does seem likely that the publicizing of social ills by widely read authors and journalists does contribute to the correction of those ills. Reform requires public awareness of the need for it, and providing that awareness is a service that writers render.

5. A folktale or fantasy is a good vehicle for social criticism because the writer can remain objective and detached. The proposition may be true enough, but there are other categories of writing that also lend themselves to objectivity and detachment. Two of these may be seen in the selections by Swift and Sansom, respectively—one gains detachment through irony, the other through symbolism. All three categories are good ones for getting around the censor when it is necessary to do so. Of course, all three require much more skill than do more direct methods.

6. Swift makes his essay more effective by pretending to advocate something that is completely unbelievable. This statement could be supported on the ground that the idea of selling and eating children is so shocking that the impact of the essay is much greater than the proposal of a reasonable reform would have produced. Once you have read this essay, it is very difficult to forget it—certainly one measure of the effectiveness of any piece of writing.

TECHNIQUES

Author's Purpose

Students are asked to discuss and decide which selections in the unit do the best job of the following:

1. Making clear and obvious what was being criticized. There may be a good deal of variety in student responses here, for whether something is clear and obvious depends upon the reader as well as the author. Most of the authors do a reasonably good job of making clear what they are criticizing. Some of the most obvious criticism occurs in *An Enemy of the People,* "Quality," "The Attack on the Mill," and "A Tale about Ak and Humanity."

2. Making you want to help the situation. Here an individual's own disposition is likely to be a critical factor in whether or not the selection creates a desire to help. It is not simply a matter of the author's effectiveness. There are other complications; for example, some of the situations are no longer relevant. Ask students to try to explore all the factors behind their choices of situations that they wanted to change.

3. Making you sympathetic with the characters. Ma Parker is probably the character who stands out most clearly as an individual and hence may be the one for whom many students feel the most sympathy. Certainly, many students will sympathize with the characters in "Children" because they themselves have probably seen or experienced irrational behavior by adults. On a more abstract level, students may feel sympathy for the Irish people in "A Modest Proposal." Others may emphathize with Ak in "A Tale about Ak and Humanity," and still others may empathize with one of the major characters in "The Attack on the Mill."

4. Making you puzzle over possible meanings. "The Long Sheet," because of its symbolic nature, is one of the obvious choices. Also "A Tale about Ak and Humanity," "The Judgments of Shemyaka," and "The Life of Ma Parker" may leave many students feeling puzzled—but each for a different reason. In short, whether a selection breeds puzzlement will depend not only on the appeal of a particular type of writing but also upon the reader's experience and interests.

5. Shaking you up and giving you a new viewpoint. The important thing here is for students to discover why they felt shaken and to determine what their new viewpoints are. It is hoped that all will have felt startled or appalled by at least one of the selections. But there may not be any change in their viewpoints, and it is not necessary that they cite one.

Irony

1. Which selection makes the best use of verbal irony? There are three strong candidates. "A Modest Proposal," "A Tale about Ak and Humanity," and "On a Journey." All use repeated contrasts between what is said and what is meant.

2. Which has the most telling example of dramatic irony? Sansom's "The Long Sheet" is a good choice for this answer. Its ending, particularly, is both unexpected and revealing. But Zozulya's "A Tale about Ak and Humanity" has similar qualities. And "The Life of Ma Parker" could be the choice of some students.

3. Which type, verbal irony or dramatic irony, is used more in these selections. Dramatic irony is relied upon for major effects considerably more often than is verbal irony.

4. Which type of irony has the greater effect on you emotionally? Which mentally? In general, one would think that dramatic irony would have the greater emotional effect and verbal irony the greater mental effect; the latter must often be figured out by using one's mind, whereas the former tends to have a direct impact. But it is wise not to make this point too dogmatically. After all, the ending of "The Long Sheet" is an instance of dramatic irony: It has an immediate emotional impact, but it is meant to have a mental impact as well. If the reader merely reacts emotionally, the author clearly has not fully succeeded.

5. Why do you think irony is such a common literary device? The simplest answer to this question is that irony provokes the involvement of the reader.

WRITING FROM READING

1. This assignment gives students practice in organizing a piece of writing that demonstrates how irony is developed.

2. From this writing task, students should learn a process that can be followed in writing an extended simile. Most of their similes will be ironic, a demonstration of how one's ideas about something are expanded when unlikes are used to describe it.

UNIT TEST

There are several options for testing your students' grasp of the unit. You may use the Summing Up section in the pupil's anthology—either whole or in part—as the unit test. For a second approach, you may select questions at random from the Study Notes at the end of each selection as a basis for constructing a final examination covering the complete unit. For a third option you may choose to use the comprehensive unit test prepared on blackline masters available in a separate test booklet ISBN 0-07-009823-9.

RELATING THE GALLERY TO THE UNIT

PAGE 565

1. Picasso said: "What do you think an artist is? An imbecile who has only his eyes if he's a painter, or ears if he's a musician, or a lyre at every level of his heart if he's a poet? On the contrary, he's . . . a political being, constantly alive to heartrending, fiery, or happy events, to which he responds in every way. . . . Painting is not done to decorate apartments. It is an instrument of war for attack and defense against the enemy." That view formed part of Picasso's philosophy, and it echoes the purpose of every painter included in this gallery as well as many others.

Read the above quotation to the class, and then examine the paintings in the gallery as visual representations of Picasso's words. Ask students these questions: How do you know that more than just the desire to paint pretty pictures motivates the artists in this gallery? Which artists are most effective in conveying their messages? Which artists are the least effective? How is exaggeration used? Color? Facial expression?

2. Goya's depiction of "The Execution of the Citizens of Madrid on the Third of May, 1808" (page 565) is a classic statement of artistic social commentary. Everything in it contributes to the overall message of horror and indignation. Examine with your students the following qualities and techniques: Notice the focusing of light on the soon-to-be-executed citizen and the whiteness of his shirt in contrast to the darkness of the soldiers. What is the effect of this contrast? Note that the faces of the soldiers are obscured, whereas the features of the citizens' faces are agonizingly shown. What effect does this contrast create? Notice also the composition of the painting: The soldiers form a straight, unbroken line, whereas the citizens are scattered in various individual postures. Why is this done? Notice the black night sky that surrounds the scene. Why was this detail included? This painting is only one of many in which Goya depicted the horrors of war. Goya's point of view is not a pleasant one. What does he have to say about the role of the individual in war? Compare this painting with the chalk drawing by Henry Moore on page 568 and the painting by Dali on page 569. What elements does the Goya canvas contain that the other two do not?

3. Daumier was a master at telling a tale through facial expression. Examine his lithograph, "The Legislative Body," at the top of page 566. Ask students the following questions: What does Daumier do to each face to give it individuality and yet link it to every other face in the drawing? Are the emotions of the artist clearly shown in this rendering? What are these emotions? What is Daumier's attitude toward the French legislature? This rendering comes closer than do any of the paintings in the gallery to the quality of a political cartoon.

4. "The Potato Eaters" by Vincent van Gogh (page 566) and "Riot" by Käthe Kollwitz (page 568) represent a gentler approach to social ills. Van Gogh chronicles as honestly as he can the starkness of peasant life, whereas Kollwitz captures an agonized moment of denial. She concentrates not on the violence of the moment but rather upon the personal agony of the people involved. In a similar way van Gogh concentrates upon the personal interaction of the peasants. Ask students the following questions: What social impact do van Gogh's and Kollwitz's depictions of poverty achieve? Do the problems of the people in these two works of art seem distant and unreal? Have each of these artists captured the problems of poverty? How would the artists treat the same subjects if they were painting in America today?

5. Orozco's mural "Zapatistas" is an imposing, rhythmic statement of support for a cause. This is social commentary on a grand scale that is designed to move multitudes through the effects of concentration and majesty. Counterparts of murals such as this are patriotic posters, patriotic music, and patriotic pageantry. Ask students the following questions: Who is the hero in this mural? How do you know? How is the hero's leadership shown? What elements of dignity are represented in the mural? What elements of dedication are depicted? What is achieved by the element of folk simplicity?

6. Despite differences in artistic style, there is a striking similarity between Henry Moore's chalk drawing "The Morning after the Blitz" (page 568) and Salvador Dali's surrealist canvas "Galacidalacidesoxiribunucleicacid" (page 569). The perspective and depth, the use of space and contrast, and the presence of light are similar. But Moore is realistic, whereas Dali deals in symbols. Ask students to decode the Dali canvas using the following questions as a guide: What does the title signify? What do the molecular models of people on both sides of the painting represent? What is the significance of the pointed guns? What is the message conveyed by the religious figures in the sky? What do the colors in the sky signify? Finally, explain to students that Dali draws his viewers into the picture by placing them behind an advancing figure. The figure, in effect, leads a procession that draws viewers into the painting. This is a Renaissance device. Why does Dali use it? Is Dali's technique more effective than Moore's? The technique of surrealism—using dream symbols—is designed to internalize the experience of the painting and thus to make it "super real." Does Dali succeed in this attempt?

THE EXPANDED EXPERIENCE: RELATING THE HUMANITIES TO THE UNIT

1. Disciplines: E, SS, A, M. Skills: LS, Rd, PS, Org.

Construct a sound-sight environment that comments upon an individual's disorientation in an industrial, urban society. Use paintings by Klee, Duchamp, Kandinsky, and Boccioni, excerpts from the composition *Iron Foundry* by Mossolov, the Dadaist poetry of Tristan Tzara, and light and sound devices that you create.

2. Disciplines: E, SS, A, M, TA. Skills: LS, Rd, PS, Org.

Obtain the book and the original cast album of the Stephen Sondheim-Arthur Laurents musical *Anyone Can Whistle,* which is a satire on restrictive and corrupt political and religious establishments. Interweaving music from the play, perform in mime several scenes that express social commentary through movement and music. As background illustration, make slides of paintings by Goya, Kollwitz, Orozco, Daumier, and Siqueiros. Give this presentation to the class, and discuss the multiple effects created by simultaneously using music, theater, and art to express a social comment.

3. Disciplines: SS, A, M, TA. Skills: Wr, LS, Rd, PS, Org.

Explain to the class the background surrounding Picasso's huge painting "Guernica." Using three slide projectors, project the painting on a wall of your classroom in a size that is close to the original. Play the funeral music from *Götterdämmerung* by Richard Wagner, as a student delivers a narrative composition that she or he has written to relate the incidents of the senseless bombing of the village of Guernica to Picasso's impassioned painting protesting against this incident. Then discuss the effect that the event and the painting have had upon individual class members. Consider the effects that artists, composers, and writers might have in bringing about social change.

RELATING ADDITIONAL READING TO THE UNIT

SUGGESTED BOOKS

Bellamy, Edward. *Looking Backward*
Camus, Albert. *The Plague*
Clark, Walter van Tilburg. *The Ox-Bow Incident*
Cleaver, Eldridge. *Soul on Ice*
Deloria, Vine, Jr. *Custer Died for Your Sins*
Dürrenmatt, Friedrich. *The Visit*
Fitzgerald, F. Scott. *The Great Gatsby*
Heinlein, Robert. *Stranger in a Strange Land*
Hugo, Victor. *Les Miserables*
Huxley, Aldous. *Brave New World*
Ibsen, Henrik Johan. *The Doll's House*
———. *Ghosts*
Le Carré, John. *The Spy Who Came In from the Cold*
Lee, Harper. *To Kill a Mockingbird*
Lewis, Sinclair. *Babbitt*
Malcolm X. *Autobiography of Malcolm X*

Miller, Arthur. *The Crucible*
Orwell, George. *Animal Farm*
———. *1984*
Sinclair, Upton. *The Jungle*
Steinbeck, John. *The Grapes of Wrath*
Shute, Nevil. *On the Beach*
Thomas, Piri. *Down These Mean Streets*
Twain, Mark. *Huckleberry Finn*
Uris, Leon. *Exodus*
Vonnegut, Kurt. *Cat's Cradle*
———. *Player Piano*
Warren, Robert Penn. *All the King's Men*
Waugh, Evelyn. *The Loved One*
Wright, Richard. *Native Son*

TWENTIETH-CENTURY BRITISH POETRY: The Present and the Past

The poetry of this period is, in some ways, as difficult as the poetry of earlier centuries. It is often densely textured and disconnected at the same time. It uses unfamiliar words, strange images, and seemingly fragmented lines. We stress the necessity of close reading and of encouraging students to examine the implications of individual words, phrases, and images. The strangeness of the poetry is balanced by its "nowness"; students will recognize that these poets are talking about their own world, the world of the twentieth century, and although the individual words may seem peculiar, the events and the ideas should be familiar.

Nevertheless, you may find that a certain amount of background is needed. When one reads Yeats, it helps to know about the civil war in Ireland. Current newspapers make the problem accessible, and you can get students to understand that the turmoil that Yeats alludes to is present today. The war poems may also need some background, because students may not have a good sense of what the two world wars were like; films, pictures, and outside reading could be considered here.

Certain poets, Yeats and Eliot especially, will take more time to cover than others. They are, admittedly, not easy to read, but they are immensely important and influential. By reading their poems carefully, students will be able to understand many of the central issues in modern poetry, especially that double-edged relationship to the past that is discussed in the pupil text.

Each poem demands its own approach, but let us again suggest that reading aloud is always the best place to start, especially with poems that may seem impenetrable. You may also want to obtain some recordings, particularly if you can find the poet reading his or her own works. There are some superb Dylan Thomas records that should delight students because of the Welsh lilt to his voice. There are also records of famous actors reading modern poetry that you may want to use. But do not feel that you must turn to professionals; students should be encouraged to produce a poetry reading. Working together in small groups, they can practice the poems, get comments from other students, and then present a group of poems to the class. Another possible exercise is to have students select poems from other units that seem to offer special insights into or contrast with one of the modern poems. Consider devoting a session to dramatic monologues, using Shakespeare's "My mistress' eyes are nothing like the sun"; Herbert's "The Collar"; Browning's "My Last Duchess"; and Eliot's "The Love Song of J. Alfred Prufrock." Students could be asked to choose a thematic topic (love, faith, responsibility, and so on) and then to find poems or even readings from the plays and short stories that illustrate and illuminate that topic.

We stress the backward-looking approach because the poems of the twentieth century are so dependent on earlier literature. You will probably find other patterns to emphasize, whether thematic or formal, that will show students the relationship between past and present.

NOTE: For some suggested reference sources, see the bibliography in the introduction to the first poetry unit, pages 34–36 in this teacher's guide.

Poems by Gerard Manley Hopkins

PAGE 617

Handbook

alliteration, assonance, imagery, meter, rhythm, symbol

Check Test 73

INTRODUCTION

Students will no doubt view Hopkins as formidable at first. However, they will probably become engaged by him once they have gotten deeply into one of his poems. It is absolutely essential to read the poems aloud because so much of what Hopkins is doing with rhythm can only be *heard.* The explanation of *inscape* in the introductory material and the explanation of *sprung rhythm* in the questions on "God's Grandeur" are simplified but sufficient. We caution against becoming over-technical about sprung rhythm. The important thing for students to understand is that it enables Hopkins to emphasize certain words that are crucial to the meaning of the poem. These two poems demonstrate the following major features of Hopkins: (1) His delight in the natural world (one of his favorite words is *fresh*), (2) his conviction that we are all versions of God/Christ and that everything that we do expresses that relationship, and (3) his use of alliteration, assonance, coined words, and images chosen from unfamiliar places. The questions treat the poems individually, but you may want to read them together and afterward talk about features that students find in both of the poems. The idea of *inscape,* extends easily into our own lives: Students may want to think about how they express themselves through particular ways of speaking, dressing, and so on.

USING THE STUDY NOTES

PAGE 618

GOD'S GRANDEUR

1. The images in the poem seem strange symbols of grandeur—the light from a piece of metal foil that is shaken, and the gathering of oil from crushed olives. Discuss: it is much more forceful for the poet to have used unusual comparisons than familiar ones. "Unusual comparisons" are by definition more forceful, more arresting, than familiar ones—unless, of course, the familiar comparisons are used in unfamiliar contexts. But students ought to see more than this. If a poem is to have organic unity, it must not use unusual comparisons merely for the sake of attracting attention. Ask students to look for the deeper purposes underlying the use of the opening images.

They should note, first, that this is a poem about "freshness"; surely the fresh images are in harmony with this theme. But Hopkins is also concerned with organic unity. Line 2 is connected by contrast with the image in lines 5 and 6; and line 3 is connected by contrast with the image in lines 7 and 8. In addition, there is clearly a connection between "shining from shook foil" and the dawning referred to in lines 11 and 12. And the warmth and "greatness" of the olive oil is surely connected with the brooding of the Holy Ghost in the last two lines of the poem.

Students should be taught to see such evidences of organic unity. Focusing attention on images for their own sake may destroy the *life* of the poem.

2. What, according to Hopkins, have human beings done to the earth? He makes this rather clear in lines 5–8. But it is not so much a matter of what human beings have done, but rather of what they have not done: They have remained passive, failed to be spontaneous, failed to feel, failed to see, failed to smell. They have wasted themselves rather than used themselves.

3. How does the poem go about illustrating the proposition stated in the first line: "The world is charged with the grandeur of God"? It illustrates it in the lines immediately following the first line and in the whole of the second stanza. It illustrates it, too, in the vigor and richness of the language—in the grandeur of the language.

4. Hopkins wrote in what he called *sprung rhythm,* a kind of meter quite different from that used in the other poems in this book. Still, there is a strong pattern to the sound. Read the poem aloud, discovering the strong beats that come naturally from the phrasing. You should find five beats to a line, even though the number of syllables varies. Notice how the sprung rhythm springs in particular on the word *ah!* in the last line.

Sprung rhythm is based on the number of stressed syllables in a line, with lesser concern for the number of unstressed. The accent typically falls on the first syllable of a foot. The monosyllabic, a single accented foot, and the first paeon, a four-syllable foot with accent on the first syllable, both occur in Hopkins's metrical system. It is also possible for a foot to continue the beginning of the following line. Here is an analysis of the sprung rhythm in the last line of "God's Grandeur":

> Wórld/bróods wǐth wǎrm/bréast ǎnd wǐth/áh!/
> bríght wǐngs.

It is the tendency for the stresses to come together—as in "World broods" and "ah! bright"—that made Hopkins call it *sprung* rhythm.

SPRING AND FALL

1. Why does autumn produce sad thoughts? What natural details are given emotional connotations? Autumn is immediately associated with loss in the poem. The word "unleaving," a Hopkins coinage, stresses both the leaves and the loss. The unusual phrase "wanwood leafmeal," for which possible interpretations are given in the notes, also suggests a kind of dying paleness. "Fall," the last word of the title, refers both to the season and to death, while "spring" has the emotional connotation of fresh thoughts and of springing forth. We notice, however, that when the word "spring" actually appears in the poem, it is in relation to "sorrow."

2. What do you understand the last two lines of the poem to mean? The last two lines argue that when Margaret weeps for the falling leaves, she is actually weeping for herself because all people must die. According to the poem, death is "the blight man was born for." Margaret's real pain therefore comes from the realization that all of us are like the falling leaves.

Poems by William Butler Yeats

PAGE 619

Glossary Word

transfigured (page 619) Made more beautiful or glorious; changed in form or appearance

Handbook

alliteration, allusion, balanced sentence

Check Test 74

INTRODUCTION

"The Lamentation of the Old Pensioner" and "The Wild Swans at Coole" are both poems about time and its effects on people. The defiance of the speaker in "Lamentation" can be compared to the more melancholy attitude in "Wild Swans." You may also wish to compare these poems to Shakespeare's Sonnet 65. Still another point of comparison is with Wordsworth's *The Prelude;* there, too, we find the poet looking back on his earlier life. "An Irish Airman" is a remarkably controlled poem, both in its form and in its feeling; it could also be taught with the poems in "Poetry and War." More advanced students might want to read Yeats's longer poem "In memory of Major Robert Gregory."

USING THE STUDY NOTES

PAGE 621

THE LAMENTATION OF THE OLD PENSIONER

1. In what sense has time transfigured the old pensioner? The old pensioner has been transfigured both physically and spiritually. He is not only physically unattractive and sexually impotent but also too exhausted spiritually to participate in political and humanistic debates.

2. Why does the speaker spit into the face of time? The speaker ends on a note of defiance because his mind allows him to contemplate the past. Time may transfigure him, but it cannot rob him of his memory and his thoughts.

3. What specific historical event is the poet referring to in lines 7–10? What is their wider meaning? The specific historical event referred to is the fight of the Irish National Brotherhood (an underground organization) to free Ireland from British rule. This event has particular relevance today in view of the current upheavals in Northern Ireland. Yet the phrases "some conspiracy" and "human tyranny" and the word "again" reinforce the idea that events are cyclical and will recur no matter what measures are taken to control or eliminate them.

4. In the last stanza, lines 13–18, the poet contrasts tranquillity with violence. What effect does this have on readers? Does line 17 succeed as a line of poetry or does its violence stop readers—forcing them to disregard the poem as a whole? The softness of line 15 provides a dramatic contrast to the harshness of line 17 and strengthens the effect of the pensioner's "spit into the face of Time." The tone of line 17 is consistent with that of lines 7–10.

AN IRISH AIRMAN FORESEES HIS DEATH

1. The speaker lists a number of reasons why he is not fighting. What are they and why does he put the explanation in the negative? The speaker discounts the customary motives of hating the enemy (l. 3), loving his country (l. 4), the call of law and duty (l. 8), the desire for approval from statesmen or the common people (l. 10); he even suggests that his death will leave no mark, either of sorrow or happiness (ll. 7–8). By eliminating the reasons that one ordinarily would think of, and that are frequently advanced as a justification for war and thus for death, the speaker focuses attention on his true motive.

2. What is the real reason for his action, which will lead to his death? He speaks of "A lonely impulse of delight," a phrase which puzzles as much as it enlightens. The speaker acts on "impulse" rather than on reason, and he joins the notion of "lonely" with that of "delight," something that may sound contradictory. But, given his evident distaste for the public values already mentioned in the poem, perhaps the need to leave the earth and "drive" to the clouds is paramount.

3. The last four lines speak of balance; how many different kinds of balance are reflected in these lines? How is balance crucial for an understanding of the poem? The formality of the poem, as seen in its carefully structured quatrains and its balanced lines ("Those that I fight I do not hate, / Those that I guard I do not love") is emphasized even more strongly in the last four lines. The word "balanced" in line 13 is echoed by "balance" in line 16; line 13 is itself a balanced line, with the alliteration of "balanced" and "brought," and each verb followed by "all." Lines 14–15 are structured in a crossing pattern:

The years to come	seemed	waste of breath
A waste of breath		the years behind

And the last line of the poem forcefully equates "this life" and "this death." One can read "balance" in several different ways: it could be argued that the tone of the speaker is resigned, accepting, balanced; or one could say that the balance comprehends the anger of finding that both past and present are both a "waste of breath" and of realizing that "this life" and "this death" may be the same thing.

THE WILD SWANS AT COOLE

1. What has happened to the poet during the nineteen years since he first counted the swans? What has happened to the swans? The poet has grown older, especially in the heart. Yet nothing has happened to the swans. Even now, nothing has changed with them; they are eternal.

2. What is the season of the year? How does it reflect the theme of the poem? The season is autumn. And the theme of the poem, too, is the autumn of a person's life.

3. What is implied by the following lines: "When I awake one day / To find they have flown away"? Realizing that the poem is about mortality, students should be able to see that the reference is to the speaker's death. They should realize, too, that only under that circumstance would the eternal swans disappear.

Poem by D. H. Lawrence

PAGE 622

Glossary Words

fissure (page 622) A long, narrow opening; a split; a crack

expiate (page 623) Make amends for a wrong, sin, etc.; atone for

Handbook

personification, point of view, rhyme scheme, rhythm, symbol

Check Test 75

INTRODUCTION

Students usually have an immediate and positive reaction to a Lawrence poem because the language is direct and strong—although they are frequently challenged to accept a point of view quite different from their own. Such may be the case with "Snake," one of Lawrence's major poems. In it he makes a number of startling assertions, for he calls the snake "a guest in quiet," "a god," "a king," "one of the lords of life," and contrasts those honorific terms with his own vulgarity and pettiness. He also implies that what we have learned from our "education" can be wrong, since it is that voice which says "He must be killed" and a similar voice which taunts him "If you were a man." Thus the poem raises the question, "What does it mean to be cowardly or perverse or even human?"

USING THE STUDY NOTES PAGE 630

SNAKE

1. Notice the way in which Lawrence uses long lines and short lines. What effects can you describe for such lines as "And must wait, must stand and wait, for there he was at the trough before me" (l. 6), "A sort of horror, a sort of protest against his withdrawing into that horrid black hole" (l. 52), "I felt so honored" (l. 34), and "A pettiness" (l. 74). The contrasting line lengths add extra emphasis to particular lines. The long lines frequently imitate the mind of the speaker as in the slightly impatient repetition, "And must wait, must stand and wait" (l. 6), or the movement of the snake, "his withdrawing into that horrid black hole." The short lines stress the speaker's point of view, "I felt so honored" (l. 34) or his feeling, as in the shamed "A pettiness" (l. 74). Other short lines such as "Silently" (l. 13) contrast with the preceding longer line; the repetition of "s" and "l" sounds in "Softly drank through his straight gums, into his slack long body" is then echoed, almost eerily, in the one word "silently."

2. What words suggest the instinctive horror Lawrence feels for the snake? What words suggest more positive feelings? What are those feelings? The words with "s" sounds: "fissure" (l. 7), "slackness" (l. 8), "sipped" (l. 11) and all of lines 12-13, emphasize the slithery quality of the snake. The image of the "two-forked tongue," the word "venomous," the description of the hole as "dreadful" and "horrid black," and the vivid verb "writhed" all imply a kind of horror. Words suggesting positive feelings about the snake fall into two categories. The first suggests the harmless quiet nature of the snake; the comparison to cattle (ll. 16–17), the description "he had come like a guest in quiet," the words "peaceful, pacified," the adverb "dreamily" (l. 42)—all these stress that the snake is essentially quiet and harmless. Moreover, the constant personification of the snake, with his looking at the speaker, and his comparison to "a god" and a "king" imply the human, even glorious, aspect of the snake. Most important is the effect the snake has on the speaker: "I felt so honored." By the end of the poem he is even calling him "my snake."

3. What are the different voices that speak to Lawrence? "The voice of my education" (l. 22), later called "the voices of my accursed human education" (l. 65), can be seen as the societal forces which teach us that snakes are bad and thus must always be killed. The inner voices (l. 25) which say "If you were a man / You would take a stick and break him now, and finish him off" may be seen as those learned prejudices which "teach" us how to fit into certain societal roles—men do such-and-such, women do such-and-such. Perhaps the voices which say "If you were not afraid, you would kill him!" are also such societal forces; perhaps they are the hidden fears within each one of us.

4. Why does he throw a log at the snake? Since the snake is leaving, throwing the log is essentially a useless act—and yet it is significant that only when the snake turns his back on the speaker can the speaker act. He calls his motive "A sort of horror, a sort of protest against his withdrawing into that horrid black hole," and it may be that he doesn't want to lose the communion he seems to have established with the snake and so, clumsily, makes a gesture which is meaningless and counter-productive. He may also be yielding to the fear he has expressed earlier—now that the snake is leaving he may feel the desire to "prove" his manliness by trying to hit ("break"?) the snake.

5. How do you understand the reference, "And I thought of the albatross"? The reference to Coleridge's poem *The Rime of the Ancient Mariner* asks us to see the similarity between the mariner who "inhospitably" (Coleridge's word) shoots the bird flying around his ship and the speaker of the poem who throws a log at the disappearing snake. In both cases, "hospitality" has been violated; in both cases, an act of violence will have to be paid for, as this speaker realizes, "I have something to expiate."

6. Is it an overstatement to call the snake "a king in exile" and "one of the lords of life"? On the literal level, there is obvious overstatement. But on the symbolic level, perhaps not. In the poem, Lawrence makes us feel that the earth in some way belongs to the snake, and that it is the man who is the intruder; thus the snake is really the king, although in exile. There may even be an ironic reference to the Garden of Eden from which man and woman were exiled, for that paradise was shared by the snake before it was made to crawl on its belly. A snake as a lord of life may seem even stranger, since snakes are often associated with death and this golden snake is said to be "venomous." But the overstatement asks us to think about the way in which life and death are connected, so that the agent of death may actually be a bringer of life.

Poems by T. S. Eliot

PAGE 624

Glossary Words

etherized (page 625) Being made unconscious with ether, an anesthetic

formulated (page 626) Being made or forced to fit a rule for doing something, especially as used by those who do not know the reason on which the rule is based

malingers (page 627) Pretends to be sick, injured, etc., to escape work or duty; shirks

obtuse (page 628) Slow in understanding; dull; slow-witted

Handbook

allusion, dramatic monologue, form, imagery, point of view, rhyme scheme, symbol

Check Test 76

INTRODUCTION

Eliot is a difficult poet to teach, but if you have already worked on Yeats with your class, Eliot will seem more accessible. The questions for "The Love Song of J. Alfred Prufrock" probe for implications about the kind of world that the speaker presents. Before going over these questions, you may want to ask students to identify words, phrases, and allusions that confuse them. Encourage students to look up the Bible references. Then you may want to discuss the imagery in the poem. What are the sources of the imagery? How many different kinds of images can one find? Discuss, too, the significance of the name J. Alfred. Why didn't Eliot use the name Alfred J.? It is also helpful to look for rhyme patterns in the poem, that is, the passages in which the poem shifts into and away from rhyme. But the most useful technique for clarifying the poem is simply to have it read aloud. Students who may have skipped over lines will be able to hear them, and those who are doing the reading must make sense of the lines in order to read them properly.

"The Journey of the Magi" is much more straightforward in its formal aspects, but it is equally complicated in terms of final attitude. Eliot is here struggling with the complex interrelationship between Jesus's birth and death. Even the scene that is described at the end of the journey is a strange combination of Bethlehem and Calvary.

USING THE STUDY NOTES

PAGE 630

THE LOVE SONG OF J. ALFRED PRUFROCK

Students are asked to consider and discuss the following propositions about the poem:

1. Prufrock is haunted by the pettiness and tri-

viality of his life. Things of a petty and trivial nature—"tea and cakes and ices," "the novels . . . the teacups . . . the skirts"—are mentioned so frequently that it seems quite fair to say that they haunt Prufrock.

2. Prufrock thinks of himself as a slightly ridiculous figure. There is considerable evidence of this attitude; see especially the stanza beginning "No! I am not Prince Hamlet."

3. He still has some desires and ambitions, but his own timidity prevents him from achieving them. In the course of the poem we learn that Prufrock has some desires and ambitions—to love a woman is one of them—but it is not clear that he has any left at the end of the poem. In any case, *timidity* is not a strong enough term to describe what prevents him from achieving his desires; *impotence* would be a more accurate term.

4. Discuss the implications of the following lines:

a. "Do I dare/Disturb the universe?" The lines imply that Prufrock believes that one properly should live within a set pattern; they also express his fear of breaking the pattern.

b. "I have measured out my life with coffee spoons." One implication of this statement could be that Prufrock has planned his life in some detail, giving a spoonful here and another there. The coffee spoon is a small measure; therefore, the line also implies the pettiness of his interests.

c. "I should have been a pair of ragged claws! Scuttling across the floors of silent seas." It is difficult to explain everything that this image implies, but it primarily conveys a sense of rapacity. Disembodied claws simply grab what they want, without pausing, without thinking, without worrying about "overwhelming questions." The bottom of the sea is a safe and uncomplicated haven, at least for ragged claws.

d. "It is impossible to say just what I mean!" Prufrock himself may not really know what he wants to say; at any rate, his inability to communicate is one of his deepest problems. To live fully one must be able to communicate with other human beings; Prufrock cannot express what he feels.

e. "I am Lazarus, come from the dead." In addition to the Lazarus raised from the dead in John 11 in the Bible, there is a Lazarus in Luke 16—a beggar who goes to heaven while the rich man at whose gate he begged goes to hell. In hell the rich man asks that the beggar be allowed to return from the dead to warn his brothers that they also could be sent to hell for lack of charity. But Abraham points out that if the brothers do not hear Moses and the prophets, they will also not hear Lazarus returned from the dead. The implication in the poem may be that the lady in the drawing room would be no more likely to listen than the rich men, even if Prufrock could be as Lazarus returning from the dead.

THE JOURNEY OF THE MAGI

1. The sermon that provides the starting point for this poem describes the journey of the Magi from the third person point of view. Eliot changes to the first person point of view. What is the effect of this change? When the journey is related from the point of view of one of the Magi, the event becomes personalized. We are no longer looking at the journey from the outside but are experiencing the irritation, the cold, and the doubts along with the speaker.

2. There are three locations in the poem—the place where the Magi live, the road, and the place being sought. How does the poem evoke the different quality of these places? The place where the Magi live is obviously somewhere in the East; it has a warmer climate ("summer palaces," "terraces," and "the silken girls bringing sherbet"). The road, by contrast, is cold; the cities are "hostile" and towns "unfriendly"; and there are continuous problems with the camels and the camel tenders. The place being sought is "a temperate valley," neither too hot nor too cold. It is a fertile, well-watered place, not as obviously luxurious as the place of "summer palaces" but clearly an improvement on the road.

3. What symbolic implications do you find in lines 24–28? At first glance these lines simply continue the description of the fertile valley. But the details have significance, for they imply the death of Jesus. The "three trees on the low sky" are like the three crosses on Calvary. (One should remember the medieval lyric "Now Go'th Sun Under Wood" with its connection of trees and crosses.) The "old white horse" may well be the "pale horse" ridden by Death that is described by St. John in the Book of Revelations. "Pieces of silver" should immediately call to mind the thirty pieces of silver for which Judas betrayed Jesus. The hands "dicing" remind us of the soldiers who played dice to determine who would get Jesus's robe.

4. The speaker asks: "were we led all that way for / Birth or Death?" What is the poem's answer? The symbolic details in the poem suggest that the place to which the Magi come contains both birth and death. In Christian terms, the Incarnation leads inevitably to the Crucifixion; that is, birth and death cannot be separated. However, if the birth of Jesus was "Hard and bitter agony" for the Magi who had to make the cold, painful journey, it was equally hard for Mary and would, on Calvary, become hard and bitter agony for Jesus. One can also argue that if birth and death are as closely joined as the poem implies, then the reverse is also true: Death is the same as birth. And in Christian terms, that is so. Jesus's death is the event that allowed humankind to be born into eternal life.

5. How would you interpret the last line of the poem? Students may have different reactions to that line. Some may believe that the speaker wants to die because he feels ill at ease in his old home. Others may see him as converted, a person who now says that his people are "alien." He may then be viewed as a Christian who longs for death so that he may be reborn in heaven. Still other students may think that the speaker is rejecting what he has seen and thought about; he would prefer *another* death to this strange and frightening birth.

Poems About Poetry and War

PAGE 630

Handbook

connotation, imagery, irony, symbol

Check Test 77

INTRODUCTION

We have grouped these four poems together both because they form a natural unit and because the subject itself is greater than any one of the poets individually. The study questions focus, first, on the poems, then, on the problem of writing poetry about something as terrible as war, and, finally, on the relationships among the poems. Because most of your students have not lived through a war, the poems may seem slightly foreign to them. But you may wish to encourage them to see how the poems relate to our own fears, defenses, and illusions today. Do we not also make up slogans to justify what we do, just as Horace did? Do we not also see ourselves as living in a sweet and pleasant country, similar to the London that Alice Meynell pictures? Cannot we imagine what the atom bomb might do? In addition to teaching these poems as statements about war, you could also connect the poems to questions about responsibility and guilt, as implied in Gunn's "Innocence."

USING THE STUDY NOTES

PAGE 634

DULCE ET DECORUM EST

1. What attitude toward war is Owen attacking? Fundamentally, he is attacking the idea that war is glorious or romantic. Note the raw realism not only in the description of the dying man but also in the rest of the poem.

2. Whom does the poem mean by "you" in the last stanza? He means you and me—all of humankind.

3. Does Owen give the last two lines the same meaning that the original author (Horace) gave them? They have the same meaning in sense but not in intention. Owen is quite clear about this, for he calls the quotation "the old lie."

SUMMER IN ENGLAND, 1914

1. How does Meynell convey a sense of happiness and prosperity in the first two stanzas? She uses images of light ("clearer light," "white," "impearled,") and images of rich harvests ("the hay was prosperous," "silken harvest"). Also, nature is personified as loving ("Caressing pencils of the sun," "Moon after moon was heavenly-sweet, / Stroking the bread").

2. What words describe the results of war? The words are: "died convulsed," "shattered," "wet corruption," "heaped," "throb of pain," and "shot through the eyes."

3. What is the effect of the short line, "Love, hide thy face" (line 23)? The effect is primarily one of shock. The shortness of the line and its three strong stresses (love, hide, face) emphasize the sudden realization of shame. This shame is felt by the poet and by the reader as well, for we all are part of "man's unpardonable race."

RESPONSIBILITY...

1. How does the speaker feel that he is different

from the pilots? How is he like them? He is different from them because he "never paid the price of their wounds." He neither directly participated nor directly suffered. (Incidentally, Spender was a fire warden during World War II.) He is like them because they "carried [his] will"—they did what he wanted them to do to the German cities. He is also like them because he shares their guilt.

2. What is the change of attitude in the speaker from the first part of the poem to the final stanza? What caused the change? In the beginning, the speaker is proud of the pilots—"Exalted expanding singing. . . ." Then comes the pivotal line, line 20; "I began to remember the lost names and faces." And the exaltation shifts to a pensive attitude as the speaker "assumes their guilt, honours, repents, prays for them."

3. Why is the poem called "Responsibility"? Students should readily see that the speaker, by assuming the guilt of the pilots, is accepting the responsibility for the destruction that they caused to the German cities. The subtitle makes it clear what the speaker feels responsible for. But, of course, he grieves not so much for Germany as for the "lost names and faces."

4. What do the figures of speech "cage," "ribbons," and "diamond bolts" symbolize? The "cage" is the formation of the planes. The "ribbons" are the smoke trails of the planes. The "diamond bolts" are the planes themselves. The bolts hold the (invisible) wires of the cage together. The imagery is bold, but if students read carefully, they should be able to understand it.

INNOCENCE

1. Is innocence a desirable quality? The question of innocence as a desirable quality should be examined both before and after reading the poem. The consensus generally is that it is desirable, especially in children.

2. What is a synonym for innocence (for example, blamelessness or ignorance)? Other synonyms for innocence are artlessness, simplicity, naiveté. Discuss the connotations of these words as well as the two synonyms suggested in the text.

3. How is the boy of the poem innocent? The boy is innocent because he is ignorant. However, ignorance of the suffering of others makes him a dangerous tool of manipulators more aware than he.

4. The poet says "no doubt could penetrate, no act could harm" his innocence. Explain. He has lost the capacity to think or to feel for himself; instead, he accepts and is directed by the simple rules of his group. Thus the effect of indoctrination is to eliminate personal choice as well as the necessity of dealing with a complex moral code.

5. Consider the following statements and decide whether the poem substantiates or refutes them:

a. Because of his good traits most people would consider the boy a desirable kind of person. Yes, the poem implies that *people* would consider the boy a good person; but the poet himself proclaims the opposite judgment.

b. After watching the torture of the partisan, the boy is still innocent. If one accepts subordination to another's code of morality, the boy is innocent. But by using understatement, the poet delivers a scathing indictment of the "innocent" boy, exposing him as an inhuman, machinelike creature instead of a compassionate individual.

c. Thom Gunn states that there is no more dangerous kind of person than the unthinking "tool" who obeys orders innocently and without questioning. Yes! You may want to relate the Calley case and the My Lai massacre to the poem.

QUESTIONS FOR DISCUSSION: POETRY AND WAR

The students are asked to discuss the following questions. It should be noted that a variety of opinions could be expressed, especially for questions 2 and 3.

1. Sometimes violent feelings do not necessarily lead to good poetry but just to polemic or propaganda. How do these poems avoid becoming merely angry or emotional?

Owen maintains control through two methods: (a) by focusing on the details of war and thus letting the emotions come through the language, and (b) by saving the ironic statement for the last two lines in which he indicts the "old lie" that dying for your country is sweet and fitting.

Meynell maintains a similar control by carefully keeping any reference to what is happening out of the first two stanzas. The title tells us that it is wartime, but the first two stanzas seem blissfully unaware of the fact. The irony is thus more powerful for being unstated.

In Spender's "Responsibility" the fact that the speaker feels partially responsible for the destruction makes the poem less an attack upon Germany than upon the speaker himself.

Thom Gunn's control comes, first, through the irony of the title. We expect innocence to be a positive quality, and the positive adjectives in the first four stanzas support that feeling. But when we realize what innocence means in the context of war, we are appalled. The shock is even stronger because the poet himself does not seem to feel that disgust. He merely describes the horror.

2. Does the modern poet have a responsibility to write about war? One would hope that students would answer yes. We hope that they will feel that poetry should be about all experiences, not just pleasant ones. If poetry is perceived as being concerned with only the pretty, the sweet, or the happy, then students will surely find it irrelevant. If poets write about all things, they have a stronger chance of reaching a wider audience.

3. What relationships do you see between these poems? One could ask how much hope is involved in these poems. Owen's and Meynell's poems offer many similarities, for both contrast romantic views of the world with the reality of war. Meynell, like Spender, accepts part of the guilt when she calls humans "unpardonable." And Thom Gunn places the guilt on those who train soldiers and on those who support that training—that is, on all of us.

Poem by Stevie Smith

PAGE 635

Handbook

quatrain, rhyme scheme, slant rhyme

Check Test 78 *(also for Auden and Thomas poetry)*

INTRODUCTION

The poem by Stevie Smith offers students much to talk about. "Not Waving But Drowning" is short but stark. It begins with the description of a man drowning and ends by extending that "drowning" to the man's entire life. The relative simplicity of Smith's language offers a good contrast to some of the more complex poems by Eliot and Yeats.

USING THE STUDY NOTES

PAGE 635

NOT WAVING BUT DROWNING

1. Much of the poem depends on the use of familiar phrases whose meanings are altered. How does Smith change the meaning? The first stanza collects several phrases that one often hears in relation to drowning—the title phrase itself, and the phrase "I was much further out than you thought" (in the Red Cross handbook, the reference usually is, "much further out than he thought"). In the second stanza, "It must have been too cold for him" and "his heart gave way" are, again, both familiar statements. The meaning is altered in the third stanza when "too cold" is joined with "always," and we realize that not only the water but the man's entire life was "too cold." Similarly, "I was too far out" turns that statement into a metaphor with several possible meanings: "I was always out of touch with human beings"; "I was always trying to accomplish too much"; "I was always doing strange things." The final repetition of the title phrase suggests that the whole of the man's life was a struggle. What looked to observers like a happy "lark" was actually a slow, painful death.

2. How would you describe the formal structure of the poem? What does that structure contribute to the poem's effect? The poem is divided into three quatrains. The first and third are fairly regular. They have no true rhyme, but there is a slant rhyme between "moaning" and "drowning." Thus these stanzas can be said to have an *abcb* rhyme scheme, which is often associated with the ballad. In the first and third quatrains we notice that the lines have similar lengths, within one or two syllables of each other.

The second quatrain, in contrast, is quite different in form. Its second line, "And now he's dead" is noticeably shorter than any line preceding it. Its brevity emphasizes the stark fact of death. The third line, the longest line in the poem, runs two cliches together. The fourth line, "They said," rhymes exactly with "dead" and is only two syllables long. This second stanza, then, is a more chaotic, less regular one. An important point to note here is that it reflects the point of view of the watching audience and that their lack of understanding is mirrored in the confusion of the patterns of the stanza.

In the third quatrain we are comforted by a return to the regular pattern of the first quatrain, only to be jolted by the change in the meaning of the familiar phrases. Thus, Smith sets a pattern, unnerves us by changing it, puts us back into a pattern, and then shakes us again.

Poems by W. H. Auden

PAGE 636

Glossary Words

forsaken (page 636) Deserted; abandoned

eugenists (page 637) Experts in the science of improving the human race by a careful selection of parents in order to develop healthier and more intelligent children

Handbook

irony, metaphor, rhyme, symbol

Check Test 78 (also for Smith and Thomas poetry)

INTRODUCTION

Teaching "Musée des Beaux Arts" offers an opportunity to let your students share the poet's experience in a special way. Often we do not know exactly what the catalyst was for a poem's creation. With Auden's poem, however, we do know the origin—it is Brueghel's masterful painting *The Fall of Icarus* (page 643). Before assigning the poem, you may wish to ask students to look at that painting and to write a poem about it. Then their poems could be discussed in class. It is likely that some of the class will see what Auden saw. It is also possible that some students will find meaning in that painting that Auden did not find. If you then assign Auden's poem, it should enrich students' experience. Should they be especially interested in how a number of poets respond to the same painting, you could also read William Carlos Williams's "Landscape with the Fall of Icarus" and Joseph Langland's "Fall of Icarus: Brueghel."

"The Unknown Citizen" works nicely with "Not Waving But Drowning." It is also a good poem to use for analyzing the comic/ironic devices of rhyme.

USING THE STUDY NOTES

PAGE 639

MUSÉE DES BEAUX ARTS

1. What is the relationship between the first and second stanzas of this poem? The second stanza illustrates the point made in the first stanza.

2. To whom does the "they" in line 9 refer? "They" refers to the Old Masters (great painters.)

3. What is the difference in attitude between the "aged" and the "children"? The suffering of the aged thrusts them away from life and toward thoughts of death. Children, as yet unmarked by life, care only for its pleasures.

THE UNKNOWN CITIZEN

1. What does the title mean? The title clearly alludes to the "unknown soldier," who was literally unknown. The citizen was unknown in the sense that the state robbed him of identity, a fact symbolized by his identification with a number rather than with a name.

2. Who is speaking in this poem? What is the speaker's concept of the good life? The speaker seems to be an official of the government. (Note the use of the royal *we.*) The speaker identifies with the state (the status quo) and with all its official agencies. It is conformity to the government that defines the good life. As the speaker implies in the last two lines, such conformity should unquestionably make one both happy and free.

3. What is Auden attacking? Students should have no difficulty with this question. Our own society continues to do much the same kind of things that Auden mentions. What Auden is attacking is the tendency to turn people into things by robbing them of their personal identities.

Poems by Dylan Thomas

PAGE 638

Handbook

form, irony, rhyme scheme

***Check Test** 78 (also for Smith and Auden poetry)*

INTRODUCTION

Thomas is accessible in a number of ways. He can be controlled and straightforward as in "In My Craft or Sullen Art," in which the lines are short, the poem is structured, and the language is plain. "Do Not Go Gentle into That Good Night" uses a highly complicated form called the *villanelle.* This structure, from sixteenth-century French poetry, is even more rigid than the sonnet. It consists of five tercets and a quatrain. There are only two rhymes, and the first and third lines (A1 and A2) are repeated in a regular pattern as follows: A1 b A2 /a b A1/ a b A2/ a b A1/ a b A2/ a b A1 A2. You may want to ask students to discuss why Thomas chose this form. What effect is gained by putting his ideas into the constriction of this very structured poem?

USING THE STUDY NOTES

PAGE 639

DO NOT GO GENTLE INTO THAT GOOD NIGHT

1. In stanza 1, what is the meaning of "good night," "close of day," and "dying light"? All these phrases refer to death.

2. What four types of people are mentioned? The four types are wise, good, wild, and grave. Students should be asked to offer specific examples of these four types.

3. What has each kind of person failed to accomplish or understand? The wise people have failed to set the world afire with their words. The good people have failed to perpetrate their "frail deeds." The wild have learned too late. And the grave have missed the chance to be gay. In each case the point is that their lives could have been more than they were. They share the feeling that the "something more" might have been realized if death had not intervened.

4. Is the poet saying that the way to die is to protest against it with every bit of strength that you have? Lines 3, 6, 9, 12, 15, 18, and 19 suggest this.

IN MY CRAFT OR SULLEN ART

The structure of this poem is as follows: There are 20 lines in the poem, and each line has 7 syllables (except lines 11, 14, and 20, which have 6 syllables). The rhyme scheme is abcdebdecca abcdeecca.

1. Examine the three lines that are each six syllables. How are all three linked in relationship to meaning? The three lines emphasize the fact that poetry does not stem from the poet's desire to achieve fame or riches, but rather from the life of the "most secret heart"—that is, from the emotions that motivate people to act and feel. Lovers have existed as long as human beings, and love often brings pain. Thomas says that the lovers' arms are "round the griefs of the ages." It is not important for the lovers to "heed [his] craft or art"; they need only understand in "their most secret heart." Human emotions endure longer than "spindrift pages," which the poet compares to the momentary salt spray that flies from the crest of a wave.

2. What is the basic irony of this poem? The irony of the poem lies in the fact that, like Yeats, Thomas writes not for fame or praise or money, but for "lovers" who do not even know that he writes. Furthermore, if they did know, they wouldn't care because they are busy living out their own griefs and joys. Paradoxically, the very humanity that he writes for ignores his "spindrift pages."

Some Modern Themes

PAGE 640

Glossary Words (for "Answers," and "Warning")

bulwark (page 640) Person, place, or thing that is a protection

sobriety (page 641) Seriousness; moderateness; quietness

Check Test 79

INTRODUCTION

Any of these poems can be taught separately. But you may want to compare them to poems of an earlier date, either from this section or from previous sections. Elizabeth Jennings's "Answers" raises the same kinds of problems as those raised in "The Love Song of J. Alfred Prufrock." In that poem, the speaker poses many questions; in "Answers," the questions are too big even to be uttered.

For "Warning" and "Duality," you may want to see what the titles alone suggest to students. Present each title to your class and ask that poems be written on each subject. The last two poems work well together because both are concerned with the problems of identity and of people who assume a variety of moods and faces. There are noticeable differences in tone that could be discussed. How, for example, does Jenny Joseph make her "Warning" sound cheerful? How does Dannie Abse create an agonized feeling in "Duality"? And how do these poems relate to earlier poems concerned with identity? Again, "The Love Song of J. Alfred Prufrock" is useful here, but one could also look at W. H. Auden's "The Unknown Citizen."

USING THE STUDY NOTES

PAGE 643

ANSWERS

1. What things seem to frighten the speaker? Is the fear justified? Size, more than anything else, is the threatening force in this poem. The answers can "bruise"; "abstractions" are "huge"; the "big answers" are noisy, clamoring; the audacity is "shouted." The last image in the poem is that of "big answers" trying to "overthrow" the protection that the speaker has built up. Students should consider whether the speaker's fear is justified. In one sense, by staying with the small answers, the speaker may be avoiding large problems. The small answers are clearly comforting ("a bulwark to my fear"), and they are to be "caressed and loved." But should one always shy away from "great audacity"?

2. Why is the last line placed by itself? Students may offer several responses to this question. It may be that the sense of impending disaster is greater when the last line is isolated, as if it were strong enough to stand by itself. But because there is an implied self-mockery (that line is clearly the "conclusion" to this poem, and it is probably not "great"), the threat that has been building up may be defused with the line's isolation.

WARNING

1. How do you feel about the behavior described in the first eleven lines? Is it irresponsible? Is it natural? Students will probably feel that the behavior is delightful, that it is precisely the way in which we all secretly want to act. It is certainly natural. The question of irresponsibility brings up the larger question—irresponsible from whose point of view?

2. What details in the poem suggest "appropriate" behavior? What is the poet's attitude toward such behavior? Lines 16–19 express the "appropriate" behavior. All the "pious teachings" in this stanza advocate very ordinary, uninteresting behavior.

DUALITY

1. Consider the following implications of the title of the poem:

a. The quality of character is twofold. People are repeatedly torn between decisions, thoughts, desires, and wishes; we are therefore in continual conflict with ourselves, a conflict that generates anxiety. Life would be easier indeed if we could be at peace with ourselves and if our conflicts came only from the outside; but we are often torn from within as well as from without.

b. The world is ruled by the antagonistic forces of good and evil. This statement is wrong primarily because the speaker specifically rules out good and evil in saying "Not Jekyll and Hyde, not good and bad."

2. Make a list of the actions, characteristics, and feelings of each of the two faces. Then discuss what the poet seems to be saying about the duality of human nature. The two faces have the following characteristics:

Face One	**Face Two**
hot	cold
cut	bleed
brass	gold
white	black
mouth eats	bites back
not what he seems	is what he is
wine	bread
East	West
dark/light	dark/light
melt	freeze
scream	sigh

The list of words suggests one idea: Although human nature is twofold, it is a gross oversimplification to define the halves as good and evil, right and wrong, or left and right. Instead of being as different as "Jekyll and Hyde," the two faces have "one profile"; yet the tugging, pulling, and warring cause immeasurable stress. Human uncertainty puts us on a tightrope, where we are always attempting to stay balanced in spite of the pressures being exerted by both "faces."

UNIT TEST

You may select questions at random from the Study Notes at the end of each selection as a basis for constructing a final examination covering the unit TWENTIETH-CENTURY BRITISH POETRY. You may also choose to use the comprehensive unit test prepared on blackline masters available in a separate test booklet, ISBN 0-07-009823-9.

Know Thyself: Scope and Sequence

Selection	Language/Vocabulary	Comprehension	Critical/Literary	Composition
THE METAMORPHOSIS	context	details, comparing/contrasting, fact/fantasy, verifying	symbol, selection of incident, organization	exposition*
"Mirrors"		inference, drawing conclusions	surrealism, selection of incident, organization	exposition*
Chekhov stories		inference, supporting conclusions, main idea	flashback, point of view, selection of incident, organization	exposition*
"Eveline"		main idea, supporting conclusions	stream of consciousness, selection of incident, identity, characterization	exposition*
Priestley essays		comparing/contrasting, summarizing, supporting conclusions	essay, theme, selection of incident, organization	exposition*, personal essay**
Jiménez essays		supporting conclusions, summarizing, main idea, comparing/contrasting	essay, setting, mood, selection of incident, organization, climax	exposition*, personal essay**
Forster essay		comparing/contrasting, main idea, sequence	essay, tone, irony, point of view, organization	exposition*, personal essay**
Lamb essay		main idea, fact/opinion, comparing/contrasting	symbol, tone, selection of incident, organization	exposition*, personal essay**
"Pavan for a Dead Prince"		main idea, cause/effect, sequence	style, selection of incident, organization, tone	exposition*, personal essay**
"The Poor Relation's Story"	context, figurative language	sequence, main idea, comparing/contrasting	tone, selection of incident, organization, climax, style	exposition*, personal essay**
"The Launch"	multiple meaning	main idea, supporting conclusions	allegory, symbol, setting, selection of incident, organization	exposition*, personal essay**
"Judas"		comparing/contrasting, supporting conclusions, sequence	allusion, narrator, selection of incident,	exposition*, personal essay**
"Seven Stories"		fact and fantasy, sequence, main idea	setting, selection of incident, organization	personal essay, description, narrative
Summing Up		comparing/contrasting, supporting conclusions, summarizing, main idea	selection of incident, organization, mood, theme, flashback	personal essay, description, narrative
Relating Composition, Gallery, and Humanities		comparing/contrasting, summarizing	identification, mood	essay

* Teachers can use the Implications in the study notes as writing assignments.
** Students may begin to write a personal essay during the study of this unit.

Know Thyself

This theme should be particularly meaningful to senior students, young people on the threshold of adulthood. To be sure, none of us ever has complete knowledge of self. Therefore, we cannot predict with accuracy how we will behave in a new or unfamiliar situation. But the more self-knowledge that we possess, the better prepared we are to meet life realistically and to find some measure of success and happiness.

The selections in this unit treat the theme KNOW THYSELF from many angles. The long selection, *The Metamorphosis,* shows a young man who has been unable to assess himself or the other members of his family and who awakes one morning to find that he has changed into a giant insect. Some of the short selections, such as Dickens's and Aub's, echo this facet of the theme—self-destruction through lack of insight into self. Another element of the theme is explored by Chekhov and Bontempelli, who present characters that are wholly in charge of themselves and meet life with confidence. Still another element of the theme is examined by Joyce and Delaney whose characters seem to grasp their strengths and their weaknesses and yet cannot change.

The essayists whose work forms a section of the unit are people who know who they are. They see themselves and the life about them with a certain degree of objectivity. A reading of their works will give students ideas about what it is like to live comfortably with self-knowledge.

The thrust of the unit is to show students that in knowing one's self it is necessary, first, to assess one's strengths, weaknesses, and limitations; then, to accept what one cannot change and to change what is possible; and above all, to meet life with a positive attitude.

OBJECTIVES

1. To study the reactions of characters who do and do not have self-knowledge in critical life situations and to observe the consequences.
2. To show the techniques that writers have used to explore the minds of their characters.
3. To encourage students to seek greater knowledge of themselves.
4. To study the personal essay as a literary form.
5. To study the selection of incident and organization in short stories and essays.
6. To develop vocabulary.

MOTIVATING THE UNIT

The following are suggested ways of opening this unit. If you have more than one class, you may wish to experiment with different approaches.

Pattern I Ask students to write autobiographies discussing who they are, how they gained their self-knowledge, and what they believe to be the advantages and disadvantages of such knowledge. Because the purpose of the essay is to encourage students to think about the theme of this unit, the compositions need not be polished; indeed, they can be done during class. You may choose to read some of the best essays to the class and to discuss the ideas presented. Be sure to check with the writers first and get their permission to do so.

It could be interesting to hold these essays until the end of the unit and then ask students to revise them in light of what they have learned from reading the selections in the unit. This approach would be particularly useful if you ask students to discuss the advantages and disadvantages of having an objective knowledge of themselves.

Pattern II If you prefer that students not be as personal as Pattern I requires, you could ask them instead to write about the advantages and disadvantages of possessing self-knowledge. The topic can be narrowed by assigning an essay on the advantages or the disadvantages. Thus, for instance, you may wish to ask students to discuss this topic: If one is a very limited person, it is better not to seek self-knowledge.

Here again, it could prove worthwhile to hold the essays until the end of the unit and then ask for a rewriting, perhaps based upon the selections as well as upon the students' own experiences.

Pattern III Speculate with the class about which one of the following types of characters and situations would provide the most interesting story material: (1) characters who are absolutely certain of who they are and who become involved in a series of interesting situations; (2) characters with confused self-images who experience crucial situations and gain some objective self-knowledge; or (3) characters who have willfully deceived themselves into believing that they are quite different from their true selves and who are confronted with unexpected situations.

Pattern IV Turn to the gallery of self-portraits. Discuss whether students agree with the commentaries in the text concerning what the artists are saying about themselves. Then ask students to imagine that they are about to paint their own self-portraits. Have them attempt to write in a few sentences what they would try to convey about themselves in such paintings.

Pattern V Most students are fascinated by the concept of people having different selves that they show at different times. Talk about the idea of wearing masks. Get students to try to identify some of the different masks that they wear in particular situations. Speculate with them about whether there is any person who never wears a mask.

Pattern VI Because *The Metamorphosis* deals dramatically with the way that one's physical body affects oneself and others, a sensitive class may find value in discussing the relationship between our physical appearance and our inner image of that appearance. Apparently the great majority of us have images of our physical selves that are different from what others have of us. Perhaps this is why most people seem to be greatly disappointed with their photographs.

The Metamorphosis

PAGE 648

Franz Kafka

With dramatic effect, the first sentence of this story plunges the reader into a horrifying situation: "As Gregor Samsa awoke one morning from uneasy dreams he found himself transformed in his bed into a gigantic insect." (Although the story never calls him such, the description suggests a cockroach.) Because he does not at first accept his metamorphosis, Gregor struggles to get up and go off to his job. We learn that he is a commercial traveler and the sole support of his mother, father, and sister. But he is dissatisfied with his job and also terrified that he may lose it. The family realizes that something is wrong because Gregor has overslept and missed his train. Their fears are confirmed when the chief clerk arrives to check on Gregor's absence. Together they implore Gregor to unlock his bedroom door. In his room, Gregor struggles desperately to his feet, twists the key with his jaws, and leans part way into the living room, revealing the full horror of his transformation. The chief clerk escapes in hysterics, and Gregor's father beats Gregor back into the room, causing him to injure his side in the process.

As time passes, Gregor's metamorphosis into an insect continues. He now eats only greasy scraps, and he learns to crawl and to hang from the ceiling. Only his sister Grete can force herself to take care of him. Whenever anyone approaches, he hides under the sofa. At night, he lies near the door listening to the family talk. He is cheered to discover that his father had saved some money each month from the sum that Gregor had given him and that his father also has a secret cache of money left over from his financial debacle. But these funds are not sufficient to prevent changes in the family's life-style. His father takes a job as a bank messenger, his mother does sewing, and Grete takes a job as a clerk.

One day Grete and her mother decide to move out Gregor's furniture to give him more room in which to crawl. So desperate is he to save a picture of a woman that he has hanging on the wall, that he places his body across it. Upon seeing him, his mother collapses. Grete rushes out to get smelling salts, and Gregor follows her, trying to be helpful. Grete turns suddenly and is startled by Gregor's presence. She drops a bottle, and a splinter of broken glass cuts Gregor's face. The two women lock themselves in his room, and Gregor climbs frantically around the living room until he collapses across a tabletop. When his father returns and hears Grete's story, he drives Gregor back into his room, hurling apples at him. One of these lodges in his back.

Gregor's condition deteriorates, as does the family's financial position. They have dismissed the maid and taken in boarders. In the evening Gregor's door is left open, and he can watch everyone from his room. One night, as Grete plays her violin for the group, Gregor is overcome by the music and creeps forward into the living room. The boarders are frightened and vow that they will leave. Grete insists that Gregor must go.

The next morning the charwoman finds Gregor dead and casually disposes of his flat, dry remains. The family takes the day off to celebrate. They realize that they all have jobs that they enjoy, that their future is opening pleasantly before them, and that Grete is in the first bloom of womanhood.

The study notes after each section are designed to help students understand what is happening in the story and, through this understanding, to grasp what Kafka is saying about the theme, KNOW THYSELF.

INTRODUCTION

The Metamorphosis usually captures readers with the very first sentence. It is therefore best not to discuss this selection before beginning it. Instead, simply read the first few paragraphs aloud. Then allow time in class for students to read the rest of the story on their own. You can divide the reading into three assignments that correspond to the three parts of the story. Or you can give the class a single period (or more if necessary) to read the story from beginning to end.

After students have read the story and before you turn to the discussion notes, it would be wise to present some information about Kafka and about critical reactions to *The Metamorphosis.* First, mention the strained relationship that existed between Kafka and his father. The son was reduced to stuttering in his father's presence. At one point, he wrote a hundred-page letter to his father articulating the failures in their relationship and his feeling of being crushed by him. Thus the relationship between Gregor and his father is probably the symbolic representation of that between Franz Kafka and *his* father. You may wish to tell students that Kafka himself is said to have gone into gales of laughter every time that he read the story. He insisted that it was an enormously funny tale that should not be taken seriously. Yet the story has provoked a vast body of critical interpretation, for almost everyone who reads it suspects that it has hidden depths of meaning. The meaning of certain details has puzzled the critics: the picture of the woman in a fur coat that Gregor has framed; the cut from the broken bottle; the description of the hospital across the street; the final description of Gregor as just a hollow tube. After this commentary, ask students to try to express in writing what they think the story means. Then you can turn to a discussion of the Study Notes.

PART I

PAGE 648

Glossary Words

malingerers (page 649, col. 2) Persons who pretend to be sick, injured, etc., in order to escape work; shirkers

reverberating (page 650, col. 1) Echoing back; resounding

plaintive (page 650, col. 1) Mournful; sad

precursor (page 650, col. 2) Forerunner; predecessor; one who goes before

dunning (page 652, col. 2) Demanding payment of a debt from someone again and again

plausibly (page 653, col. 1) Apparently true or reasonable

entreaties (page 653, col. 1) Earnest requests; pleas

presentiment (page 653, col. 2) A vague sense or feeling of approaching misfortune

incapacitated (page 655, col. 2) Being deprived of ability, power, or fitness; disabled

injunction (page 655, col. 2) An authoritative or emphatic order; a command

Handbook

chronological organization, incident, symbol

Check Test 80 (for Part I)

Check Tests for each selection—in the form of blackline masters—are available in a separate test booklet, ISBN 0-07-009823-9. Each test is titled and numbered for easy filing after use.

Give the Check Test after students have read the selection(s) and before you begin the discussion of the work(s).

USING THE STUDY NOTES **PAGE 657**

DISCUSSION FOR UNDERSTANDING

1. Describe Gregor Samsa at the beginning of the story. He is lying on his "hard, as it were armor-plated, back and... he could see his dome-like brown belly, divided into stiff arched segments...." There are numerous legs, pitifully thin, that he can't seem to control. When he feels an itch on his belly, he discovers little white spots.

2. What details are given about Gregor and his job? He is a commercial traveler and has worked for five years trying to support his family and to pay off the debt that his father had contracted in his financial debacle. He is tense and nervous about his job and works hard at it. Basically, he seems to dislike the work. Apparently he must get up at four every morning to reach the office on time.

3. What is the evidence that Gregor does not accept his change as permanent? He thinks continually about his job and of how he must get out of bed and get dressed to catch the next train. He worries that the chief clerk will think that he is malingering. And he tries to talk reassuringly to his parents and to the messenger.

4. How does Gregor open the door? Gregor hitches himself up onto a chest of drawers and then falls against the back of a chair. By shoving the chair forward, he reaches the door and catches hold of the frame for support. He finds his feet are sticky and adhere to the wood. Then he manages to turn the key in the lock with his mouth. He has no teeth, but his jaws are very strong, and his maneuvers finally unlock the door. He pulls the door toward him, but he is still invisible to those in the other room. Students need to realize that this is a French door and that only one side opens; thus the passageway is much narrower than that through a regular door.

5. How do his parents and the chief clerk react on seeing Gregor? The chief clerk utters a loud "Oh!" and, clapping his hand to his open mouth, backs away. His mother clasps her hands, looks at her husband, takes two steps toward Gregor, and then slips to the floor, hiding her face on her breast. His father makes a fist as if he is about to knock Gregor back into his room, then covers his eyes and weeps.

6. How does Gregor get back to his room? Gregor attempts to pursue the fleeing chief clerk and to persuade the frightened man to return. Suddenly the father, completely upset by the clerk's flight, picks up in one hand the clerk's forgotten walking stick and in the other a roll of newspaper and proceeds to drive Gregor back to his room. Gregor's pleas to his father go unnoticed, for his language is no longer intelligible to the family. Because he is now in his crawling position, he finds the door too narrow to pass through. But his father keeps up loud hissing noises behind him. When Gregor gets stuck half way through, his father gives him a strong push that bruises Gregor's body.

PART II

Glossary Words **PAGE 657**

palpitating (page 658, col. 1) Throbbing; beating

collaboration (page 658, col. 1) Act of working together

concierge (page 660, col. 2) A person living in an apartment who serves as doorkeeper, landlord's representative, and janitor

execrate (page 662, col. 1) Loath intensely; detest; call down curses upon

ministrations (page 662, col. 1) Help; aid

admonitions (page 663, col. 2) Advice against something; gentle scolding or reproof

recalcitrance (page 664, col. 2) Refusal to submit, conform, or comply; disobedience

ejaculations (page 665, col 1) Remarks said suddenly and briefly; exclamations

propitiate (page 666, col. 1) Pacify; reduce the anger of; win over

visage (page 666, col. 2) Face; appearance

Handbook

chronological organization, incident, symbol

Check Test 81

USING THE STUDY NOTES

PAGE 667

DISCUSSION FOR UNDERSTANDING

1. What changes have taken place in Gregor's food preferences, healing ability, vision, sleep needs? He no longer likes milk but prefers dried cheese, leftover vegetables, and sauce. He seems to heal more quickly than usual. His vision is becoming worse, and he can no longer distinguish things at a distance. He needs less sleep.

2. How does Grete act toward Gregor? She begins by treating Gregor almost like an invalid. But she uses a cloth to handle the dishes he uses. She sweeps up leftover food and throws it away. She allows nobody else to serve Gregor or to clean his room. But whenever she comes in, she first rushes to the window and opens it, breathing deeply as if the air in the room were impure. One day he is in the chair, and she cannot get to the window, and so she quickly leaves the room.

3. What does Gregor find out about the family's financial situation? Their financial situation is not as desperate as Gregor had imagined. His father had saved something from the financial ruin that had forced Gregor to take over. Furthermore, the father had put aside a small amount each month from the money that Gregor had given him, and so the family has a small nest egg to help them while they adjust to the loss of Gregor as their breadwinner. Surprisingly, this news cheers Gregor.

4. Why does Grete decide to move the furniture from Gregor's room? Why does his mother object? What is Gregor's reaction to this? Grete thinks that the furniture is an obstacle to Gregor's movements. The mother objects, feeling that this action makes Gregor's metamorphosis seem permanent. At first Gregor is pleased to have the two women in his room. Then he becomes disturbed at their removing all his possessions. Their loss makes him feel less human.

5. What happens when Gregor tries to save his furniture? When his mother sees the great brown mass of Gregor's body on the wall, she faints. Grete runs for medicine, and Gregor follows in order to help. When she turns and sees him, she drops the bottle. A piece of glass cuts Gregor's face, and the medicine splashes over him. Grabbing a bunch of bottles, Grete flees to his bedroom and locks the door, leaving Gregor madly running over the walls and the ceiling until he falls exhausted onto a table.

6. Describe the scene between Gregor and his father. The father is stiffly dressed in his bank messenger's uniform with gold braid. Throwing off his cap, he advances purposefully toward Gregor, lifting his feet high. Alarmed, Gregor moves away, and they circle the room several times. Then his father begins pitching apples at Gregor, and one lodges in his back, causing excruciating pain. At this moment Gregor's sister and mother burst from his room screaming. His mother has only one purpose—to reach her husband and safety. Here Gregor's eyesight fails and he sees no more.

PART III

PAGE 667

Glossary Words

behest (page 669, col. 1) A command; an order

allocutions (page 670, col. 1) Encouraging remarks

chagrin (page 670, col. 2) A feeling of disappointment, failure, or humiliation; annoyance

scrutinize (page 671, col. 1) Examine carefully; inspect carefully

masticating (page 671, col. 2) Chewing thoroughly

susceptible (page 673, col. 1) Open to; capable of being affected by

vehemently (page 674, col. 1) In a manner showing strong feeling; passionately

respite (page 676, col. 2) Time of relief and rest

Handbook

chronological organization, incident, symbol

Check Test 82

USING THE STUDY NOTES PAGE 677

DISCUSSION FOR UNDERSTANDING

1. In the month since Gregor's injury, what has happened to each of the following: the father? the mother? Grete? Gregor? Father: He is so proud of his bank messenger uniform that he insists on wearing it even at home. He is so tired now that he falls asleep as soon as dinner is finished. Mother: She is doing piece-work sewing for an underwear firm. Grete: Gregor's sister has a sales job and is studying shorthand and French in the evening to improve her situation. Gregor: He can no longer climb the walls and has lost his appetite, which causes him to grow thin and listless. He seldom sleeps.

2. What are the attitudes of the family and the charwoman toward Gregor? Grete no longer takes pains to bring Gregor food that may please him. She shoves into the room with her foot anything that is available. At night she sweeps up the leftovers with one motion, paying no attention to what is left. As for cleaning the room, Grete simply ignores the chore. His mother gives it a thorough cleaning one day and creates a disturbance that awakens the father. He berates the mother for taking over the cleaning of Gregor's room and orders Grete never to clean it again. The charwoman takes to opening the door each morning and shouting words such as "Come along, then, you old dung beetle!" She seems to think of Gregor as a pet in the house.

3. What happens when Grete plays the violin? Gregor creeps farther and farther into the room until he is behind her. He feels that his love of music is his last assurance that he is really not an insect. His appearance causes the boarders to insist on leaving without paying the money that they owe.

4. What are Grete's reasons for getting rid of Gregor? Does Gregor agree or disagree? She feels that this insect is not really Gregor after all, that they have all simply been fooled into thinking it is he. Were it Gregor, he would have seen how he was harming them, and he would have gone away of his own accord. Gregor, herded back into his room, decides that Grete is right—he must disappear. Then, he simply dies.

5. How do the Samsas feel about Gregor's death? Although somewhat saddened, they are basically grateful and relieved. But they cannot bring themselves to bury his remains; the charwoman disposes of the body. And the family has a kind of celebration, taking a holiday from their jobs and going for a walk.

USING THE STUDY NOTES PAGE 677

I. THE REAL AND THE UNREAL

Students are asked to discuss how Gregor is affected by the following identity crises:

1. Physical appearance. Much of the story deals with physical appearance and its effect on others. Gregor himself never reveals how he feels about his new form, but he is made acutely conscious of its effect on others. On his first appearance, his mother faints, his father drives him back into his room, and the chief clerk flees in hysterics. Yet Gregor seems to accept his new form placidly. Trying to learn how best to manage his body, he attempts at first to stand upright. He gradually becomes more comfortable with his insect's body. But sensitive to how the others react at the sight of him, he hides under the sofa whenever anyone enters the room. Only near the end of the story is he indifferent to how the others will react as he crawls into the living room.

2. Family relationships. Because Gregor has always thought of himself as the sole support of his family, he is immediately concerned about how they will survive. Thus, he is relieved rather than angry when he overhears that his father had saved a bit out of his financial debacle and had put something away from Gregor's earnings every month. Gregor still responds with tenderness toward his sister and mother, always hiding to spare them from seeing him. He continues to think of his father as sickly, old, and inadequate and cannot believe that he is holding a job. He gets angry at Grete when she does not bring him the kinds of food that he craves and when she does not clean his room well. And he loses control when the women start to remove everything from his room that reminds him of his life as a human being. His main concern is always the welfare of the family, even though at times he rages at their neglect. Did he perhaps will himself to die when he heard Grete say, "Things can't go on like this . . . we must try to get rid of it"?

3. **Physical surroundings.** Note the details of Gregor's room. Also, note that he desperately tries to protect his possessions when the women decide to remove them. The articles in the room seem to constitute a tie to his life as a human being. Are possessions an integral part of one's picture of self? Experience suggests that they are. When one's environment is changed, one may feel confused and dislocated. You may want to mention the sense of unreality that people have noted, for example, in space, in a cave, or in any setting different from what they are accustomed to. Notice that Gregor's room eventually becomes a storage catchall. How does this affect Gregor?

4. **Response to the arts.** There are two things that Gregor continues to appreciate throughout his life: music and the picture of the woman in furs. The suggestion seems to be that the arts remain important to a person long after other needs fade.

5. **Food preferences.** A famous natural food advocate uses the adage, "We are what we eat." Does Gregor's change in food tastes support this statement? He rejects what he formerly liked and craves what would once have been repulsive to him. Does a person have a different image of self as a vegetarian than as a meateater?

6. **Ability to communicate.** Step by step Gregor loses his ability to speak. Although he can understand what the others say, they assume that he cannot. The only way that he can communicate is through direct actions such as his attempts to save his picture and to hear the music. If Gregor could have expressed his feelings, would his family have treated him differently?

II. IMPLICATIONS

Students are asked their reactions to the following statements:

1. **It is natural to assume, as Gregor does, that even after a change, things will go on as usual.** To get students to understand this statement, suggest that in the first throes of illness, a person assumes that things will soon be normal again. Immediately after an injury, the individual often continues to act as if nothing had happened. After a death, it is hard to accept the break in relationships. Therefore, Gregor's desperate attempts to get to his job are not so bizarre as they at first seem.

2. **The real metamorphosis is what happens to the family, not what happens to Gregor.** The introduction suggested that a metamorphosis is thought of scientifically as a change to the adult stage of life. From this point of view, the family members could be said to have metamorphosed.

3. **The father's treatment of Gregor represents the usual father/son relationship.** Try to get students to think about this statement on more of a symbolic than a literal level. What does Gregor's father want? Seemingly, he feels that Gregor should be kept in his room, out of sight, and away from the family. Kafka might have felt that this was his own father's attitude toward him. Psychologists, biologists, and anthropologists indicate that there is always submerged resentment between a parent and children of the same sex. It is a natural kind of rivalry that civilized people have tried to overcome. Perhaps the father hasn't completely succeeded but has merely covered over these feelings.

4. **Gregor's sister is the only member of the family who seems *human* in her treatment of Gregor.** This is not entirely true. After the first shock at seeing Gregor has worn off, his mother begs to be allowed to go into Gregor's room because he is her "unfortunate son." But the father refuses. The mother does help Grete move out the furniture, but she is concerned that its removal might make her son feel that the family has given up hope for his recovery. It is certainly Grete who does everything else for Gregor. Yet even her humaneness falters.

5. **The charwoman, although uneducated and probably not too bright, is basically the most admirable person in the story.** Because the charwoman probably did not know Gregor the human being, she is in a better position to accept him as an insect and nothing more. Hence her whole attitude toward Gregor is one of matter-of-fact acceptance. She does what needs to be done. Whether this makes her admirable is a moot point. Some students may believe that it is Gregor who is truly the one to admire, for he is sensitive, is aware of others' feelings, and wishes to offend no one.

6. **The family is better off because of Gregor's metamorphosis.** This discussion may center on the value of the work ethic. Was the family really better off in having leisure and servants when Gregor was the breadwinner? Or did they move to a more fulfilling life-style when each was working and obtaining a certain satisfaction from it? Some may see Grete's giving up her musical pretensions and working toward a more realistic vocational objective as a wise change.

Students are asked to react to seven different interpretations of the story, which are presented to provoke students to think for themselves. It may be helpful to divide the class into small discussion groups, asking each group to state the strengths and the weaknesses of one of the interpretations.

Or you may prefer to read the statements aloud, pausing after each one to say a few words about its relationship to the story. Then suggest that a literary symbol should evoke multiple relationships and many facets of human existence. Thus a symbol is much like a general concept such as *government.* Although there are many varieties of government, there is a limiting factor operating—for government refers only to a particular aspect of human activity. Similarly, it is possible to have many specific interpretations of a literary symbol or story; however, they should all fall within one area of human interrelationships—in this case, the family (or group).

III. TECHNIQUES

Selection of Incident

Students are asked to answer the following questions about selections of incidents in the story.

1. Suppose a television writer created a character who woke in the morning to find a greatly changed body. Typically, what would the character do? The character, horrified, would likely rush to the mirror, shriek for help, moan, do anything that would create both confusion and excitement. It should be interesting to see what reactions students will suggest.

2. How is Kafka's selection of incidents different from this? Gregor has a matter-of-fact reaction to his metamorphosis. He does not try to discover what he looks like nor does he call for help. Instead, he quietly struggles to handle his body and thinks only of getting to work.

3. In the first section, what are the three phases in Gregor's reaction to his situation? What effect do these incidents create? The three phases in his reaction are *(a)* his struggle to get out of bed *(b)* his attempt to talk to his parents and the chief clerk through the door and *(c)* his appearance in the doorway. The effect of this arrangement is to build suspense. After reading the first sentence, the reader probably wants to know why Gregor has been transformed and how other people will react to him. Kafka graphically answers the second question but leaves the first for the reader to ponder.

4. What are the incidents that show other people's reactions? The chief clerk backs away, his shoulder twitches, and he inches toward the door. Once there, he runs away hysterically. Gregor's mother sinks to the floor, speechless, her head down. When Gregor falls to his feet, he lands almost in front of her, which makes her jump to her feet, scream for help, and bump into the breakfast table where the coffeepot overturns. His father remains relatively calm until Gregor starts to pursue the chief clerk. Then, seizing in one hand the clerk's abandoned walking stick and in the other hand a large newspaper, he stamps his feet and drives Gregor back to his room.

5. Consider the first section. What incident is most vivid for you? Different people will have different answers. It should be interesting to see how much commonality of opinion there is.

Organization

Students are asked to answer the following questions about the story's organization.

1. How much time elapses in each of the sections? Part one is continuous and covers only an hour or two. Part two covers a period of two months. Part three also covers a time span of about two months.

Are the incidents arranged chronologically or in some other pattern? The arrangement is, generally, a chronological one interrupted by a short flashback as Gregor considers his job as a commercial traveler.

2. A modern play is often divided into three acts that are designated as: the situation, the development or complication, and the resolution. *The Metamorphosis* is divided into three parts. Does it basically follow the three-act play pattern? Yes, clearly. Part one presents the metamorphosis and the reactions of the other characters to it. Part two shows the family struggling to meet the changes in many aspects of their lives, from Grete's care of Gregor to his father's getting a job. In part three, the family, and especially Grete, recognize that something must be done about Gregor. But before they take any action, he conveniently dies.

IV. WORDS

Students are asked to use the defined vocabulary words in sentences of their own. Their responses will, of course, vary widely.

Mirrors

PAGE 680

Massimo Bontempelli

Glossary Words

baffling (page 680, col. 1) Puzzling; bewildering

suffice (page 680, col. 2) Be enough; be sufficient

Handbook

flashback, form, incident

Check Test 83

INTRODUCTION

Related by the author as an incident that once happened to him, this story is a lighthearted comment on self-knowledge. Massimo, it seems, is in the habit of receiving strange telegrams. Once his lost umbrella sent him a message that it was returning. Now he receives a telegram from Vienna signed with his name saying, "Leave for Rome day after tomorrow stop *arrivederci* stop." He immediately knows that the telegram has come from his image, which has been missing from mirrors. He first noticed the disappearance two months ago in Vienna when a mirror broke while he was shaving during a storm. As expected, on the day designated, the image returns to its proper place. But Massimo is careful not to give his image the impression that he has missed it.

Little needs to be said to introduce the story. You may want to point out that modern writers often use bizarre situations to explore identity problems, as students have just observed in Kafka's *The Metamorphosis*.

USING THE STUDY NOTES

PAGE 682

I. HOW IMPORTANT IS YOUR IMAGE?

Students are asked to imagine that they are blind and have no way to gain a visual image of themselves. Would this make a difference in their self-identity? This proposition is designed to make the class think about mirrors and whether they are important to us in gaining a picture of ourselves. There should be varied opinions here. Some students may even feel that blindness is an advantage. An interesting assignment is to ask them, first, to use their fingers to trace their facial features and their hair and skin and, then, to write a paragraph describing themselves using this information only. How close did they come to actual appearance? Ask students if they think that lack of visual knowledge would damage their concepts of self?

II. IMPLICATIONS

Students are asked if the ideas implied by the following quotations are valid or false.

1. "Rather I would prefer not to have some malicious person think that I spend most of my life before a mirror." This is a sly comment. We all know people who continually want to look at themselves and who use any shiny reflective surface as a mirror. As they walk down a street, they watch their progress in plate glass display windows, in the doors of automobiles, and in decorative mirrors. There is a Greek legend of a beautiful young man, Narcissus, who angered the gods. As his punishment, he was fated to pine away for love of his own reflection. There is a suggestion that this story is connected with the widespread superstition in Greece that it was bad, even fatal, to look on one's own reflection. Hence the term *narcissistic* is used in psychiatry for persons morbidly interested in their own bodies. The speaker in this story does not want anyone to think that he has this kind of attachment to self. Do we perhaps all have to fight this tendency to study ourselves?

2. "...it is not an uncommon thing (even if science has not as yet explained it) to find a lost article in the very place where one has looked for it many times before." Yes, this does happen. Students should be able to relate instances that have happened to them or to someone in their families. We do know that at any one time we are selective in what we perceive. This selective perception is probably what operates when we finally find an object where we had looked for it before.

3. "All those who use a mirror... must have noticed, I believe, that the moment they pull themselves away from it, from the mirror into which they are looking, they feel a slight sense of discomfort." This statement is also a sly inference that we really enjoy looking at ourselves. Do students think that this is true?

4. "I did not want to give my image the satisfaction of knowing that I care very much about it, that I have been waiting for it impatiently, that I cannot do without it." Ask students to recall that often when we are upset about the lateness of someone, we try to appear as though we have not noticed the tardiness when the person finally arrives. This behavior is an example of rationalization—the refusal to admit certain things about ourselves. The speaker indicates that he *has* been waiting impatiently, but he hates to admit this dependence on his image.

III. TECHNIQUES

Selection of Incident

The incident with the umbrella seems to intrude into the story. What does the author gain by including it? It prepares the reader for the telegram from Massimo's image. Also, it is amusing. Finally, it adds an element of suspense because it delays the main incident (the loss of the image).

Organization

This story provides an example of a particular type of organization. Can you identify its organizational method? The method is the flashback. There are two examples of it that span almost the entire story. The first is the incident of the umbrella. The second is Massimo's description of how he lost his image and how he behaved in the interval between the loss and the receipt of the telegram.

After the Theater

PAGE 683

Anton Chekhov

INTRODUCTION

In "After the Theater" the sixteen-year-old Nadia has just returned from the opera where she and her mother saw *Eugene Onegin*. Nadia is a romantic young woman who identifies easily with Tatiana of the opera story. She thinks Tatiana's suffering in her unrequited love for the hero and Onegin's eventual suffering when Tatiana is rich, married, and unavailable are very beautiful and perhaps comprise the real meaning of love. Nadia goes to her room to write the sort of letter Tatiana wrote to Onegin when she first declared her love.

Nadia tries out all the emotions she imagines go with love. She pretends to doubt the declarations made by the two young men who are in love with her. She writes a letter responding to rejection and begins to cry. She enjoys this little drama and begins thinking of how interesting men are. She is soon laughing excitedly.

Nadia realizes that the possibilities of romance hold many wonderful moments in store for her. She can hardly contain her joy as she soberly contemplates the religious image hanging over her bed.

Students may recognize Nadia's state of trying to know her own emotions. She knows something of what other people feel and what she should perhaps feel. She tries to manufacture some concrete reasons for her awakening sexuality and emotional unsteadiness.

Glossary Words

abyss (page 686, col. 1) Chasm; anything too deep to be measured

rive (page 686, col. 1) Tear apart; split

Handbook

incident, point of view

Check Test 84 *(also for "The Trick")*

The Trick

PAGE 685

Anton Chekhov

Handbook

flashback, narrator

Check Test 84 *(also for "After the Theater")*

INTRODUCTION

The second story by Chekhov, "The Trick," is another study of a character's psychological reactions but quite different from the first story in its organization.

"The Trick" is a flashback told in the first person by an unnamed narrator. He tells of an event years before when he rather inadvertently started a trick and then, for some reason he still cannot explain, continued it.

On that day long ago, after the narrator has persuaded Nadenka to ride down a steep hill on a toboggan, he whispers with the wind that he loves her. When they reach the bottom of the hill safely, neither rider acknowledges the words spoken on the ride. Nadenka wants to ride again. Again the narrator whispers he loves her. This event is repeated again and again. Since there is never any sign from the narrator that he does love her, Nadenka must be left to think she could have imagined the words, or she must think the wind could be the speaker. The narrator has seen Nadenka experiment with riding down the hill without him.

One evening in March when tobogganing is over and the narrator is about to leave for Petersburg, he sees her standing by her fence in the wind. He is standing close enough to be heard but not be seen, and he once more whispers that he loves her. The narrator observes Nadenka's great joy.

The narrator reports that although Nadenka is now married and presumably happy, her happiest memory is of the wind speaking words of love to her that winter season years ago.

Introduce the two stories merely by asking students to consider as they read how the characters in each attempt to get to know themselves.

USING THE STUDY NOTES

PAGE 688

I. FOOLING ONESELF

Students are asked how the women in the stories fool themselves, whether they do it intentionally, and how that helps them to know themselves.

The women in both stories do fool themselves. Nadia in "After the Theater" intentionally tries to make herself feel rejected by her lovers. Nadenka apparently lets herself believe the impossible, that the wind told her it loved her.

Nadia is experimenting with emotions trying to grow into feelings she knows adults have. She probably has better knowledge of herself as a result. Nadenka may have felt in fact loved by hearing the declarations so clearly. The narrator seems to think this has contributed to her present contentment.

Students may also consider whether the narrator of "The Trick" is trying to get to know himself better by telling about the trick and wondering why he carried it out.

II. IMPLICATIONS

1. Students are asked to discuss whether they agree or disagree with the implications of the following statements from the stories:

a. "When one loves greatly but the other is indifferent, there is something beautiful in that, affecting and poetic." Nadia in "After the Theater" obviously believes this to be the major ingredient in romance. Students may agree that an unequal attraction makes the best stories (hence, the popularity of soap operas, romance novels, and popular songs). They may also appreciate the fact that Nadia did not need to feel rejection at all, and hers was only temporary and in her imagination.

b. "In a society where indifference and chill arrogance are counted signs of breeding and of noble manners men have to hide their passion." Even Nadia did not really believe this as she described Gorni's attempt to adhere to it. Nadia is speaking specifically of men, not of mankind, and discussion may lead to a consideration of whether men are more or less likely to show emotions and whether there is a change in society's acceptance of men's emotions. Do students feel "indifference and chill arrogance" are signs of noble manners in men? In women? In both? In neither?

c. **"...fear and danger gave peculiar force to fascinating words of love...."** This opinion attributed to Nadenka in "The Trick" might seem similar to Nadia's feelings that rejection is romantic. Do students agree that romance thrives on fear and conflict? Does Nadenka find the words of love stronger because of the terror of the ride? Or, would she have been as taken with them in any other mysterious circumstance?

2. **In the last paragraph of "After the Theater" what is meant by "the great joy that oppressed her"? Can joy be oppressive?** Although oppressive joy would seem to be contradictory, it should be clear from the story that Nadia was in fact carrying a heavy burden of giddiness. The last line seems to be full of a plea for help in understanding herself and her youthful need for passion with conflict.

3. **Do you agree or disagree?**

a. **Romance cannot thrive on happiness.** It might be inferred that Nadia would agree at this point in her life with the statement. Do students think romance depends upon conflict and that long-term relationships are dull?

b. **Nadia was basically an unhappy person.** The story does not support this statement. Nadia gloried in the melodrama she made up for herself.

c. **Nadenka believed that the wind whispered to her.** Certainly the narrator thinks this is so. Nadenka's behavior would also indicate this. Do students think the narrator could be wrong? Could he need to feel for some reason that he had been responsible for the happiest moment in Nadenka's life?

III. TECHNIQUES

Selection of Incident

Both stories cover one event. "After the Theater" takes place in one room in a short time and is the reaction to an operatic production. The one character has many changes of mood. "The Trick" takes place over a few months in several places but is the same event over and over.

1. **How would "After the Theater" be different if Chekhov had begun it while Nadia was still at the opera?** The story could still run through a range of emotions, but it would not have as great an impact as it does with the incidents all in the same time and place setting. If the story started at the opera, there would have to be more description of the setting. The story as it is can be entirely concerned with exploring Nadia's feelings.

2. **Why does "The Trick" need to take place over a period of time? Would it have worked as well if Chekhov had told about only one trip down the slope?** The repeated incidents of Nadia listening for the words of love contribute to the narrator's case of how dependent she has become on hearing them. The story would not be as effective with only one incident.

Organization

1. Students are asked if Nadia's changes in mood are handled smoothly and why they think the story is organized as it is.

The changes in Nadia's mood are abrupt, but the writing style is smooth. Chekhov describes a simple movement which is accompanied by a change in mood which becomes exaggerated before another change begins.

Having all the changes occur in a short time emphasizes Nadia's volatile, romantic nature.

2. Students are asked how "The Trick" would be different if it had been set all in the present instead of being presented as a flashback. They are also asked how the effect would be different if the narrator were not in the story.

The effect of the story depends on the narrator's point of view. He started the trick, he carried it out, he observed the reaction to it, and he now wonders why he did it. If there were no flashback, there would be no reason for the retrospection. The series of events stretching into months and observed years later let the reader know the illusion was of long duration.

Eveline

PAGE 689

James Joyce

Glossary Words

palpitations (page 690, col. 2) Rapid beatings of the heart; tremblings

squander (page 690, col. 2) Spend foolishly; waste foolishly

melancholy (page 691, col. 2) Causing sadness; depressing; deplorable
nausea (page 692, col. 1) A feeling a person has when about to vomit
frenzy (page 692, col. 1) A state of near madness; a frantic condition

Handbook

atmosphere, characterization, incident, stream of consciousness, symbol, theme

Check Test 85

INTRODUCTION

There is very little action in "Eveline"—as befits a story whose main theme is paralysis. Through most of the story, Eveline is merely sitting at the window of her home, thinking about her past and possible future. She is a simple nineteen-year-old whose adolescence has been spent keeping house for her father. But she has met a young sailor, Frank, who wants to marry her and take her with him to Buenos Ayres (Aires). Her father, however, is opposed to her even seeing the young man. A second reason for not marrying him occurs to her as she reviews her life: She made a promise to her mother on her deathbed that she would keep the home together as long as she could. Eveline further recalls her mother's life of "commonplace sacrifices closing in final craziness." And she jumps up, determined to escape from a possibly similar fate.

She goes with Frank as far as the ship's dock, but at the last moment the "paralysis" strikes, and she grips at the railing "in frenzy." Frank begs her to follow him on board, but she sets a passive face to him. "Her eyes gave him no sign of love or farewell or recognition."

Although a brief story, "Eveline" may be used to illustrate virtually all of Joyce's characteristic techniques. One is instantly impressed by the story's power to evoke atmosphere and emotion. One may see many Joycean epiphanies in the tale, such as the one about the photograph of the priest who has gone to Melbourne. (Note how nicely the "casual word" uttered by Eveline's father is immediately followed by her own questioning about going away: Can she stand to become no more than the subject of a "casual word" in her own home, if she settles—like the priest—in the southern hemisphere?)

Joycean understatement may be observed in many places, notably in Eveline's memory of the happy moments in her life at home—one that had occurred "not long before" and the other "another day, when their mother was alive." The wide separation in time helps to show how tragically few pleasant memories Eveline actually has had. Even Joyce's symbolic techniques may be seen in the tale. For example, as Richard Levin and Charles Shattuck point out, "Eveline" has a great number of parallels to Homer's tale of Odysseus and Calypso: Eveline is Calypso, Frank is Odysseus, and Eveline's father is Zeus.

If you wish to study "Eveline" as an illustration of the artistry of James Joyce, you could discuss some or all of the considerations just mentioned. It may constitute a welcome change of pace for the students. As far as the theme is concerned, however, you could ask students to read the selection with these key questions in mind: Does Eveline know who she is? How does her self-knowledge or lack of it help or hinder her?

USING THE STUDY NOTES PAGE 692

I. A NEW LIFE

The story brings up some very interesting questions relating to personal identity. Eveline is certainly identified with her father, her mother, and her home environment generally. Can we say that she possesses a sense of identity?

The answer is No. The proof that she does not is the fact that she is incapable of acting spontaneously and of accepting joyously a new life. One cannot have a sense of personal identity and be a slave; Eveline's real self is trapped within—as the last line of the story so well reveals.

II. IMPLICATIONS

1. Students are asked to use the following questions to explore the far-reaching implications of the story.

a. What suggestion is there of how Eveline will pass the rest of her life? The implication is very clear that if she does not escape, she will pass her life as her mother did—in "commonplace sacrifices." Indeed, she is already living that sort of life, as her characteristic occupation of dusting reveals.

b. How is the world Joyce portrays in "Eveline" a reflection of the "paralysis" he wished to examine in *Dubliners?* What sort of paralysis did he mean? Moral paralysis is chiefly what Joyce meant. Eveline is so morally paralyzed that she is incapable even of seeking her own happiness. She is a completely dependent person—dependent upon her father's will, her mother's wishes, her fruitless prayers for direction from God.

2. Students are asked whether they agree or disagree with the following statements:

a. **One's first duty is to oneself.** It often seems to us that if one does not fullfill one's duty to self, one's duties to everyone else will be flawed. And of course one of the primary duties to self is to come to know oneself. To be sure, once one does know oneself, she or he may cease sacrificing for drunken, passive fathers like Eveline's. But then one may well ask what duty is really owed to such a parent.

b. **Eveline was unable to escape from her dreary life because in reality it suited her.** Students must first ask what "in reality" means. There are many levels of reality. In the deepest reality every human being wants to be free and happy. Eveline's life clearly did not suit her on this level of reality. Her problem was that she could not reach this level.

c. **Eveline's character is so weak that she would have been just as unhappy in Buenos Ayres (Aires) as in Dublin.** Often dependent people when removed from the chief source of their dependency, become much happier. And of course Eveline's running to Buenos Ayres was (or would have been) a running toward rather than a running away from, for her escape was not merely a matter of place but a matter of Frank and of love.

d. **Happiness belongs to those who are strong enough to take it.** It may seem strange to students to think of happiness as requiring strength. Yet it sometimes does, as the case of Eveline very well illustrates. Perhaps one of the reasons why we find it difficult to associate happiness and strength is that we too frequently connect the former with acquiring material possessions. It does not require strength to "take" this kind of happiness.

III. TECHNIQUES

Selection of Incident

Students are asked what each of the following incidents shows about Eveline.

1. **The children playing games in the fields.** It shows, for one thing, that Eveline naturally enjoyed the company of others when she was young and that she was more spontaneous than she is at the time of the story.

2. **Her thoughts about her job at the Stores.** These thoughts show that she has a little spirit left in her. However, they also reveal her to have been a somewhat passive worker, whom it was easy to "pick on."

3. **The Saturday night squabble over money.** It reveals that she has to take a great deal from her father, that she is rather passive in the face of his drunken anger.

4. **Her romance with Frank.** This romance illustrates that Eveline is by no means dead emotionally. She appears to be somewhat shy, as one would expect. But in most respects their romance is quite normal.

5. **Her mother's death.** Her promise to her mother to keep the house together indicates most probably her sympathetic feelings toward her mother. Her musings on her mother's life show that she has good insight—at least into the lives of others.

6. **Her inability to follow Frank through the gate at the dock.** This incident shows many things. It shows some fear of the unknown—she has a flash of fear that she may drown, for instance. It shows, perhaps, that she is actually incapable of feeling love. At the end, she gives him "no sign of love or farewell or recognition." It shows that she is dependent upon the past to such an extent that she cannot grow or change, even though this would bring a much richer life than she has ever known.

THE PERSONAL ESSAY

Make sure that students read the statements about the personal essay on page 699 before they read the essays themselves. You may want them to take notes on the main points of the commentary and then let them see how these main points are illustrated in the essays that follow. Or let them return to page 699 after they have read the essays.

As far as our theme is concerned, perhaps the most important thing about the personal essay is that it introduces the reader to writers who know themselves. In comparing their own reactions to those of the authors, readers, too, may learn about themselves. Sometime during this unit, it would be good for students to try to write personal essays, perhaps on subjects similar to those used by the authors represented. Through this means students may learn still more about themselves.

from Delight

PAGE 700

J. B. Priestley

Glossary Words

burlesques (page 701, col. 2) Literary compositions that treat serious subjects in a ridiculous manner or trivial subjects as if they were important

dubiously (page 702, col. 2) Doubtfully; uncertainly

dubiety (page 702, col. 2) Doubtfulness; uncertainty

pessimist (page 703, col. 1) A person inclined to look on the dark side of things or to see all the difficulties and disadvantages

optimist (page 703, col. 2) One who looks on the bright side of things

insufferably (page 703, col. 2) Unbearably; detestably

portentousness (page 703, col. 2) Great importance

daft (page 704, col. 2) Without sense or reason; silly; foolish; also, crazy or insane

aptitude (page 705, col. 2) Natural capacity; talent; ability

egotistical (page 706, col. 1) Talking too much about oneself; conceited

Handbook

essay, form, incident, theme

Check Test 86

THE SELECTIONS

In ''After Finishing Some Work,'' Priestley recaptures that moment of delight and satisfaction that comes after completing a difficult piece of work. There is a sense of being released, a sense of new-found freedom. Tomorrow and all its infinite possibilities are open wide for the taking. And so for a short time ''before the key grates in the lock again,'' one is free.

''My First Article'' is a humorous-serious piece about Priestley's first published article and the reaction that he saw on the face of a woman who was about to read his first article as she sat near him on a tram. Priestley tries to describe the look of a reader about to read an article. It is a look that causes authors to realize the wide gulf likely to exist between their own opinions of their work and those of casual readers.

''Waking to Smell Bacon, etc.'' illustrates the fact that some of our most intense delights come from the little things of life. In this case, the little thing involves the use of the sense of smell—the smell of bacon, eggs, and coffee upon first getting up in the morning. It is an animal delight whose pleasure comes in part from the realization that we are simple animals at bottom, sharers in ''a smaller, plainer but more companionable world.''

In ''Giving Advice'' Priestley contends that he is the last person in the world from whom advice should be sought, for his own life is so badly organized. But because he smokes a pipe, has a deep voice, and weighs two hundred pounds, his advice is sought. Like all of us, he enjoys giving it in spite of his lack of qualifications. The key sentence in the essay is the last one. From it, we may gain a sudden flash of what it is to be human, to be fallible, and yet at the same time to act as though one were a god.

Priestley tells of some of his own absurd weaknesses and some of those of others that he knows in ''Other People's Weaknesses.'' Then he philosophizes on the matter, asserting that nearly all of us are pleased by our own admissions and the admissions of others concerning such weaknesses. They prove us mortal; they show that we are all still children underneath our facades. People who do not possess such weaknesses, Priestley says, are ''not one of us at all.''

Priestley complains in ''Dreams'' that most West

Europeans do not accept dreaming as important parts of their lives. He insists that dreaming is very important, and he speaks of some of its advantages as well as of some of its strangenesses. Ultimately, what comes across most strongly in this essay is Priestley's insistence on seeing life as all of a piece and his refusal to reject any of it as trivial. One may also be pleased by his treatment of dream life as an entity interesting in itself rather than for what it can reveal of the waking self. This is a very refreshing, un-Freudian point of view.

"No School Report" is a highly humorous piece in which Priestley thanks heaven that no one can write school reports about him anymore. At the same time, he suggests what kind of a report he would now get. It seems to be an unflattering but honest appraisal mixed with a good deal of pure fun. He also imagines how his father would confront him if he had such a report to show. One senses in this essay that he would actually be a very understanding and forgiving father if his own son brought a bad report from school. He would be able to perceive the essentials, which, unfortunately, school reports rarely if ever present.

Naturally, one's reactions to the essays will be conditioned by one's own character as well as by Priestley's. Our own dominant feeling is that the author is someone whom we should very much like to know. We hope that many students will develop the same feeling.

Students should be asked to read the headnote in the text. It consists mainly of a statement by Priestley in which he describes his public image, and it helps to explain why he wrote a book of essays entitled *Delight.* You may also want students to discuss the subject of the public versus the private self. This is a topic that should be of considerable interest to many students.

The essays are short enough to form a single assignment. If time permits, however, we suggest that you break up the reading into at least two and perhaps even three assignments. Students will get much more from their reading if they can savor each essay before moving on to the next. Perhaps some of the essays can be read and discussed in class. The discussions should reveal what is to be savored. Several of the essays could well be read more than once, as one would read a letter from a good friend more than once.

USING THE STUDY NOTES PAGE 706

I. SECRET PLEASURES

Students are asked to tell what the following lines reveal about Priestley and whether they share the feelings or traits with him.

1. **After finishing a piece of work that has been long and rather difficult, I have a sense of satisfaction that can expand into delight. . . . I have been in prison with this one idea, and now, I feel, I am free.** The line shows that Priestley has the capacity to take pleasure in a difficult job completed and well done. It is hoped that some students, especially the more mature ones, will be able to share this feeling with him and take pride in their own abilities to carry tasks through to completion.

2. **So ever since that tramride I have never caught a glimpse of the reader, the audience, the customer, the patron, without instantly trying to wedge myself into the rocks above the black tarn of doubt.** The basic idea is that the sight of a real reader—as opposed to the imagined reader that an author may have in mind when writing—causes the author to have self-doubts and to wonder whether the work will have its intended effect. Such doubts must plague many authors, who work at what is essentially a very lonely craft. These doubts plague student authors as well when they turn their essays in to their teachers.

3. **Most of us could do with a smaller, plainer but more companionable world.** The implication is that most of us live in a world that is too large, too complex, and too unloving. As Wallace Stevens says in one of his poems: "There is so little that is close and warm./It is as if we were never children." This must certainly be a universal feeling, at least in contemporary society.

4. **A man or woman whose personality had not a speck of such weakness would be intolerable. . . .** Priestley feels that he is weak and human; he does not like those who put themselves above the human condition. Perfection is something that we may admire in the abstract, but most of us don't care to get very close to it. For one thing, we suspect it to be a masquerade in human beings. Students will doubtless share Priestley's feelings on this matter.

II. IMPLICATIONS

Students are asked to explain their reasoning in agreeing or disagreeing with the following statements:

1. **One of the best ways to know yourself is to tally up the things you take delight in or the things you dislike. You can learn to know yourself better by tallying the things you like rather than the things you dislike.** Students' opinions will probably differ, and their expressions of preferences may lead to a lively discussion. Perhaps the class will see that our natural inclinations seem to run contrary to Priestley's advice. We all seem inclined to list unfavorable things before the ones that we consider favorable.

2. **Most of us build our own picture of self by little everyday judgments rather than by blinding moments of revelation.** There may be a lively difference of opinion between the two alternatives. The

Judeo-Christian tradition is filled with stories of sudden revelation. Remind students of some of these: Moses and the burning bush, Peter and Jesus, Paul on the road to Damascus. This same theme appears elsewhere in literature. James Joyce's concept of epiphany is a case in point. Have students had such experiences in their own lives? Perhaps, on the other hand, their self-understanding has developed in the same way that Holden Caufield's does in *The Catcher in the Rye*. Even at the end of the book he doesn't really know what he is like.

III. TECHNIQUES

Selection of Incident

Students are to discuss the following questions:

1. What kinds of incidents does Priestley use in an essay to support his picture of a particular delight? Do you feel he has been selective? Generally, Priestley builds upon a single incident—the smell of bacon, coffee, and eggs; the woman in the tram reading his first article. In "Dreams," however, there are several "incidents" and in "No School Report" there is a good deal of wandering. In these cases one could argue that multiplicity is required by the nature of the subject: "Dreams" is about dreams, and a report card contains marks on many subjects. The selection in these cases is not what we would call tight, but tight selection does not seem to be required by the personal essay form.

2. Do you actually share his remembered delights with him? Have students jot down the specific delights that they remember from the essays. Speculate with them about why some of them have longer lists than others and why different people remember different things.

Organization

Students are to consider the following:

1. Take any three essays and decide what the pattern of organization is in each. Are they all alike? Does it matter how he arranges examples in them? A mere glance at the beginning and the end of each of the essays will reveal one rather strong pattern: Each essay almost invariably begins and ends with references to delight. Quite frequently, the word itself is used. If not, Priestley cites an instance of delight. Other than this theme, the patterns differ. For instance, some tend to begin with general statements and work toward specifics. Others begin with specifics and work toward generalizations. The endings are often climactic, but not always.

There is nothing special in the arrangement of examples. In "No School Report," for instance, the examples could have been arranged quite differently.

2. All of us have moments when we feel twinges of delight. Take any one of your private delights and, using Priestley's pattern of organization, write an essay describing it. By "Priestley's pattern of organization" we mean beginning and ending with a reference to delight and using examples between. In addition, students should challenge themselves by working toward some sort of generalization, as Priestley does. That is, private delight should not be altogether private.

from Platero and I

PAGE 707

Juan Ramón Jiménez

Glossary Words

guileless (page 708, col. 2) Without deceit or trickery; honest; frank; straightforward

indigo (page 709, col. 1) Deep violet blue

quietude (page 709, col. 1) Stillness; calmness

sonorous (page 710, col. 1) Full and rich in sound

cadence (page 710, col. 1) Rhythm; rise and fall of the voice

delirium (page 711, col. 2) A temporary disorder of the mind that occurs during fevers, insanity, etc., characterized by restlessness, excitement, etc.

disoriented (page 711, col. 1) Loosing one's bearings; confused as to time, place, identity, etc.

arabesques (page 712, col. 1) Elaborate and fanciful designs of flowers, leaves, geometrical figures, etc.

Handbook

climax, form, incident, mood

Check Test 87

THE SELECTIONS

"Platero" is a brief, poetic description of Jiménez's donkey. The images that he uses are of both hardness and softness—"tender and loving" but "strong and firm"; "soft to the touch," yet with eyes "hard as two beetles of dark crystal." The people from the country see only the hard side of Platero; they say that he is made of steel. Jiménez knows that he is made of both steel and quicksilver.

"White Butterflies" tells of a twilight confrontation between Jiménez and Platero and a tax collector who asks what merchandise they are carrying in the saddlebag. Jiménez answers "white butterflies." When the saddlebag is opened and the agent sees nothing, Jiménez comments that the stuff of dreams is free and untaxable.

"The Crazy Man" contrasts earthly and heavenly realities. One is represented by the gypsy children who shout "The crazy man!" after Jiménez as he rides through the streets. The other is represented by Jiménez's vision of the "divine, harmonious serenity which lives in the endlessness of the horizon." Jiménez is a kind of Christ figure, in mourning for the world that jeers at him.

"The Grape Harvest" implicitly comments upon the effect of economic conditions on people and animals. In the past, harvests were bountiful. There was plenty of work for people and for donkeys, and there was madness, dizziness, optimism, and affection among the workers. This year, however, the harvest is meager, and most donkeys and most workers are unemployed. So that the few donkeys that are working will not think badly of Platero, Jiménez loads him with grapes and leads him to the wine press. Then he leads him away inconspicuously.

The first two paragraphs of "The Little Girl" tell of the love between Platero and a young girl. Then suddenly the essay shifts to the long, lingering, summertime death of the girl, who calls to the donkey in her delirium. Finally she dies and is buried on a splendid day in late September. Coming home from the burial, Jiménez flees people and sits down in the stable to weep with Platero.

"The Old Donkey" touches upon the helplessness of people in the face of death. Jiménez and Platero come upon an old donkey that has got out of the boneyard and is standing motionless. First Jiménez tries to call him and then pull him, but the beast stands as if the death struggle had rooted him to the spot. Jiménez knows that the donkey will die at night in the cold. He does not want to leave. Yet he does not know what to do.

In "Carnival" Platero, dressed in costume by some children, is met by a group of women dressed as lunatics. They dance around him wildly while some children bray at him in order to make him bray. Platero is confused and nervous, but finally he breaks through the circle and comes crying to Jiménez. They do not want to have anything to do with Carnival. They "were not made for this sort of thing"—inhumanity.

In "Melancholy" Jiménez visits Platero's grave on a day in April. He asks Platero whether he has forgotten him. As if in answer, a butterfly flies around, like a soul.

Let students read the introduction in the text. No other introduction ought to be necessary. You will probably not want to read these essays in class. Assign them to be read at home. If you divide the assignment into two parts, use the first four essays for the first assignment, the second four for the second assignment. The latter group will then contain all the sadder essays.

USING THE STUDY NOTES PAGE 713

I. A POET'S ISOLATION

How different to be born and raised in twentieth-century Spain than in twentieth-century England. That contrast alone may well explain the differences in temperament between Jiménez and Priestley. Their origins must have affected how they saw the world, just as it necessarily affected what they saw of the world.

Discuss with students the differences between these two essayists (both of whom seem to have developed strong senses of identity), as an example of how different people may become from one another. Yet do not neglect the similarities between the writers: love of nature, contempt for inhumanity, interest in dreams and dreaming. These are things shared by all people who have profound self-knowledge.

II. IMPLICATIONS

1. Students are asked what insights into Jiménez's life and personality are revealed in the following lines:

a. He is made of steel. Both steel and quicksilver. These words refer to Jiménez as well as to his donkey. They suggest that there is both a hard and a soft side to their personalities, that they are both realists and dreamers.

b. "The cra-azy man!" When one reads this epithet in context, one gets the impression that Jiménez would answer, "Yes, crazy as Jesus was crazy." He is crazy, "different," unsettled because the world is such a place as it is, whereas it could and should be a place in which love and brotherhood prosper.

c. And now, Platero, you must do something, for you are not going to be an idler forever. It is not Platero alone who has been an idler and who should feel guilty about it. Recall, too, that when the grape harvest was richer, Jiménez also worked and benefited from the affection of the workers.

d. Like me he wants to have nothing to do with Carnival. We are not made for this sort of thing. Fundamentally, the statement means that Jiménez wants nothing to do with the kind of inhumanity exhibited by the children and the women. Another defect of Carnival is that it enforces gaiety; one ought not to need an excuse for being merry.

2. Students are asked whether they would agree or disagree with the following statements:

a. In spite of the fact that there is a tone of sadness in Jiménez's essays, they reflect a mind at peace with itself, the mind of a man who knows who he is and is comfortable in that knowledge. Jiménez does seem to be a man who knows who he is. And on the whole, he is at peace with himself. He certainly is not at peace with the world, and we hesitate to use the word *comfortable* to describe him. One is never comfortable, really, unless—as Socrates put it—the inward and the outward are as one.

b. "This world is a comedy to those that think; a tragedy to those that feel." This statement is epigrammatic. Students should be informed that an epigram often uses hyperbole (extreme overgeneralization) to make a point. Therefore, it is not necessarily applicable to every situation. This statement suggests that if one looks objectively at people and their customs, at what they prize and what they despise, one realizes that they are basically absurd. But if one becomes emotionally involved, people seem tragic. Jiménez seems to balance the two approaches. He sees that things are funny but also that they always teeter on the brink of being tragic.

c. The author's feeling for his donkey is too sentimental. Sentimentality involves emotion in excess of objective cause. How one responds to the statement will depend upon how one sees Platero: If the latter is no more than a dumb beast, the feeling—especially in "Melancholy"—will be perceived as sentimental. But if one accepts Jiménez's picture of Platero, one is less likely to accuse the author of sentimentality.

III. TECHNIQUES

Selection of Incident

In "White Butterflies," "The Crazy Man," and "Carnival," Jiménez pictures himself as alienated from the human community. However, what he shows us of the human community tells that he is alienated because the community itself is alienated from fundamental humanity.

Organization

The essays do tend to rise to a climax. The last sentence frequently serves as a summary of sorts.

My Wood

PAGE 714

E. M. Forster

Glossary Words

asceticism (page 714, col. 2) Unusual or extreme self-denial or severe discipline over oneself, especially for religious reasons

antithesis (page 715, col. 1) The direct opposite

depreciating (page 715, col. 1) Lessening or lowering the value of

pretentious (page 715, col. 2) Making claims to excellence or importance

traverses (page 716, col. 1) Cuts through; crosses from one side to the other

avaricious (page 716, col. 1) Greatly desiring money or property; greedy for wealth

pseudocreative (page 716, col. 1) Being falsely original or inventive; pretending to be original or inventive

Handbook

essay, form, irony, tone

Check Test 88

INTRODUCTION

"My Wood" begins with a paragraph briefly outlining how Forster acquired a piece of property, and it sets forth the main question of the essay: What is the effect of owning property on the owners? Forster describes four effects: (1) It makes owners feel heavier; (2) it makes them want more; (3) it tends to become a substitute for creation and enjoyment; (4) it makes owners possessive. Forster characterizes these effects very well in his last sentence: "Enormously stout, endlessly avaricious, pseudo-creative, intensely selfish...."

You may wish to introduce this selection with a key question: How does it differ *in tone* from the work of Priestley and Jiménez? To challenge students further, ask them in what way Jiménez and Priestley are closer in tone to each other than either is to Forster. The point is that the tone in both *Delight* and *Platero and I* is straightforward. In "My Wood," the tone is indirect, ironic, even irreverent. (This is not implying, of course, that Jiménez's and Priestley's tones are identical.) You may also wish to ask about the differences in tone among all three writers; Jiménez's tone is melancholic, Priestley's is jovial. Ask students to cite examples of tone, and discuss with them its importance.

You will probably want to ask students to read the headnote to this selection because it tells something about the novel to which Forster refers in the first sentence of the essay.

USING THE STUDY NOTES PAGE 716

I. POSSESSOR OR POSSESSED?

As the commentary suggests, one's views on a subject are determined by the angle of one's perspective. Ask students how this point relates to the matter of self-knowledge. That is, does it necessarily hold true for an individual who has self-knowledge? Or does having self-knowledge imply having a very firm basis—the "known self"—from which to view things, a basis that is relatively unaffected by whether or not one is a "have" or a "have not" in a material sense? This is a very delicate and interesting question that is closely related to the selection.

II. IMPLICATIONS

1. Is Forster either "for" or "against" the ownership of private property? Or does he commit himself to neither side? What, in your own words, is the point he is trying to make? He is trying to make the point that owning private property is likely to change one's character. His irony makes it clear, however, that ownership of the wood hasn't really changed him very much. This becomes especially clear through the use of the word *perhaps* in the third-from-the-last sentence, which modifies all three of the final sentences.

On the matter of being for or against ownership, Forster does not seem to commit himself unequivocally. He is concerned about private ownership, and he is issuing a warning. Yet, we find nothing in the essay to suggest that he would favor abolishing private property. His reference to communists as "those nasty Bolshies" certainly does not indicate a very favorable view of Russian communism.

2. Students are asked to recall having owned something that had value for them. Then they are asked to compare their reactions toward what they owned with Forster's reactions toward ownership of the wood. Specifically, they are asked to think about whether their property made them *(a)* feel heavy, *(b)* feel that it ought to be larger, and *(c)* feel that they ought to do something to it.

Students may think of such things as a car, a stereo, a bicycle, expensive clothes, as well as other items. They should refer to the essay, if necessary, to be sure that they know exactly what Forster means by something's making one feel "heavy," and so on.

III. TECHNIQUES

Organization

Students are asked to try to rearrange Forster's reactions to see whether any other arrangement leads to the same point or changes the effect of the essay. They are also asked whether Forster placed his reactions in a natural order. There is an order from least to most with respect to the seriousness of the effects of ownership. There is, of course, no absolute standard by which such effects may be judged, but it is hard to see how anyone would want to change the order of the first or the last effect. Some students may think that the second and the third effects could be interchanged. But the second is related to the first by the shift from the owner's feeling of heaviness to the idea that the property ought to be "heavier" (that is, larger). Also, a creative person like Forster is likely to believe that what he calls endless avarice (point 2) is less damaging than pseudocreativity (point 3).

Old China

PAGE 717

Charles Lamb

Glossary Words

partiality (page 717, col. 1) A particular liking; great fondness; preference

repugnance (page 717, col. 2) Strong dislike, distaste, or aversion

tinctured (page 717, col. 2) Colored or tinted with

decorous (page 718, col. 1) Acting properly; in good taste; well-behaved; dignified

mandarin (page 718, col. 1) A high-ranking official in ancient China

finical (page 719, col. 1) Too dainty or particular; too precise; fussy

relish (page 719, col. 2) Keen enjoyment

precarious (page 719, col. 2) Doubtful; uncertain; dependent on chance or circumstance

rhetorical (page 720, col. 2) Having to do with making a speech and using language skillfully

insipid (page 721, col. 1) Lacking interest or spirit; dull

Handbook

essay, form, incident, symbol, tone

Check Test 89

INTRODUCTION

This essay deals with the change in the Lambs' fortune from comparative poverty to comparative wealth and the question of whether this change has brought them less happiness. The essay begins with a brief discourse by Lamb—in the person of Elia—on his fondness for old china. This leads him to the observation that he and his cousin Bridget (Mary Lamb, his sister) had used a new set of china for the first time on the preceding evening. He remarked at the time that he was happy that their fortune had changed to the extent that they could afford such trifles as good china. But Bridget remarks that she wishes that the good old times would come again. The rest of the essay, except for the final paragraph, reports Bridget's description of the good old days, especially the small pleasures that they used to share.

When she is finished, Lamb realistically points out that they are really not all that wealthy now. However, it is good to have what they do have because they are older and should "live better and lie softer." Lamb ends on a tender note by saying that he would give anything to purchase a return to their younger, poorer days. At last, he shifts his "cousin's" attention at this dramatic moment to one of the pieces of china. And old china becomes a symbol of Lamb's tenderness and solicitude.

The opening sentence of this selection—"I have an almost feminine partiality for old china"—as well as the announced subject is likely to alienate students. It will be well, therefore, to tell them in advance that the true subject of the essay is not old china. It would indeed be a pity if the opening were to turn students away from what is essentially a deeply felt and moving essay. Perhaps you should read the first seven to nine paragraphs in class to get students started on the essay and to acquaint them with Lamb's style. (The style is easier in the middle of the essay because dialogue is used.)

As with the previous essays, tone is an important consideration here, especially the tone of the last paragraph. Students must be attuned to the tenderness and the sympathy expressed in the speaker's voice, or they will not fully appreciate the essay.

USING THE STUDY NOTES PAGE 721

I. "A MIDDLE STATE"

The commentary raises the underlying question of the essay: As we grow and change, should our perceptions of ourselves change too? The kind of poverty that Bridget describes is delightful for the young, debilitating for the old. Get students to relate similar instances. Are their clothing styles, dance steps, and social customs appropriate for their parents? Their grandparents? As they age, will they continue to pursue the same life-styles, the same ways of looking at things?

II. IMPLICATIONS

1. Students are asked how true of people in general and of themselves the following comments are:

a. "A purchase is but a purchase, now that you have money enough and to spare. Formerly it used to be a triumph." Students may remember having worked and saved for something—a bicycle or a special pair of shoes. They should recognize readily the special feelings that they had for these objects and the triumph of their acquisitions. Ask them if they had the same feelings about things that were simply given to them. The point to be emphasized is not the mere possession of something but the sense of achievement when one has earned something through personal efforts. Why do some people work on their cars themselves, even when they can have them repaired by experts?

b. "Now, you have nothing to do but to walk into Colnaghi's, and buy a wilderness of Leonardos. Yet do you?" There must be some truth in the idea—at least for some people—that one loses interest in those things that become too easy to acquire. But there are other people who can never get enough of one thing or another, even though it may be quite readily accessible.

2. Students are asked whether they agree or disagree with the following statements:

a. Delving back into memories of bygone times is a good way to find out what you are. Why do you remember some things more vividly than others? Are these things more significant to your personality? How do you remember them? This exercise should provoke a worthwhile discussion.

b. Bridget is not satisfied with what she has become. This seems to be true. On the other hand, her main complaint seems to be about what has been lost of the past rather than about what is wrong with the present.

c. The delights of being poor are more fun to remember than actually to live through. Being poor is certainly not fun. But the delights of the poor might be as much fun to live through—perhaps more fun—than to remember. Indeed, these delights—bound up, as they were, with his youth—are so appealing to Lamb that he says he would give anything to purchase them back.

III. TECHNIQUES

Selection of Incident

Students are asked what the following incidents reveal about Bridget and her brother. Do her memories tend to "rose-tint" the past? Do the incidents convince the reader that her argument is valid?

1. **The Beaumont and Fletcher folio**
2. **The print they called Lady Blanch**
3. **The holiday expeditions**
4. **Their viewing of the plays from the one-shilling gallery**
5. **Their little food extravagances**
6. **Their struggle at the year's end to make the accounts balance**

Items 1, 2, and 4 reveal a love of culture and a willingness to sacrifice material comforts to acquire or experience fine things. The third item reveals a fondness for the outdoors and an adventuresome spirit. The fifth item reveals that they took pleasure in little things. The final item reveals general good humor, for the struggle always ended with hope and "laughing spirits." In all the items, one senses, also, the intimacy of sharing and their love of life. The incidents themselves do not impress us as being unusually "rose-tinted," except that perhaps the pleasure is remembered more vividly than the pain.

Bridget's argument is that they were happier then

than they are now. In this assessment, Lamb agrees with her: "It is true we were happier when we were poorer. . . ." But she also argues that they were happier *because* they were poorer, and Lamb does not completely agree with that. He recognizes, for one thing, that their youth also had a great deal to do with their happiness.

Organization

The remarks about old china help Lamb to approach his subject, but they do much more than that. They reveal a love of delicate things and therefore are suggestive of his love for his sister, who is delicate. He also asserts that his love of old china began before he can remember and that it continues as strong today as it ever was. This, too, characterizes his love for Mary Lamb. At the end of the essay, the love of china becomes a symbol. The talk of china is thus not to be seen merely as a device of organization; it is an integral part of the essay. Lamb would not have titled his essay "Old China" if his remarks on that subject were purely peripheral.

Pavan for a Dead Prince

PAGE 722

Shelagh Delaney

Glossary Words

pavan (page 722) A slow, stately dance and also the music for it

dynamic (page 723, col. 1) Active; energetic; powerful; vigorous

auspices (page 723, col. 2) Patronage; approval or support

distraught (page 723, col. 2) Very distressed; distracted; frantic

engrossed (page 726, col. 1) Being occupied wholly by something; giving all one's attention to something

feigning (page 727, col. 2) Making believe; pretending

Handbook

dialogue, form, incident, tone

Check Test 90

INTRODUCTION

This selection opens with a discussion about the practice of funeral sightseeing, a sport indulged in by a woman who calls herself a friend of Shelagh's mother. After viewing a corpse, this woman would come to the Delaneys' home to tell about it. Shelagh's mother would have liked to shoot this creature.

Then the story shifts to a young neighbor of the Delaneys, a miner named Benjamin, whom Shelagh loves. Benjamin has an "elegant and graceful and subtle" body, and he loves to dance. He takes Shelagh to see some dancing by several "Genuine Spanish Gipsies" on one occasion. Although the dancers are not Spanish at all, the couple enjoy themselves very much, probably because the dancers themselves are having such a good time.

Shortly after this, Shelagh sees Benjamin practicing a Spanish dance routine in his bedroom (which is directly across the street from her own). She says nothing to anyone about this.

Then, at Eastertime, Benjamin gets rheumatic fever and has to go to the hospital for several months. After his release, he continues to convalesce at home, sitting in his bed and looking out the front window. Shelagh visits him a great deal and usually leaves him in extreme laughter or in extreme anger: "Everything had to be extreme with that boy."

Eventually, Benjamin is able to go outdoors briefly. But the news that his mining and dancing days are over for good upsets him greatly. So bitter is he over his bad heart that he sometimes stands with his hand upon his breast reciting every profanity he knows.

One night Benjamin invites Shelagh to his house to watch him do a Spanish dance. He tells her, "It'll be the high spot of your existence and mine too." The dance, which is the one that he had started practicing before his illness, is brilliant. Both of them are lost in it. Then it stops, and they hate each other for a moment. He falls across the bed in exhaustion, and it occurs to her "without fear or surprise" that he is going to die. They then have a brief conversation in which they discuss how he looked, whether he looked funny, and what "people" would think if they saw him. Benjamin says that solo dancing "means more," you can put more feeling into it.

The next reference is to his funeral procession, a reference that includes some lines of dialogue spoken by the sightseers at the funeral. The story concludes with Shelagh's observation that Benjamin's face had shone again and with the following snatch of dialogue: "What's funny, kid?" "Nothing."

The story is about a beautiful moment in the life of a young man who consciously chooses to live that one moment, even though he knows it may bring about his death. It was necessary to his being, his identity, that he dance that dance. The story is also about the society in which the boy and the girl live, a society whose members are sightseers, not participants in living. They say that Benjamin's death is tragic and a waste, but the author suggests that it is their living, not his dying, that is tragic and wasteful.

INTRODUCING THE SELECTION

As noted in the last paragraph above, this story has both a personal and a social context. Most students will appreciate the former without great difficulty, but you may have to help them to see the latter. Perhaps the simplest way to do this is to ask them to turn back to the beginning after they have read the whole story. Ask them to think about the connections between the opening and the closing parts, or perhaps merely the connections between the sightseers' dialogue at the end and the first line of the story.

The only other aspect that may trouble the students is what can be called the abruptness of the style. Often Delaney completely ignores transition. Therefore, much in the story hits the reader quite suddenly, for example the story's beginning, the fact that Shelagh loves Benjamin, Benjamin's getting rheumatic fever, and the funeral procession. This abruptness is quite conscious, but students may be so used to hearing that they must have coherence in their own writing that they may consider the lack of coherence in Delaney's writing a defect. To forestall such a reaction, you may want to focus attention on this stylistic peculiarity. Ask students why she might have used such a rhetorical device.

We suggest several possible answers. For one, the story opposes conventionality, and few things are more firmly rooted in convention than the notion that a writing style must possess coherence. Another possible explanation is that the abruptness shows that in lower-class life things happen to people suddenly because they have little control over their environment. Still a third possibility is that Delaney may be rejecting the notion that life unwinds like thread from a spool. In fact, we really live life only in discrete moments and are unconscious of living most of the rest of the time. A style that reflects this notion would be a more realistic style. Finally, one could say that *all* of these are reasons for the abrupt style. Perhaps students will be able to add other reasons to explain the use of this highly effective technique. What is probably most important, however, is that they understand that it is conscious and that it is effectively used in this story.

USING THE STUDY NOTES PAGE 727

I. LIFE WITHOUT COMPROMISE

There is a sense in which the things that we do best and enjoy most "define" us and give us a large part of our identity. Everything in this story suggests the idea that Benjamin defines himself as a dancer (and as a miner during the working day). It is important that we see this as his *essence.* The extended dialogue on page 725 shows that dancing and mining are the only things he does well, the only things he really enjoys doing. He cannot simply change his identity and paint or read as an alternative. To help students to understand the concept of self-identity, you could ask them these questions: Does the fact that Benjamin cannot change prove that he is a limited person? Should all people be able to find intense pleasure in several things rather than in only one?

On the surface it may seem that the answer to both of these questions should be yes. But suppose that there is such a thing as an essential identity. Everyone, after all, is limited in many ways—by heredity, by environment, by other people, and so on. And don't all of us seek fulfillment by looking for ways to satisfy our core selves? Not to be able to do so would mean not to live; to do something else would be to live only partially. And perhaps, Delaney implies, it is better to die living than to live dying.

II. IMPLICATIONS

1. Even though Shelagh and Benjamin know that the traveling dancers they saw are "fake" it doesn't seem to bother them. Why not? It did not make any difference whether or not the dancers were actually Spaniards. They were enthusiastic dancers, and their enthusiasm was far more important to the couple than was their national identity. The important thing in life is not where you were born but that you discover what you do best and then do it.

2. Can you find any indications in the story that Shelagh is a "rebel" against the world she lives in? The story is weighted with such indications; we have already discussed many. In addition to those, we should note what is probably the most explicit indication of her rebellious nature—her reactions to Benjamin's visitors (as detailed in the first paragraph, page 725).

3. Do you agree or disagree with these propositions:

a. When you know the things you want from life, it is better to die than compromise. The "things you want from life" does not mean material objects, of course, but rather the things that make up an individual. We suspect that few persons would have the courage to die rather than to compromise if they were in such a position. But then one could perhaps cynically add that few ever discover what they really want from life.

b. It would have been better for Benjamin to seek a goal that contributes more to society than does Spanish dancing. This is the kind of remark that only a "sightseer" would make. It might have been better for society, but it would not have been better for Benjamin.

c. In most people there is a deep desire for something beautiful. Yes, we agree, but too frequently it is a *very* deep desire.

III. TECHNIQUES

Selection of Incident

Students are asked to answer the following questions:

1. Why does the author begin with a discussion of funerals? An inspection of the opening section will reveal that she does not begin by discussing funerals. She begins by discussing "sightseers" and "deadwatching." She does this because this is, in part, what her story is about.

2. What was your reaction to Benjamin's attempts at dancing? We believe everything Delaney tells us about his dancing, especially that there was nothing funny about it.

3. In what scene did you sense that the mood of the story was darkening? It certainly darkens when Benjamin comes home from the hospital; the narrator literally says, "All the shine had gone off him." In the immediately preceding paragraph (page 724) there is also some gloom in the description of their living conditions.

4. How vivid is the funeral? The funeral is merely sketched in, because to make the funeral vivid would not suit the author's purpose. This is a story about life, not death. The reactions of the sightseers are not vivid, either, but they are memorable, partly because one connects them with the specific portrait of the vulture at the beginning of the story.

Organization

Students are told that the vibrant part of the story is bracketed by death. Then they are asked how this concept served to accomplish the following:

1. make the central moments stand out

2. set the tone of the story

The bracketing of the central moments by death should help to make them stand out through contrast. But it does more than that. In particular, it relates to the central paradox of the story, which focused upon life and death. The final three lines of the story imply that the dead boy is still alive. The lines immediately preceding these three lines imply that the living are dead.

Strickly speaking, it is only the opening section that sets the tone of the story. It hints that the story will involve a death. And the spit bouncing off the iron "like lead shot" more than hints that the story will be very hard on "dead-watchers."

The Poor Relation's Story

PAGE 728

Charles Dickens

Glossary Words

precedence (page 728, col. 1) The act of going first; the lead

diffident (page 730, col. 1) Lacking self-confidence; shy; bashful

genteel (page 730, col. 2) Belonging to polite society; well-bred; well-mannered

baronial (page 731, col. 2) Suitable for a nobleman; splendid, stately, and grand

mercenary (page 731, col. 2) Acting with money as the motive; money-loving

avarice (page 731, col. 2) Too great a desire for money or property; greed for wealth

contemptible (page 732, col. 1) Worthless; despicable; deserving scorn; mean; low

abhorrence (page 732, col. 2) A feeling of great loathing, revulsion

repudiated (page 732, col. 2) Rejected; cast off; disowned

palpable (page 734, col. 1) Readily seen or heard and recognized; obvious; actual; real

Handbook

climax, form, incident, mood

Check Test 91

INTRODUCTION

The members of a family are gathered around a Christmas fire, and it is decided that each will tell a story for entertainment. The poor relation is prevailed upon to begin the round.

He starts by saying that he is not what he is supposed to be. Nevertheless, before going on, he proceeds to tell what he *is* supposed to be. The picture that he presents in this part of the story is largely factual. It does begin, however, with a brief recounting of how others think he became what he is—mainly through being "nobody's enemy but [his] own." It was through this "fault" that he failed in his "expectations from [his] Uncle Chill" (expectations of inheriting money), that he failed in his business, and that he failed in love.

The poor relation then gives a realistic description of himself and of a typical, dreary day in his life. He concludes this description by noting that he is not "an attractive companion." But there is one exception—his relationship with little Frank, the child of his first cousin. It is clear from his description of this relationship that he is a very kind and sincere human being, although obviously a social outcast, even within his own family circle.

Then the poor relation explains what he actually is—the resident of a castle. This part of the story begins with an account of how he was disinherited by his Uncle Chill because the latter suspected that Christiana and her mother wanted not a husband and son-in-law but rather the uncle's money. This part of the story is factual, including the uncle's idea of the true motives of Christiana and her mother.

In the next two sections, the poor relation shifts from the facts to what might have been—first with respect to Christiana, then with respect to his association with his business partner, John Spatter. In reality, both of them wronged him after discovering that Uncle Chill had disinherited him. But he tells how Christiana and he were married and raised a fine family and how John Spatter and he formed a stronger and friendlier partnership. At the end he speaks of how good life is in his castle. But when a member of the group says, "and the Castle is—," the poor relation admits it is "in the Air."

The frequently repeated phrase "Nobody's enemy but my own" is in many ways the key to the story. The simple fact is that the poor relation's only real fault was in assuming that other people were as gentle and giving as himself. The implication is that in society one must have enemies—other than oneself—if one is to avoid becoming a poor relation. Society and most individuals, Dickens implies, reward the vicious rather than the virtuous. Thus the reader may be tempted to ask: If this is the shape of reality, would it be better to live in a dream?

Many students will have difficulty following this story. To help them, we suggest that you read the opening in class—perhaps down to the end of the first paragraph on page 730. Be sure that all students understand that, in general, what the poor relation is supposed to be is what he is in reality, except that the "failures" detailed in the second full paragraph, page 729, might not entirely have been his own fault.

Perhaps you will also want to warn students that the first part of the poor relation's second story—which begins on page 731—is also factual down to the break on page 733. Only after this does the narrator indulge in what might have been. If you do not inform students about this, you will find that many will be quite confused over whether or not Christiana actually married the poor relation, and they will be confused about the business partnership. This is not because Dickens is purposely ambiguous (and a very careful reader will not be misled). But it may be partly the author's fault, for after the poor relation shifts from what he is supposed to be to what he is, he talks at considerable length before beginning to fantasize. There may also be confusion over the fact that John is the first name of both the poor relation's business partner and his host. They are definitely not the same person, however.

USING THE STUDY NOTES

PAGE 736

I. A CASTLE IN THE AIR

Is Dickens saying that individuals can truly know themselves and be at peace only in a dream world? In attempting to evaluate this interpretation, students should begin by asking whether the poor relation is truly at peace. They can study the last few paragraphs of the relation's story in order to decide. For instance, when he says, "I really do not know, in my Castle, what loneliness is," are we to take him literally? Or is it a fact that just the opposite is true—that the man is almost utterly lonely?

Everything points to the latter interpretation: His children and grandchildren—who he says keep him from loneliness—are nonexistent. His tears at the theater show that he is still not reconciled to bachelorhood or to the loss of Christiana. And of course we should remember his earlier description of the loneliness of his typical day and of his solitary lodgings in the Clapham Road.

Consequently we do not accept his word when he tells us that he doesn't know what loneliness is. But we do believe him when he reports, "I have got in the habit of speaking low, and being rather silent, and my spirits are not high, and I am sensible that I am not an attractive companion." (page 730) These are neither the words nor the tone of an individual at peace; they are the words and the tone of a beaten person. To be sure, the poor relation does have self-knowledge, and thanks to little Frank, he is not utterly lonely. But he is certainly not at peace with himself.

Finally, one may ask how it can be that a person may have self-knowledge and yet not be at peace? The answer, Dickens seems to suggest, is that self-knowledge is not enough to guarantee peace. One must also have satisfying relationships in society. These are impossible for the poor relation (except for his relationship with little Frank), for, as Dickens notes elsewhere, "Society is a prison." It is especially hostile to people like the poor relation, to people of feeling.

II. IMPLICATIONS

1. Students are asked to take *one* of the following lines and to explain why they think that it is the best expression of the poor relation's evaluation of himself.

a. "I am not what I am supposed to be." We all have two lives: one that the world sees and one that we live in our own minds. Sometimes one predominates, sometimes the other. Although basically honest in admitting his shortcomings in his public life, the poor relation reveals that inside himself he lives quite a different life.

b. "I am nobody's enemy but my own." The poor relation himself evidently believes that this statement describes his character. On page 729 he says that he failed in business because he was "unbusiness-like and credulous," that he failed in love because he was "ridiculously trustful," and that he failed in his expectations from his uncle because he wasn't as sharp in worldly matters as his uncle wanted. One could say that he is unflattering to himself in this analysis but that he is probably accurate.

c. "Yes. My Castle is. . . is in the Air." In spite of his dream life, the poor relation is basically honest. This can lead to real knowledge of self, for a person must be able to separate the real from the dream.

2. Students are asked to give their reactions to four statements.

Because all four statements are controversial, it may be well to divide the class into groups and to let each group discuss one of the statements. Ask them to think about the statement as an evaluation of the poor relation and then to consider its validity and relevance today.

III. TECHNIQUES

Selection of Incident

Students are asked to tell whether in this selection Dickens was using Collins's formula for writing successful fiction ("Make 'em laugh, make 'em cry, make 'em wait"). As readers of Dickens know, he generally does use this formula in his work. But in this case he has not tried to "make 'em laugh" and he has not used "make 'em wait" as extensively as he often does, that is, there is not a great deal of mystery. The "make 'em cry" part of the formula is very much used, however.

Students are also to answer the following questions:

1. **Does Dickens use the incidents here to reveal character or to move toward the climax?** He uses them for both purposes, perhaps more for the former than for the latter.

2. **Dickens, in his stories, moved from attacking the particular evils of society such as the poor law and the iniquities of private schools to an all-out attack on the evils of money. Are there incidents in this story that point out the evils of money?** Yes, Christiana left the poor relation to marry a wealthier man when he was disinherited by Uncle Chill. Also, John Spatter began edging the poor relation out of the business because he had lost his pecuniary "expectations." Avarice is also specifically identified as Uncle Chill's master vice.

Organization

Students are told that Dickens, in effect, tells the

same story twice. Then they are asked whether the retelling is as detailed as the first telling, whether the details are more simplified or more elaborate, and whether he uses as many incidents in the second telling.

The first story refers very briefly to the main events of the second story—the events focusing upon Uncle Chill, Christiana, and John Spatter. The retelling is much more detailed and elaborate and uses many more incidents. The only really elaborate part of the first story concerns little Frank, and he plays a very small role in the second story.

Next, students are asked to consider the effect of "this kind of arrangement." In particular they are asked about their pictures of the poor relation at the end of the first story and at the end of "the dream story." Finally, they are asked to tell what the second story does to change their first impression.

At the end of the first story we feel very sympathetic toward the poor relation. He elicits our sympathy because he has been ill-treated and because we see from his relationship with little Frank that he is a very decent human being, although somewhat drab. He seems to have accepted his dreary status in life rather completely.

The second story changes the impression. We find a person not at all content with his pattern of life, a person whose imagination and mind are alert, alive. As a result, his plight becomes even more poignant. He is aware that life *can* be better, but he experiences that better life only in his imagination.

IV. WORDS

A. Using context clues, students are to find the meanings of these words.

1. **palpitations**—throbs
   nausea—extreme disgust
2. **saurian**—any of a class of reptiles, including lizards
   dour—stern; harsh; gloomy
   dubiety—uncertainty
   daft—silly; foolish
3. **quietude**—repose
   sonorous—resonant
   cadence—a beat of rhythmical motion or activity
   arabesque—ornaments that employ flowers, foliage, or fruit to produce an intricate pattern of interlaced curved lines
4. **asceticism**—practice of self-denial as a religious discipline
   antithesis—the direct opposite
   avaricious—greedy to gain wealth
5. **tinctured**—tinted
   decorous—marked by propriety and good taste
   mandarin—a high public official in the Chinese Empire
   finical—finicky
   rhetorical—verbal
6. **dynamic**—active
   catcall—a noise made to express disapproval
7. **genteel**—having an aristocratic quality
   baronial—stately
   mercenary—greedy

B. Students are to look up the meanings of the following terms:

The Bohemian Girl—an opera written in 1843 by M. W. Balfe

Patagonians—(see footnote 4, p. 691)

The West Riding of Yorkshire—Yorkshire, the county in England bordering on the north, was divided into three ridings or administrative divisions, the North, the East, and the West.

Victoria—Victoria, Queen of Great Britain from 1837 to 1901

Edward the Seventh—King of Great Britain from 1901 to 1910

Fleet Street—(See footnote 1, p. 700)

Sinbad the Sailor—a citizen of Baghdad whose adventures are cataloged in the *Arabian Nights Entertainments*.

Polonius—(see footnote 1, p. 703)

A Comedy of Errors—(see footnote 1, p. 706)

C. Students may be assigned to search for other examples in both stories.

The Launch

PAGE 738

Max Aub

Glossary Words

recondite (page 739, col. 1) Little known; obscure

stratagems (page 739, col. 1) Careful, often complicated schemes for gaining an advantage

absurdity (page 740, col. 1) Condition of being ridiculous; senselessness

Handbook

allegory, form, incident, symbol

Check Test 92

INTRODUCTION

"The Launch," a frequently reprinted Spanish story, is obviously a parable or allegory. Erramón lives near the sea and makes his living from it, but he gets violently seasick whenever he ventures out in a boat. He has tried, to no avail, all remedies from medicines to magic. People laugh at him for his weakness, but Erramón learns to cope with his problem.

The one joy in his life is a great oak that grows in his yard; between this tree and him there is an understanding. One night he dreams that he is in a boat and is not seasick. He perceives that the boat is made from the wood of his oak tree. The idea is in his mind, and although he fights against the thought, he finally cannot resist the temptation of cutting down his oak. He is ecstatic when he ventures out to sea in a boat made from the oak, for he is not seasick. But he soon notices that the wood is oozing water, which he tastes and finds sweet. Erramón tries desperately to row but cannot move the boat. And the hull continues to leak more and more water.

Erramón is not heard from again, although some people claim that he has been seen in nearby towns and later, that he has gone to America. The oak starts to grow again from its roots.

The story, like *The Metamorphosis,* will generate some confusion and multiple interpretations. It presents no difficulties in reading other than the Spanish place names. Certain classes may benefit from viewing a map on which they can locate the towns. The point to be made to students is that Erramón's life is very circumscribed; he has never ventured beyond a small geographical area. No further introduction is needed for this selection.

USING THE STUDY NOTES

PAGE 741

I. AMBIGUITIES ENRICH INTERPRETATION

It may be wise to check on students' understanding of the word *ambiguity.* In literature, ambiguity suggests the possibility of multiple interpretations because two or more meanings may arise from the language used. The author has used the term launch, which is both a noun that describes the kind of boat built by Erramón and a verb meaning to propel a boat into the water or to initiate. What does this ambiguity do to the meaning of the story? The author goes to great lengths to tell the reader what a narrow, circumscribed life Erramón lives. He calls it his *world.* But there is a larger and more complicated world that Erramón has been unable to explore—the sea. The boat launches Erramón into that larger world where he dies. What is the author suggesting—that we should be satisfied with our limitations? Or that we must break out of our bonds even though death may result?

II. IMPLICATIONS

What reactions are generated by the following statements? Use either your experiences or the story for support.

1. There are two major symbols in the selection—the sea and the oak tree. What are the possible implications of each? What are Erramón's reactions to each? The sea often symbolizes the unknown. In modern times, it thus often stands for the subconscious. Other possible meanings are the source of life, the mysterious, and the infinite. If one uses the sea as a symbol for the subconscious, one should note that Erramón is acutely sick when he is at sea. Evidently, he cannot handle what lies in his subconscious. Because he has lived in a very tiny area most of his life, his experience has been restricted. On a symbolic level, he has not had the kind of experience that would have enabled him to know how to handle his inner fears, hopes, and so on.

The oak tree could stand for life-force, strength, beauty, nature, shelter, warmth, a hanging tree, love, or nobility. Some students may call the class's attention to the fact that oak was the wood used for Jesus's cross and for coffins. To Erramón the tree represents everything that is good and beautiful in life. He touches it in passing, and the bark seems warm. Sometimes he speaks to it, and the man and the tree seem to share perfect understanding. Yet he fights only briefly the temptation to cut it down. He is willing to sacrifice the oak in the hope of overcoming his weakness.

2. Oscar Wilde wrote, "Each man kills the thing he loves," but this story suggests that the thing you love may kill you as well. There is no doubt that Erramón loves the oak tree. His caressing it, talking to it, and admiring it indicate this sentiment. Yet when he thought that he had found a way to conquer a weakness in himself, he quickly overcame his revulsion at killing the tree. There is every suggestion that the tree drowns him. Or does this take place in Erramón's mind because of his guilt feelings?

3. There are some weaknesses that a person should learn to live with. Students may argue both for and against this statement. The story suggest that Erramon is not a person to give up easily. The astounding number of cures that he tries for his seasickness demonstrates his great perseverance. In light of his past behavior, it is probably not surprising that he elects to try yet one more cure. Try to refrain from focusing on absolutes in discussing this question.

4. There is no reason for Erramón's desperate urge to go to sea. There is a symbolic reason. Erramón's urge suggests that even for someone living such a circumscribed life, there is still a need to break away and have new experiences. To do this, Erramón must come to terms with himself. Also, the fact that people laugh at his problem is unsettling. However, on the surface, the statement is true. The sea gives Erramón his food and his work, and there is no need for him to go out in a boat.

III. TECHNIQUES

Selection of Incident

What does each of the following reveal about Erramón?

1. The first sentence. The town in which Erramón was born has no name, and so he picks the most important city in his area as his birthplace. This decision could indicate his wish to appear less provincial.

2. The long list of cures for seasickness that he tries (three paragraphs in this short, short story). This long list of attempted cures indicates Erramón's desperate need to conquer his weakness, as though his worth as a person depends on overcoming his seasickness. Among the sources that he tries are: a druggist; a doctor; a politician; a maid; religion; magic; willpower; going out with a full stomach, an empty one, drunk, and sleepless; and, finally, following a vision from a dream.

3. The song he sings. It reveals an enigmatic quality characteristic of the Basque people. He seems to be saying that what is is not; that all of us are the same; and that people are not what they appear.

4. The last few sentences. No one appears very concerned about Erramón's disappearance. The townspeople shrug their shoulders and go on with their lives. Even the rumors about Erramón eventually cease. It is almost as though he never was. But the oak tree grows again.

Organization

Students are asked the following questions about the two step-by-step action scenes in the story.

1. What are the two scenes? The dream and the trip in the boat.

2. At which points in the story do they occur? Both come near the end, one following the other.

3. How much space do they occupy in the story? About half the story.

4. Do you prefer a story consisting primarily of action scenes? You will probably receive more affirmative than negative answers. Most people think that they prefer detailed narrative.

5. Would such a pattern of organization have been possible here? Point out all that is told about Erramón, information that would have required a great many scenes to present. Could the story carry such a great amount of action, or is this information more effective in this concise form?

Judas

PAGE 742

Frank O'Connor

Glossary Words

callous (page 745, col. 2) Unfeeling; insensitive; hard-hearted

intriguer (page 745, col. 2) A plotter or schemer

Handbook

chronological organization, flashback, incident, narrator

Check Test 93

INTRODUCTION

The narrator, Jerry Moynihan, is telling a friend about the happenings on a long ago night. Living with his widowed mother, he had had very few contacts with young women until he met Kitty Doherty, a hospital nurse. They had met each other while out walking one night and they continued to meet and walk and talk. Then for three weeks he had no contact with her. He was so desperate that the week before the night in question he had called her at the hospital. When she answered, he had been so appalled at his forwardness that he pretended to have the wrong number. So on this particular evening he walked about hoping to run into Kitty again. He spotted her on the tram and started running after it, hoping to jump on and ride with her. He kept the tram in sight and managed to spot the house she entered. Then he walked up and down outside, waiting for her return. A friend came by and, embarrassed, he pretended to have another engagement and went to the tram stop to wait there for Kitty. When she spotted him coming out of the darkness, she was frightened and started to run, and he ran after her. Then she began to outdistance him, and he called out her name. She was very angry but stopped to talk. She told him that since he would never come into her house and meet her family, her mother thought he was up to no good. Her description of her behavior with earlier boyfriends shocked him. Then after more revelations, they discovered how attracted they were to each other. Going home in a rosy glow, Jerry found his mother frightened and complaining. Feeling guilty at neglecting her and at the same time hating his responsibility for her, he shouted a nasty retort to her questions and stomped off to bed. That night he couldn't sleep, and in the morning when he went into her bedroom to apologize, he broke down and wept as she rocked him in her arms, murmuring the love names of his childhood.

In introducing this story, you might ask the students to explain who Judas was and what the term means to them today. If their explanations are somewhat inadequate, have someone read the definitions of Judas from the dictionary. Once the definition is established, ask students what kinds of situations they can imagine in which a person might feel like Judas. There are many possibilities, such as dating your best friend's girlfriend or boyfriend, lying about a friend to keep him or her from getting the job you want, etc. Then suggest to students that they read the story to see what made a young Irishman feel like a Judas.

USING THE STUDY NOTES

PAGE 747

I. THE STRANGER WITHIN

As the Implications will bring out, the story seems to say that the turmoil teenagers experience is the result of learning to know oneself. There seems to be a stranger lurking within a person who may momentarily emerge in moments of stress.

II. IMPLICATIONS

Discuss the following by exploring what the story indicates about each and how you interpret the statement.

1. The turmoil and stress of the teenage years comes from not knowing oneself. The story supports this statement. Jerry suffers self-doubts throughout the story. He does not know how to react to his friends, to Kitty, or to his mother; he has little confidence in himself and his values. In the teenage years, young people are generally trying to find their first job for pay, break away from parental control, relate to the opposite sex, establish new relations with their peers, etc. This is the maturation process —a getting to know oneself and one's values—and few can pass through it without turmoil. Since students in your class are in the midst of this process, they may see the statement from a different perspective.

2. **A young person today would not feel the guilt and distress that Jerry does toward his mother.** Most of your students may accept this statement as true since the young always feel that they would handle problems differently than other generations. If there are youngsters in the class with a single parent, they may add a different facet to the discussion.

3. **Growing to adulthood makes every child a Judas toward his or her parents.** Not intentionally. But since the young must go their own way, eventually to lead an adult life with their own goals and own relationships, they may seem like traitors to very dependent parents since they will no longer have the same time to devote to them.

4. **In moments of stress individuals often learn something surprising about themselves.** See if students can think of a crisis with parents, friends, a coach, police, a teacher, or an employer; it could be an event such as an auto accident, an encounter with a fierce dog attacking a child, or getting the ball in a stressful moment in a game, etc. Did they find out something about themselves from their reaction? Did they respond with clear thinking or emotion? Courage or cowardice? Cleverness or awkwardness? Quick action or no response? Were they surprised by what they did? What did the crisis reveal?

III. TECHNIQUES

Selection of Incident

After the narrator establishes the attraction of Jerry for Kitty, there are six major incidents, almost like separate scenes in a play. What does each of these reveal about Jerry? 1. Calling the hospital. His insecurity and resultant embarrassment. **2. Following the tram.** His need and determination to talk to Kitty. **3. Waiting outside the house for Kitty to come out and meeting Paddy there.** His need to keep his real feelings for Kitty a secret from his peers. **4. Talking with Kitty after the chase.** His horror at what Kitty's mother thinks of him; his shock at how Kitty has behaved with earlier boyfriends; his elation that she seems to like him as much as he likes her. **5. Finding his mother waiting up for him.** Anger at being treated like a child when he's working to support her. **6. The next morning.** Guilt that he had blown up at his mother the night before when she was probably only showing her love and concern.

Organization

The narrator is telling the story about an event in his life to someone called Michael John. So the story itself is a flashback though it does not return to the present at the end. What does this pattern allow the author to do that he could not do if the story had been told in a straight chronological order? In looking back at this earlier period the narrator can understand what was happening to himself at that time in a way that would not have been possible when it was actually happening.

Seven Stories

PAGE 748

Dino Buzzati

Glossary Words

competence (page 748, col. 1) Ability; fitness

prospectus (page 748, col. 2) A printed description of something; an advertising brochure

stratification (page 749, col. 1) An arrangement in layers or levels

homogeneous (page 749, col. 1) Similar; of uniform character or nature throughout

enunciating (page 749, col. 2) Speaking clearly and distinctly

analogous (page 751, col. 2) Similar in certain qualities, circumstances, or uses; comparable

manifestation (page 752, col. 2) Something that becomes apparent to the eye or mind

efficacious (page 754, col. 2) Producing the desired results; effective

avidity (page 756, col 1) Great eagerness

debility (page 756, col 1) Abnormal weekness of body; feebleness

Handbook

form, incident, realism, setting, symbol, theme

Check Test 94

INTRODUCTION

Like other selections in this unit, "Seven Stories" is open to many interpretations. As in *The Metamorphosis,* the story is told with complete realism; only the situation is strange. Giuseppe Corte has a minor but persistent ailment and goes to a magnificent sanatorium specializing in the disease. The building is seven stories high and is organized in an unusual way—the lower the floor, the more seriously ill are the patients. Those on the first story are the terminally ill.

When he arrives, Corte is assigned a room on the seventh floor. Then, through a series of intriguingly plausible situations, none of which is connected with his disease, he is moved down one floor at a time, always with assurances that he will shortly be moved back up. At the end, seemingly through an administrative error, he is on the first floor. As the story ends, the shutters in his room are slowly closing, implying that he is dying.

The story is placed in the theme KNOW THYSELF for two reasons. First, Corte deceives himself, for at no time does he acknowledge the seriousness of his illness. Also, the story is a portrayal of the desperate struggle of a person to hold on to his identity. In this way, it is very like Gregor's struggle in *The Metamorphosis.*

The selection needs no introduction. However, it may be helpful in some classes to discuss how a sanatorium differs from a sanitarium. The former deals with a single illness. In the past there were hundreds of tuberculosis sanatoriums, and a few exist today. See if students can think of other centers that specialize in the treatment of one disease. Alcohol, cancer, and drug addiction are a few that may be mentioned. In general, the word *sanatorium* has gone out of American usage, and we use substitutes instead.

USING THE STUDY NOTES PAGE 757

I. SLOW RETREAT FROM THE WORLD

It is an experience common to hospitalized patients that the world outside becomes less important as the hospital routine of eating, sleeping, and treatment becomes all-engrossing. Bit by bit patients lose touch with the outside world as their vision of life constricts to one small space. Writers have used prisons, factories, islands, and small towns as settings of withdrawal from the larger world, a withdrawal that is symptomized by a loss of will and a deadening of the spirit. Ask students if they have experienced this kind of withdrawal?

II. IMPLICATIONS

Students are asked to discuss the ideas triggered by the following statements:

1. The story can be interpreted literally or symbolically. Yes, it can be interpreted either way. Some students may insist that only a physical disease is meant. But the more imaginative may see that the disease could symbolize, among other things, life itself, the process of aging, or the loss of physical beauty. Let students explore other possible meanings.

2. The disease you think of first in reading the story is the thing most troubling you at the time you read it. This is a startling idea. Yet in reading great literature, it is generally true that you project your own insecurities onto the symbol. Few students will want to discuss this, but they may be willing to explore the idea in writing.

3. We tend to change and become the way we are classified by others. This statement should generate a good deal of discussion. Consider that the doctors frequently assure Corte that his physical state has not worsened. Yet with each step downward, he becomes progressively sicker. Also, there is some evidence to indicate that a normal child put in a retarded group will tend to act outwardly as though retarded. People who are labeled a certain way—as stupid, mean, bright, beautiful, brave, and so on—often grow to fit these labels. Or do they?

4. There is no good reason why Corte does not simply walk out and leave the sanatorium. Corte is a lawyer, an educated person intelligent enough to realize that he is ill. This awareness counterbalances his emotional reactions to what is happening to him.

5. Corte is really destroyed by his own fear of the first floor. Corte is repeatedly told that tranquility is essential in the treatment of his disease. Yet he is visibly upset at the time of the first move, and he becomes progressively angrier and more acutely nervous with each succeeding move. He is morbidly concerned with the first floor from the moment that he hears about the hospital's pattern of organization. And he loses his ability to enjoy pleasures around him such as the view and the pleasant spring weather.

6. There are indications that Corte is personally insecure. Have the class look at the first three paragraphs of the story and speculate about what they suggest. Corte walks and carries his bag although he has a slight fever. He has chosen this hospital because he will be assured of the best possible care. On seeing the building, he is impressed by its appearance. Yet later, after his first physical, he expects the worst and is inwardly prepared for a harsh verdict.

III. TECHNIQUES

Selection of Incident

The story is built around Corte's six moves to lower floors in the hospital. How are the reasons for these handled so that they do not become monotonous for the reader? Each move is surrounded by different circumstances. **The first move:** A woman and her two children are entering the sanatorium, and three adjacent rooms are needed. The two rooms on either side of Corte's are free, and he moves to the sixth floor to accommodate the family. **The second move:** Each patient's severity of disease is evaluated one-half point lower. Because Corte is included among the more seriously ill on the sixth floor, he is moved to the fifth. At the same time he is assured that the competence of the doctors increases as one moves down; therefore, on the fifth floor he will get better care. **The third move:** Corte is afflicted with a bad rash that shows no sign of healing. He is shifted to the fourth floor, which contains special apparatus to handle his rash. **The fourth move:** Corte listens to his doctor's suggestion that the digamma-ray machine on the third floor is far more powerful and will certainly rid him of his eczema. Then, too, the care on that floor will be so much better. Again, Corte succumbs and moves. **The fifth move:** The personnel on the third floor are going on vacation. Corte agrees to move to the second floor during their two-week absence. **The sixth move:** At the end of a week, Corte is transferred to the first floor on Professor Dati's orders. The doctor in charge of the floor feels certain that an error has been made; however, the professor's orders cannot be countermanded, for he has left on a short holiday.

Organization

Which of the following dominates the external organization of the story: the characters, the setting, the theme? This story is somewhat unusual in using the setting as the pattern of organization.

SUMMING UP: KNOW THYSELF

THE MASKS OF THE SELF

This section is intended to help students review their understanding of the selections in the unit. They are asked to specify in which stories the authors have presented characters who exemplify the following situations.

1. People who discover that they cannot act against their inner nature. One could include in this category Gregor, Eveline, Benjamin, the poor relation, Erramón, Corte, and Jerry. Gregor has allowed his family's treatment of him and his sense of duty toward them to transform him into something nonhuman. Eveline can find nothing in her situation that should make her want to stay and yet at the last moment, something deep inside her will not let her leave. Benjamin follows his inner drive even though it results in his death. The poor relation does not really "discover" that he cannot act against his inner nature, but it is because he does not act against it that he becomes the man that he is. Erramón is an example of someone who actually goes against his inner self in killing the tree and is killed by it in turn. Corte seems outwardly to be a sophisticated, educated man, yet his inner fears help to destroy him. Jerry acts flip to his mother upon returning from the meeting with Kitty and spends a sleepless night regretting his action.

2. People who attempt to build up their own egos. In "The Trick," the narrator could be chosen as a character who wants to build his ego. Forster could be said to be trying to build his ego by acquiring property; at any rate, it has that effect—it makes him feel "heavier." Christiana and John Spatter (minor characters in Dickens's story) in a sense attempt to build up their egos, the one by a wealthy marriage, the other by taking over the business. Corte, as he moves downward in the hospital, tries to build a self-image of good health by announcing to everyone that he is only there temporarily; this behavior in a sense builds his ego.

3. People who do not really know themselves. Gregor does not really understand the kind of person that he is and what he has permitted his family to do to him. Nadia uses fantasy to experiment with her feelings about who she is. The narrator in "The Trick" still does not know why he behaved as he did toward Nadenka. Forster discovers that ownership is likely to change one's character in unwholesome ways. Dickens's poor relation discovers how vicious and heartless society may be. Erramón is unable to put his seasickness into a proper perspective and thus makes a fatal decision. Corte cannot acknowledge the true seriousness of his illness. As is true of most adolescents, Jerry is in the process of learning to know who he is.

4. People who discover something about themselves that they did not previously know. Almost all the characters could be said to make discoveries about themselves except perhaps for Jiménez and the poor relation.

5. People who truly know themselves. Priestley, Jiménez, Forster, Lamb, Shelagh, Benjamin, and Massimo fit this category. But arguments could be made for some of the other characters as well.

IMPLICATIONS

Students are asked to tell how the selections either support or negate the following statements:

1. People try to hide their weaknesses even from themselves. The relative truth of this statement seems to depend a great deal on a person's character as well as on the degree of self-knowledge possessed. The essayists in the unit do not try to hide their faults; indeed, one can almost say that they parade them. Priestley, for instance, is quite open about his weaknesses; furthermore, he claims that many persons enjoy confessing their weaknesses. The poor relation could also be said to be parading his weak points. Massimo hides the fact that he has lost his image. The fact that everyone knows Erramón's weakness is the reason for his tremendous need to overcome it. Corte certainly hides from his weakness, as does Gregor.

2. Knowledge of self is essential to be a free person. Gregor is so driven by his need to pay back his father's debts and to take care of his family that he never once considers what he wants to do. Eveline's lack of knowledge of herself keeps her from escaping her dreary life. As for Jerry, could his explosion at his mother's checking on why he was late be an instinctive effort to break the silver cord? Or does he know what he wants to do but is unable to do it? And Corte's lack of knowledge about his condition moves him farther and farther from freedom with each move downward in the hospital.

3. Learning about one's self can change behavior. Many of the selections indicate that changes in self-knowledge do change behavior. Jerry's discovery of Kitty's feelings towards him and his response indicate he is coming to terms with his maleness and needs. But probably his irritation and anger at his mother is a short-lived, momentary expression after his lovely evening. When Corte is moved to the first floor, he gives up; the seriousness of his disease can no longer be shrugged off.

4. Self-knowledge gives a person confidence in facing a crisis. Those whose actions would give support to the statement are Shelagh and Benjamin, Priestley, and Massimo. Gregor and Erramón are examples of people who do not know themselves and who therefore do not meet crises with intelligent action.

5. To know oneself completely is an impossible task. Even a psychiatrist would agree with this statement. But the statement should lead to an evaluation of the theme of the unit, KNOW THYSELF: What does the theme now mean to students? How important is self-knowledge to a happy life?

TECHNIQUES

Selection of Incident

Students are to discuss the following questions:

1. Which selections are stripped down to a bare minimum of incident? The most stripped-down selections are probably the essays of Priestly, Jiménez, and Forster; the biographical piece, "Pavan for a Dead Prince"; and the stories, "The Launch," "Mirrors," and "After the Theater."

Which selections are jammed with incidents? Jammed with incident are "Old China," "The Poor Relations's Story," "Judas," and "Seven Stories." Oddly enough, *The Metamorphosis* may seem stripped down to some students and jammed to others.

Do you prefer one kind of writing to the other? Why? It is not necessary for students to choose one kind of writing over the other. The discussion may lead to the observation that the number of incidents that an author includes has little effect on most readers' enjoyment.

2. Choosing one or two selections, show how the selection of incidents affected the mood of the piece. This is perhaps particularly revealed in the contrast between the incidents chosen by Priestly and those chosen by Jiménez. The mood of delight could hardly have been maintained by Priestley if he had chosen the subjects or incidents used by Jiménez in "Platero," "Carnival," or "Melancholy." The contrary is also true. "Seven Stories" and "Mirrors" are also good selections to explore in discussing the connection between choice of incident and mood.

3. Which selection in this theme seemed the most tightly plotted? That is, in which does everything selected seem absolutely necessary to the movement of the writing? "Eveline" and "Seven Stories" are perhaps the best choices. But students should be allowed to choose others if their reasons prove valid in discussion.

Organization

1. **In the preceding group of selections, which stories present events in chronological order? Which selections use a "stream-of-consciousness" pattern?** "Pavan for a Dead Prince" and "Seven Stories" are chronological. In "Judas" the writer begins in the present with Jerry Moynihan telling his story to a friend, but the story he tells is in chronological order. It is, in effect, an extended flashback. "Eveline" has a stream-of-consciousness pattern.

2. **Which stories employ the flashback technique?** One or more flashbacks are used in *The Metamorphosis,* "The Trick," "Eveline," "Old China," "The Poor Relation's Story," "Mirrors," and "The Launch."

3. **Students are asked to make an outline of one of the essays in order to learn something about the structure of the essay.** This should prove a useful exercise for students. You may want to go over one or more of the outlines in class, pointing out how important structure can be to meaning.

WRITING FROM READING

1. This assignment is intended to give the student an opportunity to write a personal essay. Having written the outline of an essay in the assignment on organization, students may have some insight into how to organize an essay, and they will now have a chance to try this kind of writing. It should be a pleasant experience.

2. This writing assignment explores the theme KNOW THYSELF and should demonstrate how complicated this process is. No matter how much we have learned about ourselves, there is always much more to learn.

3. This assignment gives students practice in selecting an incident to tell a story. It should also give their imaginations a workout as they try to describe how a different life form would hinder or help them. Reading some of these compositions aloud should be fun for the class.

UNIT TEST

There are several options for testing your students' grasp of the unit. You may use the Summing Up section in the pupil's anthology—either whole or in part—as the unit test. For a second approach, you may select questions at random from the Study Notes at the end of each selection as a basis for constructing a final examination covering the complete unit. For a third option you may choose to use the comprehensive unit test prepared on blackline masters available in a separate test booklet, ISBN 0-07-009823-9.

RELATING COMPOSITION TO THE UNIT

SUGGESTED ACTIVITIES

1. Sometimes situations arise in our lives that force us to reevaluate our sense of self. Describe such a situation in your own life and explain what it taught you about yourself. Look back at the selections in the unit. Do any of them trigger memories of a moment when you came to know something about yourself?

2. Draw a caricature (a distorted, exaggerated likeness) of yourself. (Suggest to students that in their portraits, they first try for some resemblance and then exaggerate a dominant feature—nose, ears, eyes, neck, etc.) Beneath the caricature, write a personal description, using adjectives and incidents to capture your personality.

RELATING THE GALLERY TO THE UNIT

PAGE 693

1. The related themes of identity and self-awareness are interpreted through the self-portraits presented in this gallery. The self-portrait embodies an artist's most personal and self-revealing exercise. It not only gives us a physical record of the external appearance of the artist, but it also freezes in time the internal emotional state that animated the artist as he or she painted the portrait. The artists represented in this gallery do not appear to be very cheerful, with the possible exception of Marc Chagall who hides behind symbols. This does not mean that most artists are morbid, but it may mean that we tend to take ourselves quite seriously when we engage in self-examination. This information is valid for a general discussion of self-portraiture. Ask the class the following questions: What does each of these self-portraits reveal about the emotional state of the artist? Does the surface seriousness seem to cover any other characteristics that appear beneath the surface? In some cases, the artists have surrounded themselves with objects or other people. Aside from obvious factual information, what do these surroundings reveal about the interests and the self-image of the artist?

2. The contrast between the self-portraits of Gauguin (page 693) and of Rembrandt (page 698) is worth noting. Gauguin sees himself at the beginning of his career; Rembrandt paints himself as an old man who has accumulated knowledge and experienced life. The questions that naturally follow are these: Are there those of us who see ourselves as old before our time, and those who see ourselves as perpetually young? Do we truly see ourselves as we really are, or do we freeze ourselves at a time that we remember most fondly? Do we see ourselves as we wish we were or as we are? Which view is true, or does each view represent an aspect of truth? What does the time of life chosen by each of the four artists tell us about that artist? At what time of your life would you like to have yourself pictured in a self-portrait?

3. Ensor's self-portrait (page 696) offers an excellent springboard for a discussion of wearing masks as a defense against revealing one's true self to the world. Try to generalize the masks in the painting. Then ask students the following questions: What masks would match what mood expressed by what artist? Do you recognize any masks that you have noticed people wearing? Which are they? Which masks would you yourself wear and in what sorts of situations would you wear them? Do you know anyone who never wears a mask? Why do human beings feel the need to wear masks? In what ways could the elimination of certain masks increase human understanding?

4. Relating oneself to another is certainly one way of defining self, and the two family portraits on page 696 are excellent illustrations of this relationship. Compare the positioning of the artist and his wife in the Rubens painting with the positioning of the artist and his mother in the Gorky canvas. Ask students the following questions: Compare the height of the two figures. Compare the size. What do these comparisons reveal about the artists' relationships with the women in the paintings? What do they say about the artists' estimations of themselves? How often do you evaluate another human being on the basis of that person's relationship with others, particularly with other family members? Is this method a valid way to judge a person? Does comparing a person with others reveal a person's true character? To what degree, and how?

5. "We are as we dress," say the couturiers of the world, and the two self-portraits by Goya and Beekmann on page 697 seem to offer partial support of this theory. Examine the portraits with the class and ask the following questions: What effect does the formal dress of the subject have upon our perceptions of who the person is? Does the choice of costume tell us anything about the artist's own self-image? How much do we evaluate others by the way that they dress? How much do we express ourselves in the way that we dress?

6. The brooding self-portrait by Chirico (page 695) and the jaunty self-study by Chagall (page 697) are attempts at portraying the self through personal artifacts. Each artist uses props and/or scenes that are designed to increase the dimensions of the self-portrait by filling in some biographical details. The interpretations of the paintings may be aided by the following questions: What does the inclusion of the bust tell us about Chirico and his own self-image? Why is Chirico looking away from his own bust? Is there a difference between a self-*creation* and a self-*portrait?* If so, what is this difference? The building rises up behind Chirico, blocking him from his own creation. What is the significance of this obstruction?

Contrast the mood of Chirico's work with the ebullience of Chagall's painting. Why did Chagall choose these colors? Is there significance in the cow within a cow? What does the cheerful encounter between human and beast signify? Why are some of the people and some of the houses upside down? (This is one of Chagall's repeated stylistic devices, but it may also suggest that memory is not always logical.) What of the bouquet held by the artist? What of the crosses on the church and around the neck of the artist?

7. Does it take longer to read a story or to look at a painting? Is it possible for a painting to hold your attention as long as a story? Do we sometimes fail at first to see things in a picture that we later discover if we look more closely? Are there things in stories that also can be overlooked? Reread "The Trick"; as you read, make a note of anything you pick up in your second reading that you missed in your first. Take a long and careful second look at "Self-Portrait with Masks" by James Ensor; make a note of anything you see that you missed before.

THE EXPANDED EXPERIENCE: RELATING THE HUMANITIES TO THE UNIT

1. Disciplines: E, SS, A, M, TA. Skills: LS, Rd, PS, Org.

The Welsh poet Dylan Thomas chronicles some of his first attempts at discovering his identity in his poem "Fern Hill." Similarly, James Baldwin, in *Notes of a Native Son,* captures his youthful efforts to distinguish himself as a person. Finally, James Agee, in his essay "Knoxville: Summer of 1915" (which has been set to music by the American composer Samuel Barber) laments "those. . . who quietly treat me, as one familiar and well beloved. . . but will not ever tell me who I am." Obtain the texts of these three works.

Then read each of them to the class. As background for the Dylan Thomas selection, take slides of scenes of the Welsh countryside from travel books and add the music of Ralph Vaughan Williams's "English Folk Song Suite." For Baldwin, use slides of photographs by Gordon Parks and the music of Charlie Byrd's "Blues Sonata." For the Agee selection, use photographs by Edward Steichen from *The Family of Man* and Samuel Barber's musical rendition of Agee's essay. Present this to the class as a study of three geographically and culturally separated but nevertheless spiritually linked searchers for identity.

2. Disciplines: E, A, M, TA. Skills: LS, Rd, PS, Org.

The Finnish composer Jan Sibelius refused to allow the music of other composers to be played in his home for fear of being influenced by that composer. Obtain articles about Sibelius's life from your school library. Excerpt details that reveal Sibelius's attempts to maintain his individual style and character. Record the last movement of Sibelius's *Symphony No. 5.* Finally, make slides of works by the Finnish artists Albert Edelfelt, Gallen-Kallela, Tyco Sallinen, and Helene Schjerfbeck. Present this to the class as a sound and sight experiece of the work of one artist who spent a lifetime protecting and expressing his own personal identity.

3. Disciplines: E, SS, A. Skills: Wr, Org.

Give students the following assignment: List, in descending order, the important things in your life. Consider what gives you pleasure, what fulfulls your needs, what makes you think, what makes you grow, what interests you. On the basis of this list, compose a self-portrait, either written, drawn, or in the form of a collage. When you have completed this composition, answer the following questions: How important is self-knowledge to me now? How much do I really care about what I am? Who do I think I am? What relation does my person bear to the person I ultimately want to become?

RELATING ADDITIONAL READING TO THE UNIT

SUGGESTED BOOKS

Aldrich, Bess Streeter. *A Lantern in Her Hand*
Bach, Richard. *Jonathan Livingston Seagull*
Baldwin, James. *Notes of a Native Son*
Buck, Pearl. *The Good Earth*
Camus, Albert. *The Stranger*
Cather, Willa. *My Antonia*
———. *Death Comes for the Archbishop*
Conrad, Joseph. *Heart of Darkness*
Ellison, Ralph. *Invisible Man*
Goethe, Johann Wolfgang von. *Faust*
Hesse, Hermann. *Demian*
———. *Siddhartha*
Holland, Isabelle. *Cecily*
Horgan, Paul. *Whitewater*
Ibsen, Henrik. *Peer Gynt*
Joyce, James. *A Portrait of the Artist as a Young Man*
Lewis, Sinclair. *Arrowsmith*
Keyes, Daniel. *Flowers for Algernon*
Mann, Thomas. *The Magic Mountain*
Maughman, Somerset. *Of Human Bondage*
McCullers, Carson. *The Heart Is a Lonely Hunter*
Neihardt, John G. *Black Elk Speaks*
O'Neill, Eugene. *Ah, Wilderness!*
Plath, Sylvia. *The Bell Jar*
Potok, Chaim. *The Chosen*
Salinger, J. D. *The Catcher in the Rye*
———. *Franny and Zooey*
Sartre, Jean-Paul. *No Exit*
Shakespeare, William. *Hamlet*
———. *Henry IV, Part I*
Solzhenitsyn, Alexander. *One Day in the Life of Ivan Denisovich*
Updike, John. *Rabbit, Run*
Wilde, Oscar. *The Picture of Dorian Gray*
Wolfe, Thomas. *Look Homeward, Angel*

RECORDS SUGGESTED IN THE ACTIVITIES

Barber, Samuel: *Knoxville: Summer of 1915* (Steber) Odyssey 32 160230
Byrd, Charlie: "Blues Sonata" Riv 6054
Rodrigo: *"Fantasia para un gentilhombre" for Guitar* (Segovia) Col MS-7063
Sibelius, Jan: *Symphony #5 in Eb* (Karajan) DG 923-039.
Sondheim: *Anyone Can Whistle* Col S-32608
Vaughan Williams, Ralph: *English Folk Song Suite* (Gould) RCA LSC-2719
Wagner, Richard: *Götterdämmerung: Funeral Music* (Ansermet) Lon 6396

FILMS SUGGESTED IN THE ACTIVITIES

"Help, My Snowman's Burning Down" McGraw-Hill Films, Inc.
The Brothers Karamazov Films, Inc.
High Noon Films, Inc.
The Magus Films, Inc.

Index of Authors and Titles